The Operas of Benjamin Britten
Expression and Evasion

The Operas of Benjamin Britten
Expression and Evasion

Claire Seymour

THE BOYDELL PRESS

First published 2004
The Boydell Press, Woodbridge
Reprinted in paperback 2007

ISBN 0 85115 865 X Hardback
ISBN 978–1–84383–314–7 Paperback

The Boydell Press is an imprint of Boydell & Brewer Ltd
PO Box 9, Woodbridge, Suffolk IP12 3DF, UK
and of Boydell & Brewer Inc.
668 Mt Hope Avenue, Rochester, NY 14620, USA
website: www.boydellandbrewer.com

A catalogue record of this publication is available
from the British Library

This publication is printed on acid-free paper

Typeset by Pru Harrison, Hacheston, Suffolk
Printed in Great Britain by
Antony Rowe Ltd, Chippenham, Wiltshire

Contents

For Michael Irwin

And the life of choice begins.
Voice of Paul Bunyan, 'Bunyan's Farewell', Act 2, Scene 2

Acknowledgements

This study began life as a Ph.D. thesis and my first debt of thanks is therefore due to tutors, colleagues and friends at the University of Kent, particularly Michael Irwin who supervised the project – and the MA dissertation which preceded it – from inception to completion, and who was a constant source of inspiration, guidance and encouragement.

I was aided throughout my research by the efficient support of the staff at the Britten–Pears Library. My many visits to the Library were immensely pleasurable and rewarding, and I should like in particular to thank Helen Risden, Judith Le Grove, Jenny Doctor and Nicholas Clark for their generous assistance.

Similarly, Anna Trussler at the Ronald Duncan Literary Institute and the archive staff at King's College Cambridge were unfailingly supportive and professional.

I am grateful to those academics, musicians and writers who made time to share their knowledge and experiences with me, including Christopher Wintle, Edward Cowie, Thomas Hemsley, Philip Langridge, Michael Holroyd, Humphrey Carpenter and Norman Platt.

Finally, I would like to thank the numerous friends with whom I have from time to time discussed aspects of the text, and whose encouragement and support has been invaluable.

Permissions

Abbreviations

The following abbreviations have been used:

BPL   Britten–Pears Library, Aldeburgh, Suffolk.

DH   David Herbert (ed.), *The Operas of Benjamin Britten: The Complete Librettos Illustrated with Designs of the First Productions.* London: The Herbert Press, 1989, revised edition.

EMF   *E. M. Forster Papers,* Modern Archive Centre, King's College, University of Cambridge.

HC   Humphrey Carpenter, *Benjamin Britten: A Biography.* London: Faber & Faber, 1992.

LL   Donald Mitchell and Philip Reed (eds.), *Letters from a Life: The Selected Letters and Diaries of Benjamin Britten 1913–1976,* 2 vols. London: Faber & Faber, 1991.

RD   *Ronald Duncan Papers: The New Collection,* University of Plymouth.

1

Introduction

I understand Ben so well and his fear that he can't. If he is only wanting a career (and I know that is not it), and a career that I know would be very short, then he need not change. But if he wants to survive, to be played with love later on, even during the later years of his life, he must search for a more personal, more interesting idiom.   Colin McPhee[1]

Music says, 'Love me'. It does not say 'Obey me'; it does not even say 'This is true'. Love me or Love with me. That is why the performer is the centre of this act of Love: he is the instrument of it . . . In making/creating music an act of Love is also undertaken. Music is the Beloved. Singer is the Lover.   Peter Pears[2]

This book examines the ways in which the operas of Benjamin Britten may illustrate his search for 'a more interesting idiom', a search which was driven by his desire for an appropriate public 'voice' which might embody, communicate, and perhaps resolve, his private concerns and anxieties. The above quotations raise several issues which may enhance our understanding of Britten's music and methodology, such as the delicate balance between private and public communication, the tension between art as self-expression and art as moral resolution, and the notion of the latent sexuality of music, particularly song.

At the heart of my investigation lies the question, 'Can, or should, music serve as a redemptive model for life?' By analysing the libretto texts and musical scores of Britten's operas from *Paul Bunyan* (1941) to *Death in Venice* (1973), the three Church Parables, and several of the 'children's operas', I seek to identify the creative links between his music and biographical events or psychological factors, in order to uncover the personal narrative encoded within the operatic narrative, and to demonstrate that, for Britten, opera was the natural medium through which to explore and express his private concerns. I shall evaluate the artistic value of the unfolding autobiographical narrative in Britten's operas, and examine the presence of a homosexual dynamic in both the verbal and musical texts. By studying the practical and creative procedures involved in the process of

---

[1]   Letter to Elizabeth Mayer, postmarked 10 July 1941, quoted in Philip Brett, 'Eros and Orientalism in Britten's Operas', in Philip Brett, Elizabeth Wood and Gary Thomas, *Queering the Pitch: The New Gay and Lesbian Musicology* (New York and London: Routledge, 1994), p. 237.

[2]   From 'The Responsibility of the Singer', found among Pears's papers after his death and quoted in Christopher Headington, *Peter Pears* (London: Faber & Faber, 1992), pp. 306–7.

composition, I shall attempt to identify the congruencies and antagonisms between text and score, and to assess the relative 'status' of word and music. By so doing I hope to demonstrate that in his operas Britten fused musical and verbal expression into a highly personal language in his search for a 'more interesting idiom', but that ultimately this language, interpreted and communicated principally by his lover, Peter Pears, may have propelled him only so far in his quest for personal integrity and artistic fulfilment.

During the 1930s, guided by his first librettist and 'mentor', W. H. Auden, the young Benjamin Britten had already begun to explore his feelings of disaffection, alienation and oppression in works such as the song-cycles *On This Island* and *Our Hunting Fathers*, in which political and sexual tensions subtly intermingled. In 1939, following the example of Auden and Christopher Isherwood, Britten travelled with Pears to America, in search of the personal and creative freedom which, as a Conscientious Objector and homosexual, he probably feared would be denied him in Britain. In the libretto of the 1941 'American' operetta, *Paul Bunyan*, Auden described this American Eden:

> It is a forest full of innocent beasts. There are none who blush at the memory of an ancient folly, none who hide beneath dyed fabrics a malicious heart.[3]

Auden urged Britten to embrace his political and sexual beliefs more honestly and openly, his advice culminating in an oft-quoted letter to the composer:

> As you know I think you [are] the white hope of music; for this reason I am more critical of you than of anybody else, and I think I know something about the dangers that beset you as a man and as an artist because they are my own.
>
> Goodness and Beauty are the results of a perfect balance between Order and Chaos, Bohemianism and Bourgeois Convention.
>
> Bohemian chaos alone ends in a mad jumble of beautiful scraps; Bourgeois convention alone ends in large unfeeling corpses . . .
>
> For middle class Englishmen like you and me, the danger is of course the second. Your attraction to thin-as-a-board juveniles, i.e. to the sexless and innocent, is a symptom of this. And I am certain too that it is your denial and evasion of the attractions and demands of disorder that is responsible for your attacks of ill-health, i.e. sickness is your substitute for the Bohemian.
>
> Wherever you go you are and probably always will be surrounded by people who adore you, nurse you, and praise everything you do, e.g. Elizabeth, Peter (Please show this to P to whom all this is also addressed). Up to a certain point this is fine for you, but beware. You see, Benjy dear, you are always tempted to make things too easy for yourself in this way, i.e. to build yourself a warm nest of love (of course when you get it, you find it a little stifling) by playing the lovable talented little boy.
>
> If you are to develop into your full stature, you will have to think, to suffer, and to make others suffer, in ways which are totally strange to you at present,

---

[3] David Herbert (ed.), *The Operas of Benjamin Britten* (London: The Herbert Press, 1989). All quotations from the librettos are from this edition, subsequently referred to as DH.

and against every conscious value that you have; ie. you will have to be able to say what you never yet have had the right to say – God, I'm a shit.

This is all expressed very muddle-headedly, but try and not misunderstand it, and believe that it is only my love and admiration for you that makes me say it.[4]

This advice was brutally honest but Britten, though disillusioned with the American 'forest of freedom' which had proved less creatively liberating than he had hoped, was not yet ready to live his life according to Auden's liberal directive. In order to escape from the immediacy of Auden's presence, which he now found domineering and suffocating, Britten returned with Pears to England in 1942. However, the poet's words of warning may have been less easy to evade or ignore. Moreover, Colin McPhee's letter to Elizabeth Mayer, quoted above, reveals that Auden was not alone in identifying potential tensions and problems that, if repressed or avoided, might inhibit Britten's musical and personal development. In the following chapters I shall suggest that, beginning with the composition of *Peter Grimes* in 1945, Britten embarked upon a life-long operatic exploration of the very problems which Auden had anticipated and articulated following their American collaboration. Unable to openly confront these issues in his life, Britten dramatised them in his music, searching for a metaphoric utopia, a magical space, place or language where his sexuality and identity could be powerfully redefined. His art thus became a 'haven', as he sublimated and transferred his emotional tensions from the real world to the creative world of his imagination. The inherent ambiguity of opera, where 'meaning' might be either enhanced or obscured by the interaction of text and music, provided Britten with a protective screen behind which he was able to return obsessively to the fruitless gratification of his desire for the unattainable, indefinable and illegitimate.

From 1941 until his death in 1976, Britten was almost continually occupied with operatic composition, completing ten operas, three church parables (*Curlew River, The Burning Fiery Furnace* and *The Prodigal Son*), the ballad opera (*The Beggar's Opera*), two children's operas (*The Little Sweep* and *Noye's Fludde*), as well as numerous smaller stage works and dramatic pieces. Before he had composed his first opera Britten had already been widely acclaimed as a composer of song. What prompted him after the success of *Peter Grimes* in 1945 to commit himself so fully to opera? A song is essentially a self-contained experience where the composer responds to a pre-existing and unaltered poetic idea. In contrast, the composer of opera is more intimately involved in the text, which he interprets and re-presents and the musical score is the embodiment of this personal involvement. Indeed, an opera libretto may positively require such interaction before it can be fully realised in dramatic terms.

Britten was not working alone but collaborated with a series of librettists – W. H. Auden, Montagu Slater, Ronald Duncan, Eric Crozier, E. M. Forster, William Plomer, Myfanwy Piper and Peter Pears – who influenced the form and

4   Auden to Britten, 31 January 1942, quoted in Donald Mitchell and Philip Reed (eds.), *Letters from a Life: The Selected Letters and Diaries of Benjamin Britten 1913–1976*, vol. 2 (London: Faber & Faber, 1991), pp. 1015–16. This edition is subsequently referred to as LL.

content of his operas in varying fashions and to different degrees. His personal and professional relationships with these librettists, as well as the extent of their influence in determining the correlation between the libretto text and the original source text, is therefore of crucial importance. Which is more 'load-bearing', the words or the music? The analyses of individual librettos in subsequent chapters pay considerable attention to the dynamics of the complex web connecting the original writer, and the source text, with the librettist and the composer. There is much emphasis on the words and how they are formulated, since the examination of the libretto drafts at various stages of composition reveals how the 'meaning' was to some extent off-loaded from the words onto the music during the process of composition. Indeed, in performance the words themselves may actually be indistinguishable, their effect or importance being musically or dramatically experienced rather than technically understood. The audience's aesthetic experience of opera is in some ways 'beyond words', intensely physical and theatrical rather than intellectual, as instinctive and conceptual communication replaces literal expression and reception.

In this context, it is interesting to note that from the earliest stages of his career Britten was profoundly interested in the 'theatrical' aspects of performance and reception, striving always for a totally unified conception. In his essay 'Designing for Britten', John Piper describes his work with Britten and the Group Theatre during the 1930s:

> A clearly announced, and accepted, aim of the Group was the achievement of a stage unity stemming from a close collaboration of the author (preferably a poet), the designer (usually a painter), the composer (if any) and the producer and cast, regardless as far as possible of individual prestige and personality. The unity wasn't always achieved, sometimes it wasn't even evident, let alone obvious, but it was an ideal . . . I believe it remained a stage-ideal for Britten all his life, and is traceable in all his works involving collaborators.[5]

Piper continues by quoting Britten's Foreword to *The Rape of Lucretia* symposium (London: Bodley Head, 1948):

> 'The composer and poet should at all stages be working in the closest contact from the most preliminary stages right up to the first night.' He very soon came to realise (if he hadn't already) that this close contact also applied to the composer and his producer and designer. As far as I am concerned, in the Britten operas that I designed, from *The Rape of Lucretia* onwards, this passionate insistence of his on the unity of the parts – that is, of all collaborating participants – only increased, through the 27 years that followed to *Death in Venice*. He came more and more to demand (always in the gentlest possible way) advance information. If you said 'I've done these sketches', he might say: 'That's wonderful, that's marvellous, that's just how I hoped it would look.' But then, having done that, he would go much further and say: 'What's going to happen at the end of Act 1, when that turns round, you know, or this goes off the

---

[5] John Piper, 'Designing for Britten', in DH, pp. 5–7.

scene, what are we going to get next, because I can't compose music until I know exactly what's going to happen.

This desire for equality and unity may have contributed to Britten's desire to create a closed and exclusive working environment, such as he established at Aldeburgh, where he could retain control over all various and potentially contradictory elements of production.

While the unity of the operatic experience may have been Britten's ultimate goal, the starting point was frequently dramatic or literary. The source texts which Britten selected are surprisingly wide-ranging and erudite given his professed lack of confidence in his ability to deal with words. Hans Keller told Alan Blyth: 'I think he felt in some way guilty about verbalising.'[6]

However, Ronald Duncan understood how essential words were to Britten's creative process:

He once told me that he never had a purely musical thought unrelated to a verbal context. In other words his method of composition was to face himself with a verbal problem and the musical answer emerged simultaneously. . .

. . . and only on one occasion did he complain to me that he was having any difficulty: that was with the Second String Quartet.

'That's because it's got no words,' I said. His frown was partial admission.[7]

A superficial examination of Britten's librettos reveals the obvious existence of a number of recurring themes – 'innocence', pacifism, social oppression, death – and symbols – the sea, the 'outsider', the 'artist'. This is striking given the variety and diversity of the source texts chosen for operatic setting and would suggest that the chosen texts were in some way in harmony with the sensibilities of the composer, that they stimulated his imagination and allowed his personality to blend with the source. Writing in *Opera* (vol. 1, no. 2) in April 1950, about a broadcast of *Peter Grimes* in Toronto, Britten himself declared: 'If the work has overtones or undercurrents, let them appear by themselves and do not emphasise them.'[8] However, this statement contradicts his actual practice of manipulating or emphasising those existing features of the sources which were in accordance with his own aims, a procedure which was often complicated by the personal agenda of the collaborating librettist. The recurrence of particular thematic ideas and symbols may be either inadvertent or intentional; such motifs may arise in response to the composer's subconscious tendencies or may be applied in a more schematic manner. Symbols such as the sea may be archetypal but their power is intensified by their personal significance to the composer, and it is perhaps impossible to ascertain whether they reveal anything of value about Britten the man or whether they simply offered him greater musical potential. One significant feature of the source texts is that there is frequently a disturbing conflict

---

6   Alan Blyth, *Remembering Britten* (London: Hutchinson and Co., 1981), p. 88.
7   Ronald Duncan, *Working with Britten: A Personal Memoir* (Devon: The Rebel Press, 1981), pp. 103–4.
8   Quoted in Blyth, *Remembering Britten*, p. 15.

between diametrically opposed forces – peace and violence, love and ostracism, youth and age, innocence and experience, art and life – which suggests that these texts were potential sites of schizophrenic anxiety which might feed Britten's own neuroticism. The source texts appear to possess inherent tensions or ambiguities which Britten dramatised both textually and musically, formulating a harmonic and structural method which embodied, supplemented and, paradoxically, occasionally contradicted the dichotomies in the text. In this way, the opera libretto may mark out a path which the music does or does not follow, and the tension between the two may increase the overall 'expressiveness' of the work.

The complex issue of the nature of musical expression or 'meaning' is irresolvable, as the non-referential nature of music renders it impossible to determine the precise or literal 'meaning' of a musical event. However, there is no doubt that, within defined cultural and artistic parameters, listeners are conditioned to invest musical sounds with extra-musical significance. Philosophers and musicologists, struggling to account for music's intangible yet undoubtedly affective power, have, broadly speaking, adopted one of three positions: firstly, that music is powerless to express anything beyond its own abstract content; secondly, that musical form is congruent with psychological form and thus music is able to communicate directly with the universal mind by avoiding the referential and representative restraints of linguistic communication; or, thirdly, that music has an associative power, which may be innate, or alternatively may be defined or strengthened by patterns of repetition within cultural contexts.

In each of these cases, musical expression is defined in terms of 'meaning'. It may be more profitable to replace this definition with the notion of 'expressivity', understood as an instinctive or physical phenomenon which has an emotional rather than intellectual effect. In this way, the immediacy and non-referentiality of music might be its most powerful attributes. Undefinable and uncontainable, it may represent and communicate tensions which words are forbidden or struggle to convey. Some musicologists, including Elizabeth Wood, Susan McClary, Gary C. Thomas and Philip Brett have explored this hypothesis and have interpreted specific instances of compositional 'irregularities' as evidence of both an individual composer's rebellion against oppression and marginalisation, and of the 'deviant' nature of musical discourse itself.[9] However, these musicologists have tended to select single compositions which stand up to their investigative methods and have seldom applied their theories more widely across a composer's whole oeuvre. The presence of an unconventional or radical gesture within a single work will not greatly increase our understanding of a composer's expressive aims or methods. More valuable is an examination of how a composer manipulates the existing musical system, over an extended period of time, creating an effective medium for personal discourse. In this way 'expression' is replaced by 'self-expression' and a composer who wishes to articulate personal concerns can

---

[9]   See for example, Ruth Solie (ed.), *Musicology and Difference* (California: University of California Press, 1993); Susan McClary: *Feminine Endings: Music, Gender, Sexuality* (Minneapolis, 1993); Brett, Wood, Thomas, *Queering the Pitch*.

formulate a subjective framework and a system of metaphor which gains 'meaning' through repetition, particularly if the musical elements are allied to textual details. In contrast to the *minoritising* tendencies of some of the above musicologists, I aim to demonstrate the way in which Britten's operatic discourse both dramatises his personal dialectic and embraces more *universal* concerns.

The analyses of Brett, McClary and so forth have often focused upon those aspects of music that lie beyond the parameters of the score. In particular, they have identified links between timbre and gender. For example, in 'Of Patriarchs . . . and Matriarchs Too',[10] Susan McClary attempts to locate a 'feminist' timbre in the works of female composers such as Hildegard von Bingen. She asks whether musical sound is arbitrary or whether timbre is in some way implicated in the 'meaning' of the work. In the latter case, this meaning could only be fully revealed in performance, and thus the role of the performer, as interpreter and communicator, would be crucial. In his provocative diary of personal recollections and ideas – *The Queen's Throat: Opera, Homosexuality and the Mystery of Desire* – Wayne Koestenbaum goes further in defining the relationship between timbre and sexuality. He describes research conducted by J.-K. Huysmans which investigated whether homosexuality could affect the quality of the vocal sound, and which concluded: 'sodomy changes the voice, which becomes almost identical in all of them [the subjects selected for his experiment]. After several days' study in that world, from nothing but the sound of the voices of people I did not know, I could infallibly predict their tastes.'[11] These ideas are interesting in the context of Britten's operas, for in each work the dramatically significant part was designed for and performed by a specific voice, that of Britten's lover, Peter Pears.

Thomas Hemsley observed[12] that Britten had a profound respect for the human voice and was instinctively able to shape his musical lines to emphasise the particular attributes of an individual singer's vocal technique and colour. He declared that Britten had 'the best sensitivity for timbre of any musician', and was uniquely aware of the infinite variety of timbre and colour which it was possible to identify in a vocally produced note. In this way, parts conceived for Pears would be deliberately shaped, in consultation with the singer, to suit the peculiar quality of his voice. Similarly, Jon Vickers has commented upon Pears's lack of a 'break' or *passagio* around the pitch E, the point in the tenor's register where a change of timbre usually occurs. Vickers remarks that Britten exploited the smoothness of Pears's voice in this range, frequently centring melody and harmony about this pitch or tonality at moments of dramatic importance.[13] In this way, an individual pitch might assume an extra-musical significance, which may be further reinforced by harmony and timbre. Once more Koestenbaum's comments are thought-provoking. He writes:

10   Susan McClary, 'Of Patriarchs . . . and Matriarchs, Too', *Musical Times*, vol. 135, no. 1816, June 1994, 364–9.
11   Wayne Koestenbaum, *The Queen's Throat: Opera, Homosexuality and the Mystery of Desire* (London: GMP Publishers, 1993), p. 14.
12   In a private interview with the author, 2 April 1996.
13   Jon Vickers, 'Jon Vickers on *Peter Grimes*', *Opera*, August 1984, 835–43.

The break between registers . . . is the place within one voice where the split between male and female occurs. The failure to disguise the gendered break is fatal to the art of 'natural' voice production . . . The register line, like the colour line, the gender line, or the hetero/homo line, can be crossed only if the transgressor pretends that no journey has taken place. By coming out gays provoke seismic shudders in the System-of-the-Line, just as, by revealing the register break, a singer exposes the fault lines inside a body that pretends to be only masculine or feminine.[14]

Another peculiar quality of Pears's tone was his reputedly unreliable pitch-centring. Responding to my suggestion that Pears's idiosyncratic timbre could lead to a sense of 'out-of-tuneness', Hemsley explained this by recalling research which he had undertaken with Professor Meyer Eppler during the 1950s into the way the pitch or colour of a sung note might vary according to harmonic context. It is this which Hemsley believes accounts for the tension between the vocal line and accompaniment which might be perceived as poor intonation. Hemsley described Britten's technique of initially establishing the harmonic colour of the music through the vocal line which would only later be complemented by the accompaniment. Whereas modern singers customarily accommodate their pitch to the orchestra, Pears did not soften the tension between melody and accompaniment; instead he emphasised this conflict for dramatic ends.

Some observers have noted that Pears's tone quality was surprisingly similar to that of Britten's mother, Edith Britten, who was a talented mezzo-soprano. Recalling how the young Britten used to accompany her during music-making evenings at the family home, Basil Reeves described: 'His mother's voice and Peter Pears's voice were fantastically similar . . . That's the first thing I noticed . . . the same voice [Britten] couldn't miss it. And I told this to Beth, and she said, "My God, yes!" '[15] Britten's sister, Beth, also remembered this incident: 'There was something about Peter's voice which gave Ben what he needed. A close friend of Ben's who had known my mother well and heard her voice, remarked to me recently, that Peter's voice was very like my mother's.'[16] Hemsley suggests that Pears's physique and register were not naturally those of a tenor but that his voice, which lacked an upper range, lay more comfortably within the baritone range. This suggests that both Britten and Pears deliberately cultivated a specific vocal colour for musical or dramatic purposes, and sheds interesting light on the fact that the part of Peter Grimes was originally intended to be sung by a baritone. Furthermore, Lucie Manén, who became Pears's vocal tutor in 1965, told Hemsley that Pears 'had a much more heroic voice than he ever allowed himself to use, but it was a psychological thing – he didn't want to sing like that. He could have sung much heavier roles, but he didn't want to.'[17] Were Britten and Pears deliberately striving for an 'ideal' timbre, one which was possibly related to

---

[14] Koestenbaum, *The Queen's Throat*, pp. 166–7.
[15] Quoted in Humphrey Carpenter, *Benjamin Britten* (London: Faber & Faber, 1992), p. 122 (subsequently referred to as HC).
[16] Beth Britten, *My Brother Benjamin* (Buckinghamshire: The Kensal Press, 1986), p. 109.
[17] HC, p. 471.

Britten's subconscious recollection of his mother's voice? Such a search for an 'ideal' might be made permanent through the 'definitive' Decca recordings made by Britten, Pears and the English Opera Group. Interestingly, Hemsley remembered that when Pears returned from his first course of lessons with Manén, Britten was overwhelmed by the changes in Pears's vocal technique and quality and expressed his desire to rerecord all his works 'the way Pears sang now'.[18]

It is certainly true that Pears acquired a sense of 'ownership' of certain roles in Britten's operas, and this was enhanced by the composer's reluctance to see any one else take Pears's parts. Keith Grant, who was the manager of the English Opera Group, remembers: 'He grew up reconciled to different interpretations, except perhaps in the case of Pears's roles, where he was bound always to hear his friend's voice, technique and interpretive powers, simply because the parts had been written with Pears's attitudes in mind.'[19] Britten's occasional hostility and prejudice was experienced by other singers, including Robert Tear, who as a young tenor was conscious that he was being 'groomed' as Pears's successor. When Tear later felt the need to disentangle himself from the Aldeburgh circle in order to establish his own musical identity, he consequently found himself condemned and shunned by the Britten clique.[20] More recently, singers have been able to temper Pears's hold on these parts; Philip Langridge, one of the foremost Britten interpreters today, writes: 'Now that P.P. is no longer with us, Ben's music has become like any other composer's music, and can be performed by anyone with the ability to sing sensitively.'[21]

The careers of Britten and Pears were intricately entwined and co-dependent. Pears's voice was an unceasing inspiration to Britten; as early as 1944, he wrote: 'I'm writing some lovely things for you to sing – I write every note with your heavenly voice in my head.'[22] At the end of his career Pears told Alan Blyth: 'He made my career, by all the wonderful works he wrote for me. On the other hand, he said he would not have achieved anything without me.'[23] Pears achieved little operatic success outside the roles created for him by Britten and sang in few operas by other composers. Inevitably, there was occasionally some antagonism between singer and composer – for example, when Pears's determination to sing a particular role conflicted with Britten's insistence that he should sing another. Pears was reluctant to take the part of Essex in *Gloriana*, and in *A Midsummer Night's Dream* he insisted on singing Flute/Thisbe, rather than Britten's preferred Lysander. It is perhaps significant that the dramatic tension in these two works is less effective than in Britten's other operas, and it raises the question of whether Pears's voice, and its potency, was 'inner' or 'outer'. Did Pears serve Britten by dramatising the possibilities encoded in his music or did he act as his alter ego, literally singing 'for him'? Is he the body which inspires or the voice which communicates? Either way,

18   HC, p. 471.
19   Blyth, *Remembering Britten*, p. 141.
20   HC, p. 507.
21   Private letter to the author, 20 April 1995.
22   Britten to Pears, 11 February 1944, LL, vol. 2, p. 1187.
23   Blyth, *Remembering Britten*, p. 23.

the relationship between singer and composer was intense and must have at times been claustrophobic. The burden of expressive responsibility which fell upon Pears, combined with the sexual tension between creator and performer, must have contributed to the strained air of unease, even neuroticism, which is reputed to have characterised Aldeburgh at this time. Each musical performance served to confirm and consummate their personal and professional dependency, reinforcing the latent sexuality in the discourse between singer, composer and listener. As Koestenbaum writes:

> The listener's inner body is illuminated, opened up: a singer doesn't expose her own throat, she exposes the listener's interior. Her voice enters me, makes me a 'me', an interior, by virtue of the fact that I have been entered. The singer, through osmosis, passes through the self's porous membrane, and discredits the fiction that bodies are separate, boundaried packages. The singer destroys the division between her body and our own, for her sound enters our system.[24]

The act of singing thus becomes a sexual act in which the distinction between the active and passive partner, or the singer and audience, is confused. The tension arising from this situation is particularly powerful when, as in the case of Britten and Pears, the composer who creates his music for the singer, then finds himself the recipient of his own gift of love. It would appear that for Britten, Pears's presence alone was sufficient, even essential, to fill the 'psycho-tension' of a carefully constructed operatic role. If Britten's music could encode the 'unspeakable' elements in the drama, then Pears could effectively communicate the 'unspoken words'.

'Silence' – verbal, musical, spatial – is indeed at the heart of Britten's expressive method. His operas proliferate with mute or semi-articulate characters who are unable to give voice to their anxieties or relieve their psychological distress. In these cases the music must bear the dramatic burden. For example, the only utterance of the mute apprentice in *Peter Grimes* is a symbolic scream, descending from a high-pitched C (a pitch often representing purity or innocence in Britten's music), which accompanies his accidental fall down the side of the cliff, and symbolises his metaphorical 'fall' at the hands of Grimes. It is in the orchestral interludes that the relationship between Grimes and his apprentice is more fully disclosed, as in the passacaglia where the repetitive structure matches the obsessive circling of Grimes's mind, and where the boy is finally given a 'voice', in the form of the viola melody. Grimes himself is only semi-articulate: despite his sporadic visionary outbursts it is his inability to adequately express his desires which leads to his defeat at the hands of the Borough. In *Billy Budd* Britten exploits the presence in Melville's text of an 'unspeakable' element which is specifically associated with Claggart but which is also manifest in Billy's stutter and which ultimately prevents him from speaking out and saving himself from death. The hidden exchange between Budd and Vere is represented by the 'interview chords', a harmonic sequence which seems to offer the listener an explication of events and motives but which in fact evades all attempts at conclusive

---

[24] Koestenbaum, *The Queen's Throat*, p. 43.

definition. In *Death in Venice* Aschenbach is a writer who, though endowed with a comprehensive command of words, cannot create. Tadzio is literally mute, and is characterised by an erotic, oriental musical motif. Verbal exchange between man and boy is impossible, thus emphasising the gap between the artist who creates beauty and the boy who is the corporeal embodiment of that beauty. Aschenbach's passion can only be expressed through music, but the all-embracing and circular nature of his opening twelve-tone melody suggests that the promise of freedom which this music proffers is illusory: Aschenbach will not be able to escape from his desires and the medium which appears to offer him freedom and liberty paradoxically contains the seeds of his destruction.

Britten appears to have had faith in the power of music to take over when words fail. In the absence of words, music may explain and justify why characters act as they do. However, there are moments when there is a sudden silencing of the musical discourse and Britten employs the unaccompanied spoken word, such as the concluding words of Balstrode in *Peter Grimes* and Elizabeth's dying recollections in *Gloriana*. These instances may represent the 'failure' of music's power to redeem or mitigate the textual violence or tension at a particular stage in Britten's on-going dramatic and personal narrative. The musical narrative, the potential healing power of which has perhaps been momentarily suggested within the individual work – as in the passacaglia in *Peter Grimes* or the lute song in *Gloriana* – must be temporarily silenced, to be resumed in subsequent compositions.

The literal silences in Britten's operas are often supported by figurative silences or 'absences' represented by recurring symbols, such as the locked room, or empty space. These include Grimes's hut which the mob find unoccupied, the empty shop in *Albert Herring* from which Albert has fled, Captain Vere's chamber in *Billy Budd* where the unseen interview between Vere and Billy takes place, and the 'haunted' room in *Owen Wingrave* where Owen meets his death. These absences are reminiscent of the homosexual 'closet' and are potent sites for an examination of the conflicts between the known and the unknown, the explicit and implicit, and for the dramatisation of the 'open secret', which is integral to the tensions surrounding homosexual identity.

Exploiting music's ability to speak without words, Britten was able to infuse his musical discourse with a homosexual dynamic. The act of hiding one's true nature might make life difficult and unsatisfying, and destroy one's sense of identity, but the revelation of one's sexuality in musical terms could enable the composer to restore his identity, while at the same time protecting himself from the inevitable social hostility which would accompany more explicit disclosure. In *Epistomology of the Closet*, Eve Kosofsky Sedgwick proposes that remaining 'closeted' is a way of revealing much about speech acts in general; by 'not saying' the individual is in fact making a specific speech act, an act of silence.[25] In this way, 'closetedness' is the opposition of what is said and what is not said, and silence may be as informative as speech; similarly, music may speak in the place of words.

25 Eve Kosofsky Sedgwick, *The Epistomology of the Closet* (Berkeley: University of California Press, 1990), p. 3.

Similarly, Koestenbaum considers the relationship between homosexuality, silence and 'voice', describing opera as the medium through which the homosexual, marginalised and silenced by a society which classifies him as sick and diseased, can regain his voice:

> Our ability to speak for ourselves has been fore-shortened; we turn to opera because we need to breathe again, to regain a right we imagine is godgiven – the right to open.[26]

> If you speak a secret. you lose it; it becomes public. But if you sing the secret, you magically manage to keep it private, for singing is a barricade of codes.[27]

He explores the notion of vocal 'crisis', which may indicate physical injuries sustained by the voice but can also imply an articulative crisis:

> in her [the singer's] interruption, hear the imagined nature of homosexuality as a rip in meaning, in coherence, in cultural systems, in vocal consistency. Homosexuality isn't intrinsically an interruption; but society has characterised it as a break and a schism, and gay people, who are molded in the image of crisis and emergency, who are associated with 'crisis' . . . may begin to identify with crisis and to hear the interrupted voice as our echo.[28]

In this way, the fragmentation of melody, harmony, textual syntax and vocal production in a scene such as Grimes's 'mad' soliloquy is a typical representation of the interruptions in performance which serve as ciphers for the disruptions and schisms which homosexuality provokes within both the social system and the individual. Paradoxically, those characters who *do* speak out suffer the same fate as those who remain silent. Thus, Lucretia, Miles and Owen Wingrave all find that their 'bravery' is rewarded with death, and the identification of public confession with self-sacrifice is intensified by their fates.

In her article 'Lesbian Fugue: Ethyl Smyth's Contrapuntal Arts',[29] Elizabeth Wood investigates issues which might illuminate Britten's case. She suggests that as a socially oppressed lesbian composer, Smyth was forced to seek an alternative way to reveal the truth about her life in her operas. Both her libretto texts and her 'Memoirs' are characterised by an obsessive repetition of phrases and stories, and Wood considers Smyth's music to be an attempt to shape the chaos and disorder of her existence into a coherent and meaningful form, to manage her anxieties and to create a structure in which she could establish a stable identity. In the face of cultural and social repression, Smyth lacked an acceptable format within which to express the nature of her forbidden desire. Consequently, Wood believes that Smyth manipulated the plots of her apparently heterosexual librettos to conceal and camouflage their autobiographical relevance, while at the same time allowing the musical scores to insinuate or reveal those elements which the texts attempted to hide. Encoding her lesbian desire in the instrumental music, Smyth

---

[26] Koestenbaum, *The Queen's Throat*, p. 16.
[27] *Ibid.*, p. 157.
[28] *Ibid.*, p. 128.
[29] In Solie, *Musicology and Difference*, pp. 164–83.

simultaneously revealed and concealed her sexual experience, and Wood concludes that we need a new interpretative strategy in order to read both text and music satisfactorily.

I hope to demonstrate that, like Smyth, Britten encoded in his musical scores the 'unspeakable' elements of his literary and personal narratives. In his operas, a pre-existing text would be carefully transformed and set to music; ideally the text and music might work together, the text bringing specificity to the music, and the music acting as a 'subtext', an interlinear version of the libretto which simultaneously comments on, reinforces and contradicts the verbal text. However, frequently the dramatic and musical endings of Britten's operas are non-congruent. Despite its abstract nature, music generates its own tensions which must be resolved, and Britten is sometimes able to exploit this compulsory musical resolution to suggest a conciliatory conclusion regardless of the inconclusiveness of the dramatic text, particularly when dramatic closure has occurred without psychological resolution. Yet there is a danger that this 'controlled' ambiguity may degenerate into inconsistency or sheer vagueness. 'Contrived' dramatic closure may appear to be upheld by a more satisfying musical closure, but although the musical finality of any Britten opera is adequate in terms of its own structure, it may never completely overcome the inconsistencies in Britten's presentation of character and drama, nor the audience's discomfort at the conclusion. Furthermore, occasionally purely musical tensions may be left unresolved, thereby ensuring that the dialectic is continued beyond the parameters of the individual opera, and is re-examined either in subsequent operas or separate instrumental or chamber works. In this way, ideas which spring initially from the written word are explored through the sung word, with musical support, before being transferred to a purely musical context, as Britten searches for resolution beyond the restrictions of language.

Smyth and Britten both appear to equivocate between an acceptance of the 'disorder' of their personal lives and a naive desire for coherence. Their experience as sexually repressed individuals contrasts with that of other, heterosexual, composers who have similarly attempted to achieve the resolution and closure which is absent from their personal lives, through their art. For example, Leos Janáček's infatuation with Kamila Stösslová, which began when he was sixty-three years old and she only twenty-five, combined with the rediscovery of a historically accurate national folk idiom, probably contributed to the revitalisation of his creative impulses and the profound transformation of his compositional style and aesthetic. The result was a series of operas written during the last ten years of his life that are an unambiguous celebration of his unconsummated passion. In contrast, it appears to be impossible for the homosexual composer to glorify his or her sexuality in opera. For Koestenbaum, opera is merely a substitute for the sexual frustration and spiritual failure of reality. He writes: 'Opera has always suited those who have failed at love.'[30]

---

[30] Koestenbaum, *The Queen's Throat*, p. 118.

Conversely, Sam Abel, in *Opera in the Flesh*, refutes the suggestion that opera is a protective closet or an unreal space where the homosexual can hide from hatred and stave off inevitable dissolution and death:

> Opera, in its glorious paradoxical tangle of undifferentiated desire, provides a fruitful outlet for both minoritising and universalising impulses . . . Opera offers a world of unique emotional intensity, free from the rules and inhibitions of 'normal' society . . . The illicit desire of opera, socially sanctioned by elite patronage and government subsidy, becomes a way, not to substitute for failed love, but instead to legitimise our 'deviant' desire and to reinforce our brilliantly diverse and freewheeling sexual lives.[31]

Despite this, Abel is unable to find any convincing examples of positive representation of homosexuality in opera.[32]

Can art, and more specifically opera, serve as a 'therapeutic model' for life? In what way might the examination of these issues enhance our understanding of Britten's operas and help us to evaluate their artistic value? Among some of the early commentators on Britten's music there appears to have been a deliberate avoidance of discussion of the sexual elements in Britten's operas. Even quite recently, Donald Mitchell, the composer's life-long friend, colleague and publisher, has disputed the significance of the homosexual dynamic in Britten's work, advising the listener to retain:

> a useful sense of proportion: and above all, not to attribute to the composer an intent which I think he did not have. He did not, in my view, write *Grimes* as a protest against, or even as a reflection of, the prevailing attitudes to homosexuality in England up to the 1950s and 1960s. Others whose seriousness I respect, take a different view . . .
>
> I shall regret it if we succeed in convincing ourselves that Britten's persistent interest in the relationship between non-conformist attitudes and the social antagonism they arouse should be attributed solely to his homosexuality. It is not Britten's sexual constitution that we have dramatised or musicalized before us, but the dramatization in an extra-ordinary variety of forms of one of the great human topics which is under perpetual debate: the pressures and persuasion to conform on those who assert different values and attitudes from those held by society at large.[33]

Mitchell assumes that music is 'expressive' but denies that Britten's music is peculiarly expressive of the condition of an ostracised minority, i.e. the homosexual

---

31 Sam Abel, *Opera in the Flesh: Sexuality in Operatic Performance* (Colorado: Westview Press, 1996), pp. 63–4.

32 Citing Wagner as a possible example, Abel proposes that: 'Above all, it is Wagner's blatant evocation of sexual transgression in his music-dramas that labels his work as queer . . . more than any other work, it is the rampant sexual ambiguity of *Parsifal* that makes Wagner an inevitable locus of transgressive sexuality.' However, he acknowledges: 'Of course no one is supposed to mention this desire openly . . . Wagner's world in *Parsifal* evokes on its surface a "normal" heterosexuality' (Abel, *Opera in the Flesh*, pp. 68–9).

33 Donald Mitchell, *Cradles of the New – Writings on Music 1951–91*, ed. Mervyn Cooke (London: Faber & Faber, 1995), p. 312.

community. His reluctance to allow that Britten's homosexuality may in some way find expression in the composer's music is typical of the critical attitude of those commentators who, following Mitchell's own example, have consistently ignored this aspect of Britten's life and work. A contrasting view is proposed by Hans Keller. Defending Britten against accusations that the presentation of homosexuality, paedophilia and pacifism in his operas weakens their artistic value Keller, whose eulogistic 1952 publication with Mitchell, *Benjamin Britten: A Commentary on His Works from a Group of Specialists*, was partly responsible for provoking a critical backlash, writes:

> Even Britten's homosexuality was drawn in in order to explain both such odd-women-in as Ellen Orford in *Peter Grimes* or Lucretia herself, or indeed his musical preoccupation with boys . . . though such critical whisper was not without malice and usually sprang from ill-repressed homosexuality on the part of the observers who simply could not bear the sound of the music of a straight-forwardly homosexual genius.[34]

Keller's comment is extraordinary for, alone among critics at this time, he appears to unambiguously identify in Britten's music the presence of specifically homo-sexual elements, and to imply that Britten's homosexuality may in fact have conferred upon him unique creative advantages, advantages which are in no way related to a political purpose: 'his psychosexual organisation placed him in the privileged position of discovering and musically defining new truths, which, otherwise, might not have been accessible to him at all'.[35]

The incompatibility of these opposing interpretations has been exacerbated by Britten's own evasiveness and his inclination to avoid all discussion that went beyond purely musical resources and techniques. Some recent commentators have condemned his unwillingness to commit himself openly to the homosexual 'cause'. For example, the writer Colin Innes has remarked: 'The theme and tragedy of *Peter Grimes* is homosexuality and, as such, the treatment is quite moving if a bit watery.'[36] More especially Philip Brett, whose 1977 article 'Britten and Grimes'[37] was one of the first to openly confront the issue of homosexuality in Britten's work, writes: 'What was the point of all those coded messages about homosexual oppression and pederasty if they prompted only further denial of their meaning, further entrenchment of the universalism and transcendentalism that make Western classical music a weak substitute for religion in capitalist society and divorce it from meaning?'[38] Brett believes that Britten was in a unique position to positively alter both the portrayal of the homosexual in art and his actual experience in life, and thus he condemns Britten's refusal to promote a political, homosexual agenda in his work. Brett considers that Britten evaded his responsibilities thereby achieving artistic, material and social success, while

[34] Hans Keller, 'Introduction', DH, p. xxv.
[35] DH, p. xxvi.
[36] Quoted in Philip Brett, 'Britten's Dream', in Solie, *Musicology and Difference*, p. 264.
[37] Brett, 'Britten and Grimes', *Musical Times*, vol. 118, 1977, 995–1000.
[38] Brett, 'Musicality, Essentialism and the Closet', in *Queering the Pitch*, pp. 9–26.

avoiding the persecution and rejection which would have been inevitable had he adopted a more confrontational stance in his life and art. His judgment echoes that of Auden who also believed that Britten had chosen success at the expense of psychological truth: 'It was what seemed Ben's lack of daring, his desire to be the Establishment that irritated Wystan most; the playing it safe, settling for amiability as a guard against his queerity, but insisting on the innocence of adolescence as if this was a courageous attitude.'[39] Brett suggests that the price which Britten paid for this self-repression was a life-long fear of 'oppression', which he perceived as an ever-present threat, and more seriously, the internalisation of this oppression and guilt. Furthermore, he deems that by disguising and diluting his subject matter Britten risked obscuring his theme, so that it was indistinguishable or confusing for his audience.

Brett appears to believe that art's primary purpose is to function as moral propaganda; consequently, he finds Britten's 'discretion model' of reduced artistic value. His hypothesis is reminiscent of Freud's theories of the sublimation by the artist of his repressed desires in his art. Freud believed that whereas the neurotic repeats his obsessions unaltered, the artist continually seeks new solutions, and in this way, the artist may be able to productively transfer potentially disruptive and destructive forces into a socially acceptable artistic medium. However, he may subsequently discover that his art is not a 'copy' of reality, and that the solutions which he achieves in artistic terms are ultimately an unsatisfactory substitute for resolution in life. Brett apparently agrees with Freud that it is possible to organise one's personal anxieties into an ordered work of art which provides creator and audience with explicit political or moral directions which may be acted upon. However, the homosexual composer and writer, Ned Rorem, contradicts this view: 'Art can make political statements, but it cannot have political effect. Art is not moral, it is something else. It cannot change us, but it can reinforce our convictions and help us get through life.'[40] Despite his apparent faith in opera's redemptive power, Koestenbaum acknowledges that ultimately music cannot liberate the individual who is burdened with guilt and self-loathing:

> Homosexuality is a way of singing. I can't be gay, I can only 'sing' it . . . The singer and the homosexual each appear to be a closed-off cabinet of urges. But the body that sings and the body that calls itself homosexual are not as sealed as we think. Nor are they as free.[41]
>
> Voice aims to purify and transcend; homosexuality is the dirt that singing, a detergent, must scour. In this sense, voice and homosexuality are adversaries: voice is evolutionary, homosexuality is devolutionary; voice is transcendent, homosexuality is grounded.[42]
>
> Queers have placed a trust in coming out, a process of vocalisation. Coming

39 Leonard Kirsten, in HC, p. 396.
40 In conversation with Leonard D. Mass in *Queering the Pitch*, pp. 85–114.
41 Koestenbaum, *The Queen's Throat*, p. 156.
42 *Ibid.*, p. 169.

out, we define voice as openness, self-knowledge, clarity. And yet mystery does not end when coming out begins.[43]

It is this 'mystery' which is the essence of Britten's art. The unsettling ambiguity of his operas need not be interpreted as creative or moral failure; indeed, the practice of maintaining many contradictory elements in permanent suspension may be artistically and personally advantageous.

To return to McPhee's advice that Britten should attempt to formulate a 'more interesting idiom', I hope to demonstrate in the subsequent chapters that Britten did indeed develop a method of opera composition which encompassed the entire creative process from choice of source text to first performance. In his operas, intellectual, political and social aspects interact with personal and sexual elements. Part of opera's allure may have been its status as a hybrid art form, one that protected Britten from the need to declare his allegiances and enabled him to maintain his belief in the potential offered by various, potentially antagonistic strands. Opera allowed him to hover between definitions, sustaining a series of polarities – public and private, male and female, youth and age, role-playing and sincerity, secrecy and disclosure, music and language. Ultimately the listener must decide whether the dualities and ambiguities which are present in Britten's operas are a positive creative force or are merely a negative outcome of the composer's refusal or inability to separate the conflicts of his dramas from his personal dilemmas. I shall attempt to show that through opera Britten endeavoured to transfer and transmute the problems of his life into art. He trusted his music to 'speak out' but at the same time refused to bring the 'real' subject into sharp focus, and the resulting approximations and hints, twisted and encoded messages, both tantalise and exasperate.

[43] *Ibid.*, p. 158.

2

Paul Bunyan

Once in a while the odd thing happens,
Once in a while the dream comes true,
And the whole pattern of life is altered,
Once in a while the moon turns blue.   W. H. Auden, *Paul Bunyan*

I've seen & am seeing Auden a lot, & our immediate future is locked with his, it
seems.   Benjamin Britten[1]

When Benjamin Britten met W. H. Auden for the first time, on 5 July 1935, the
young composer was immediately awed by the charismatic poet who, seven years
Britten's senior, was already a renowned writer, intellectual, left-wing spokesman
and homosexual. Soon after returning to England to take up a teaching post in
1930, after two years in Germany, Auden had become involved with Rupert
Doone's Group Theatre, and in 1935 began writing for the GPO Film Unit. When
he heard the incidental music that Britten had written for the song 'O
lurcher-loving collier' for the film *Coal Face*, Auden was convinced that he had
found *the* composer to complete the 'group' of writers, poets, directors and
designers who were collaborating on various projects at this time. He praised
Britten's: 'extra-ordinary musical sensitivity in relation to the English language.
One had always been told that English was an impossible tongue to set or sing . . .
Here at last was a composer who set the language without undue distortion.'[2]
Britten was similarly filled with admiration for the poet; he wrote to Marjorie
Fass, 30 December 1935: 'I haven't had time to read much of the Auden yet – but I
feel that most of it is definitely going to be for me – knowing him as I do, & feeling
quite a lot in sympathy with his ideals. I am working with him on various projects
outside films – it is a treat to have someone of his calibre to think with!'[3] However,
he was somewhat oppressed by Auden's intellectual dominance, recording in his
diary: 'Spend day with Coldstream and Auden . . . I always feel very young and
stupid with these brains – I mostly sit silent when they hold forth about subjects in
general. What brains!'[4] Auden's guiding influence was immediately evident. Until
this time Britten had shown little public interest in politics; now, introduced into

---

[1] 3 September 1939, to Barbara Britten; LL, vol. 2, p. 696.
[2] HC, p. 67.
[3] LL, vol. 1, p. 391.
[4] 17 September 1935; *ibid.*, pp. 380–1.

a circle of intellectuals and artists that included among others Basil Wright, Rupert Doone, Christopher Isherwood and Stephen Spender, he adopted a more left-wing position and even began to criticise music from a political standpoint. For example, after a performance of Elgar's First Symphony at the 1935 Promenade concert season, Britten remarked, 'I swear that only in Imperialistic England could such a work be tolerated.'[5]

However, Auden's encouragement that he should openly embrace political radicalism, and should acknowledge his own homosexuality, left Britten exposed and vulnerable to attack from without and within, and probably provoked feelings of self-doubt and guilt. At this stage, Britten's ethics were too conventional for him to come to terms with what he saw as a 'deviation'; and even Auden, who in public blazoned the ideas of the man free from social and sexual repression, expressed in private the belief that his sexuality was an inner disorder which was symptomatic of a deeper failure of intimacy and trust.

In *The New Statesman*, 15 October 1932, Auden had declared: 'It would be presumptuous of me to pretend to know what the proletariat think of Communism; but its increasing attraction for the bourgeois lies in its demand for self surrender for those individuals who, isolated, feel themselves emotionally at sea.'[6] By 1939 there was a growing feeling among Britten's contemporaries that Europe was no place for an artist to live, and that a brighter future lay in the New World, a fresh continent where the possibility of recovering a lost world of childhood innocence and freedom from persecution beckoned. In many cases, political and sexual factors mingled, and Britten's own feelings on this matter were probably strengthened by his homosexuality, which heightened his awareness of intolerance and alienation.[7] The 'stranger' or 'outsider' is a figure who reappears in many Auden poems, such as 'The Watershed' and 'Look, stranger' (the latter set by Britten in the song-cycle *On This Island*). Likewise, Britten's subsequent operatic works were frequently to explore the struggle between the individual and the mass, between self-integrity and the desire to belong to, and be accepted by, the social group. An increasing sense of personal and political 'isolation' may have contributed to Britten's decision to leave England and embark upon a new life in America, a feeling strengthened by the disillusioned departure of Auden and

---

5 HC, pp. 68–9.
6 Edward Mendelson (ed.), *The English Auden: Poems, Essays and Dramatic Writings 1927–1939* (London: Faber & Faber, 1977), pp. 314–15.
7 Britten's diary entries from the late 1930s hint at the guilt and anxiety which his sexuality provoked. For example, he described his friendship with the thirteen-year-old Piers Dunkerley: 'He is a nice thing and I am very fond of him – thank heaven not sexually, but I am getting to such a condition that I am lost without some children (of either sex) near me' (LL, vol. 1, p. 403). The diary entry for 3 July 1937 recounts a visit with Isherwood to the Jermyn Street Turkish Baths, a well-known meeting place for homosexuals, and suggests that Britten was indeed coming to terms with his sexuality: 'get slightly drunk, & then at mid-night go to Jermyn St. & have a Turkish Bath. Very pleasant sensations – completely sensuous, but very healthy. It is extraordinary to find one's resistance to anything gradually weakening' (LL, vol. 1, p. 18).

Isherwood three months previously. Yet when Britten, accompanied by Peters Pears, sailed from Southampton for North America on 29 April 1939, his motives and hopes were probably various, somewhat confused and ambiguous. Undoubtedly the acclaim that his musical mentor, Frank Bridge, had received after his American visit of 1923, and the success of Pears's tour in 1937, encouraged Britten to make his own voyage. Moreover, as he explained to Lord Harewood in a BBC interview, 1960: 'I was very much influenced by Auden . . . He went to America, I think it was '38, early '39, and I went soon after. I think it wouldn't be too much oversimplifying the situation to say that many of us young people at that time felt that Europe was more or less finished . . . I went to America and felt that I would make my future there.'[8]

Thirty-five years separate the first and second performances of *Paul Bunyan*, and this 'absence', in score and on the stage, has given rise to much curiosity and speculation about Britten's earliest opera. Premièred in May 1941 in Brander Matthews Hall, Columbia University, by the Columbia Theatre Associates, this 'choral operetta' on the quintessentially American theme of the legend of the pioneer lumberman, Paul Bunyan (perhaps intended by composer and librettist, W. H. Auden, as a naïve offering of their artistic credentials for American citizenship), was subsequently 'suppressed' by Britten. It remained unheard and unseen until 1974 – attracting much speculative comment concerning its status as a 'trial run' for Britten's later, successful operas. Following Auden's death the preceding year, the composer was persuaded to unearth this youthful work from the oblivion where it had languished, and to revise several excerpts for performance at the 1974 Aldeburgh Festival. The success of these excerpts encouraged Britten to undertake more extensive revisions: the fully revised version was broadcast in a concert performance by the BBC in February 1976, and staged at the Aldeburgh Festival later that year.

The critical reception which *Paul Bunyan* received in 1941 was rather hostile: although the composer's technical deftness and skill in handling a variety of musical forms and idioms were admired, the operetta was judged to be weak in terms of the overall structure and theme. Contemporary critics disparaged Auden's characterisation and plot, Virgil Thomson writing in *New York Herald Tribune* on 6 May 1941:

> What any composer thinks he can do with a text like 'Paul Bunyan' is beyond me. It offers no characters and no plot. It is presumably, therefore, an allegory or a morality; and as either it is, I assure you, utterly obscure and tenuous. In addition, its language is not the direct speech of dramatic poetry. It is deliberate parody . . . Every sentence is indirect and therefore unsuited to musical declamation. Every dramatic moment has the afflatus taken out of it before the composer can get it over to the audience . . . it never did get going, and I never did figure out the theme.[9]

---

[8]   LL, vol. 1, p. 619.
[9]   LL, vol. 2, p. 916.

Writing in *New York Times*, Olin Downes echoed some of Thomson's criticisms:

> the libretto . . . seems to wander from one to another idea, without conviction or
> cohesion. In the plot, as in the score, is a little of everything, a little symbolism
> and uplift, a bit of socialism and of modern satire, and gags and jokes of a Holly-
> wood sort, or of rather cheap musical comedy . . . the operetta does not have a
> convincing flavor of inevitable conglomeration. It seems a rather poor sort of a
> bid for success, and possibly the beguilement of Americans.[10]

Downes did, however, find more than Thomson to praise in the musical score:

> Mr. Britten . . . is a very clever young man, who can provide something in any
> style or taste desired by the patron. He scores with astonishing expertness and
> fluency. He has a melodic vein which is perfectly plausible . . . He shows what
> could be done by a composer whose purpose was deeper and more consistent
> than Mr. Britten's appears to be. The flexibility and modernity of the technical
> treatment were refreshing. That they are derivative does not alter this salient
> and striking fact . . . He knows how to set a text, how to orchestrate in an
> economical and telling fashion; how to underscore dialogue with orchestral
> commentary . . . Then the music begins to fail, the set numbers to become
> wearisome and the listeners to tire of ingenuities which are seen before the
> evening is over as platitudes and notion-counter devices of salesmanship.

While it may be extreme to suggest that there are no characters and no plot, the
charge that the libretto is incoherent may be justified. *Paul Bunyan* grows from
the music for film and theatre which Britten composed for Auden during the
1930s, and it is true that *Paul Bunyan* lacks the obsessive focus characteristic of
Britten's later operas. It is essentially a 'choric opera' whose 'message' is rooted in
collective rather individual expression; indeed, the depiction of the 'chorus as
protagonist' looks forward to the dramatic representation of the power of the
choric community in *Peter Grimes* and *Albert Herring*.[11]

The operetta is constructed as a series of episodes rather than as a cumulative
drama. Britten uses one predominant motive to unite the fragmentary structure –
the simple, limpid, swinging gesture in C major which is sung in unison by the chorus
of Old Trees at the start of the Prologue. [Example 1] This lilting phrase evokes the
calm, seamless state of eternity which existed before man's arrival on earth. The
repetition of this motif in E major at Fig. 1 establishes a tonal juxtaposition which will
be employed both melodically and harmonically throughout the opera (and
which assumes musico-dramatic significance throughout Britten's works);
furthermore, it highlights the tension between the major/minor third interval
which is also an important motif. For example, the geese's melody at Fig. 10 grows
from their opening chain (Fig. 5) of alternating major and minor thirds: the geese
are a step nearer to 'consciousness' and their melody presages man's arrival:

---

10 *New York Times*, 5 May 1941; LL, vol. 2, p. 915.
11 In a programme note, the authors themselves downgraded the importance of the 'soloists',
    describing the work as an operetta without 'star roles' (see Donald Mitchell, 'The Origins,
    Evolution and Metamorphosis of *Paul Bunyan*: Auden's and Britten's "American" Opera',
    in W. H. Auden, *Paul Bunyan* (London: Faber & Faber, 1988), p. 121).

2. PROLOGUE In the forest

Example 1

> *A man is a form of life*
> *That dreams in order to act*
> *And acts in order to dream.*

The community is building a new world, discovering personal freedom, learning to value the individual's choices, to tolerate 'difference' and to protect the 'outsider' against the words and pressures of the community. The Young Trees are bored and impatient for the growth towards consciousness. They are dismissed by the Old Trees as 'silly', 'crazy' and 'sick'; but as the Prologue progresses, the modulation to E major (Figs. 13 and 16) implies that the Old Trees must learn to accept the changes which they feel are being forced upon them:

> *CHORUS OF OLD TREES:*
> *But once in a while the odd thing happens,*
> *Once in a while the dream comes true,*
> *And the whole pattern of life is altered,*
> *Once in a while the moon turns blue.*
> *SEMI-CHORUS OF OLD TREES:*
> *We can't pretend we like it, that it's what we'd choose,*
> *But what's the point in fussing when one can't refuse.*

In this way, Britten uses a feature of the opera's tonal and structural organisation to translate into music the emotions of the text.[12]

Britten's ability to transform a musical phrase (and thus its expressive or emotional associations) by altering only a few small details, such as instrumentation, tempo and dynamics is illustrated at the end of the Old Trees' third verse. The *pianissimo*, plodding, scalic descent, 'We like life to be slow', is radically translated into a more rapid, *marcato* accompaniment for pizzicato strings, harp and piano. As the scalic descent is converted into an emphatic vocal rise articulating

---

12 In the 'Litany' at the end of Act 2, the choral melody is formed from chains of thirds, and a harmonic progression from A major to C major perfectly balances – musically and dramatically – the move from C major to E major in the Prologue.

the Young Trees' agitated cries, 'We do NOT want life to be slow', so the dynamic increases, culminating in the declaration, 'We want to see things and go places' (which is further emphasised by the use of syncopation in the accompaniment).

Britten's command of both text-setting and musical characterisation is displayed in this scene – for example, the elongated rhythm for the Young Trees' *fortissimo* cries 'We're *bored*'. Although he sometimes sets Auden's complex textual rhythms in direct imitation of ordinary speech, he does not avoid unnatural stresses if the prosody or the emotional situation so demand. In this way, he transforms the intonation and rhythm of speech into a 'stylised' melody of memorable musical phrases which complements and conveys the meaning of the text. A good example of this is the song of the two wild geese: the lengthening of the final syllable of their phrase (Fig. 6) enhances the musical characterisation, for this gesture recalls the geese's opening wordless melody, and further contributes to the overall cohesiveness of this section, as the chains of major and minor thirds are harmonically and melodically related to the opening bars of the Prologue. Thus, by developing a rudimentary musical feature, Britten suggests the 'intermediary' position of the geese, between the 'preconscious' trees and 'conscious' man, and so prepares for man's transformatory arrival.

Another aspect of the opera to be attacked by the early critics was Auden's characterisation of the eponymous 'hero', who was perceived to experience no cumulative interaction or traditional development, but rather to be a static, and therefore 'undramatic' definition of a 'pure' state of mind. Paul Bunyan has grown to such a size that his appearance on stage is impractical. He is more than just an adventurous individual who has conquered and opened up new country without violence or bloodshed; rather he has become an embodiment or incarnation of mankind's spirit of conquest. Presented as a disembodied voice, his melodramatic spoken text inevitably creates problems of musical and dramatic integration.

Auden's libretto lacks satisfactory links between its essentially self-contained scenes, and this to some extent inhibits the development of narrative and character. Weaknesses in a spoken drama may, however, benefit an opera libretto which can be arranged as 'set-pieces': the music can heighten the emotional immediacy and rhetoric when continuity is missing in the drama. Britten's music for *Paul Bunyan* is divided throughout into clearly defined 'numbers'. While structural repetitions enhance the musical cohesion (for example, the return of the Western Union Boy's music at the end of Act 2 symmetrically balances the opening act), Britten rejects Wagnerian 'permanent melody' for the classical practice of separate musical numbers which crystallise and hold the emotion of the drama at chosen moments, and exploit the contrasts of the text. This is emphasised by the eclecticism of musical styles, which include the English ballad form, jazz and blues, Italian grand opera, the musical comedy of Gilbert and Sullivan, and the music theatre works of Brecht and Weill.

Stylistic juxtaposition may occur within a single number. In 'The Fight' in Act 2, Britten is not content with a mere replica of the Broadway idiom but contrasts the 'love theme' of Slim and Tiny, which is derived from their earlier solo numbers, with an intense Stravinskian ostinato pattern. Auden's text draws attention to the opposition of material:

> TINY: *That I may be left alone*
> *With my true love close to my heart.*
> *(Thunder and shouts off.)*
> SLIM: *Tiny.*
> TINY: *Yes, dear.*
> SLIM: *Did you hear a funny noise?*
> TINY: *I did, but I don't care.*

This variety is endemic to the theme of the opera for it suggests that the raw newness of America is essentially a miscellany of European fragments, an idea which is reinforced by details such as the European origins of the lumberjacks.

The works composed by Britten in collaboration with Auden during their early years in America embraced popular forms and pastiche. Indeed, even before his departure for America Britten's musical language had assimilated some elements of the American popular idiom. In a letter to Enid and Montagu Slater, 29 December 1938, he declared, 'I am now definitely into my 'American' period, & nothing can stop me. I hum the tunes & mutter the words all day, & all my ideas now seem to be that way too.'[13] Similarly, he indicated his intention to formulate an 'authentic' American voice in a letter to Ralph Hawkes, 7 December 1939: 'PAUL BUNYAN is progressing well . . . It is very witty but nevertheless serious in the fundamental idea. I have sketched one or two tunes already, a little bit more serious than the Hedli tunes[14] but very direct and simple, which is the kind of style I propose to use throughout the work.'[15] The *Cabaret Songs*, composed in the style of classic American popular song, are predecessors of many of the set pieces and Broadway-style choruses found in *Paul Bunyan*. The richly chromatic melody and exaggerated vocal gestures of 'Funeral Blues' (which was adapted from the number 'Stop all the clocks', written in June 1937 for Auden and Isherwood's play, *The Ascent of F6*), is a pastiche of the stoical lamentations and flamboyant imagery of a blues lyric. It looks forward to the 'Quartet of the Defeated' in *Paul Bunyan*, which tells of the hopes and perils involved when forging civilisation from chaos, and whose bass rhythm is more funereal than jazz-like:

> TENOR SOLO:
> *Gold in the North came the blizzard to say,*
> *I left my sweetheart at the break of day,*
> *The gold ran out and my love grew grey.*
>   *You don't know all, sir, you don't know all.*

The eclectic idioms of the *Cabaret Songs* and *Paul Bunyan* encompass both humorous, light-hearted entertainment and more serious political and sexual

---

[13] LL, vol. 1, p. 603.
[14] The *Cabaret Songs* composed for the soprano, Hedli Anderson.
[15] LL, vol. 2, p. 740.

references. For example, Auden's libretto contains much contemporary satire –
such as the revolutionary politics of the Young Trees:

> *CHORUS OF OLD TREES:*
> *Reds.*
> *CHORUS OF YOUNG TREES:*
> *We are bored with standing still,*
> *We want to see things and go places.*
> *CHORUS OF OLD TREES:*
> *Such nonsense. It's only a phase.*
> *They're sick. They're crazy.*

This contrasts with the 'Cooks' Duet' which comically parodies the affected style
of Italian grand opera.[16] The text comments on the vulgarities of the advertising
culture which plays on man's physical and commercial insecurities, and on the
vacuity of the glamourised dream-life represented by Hollywood and magazines:

> *SAM SHARKEY: The Best People are crazy about soups!*
> *BEN BENNY: Beans are all the rage among the Higher Income*
> *Groups!*

Britten mimics the hypnotic quality of advertising slogans and clichés by his
use of drone-like intoning on a single pitch, a device which recurs in the 'Litany'
where men, women and animals join together to ask for salvation, and the
animals are given the task of cataloguing a series of 'Audenesque' social ills:

> *FIDO, MOPPET and POPPET:*
> *From a Pressure Group that says I am the Constitution,*
> *From those who say Patriotism and mean Persecution,*
> *From a Tolerance that is really inertia and delusion*
> *CHORUS:*
> *Save animals and men.*

The realities of the present are thus contrasted with Paul Bunyan's prophetic
dreams of man's contented natural state, and in this way the satire contradicts the
epic, for Paul Bunyan brings man to a world he cannot enjoy.[17]

Although it is a 'youthful' work, there are many elements in *Paul Bunyan* that
would later become characteristic of Britten's technique, such as the supremely
assured handling of an eclectic range of musical idioms and styles, and the richly
melodic vocal style. The skilful writing for large chorus and the imaginative
approach to orchestral textures and instrumental groupings (for example,
Inkslinger's music is characterised by the absence of strings in the

---

[16] This duet looks forward to the rustics' music in Act 3 of *A Midsummer Night's Dream*.

[17] Peter Evans observes that the Litany epitomises a major problem resulting from the stylistic
and expressive eclecticism of Auden's and Britten's opera: the refrain – 'Save animals and
men' – 'is of an unaffected, even touching, melodic simplicity, whereas the conceit of setting
a catalogue of abominations of modern life as a litany intoned by the three animals invites
titters that are difficult to reconcile with the sombre mood of valediction' (Peter Evans, *The
Music of Benjamin Britten* (Oxford: Oxford University Press, 1996), p. 103).

accompaniment) demonstrate Britten's effortless technical facility and superb dramatic awareness. Moreover, the innovative use of Far Eastern sonorities, tonalities and textures – the pseudo-gamelan ensemble and layering of the Prologue – look forward to the more extensive use of such techniques in *A Midsummer Night's Dream*, *Death in Venice*, *The Prince of the Pagodas*, and the church parables.[18] Most individual is the distinctive 'harmonic voice' which combines traditional tonal writing with more dissonant, astringent harmonies (for example, in the 'Mocking of Hel Helson' the choral monotones strike obliquely against the harmony thereby emphasising Helson's position 'outside' the community).

More important, perhaps, than these musical features is the nascent appearance of several dramatic themes and issues which would preoccupy Britten in subsequent years. Auden professed to believe that 'Opera . . . cannot present character in the novelist's sense of the word, namely, people who are potentially good and bad, active and passive, for music is immediate actuality and neither potentiality nor passivity can live in its presence'.[19] Auden's conviction that the opera libretto was a genre in which psychological complexity and self-deception were impossible is, as I shall demonstrate in the following chapters, emphatically challenged by each of Britten's subsequent librettos. Auden did believe, however, that music could portray the relation of immediate and simultaneous states to one another, and this is exemplified in *Paul Bunyan* by 'Inkslinger's Song', where Johnny reflects upon the precarious equilibrium between the simplicity of nature and the sophistication of human culture. The form and melodic style of the song is reminiscent of the *Cabaret Songs* but Britten employs a more complex harmonic palette that boldly contrasts with the strict diatonicism of the narrator's preceding ballad interludes. The shifting modulations and chromaticism of the accompaniment underline the intellectual sophistication of Inkslinger's speculations; the forlorn orchestral cadence of the opening bars (xylophone and celeste supported by woodwind and harp) colours the number and is taken up by the voice, which steadily grows in intensity from a subdued recitative style in the opening verse into the expansive melody of the third stanza. The refrain which concludes each strophe – 'But I guess that a guy's gotta eat' – is harmonised by the motif from the opening bars of the song. This motif is transformed at Fig. 6 into the major mode and, accompanied by a radiant instrumental texture spanning three octaves, expresses a Utopian vision which suggests that Inkslinger's personal predicament is transcended by the universal dilemma of the creative individual's responsibility and 'usefulness' to society. At this point Auden articulates the social conscience of the 1930s:

> INKSLINGER:
> *Oh, but where are those beautiful places*
> *Where what you begin you complete,*

---

[18] For a full consideration of 'orientalism' in Britten's music, see Mervyn Cooke, *Britten and the Far East: Asian Influences in the Music of Benjamin Britten* (Woodbridge: The Boydell Press, 1998).

[19] W. H. Auden, *The Dyer's Hand* (London: Faber & Faber, 1946), p. 470.

> *Where the joy shines out of men's faces,*
> *And all get sufficient to eat?*

'Inkslinger's Song' is remarkable for its complexity of feeling, as the protagonist strives for the ambiguous, the unattainable, the unknowable. Johnny Inkslinger is a man of 'superior intellect' who possesses a speculative and critical intelligence: in some ways he foreshadows Britten's subsequent tortured 'heroes' – Peter Grimes, Albert Herring, Billy Budd, Nick Bottom, Owen Wingrave, Gustave von Aschenbach – in that we sense a richer experience painfully eluding his grasp.

Inkslinger's 'Regret' (No. 16) encapsulates the poignancy of his impotence and self-knowledge [Example 2]. The chamber scoring is very controlled: as solo oboe, clarinet and bassoon trace rising and falling scales in C minor, Inkslinger's vocal line returns repeatedly to the pitch C, a false relation embodying the pain of his 'failure'.

> *All the little brooks of love*
> > *Run down towards each other*
> *Somewhere every valley ends*
> > *And loneliness is over*
> *Some meet early, some meet late,*
> > *Some like me have long to wait.*

The simultaneous sounding of E♮ and E♭ in the final bars perhaps indicates the strain between man's eternal hope and his indomitable will to strive against adversity and misfortune; as Paul Bunyan reassures Johnny:

> PAUL BUNYAN: *I know what you want. It's harder than you think and not so pleasant. But you shall have it and shan't have to wait much longer, Good night, Johnny.*

'Bunyan's Goodnight (iii)' (No. 17) which follows the 'Regret', was added by Britten during revisions to the score in 1974:

> *Now let the complex spirit dissolve in the darkness*
> *Where the Actual and the Possible are mysteriously exchanged.*
> *For the saint must descend into Hell; that his order may be tested by its*
> > *disorder*
> *The hero return to the humble womb; that his will may be pacified and*
> > *refreshed.*
> *Dear children, trust the night and have faith in tomorrow,*
> *That these hours of ambiguity and indecision may be also the hours of*
> > *healing.*

Donald Mitchell explains that Auden's unaccompanied text had originally followed a 'Lullaby of Dream Shadows'; Britten excised this 'dream sequence' in 1974 and recomposed the passage for voice and orchestra. Perhaps we may see in the hero's 'return to the humble womb' a foreshadowing of Peter Grimes's resigned return to the safe depths of 'calm water'; indeed, the static C major string chord, with flattened seventh recalls the harmonic and instrumental colour associated with Grimes from his first appearance in the Prologue of *Peter Grimes*.

16. INKSLINGER'S REGRET

Example 2

Likewise, the 'hours of ambiguity and indecision' which may also be 'the hours of healing' look forward to Captain Vere's struggle with the mists of conscience and his ultimate vision of the 'far-shining sail'. In Britten's final opera, *Death in Venice*, Aschenbach was to discover the inescapable truth of the line, 'For the saint must descend into Hell; that his order may be tested by disorder'.

'Bunyan's Goodnight (iii)' effects a symmetrical, harmonic closure to the Act [Example 3]. Britten instructs that the final bar of the Act should be repeated 'many times with dim. but no rall.'. Thus a pure, still major third, C–E, marked *pppp*, is destabilised in perpetuity by a 'lively' violin solo, whose leaping melody, G♯–E–D♯, intimates the E major tonality which had challenged the preternatural C major at the opening of Prologue. The conflict between Nature's instinctive acceptance and man's questing intellect will continue.

Example 3

Britten's musical intensification and lucid instrumental textures endow Inkslinger with a human profile and conscience which elevate him to the central role in the opera.[20] However, his search for self-knowledge is intimated to a lesser extent in Slim's Song (No. 12):

[20] Mitchell notes that in the 1941 performance, Inkslinger's song was heard after the 'Exit of the Lumberjacks', near the end of Act 1, with the result that it was separated from his 'Regret'; Mitchell surmises that this was primarily a production decision, designed to space out the solo numbers on a more even basis throughout the work. However, when *Bunyan*

In fair days and in foul
    Round the world and back,
I must hunt my shadow
    And the self I lack.

One winter evening as I sat
    By my camp fire alone,
I heard a whisper from the flame,
    The voice was like my own:

'O get you up and get you gone,
    North, South or East or West,
This emptiness cannot answer
    The heart in your breast

'O ride till woods or houses
    Provide the narrow place
Where you can force your fate to turn
    And meet you face to face.'

In fair days and in foul
    Round the world and back,
I must hunt my shadow
    And the self I lack.

Slim's sense of his 'other self', a voice from which he turns but which he ultimately must face, perhaps foreshadows the torments suffered by Britten's later protagonists – Peter Grimes, Captain Vere, Gloriana and Aschenbach – who, similarly 'divided', must heed and assimilate the voices of their 'other selves' in order to achieve self-reconciliation.

In *Paul Bunyan*, Inkslinger's 'other self' is represented by Hel Helson, the strident, arrogant Foreman who cannot recognise that he will never be 'great', and who resents being superseded by the farmers. He has no proper 'aria', although in the 'Mocking of Hel Helson' he brashly puts forward 'slogan-like' estimates of himself – Helson the Brave, the Fair, the Wise, the Good and the Strong. Helson is taunted by the farmers, just as Peter Grimes is persecuted by the Borough. Possessing brawn but no brains, Helson is dangerous only when his awareness of lacking intelligence turns to suspicion and hatred of those who possess it. Helson's viciousness when threatened by others, or when faced with his own sense of inadequacy and failure, looks ahead to the spite and cruelty of Peter Grimes, Tarquin, Claggart and Oberon.

Believing himself to be misunderstood and undervalued, Helson launches a violent attack on Paul Bunyan. Their confrontation is juxtaposed with a love duet between Slim, the country boy who has learned to dream, and Tiny, Paul Bunyan's daughter.[21] In a comic operetta which emphasises the power of

---

    was revised in 1974, Britten returned to the original sequence as composed, thus reuniting Inkslinger's 'Song' and 'Regret' in Act 2.

[21] This number anticipates the relaxed lyricism of the music Britten would compose for Sid

communal effort and endeavour, it is natural that Helson does not suffer Grimes's tragic fate; awakening with a sore head and a stiff chin, he is reconciled with Bunyan:

> *PAUL BUNYAN: I'm sorry, Hel, I had to do it.*
> *I'm your friend, if you but knew it.*
> *HELSON: Good heavens! What a fool I've been!*
> *PAUL BUNYAN: Let bygones be bygones. Forget the past.*
> *We can now be friends at last.*
> *Each of us has found a brother.*
> *You and I both need each other.*

The more sinister face of communal pressure and oppression would be dramatised in Britten's later operas.

To what extent is *Paul Bunyan* a 'serious' opera? How seriously should we take the covert 'messages' – political, social and personal – that we suspect reside in Auden's libretto? The popular idiom is always distanced, which may imply the creators' own reluctance to fully commit themselves. It was the inconsistency and seeming lack of commitment that the critics vilified and, indeed, it is difficult either to discuss any one element of *Paul Bunyan* in isolation, or to convincingly talk about 'the whole'.

'Inkslinger's Love Song', discarded by Britten when the opera was revived in 1974, illustrates this difficulty. It perfectly demonstrates Auden's lexicographical dexterity and mastery of the 'Gilbert and Sullivan' idiom; indeed, Inkslinger's first words are, 'Think of a language and I'll write you a dictionary':

> *CHORUS: But how do you think we should address her*
> *What can we of to impress her?*
> *INKSLINGER: You must sing her a love song.*
> *CHORUS: That's too hard and takes too long.*
> *INKSLINGER: Nonsense. It's quite easy, and the longer it is, the more*
> *   she'll like it. Use the longest words you can think of. Like this.*
> *In this emergency*
> *Of so much urgency,*
> *   What can I do*
> *Except wax lyrical?*
> *Don't look satirical;*
> *I have empirical*
> *   Proof I love you.*
> *Like statisticians, I*
> *Distrust magicians, I*
> *   Think them a crew,*
> *That is, collectively;*
> *Speaking objectively*

and Nancy in *Albert Herring*; similarly, the welcoming of Helson back into the community is reminiscent of Albert's reacceptance by the Loxford worthies following his night of drunken excesses.

> *If not effectively,*
> *I feel protectively*
> *Mad about you.*

Such effortless and exuberant flippancy, reminiscent of Auden's lyrics for 'Tell Me the Truth About Love' (*Cabaret Songs*), may be deceptive. Despite his professed satisfaction with his emotional life, in his private journals Auden analysed his homosexuality as a disorder whose cure he could never find, believing that this own path to love was blocked by the psychological detritus of his childhood: 'the bugger got too much mother love, so sheers off women altogether, the whorer too little, so must always have another'.[22] Such apparent self-knowledge may have been of little comfort; Donald Mitchell suggests that 'Tell Me the Truth About Love' reveals Auden's preoccupation with his ignorance of love, a term capable of infinite definition – the concluding words are 'Will it alter my life altogether? O tell me the truth about love.'[23]

There are other moments in *Paul Bunyan* which seem to have an affecting personal significance, most especially the Act 1 chorus of Old Trees, 'But once in a while an odd thing happens'. Recalling the phrase 'the moon turns blue', Britten once remarked to Donald Mitchell, 'That was Peter',[24] and indeed a letter from Pears to Britten, 9 January 1940, declares, 'as long as I am with you, you can stay away till the moon turns blue'. At this point in *Paul Bunyan* (Fig. 13) Britten employs a musical technique which is closely related to Balinese gamelan techniques; and it is no accident that the operetta was written in 1940 at a time when Britten was in close contact with the composer and ethnomusicologist Colin McPhee. In 'Catching on to the Technique in Pagoda-land',[25] Donald Mitchell remarks that the importation of an exotic technique into *Paul Bunyan* was probably an attempt to find and 'alien and unexpected' musical idiom to match the 'exceptional dramatic moment (a blue moon)'. Perhaps this passage is an early sign that the assimilation of oriental techniques and colours into Britten's music may have carried some musico-dramatic 'meaning'. Man will be born at the next blue moon, and the whole pattern of life will be altered.

The search for love is perhaps the most 'subtle' theme in *Paul Bunyan*. Although Auden had earlier protested that his crooked sexuality made love impossible for him, he later realised that his homosexuality did not necessarily have to isolate him, and that love was a matter of choice. In a world where in a material sense almost anything is possible, modern man faces a boundless moral choice; how is he to know what is the right action?:

> *VOICE OF PAUL BUNYAN:*
> *The pattern is already clear*
> *That machinery imposes*

[22] Mendelson, *The English Auden*, p. 59.
[23] When Auden did eventually find love with Chester Kallman in May 1939, he was inspired to write 'Calypso' which became the fourth of Britten's *Cabaret Songs*.
[24] HC, p. 150.
[25] *Tempo*, 146, 1983, 13–24.

> *On you as the frontier closes,*
> *Gone the natural disciplines*
> *And the life of choice begins . . .*
> *As at freedom's puzzled feet*
> *Yawn the gulfs of self-defeat;*
> *All but heroes are unnerved*
> *When life and love must be deserved.*

The libretto is most obviously concerned with this at the end:

> *VOICE OF PAUL BUNYAN:*
> *Every day America's destroyed and re-created,*
> *America is what you do,*
> *America is I and you,*
> *America is what you choose to make it.*

Auden may have addressed these lines to Britten, as a reply to his frequent complaints that America was not living up to its promise: 'America seems to be letting us down in every way . . . She is so narrow, so self-satisfied, so chauvinistic, so superficial, so reactionary, & above all so ugly . . . This country is dead, because it hasn't been lived in, because it hasn't been worked on . . . Everything comes too easily – success, wealth, luxury. They have no standards; no culture –'.[26] In this context, Inkslinger may be seen as an 'outsider' who initially refuses to partake in the American way of life, yet who eventually submits and is rewarded with a share in the American Dream. Auden's conclusion to *Paul Bunyan* may have been intended to alter Britten's attitude to America, and to bring about his 'rebirth' both as an American and as someone who was comfortable with his own sexuality. In this way, the overtly allegorical structure encloses more personal feelings. In representing the move from an uncivilised to a civilised society, Auden is encouraging Britten to progress from 'raw' feeling to a manifestation of that feeling. Thus, *Paul Bunyan* reiterates the theme of *Our Hunting Fathers*:

> *Saw in the lion's intolerant look,*
> *Behind the quarry's dying glare,*
> *Love raging for that personal glory*
> *That reason's gift would add.*

The earlier work's proposal that love and hate are part of the same basic animal instinct is echoed in the 'Hymn' in Act 2 of *Paul Bunyan*, 'O great day of discovery':

> *VOICE OF PAUL BUNYAN:*
> *Often thoughts of hate conceal*
> *Love we are ashamed to feel;*
> *In the climax of a fight*
> *Lost affection comes to light.*

Auden may be urging Britten to free himself from the sexual guilt which

---

[26] LL, vol. 2, p. 800.

'imprisons' him.[27] At this point in the opera the 'love theme' of Slim and Tiny is recapitulated, suggesting that any 'New World' must be based on personal acts of love, as the collective experience is exchanged for unique human relationships:

> Lost, lost is the world I knew
> And I am lost, dear heart, in you.

In *Paul Bunyan* man's search for individualism and personal love is further explored through the depiction of man's relationship with the animal world. Fido, the dog, and Moppet and Poppet, the cats, are incorporated into the libretto ostensibly to allow the introduction of female voices (high soprano and two mezzo sopranos respectively) into an otherwise male-dominated opera. However, in the 'Cats' Creed' the theme of man's necessary choices is brought to the fore:

> Let Man the romantic in vision espy
> A far better world than his own in the sky
> As a tyrant or beauty express a vain wish
> To be mild as a beaver or chaste as a fish . . .
> But the cat is an Aristotelian and proud
> Preferring hard fact to intangible cloud;
> Like the troll in Peer Gynt, both in hunting and love,
> The cat has one creed: 'To thyself be enough'

Such sentiments are reminiscent of Auden's verse 'Underneath an Abject Willow', set by Britten in 1937, which similarly compares the instinctive life of natural phenomena with the human life of conscious choice:

> Geese in flocks above you flying,
> Their direction know,
> Icy brooks beneath you flowing,
> To their ocean go.
> Dark and dull is your distraction:
> Walk then, come,
> No longer numb
> Into your satisfaction.[28]

---

27 Such 'shame' and 'guilt' were to torment a chain of Britten's protagonists – Peter Grimes, Lucretia, Captain Vere, Claggart, Gloriana, Owen Wingrave and Aschenbach.

28 Similar ideas were expressed in another Britten setting of Auden's verse of the 1930s, 'Fish in the Unruffled Lakes':

> Fish in the unruffled lakes
> Their swarming colours wear,
> Swans in the winter air
> A white perfection have,
> And the great lion walks
> Through his innocent grove;
> Lion, fish and swan
> Act, and are gone
> Upon Time's toppling wave.
>
> We, till shadowed days are done,
> We must weep and sing

Auden's 'message' – that man, able to distinguish between the 'self' and his environment in a way which the animal kingdom cannot, can consequently choose between alternative actions – had received a rather more enigmatic expression in the Epilogue of *Our Hunting Fathers*, a song cycle composed for the 1936 Norwich Festival. The first stanza of Auden's Epilogue pities the instinctive innocence of the animal world, an undirected force which contrasts with the second stanza's view of a modern human love which, tempered by reason, is the power which motivates the individual's choices. However, such 'power' can lead to guilt and self-regard, and the lines, 'To hunger, work illegally/ And be anonymous', adapted from Lenin, reveal the dissatisfaction that man inevitably experiences, since although his capacity for choice enables him to gain knowledge and freedom, both seem perpetually too limited and incomplete. Britten's vocal setting of these verses lacks any real lyrical quality, until the lines:

> *That human company could so*
> *His southern gestures modify.*

Auden moralises the points of the compass; he had notably declared that 'North must seem the "good" direction, the way towards heroic adventures, South the way to ignoble ease and decadence'.[29] Such sentiments would be recalled by Britten in his final opera, *Death in Venice*, in his depiction of Aschenbach's temptation, liberation and decline amid the warm, hedonistic, southern vistas of Italy. Britten concludes his setting of the Epilogue of *Our Hunting Fathers* with an extended melisma which flowers on the word 'anonymous', suggestive of the guilt which is concealed within the private individual. The final sentiment of *Our Hunting Fathers* is pessimistic, in keeping with the sombre spirit which prevails at the conclusion of *Paul Bunyan*: the animals live in ignorance of a future that they cannot alter, while man remains in a constant state of anxiety.

> *Duty's conscious wrong,*
> *The Devil in the clock,*
> *The goodness carefully worn*
> *For atonement or for luck;*
> *We must lose our loves,*
> *On each beast and bird that moves*
> *Turn an envious look.*
>
> *Sighs for folly done and said*
> *Twist our narrow days,*
> *But I must bless, I must praise,*
> *That you, my swan, who have*
> *All gifts that to the swan*
> *Impulsive Nature gave,*
> *The majesty and pride,*
> *Last night should add*
> *Your voluntary love.*

29 W. H. Auden, 'England: Six Unexpected Days', *Vogue*, CXXVIII, 15 May 1954, 62; in J. G. Blair, *The Poetic Art of W. H. Auden* (New Jersey: Princeton University Press, 1965), p. 89.

*

Britten's years in America were a time of reappraisal and reassessment of his personal and professional goals. Bouts of depression alternated with feelings of creative well-being. Far from being 'reborn' as an American, it was during the unhappy summer of 1941 that Britten's discovery of the poetry of George Crabbe reawakened his need for roots which he had first expressed to Kit Welford, 4 April 1940: 'You see, Kit, in so many ways this country is such a terrible disappointment . . . I'm gradually realising that I'm English – & as a composer I suppose I feel I want more definite roots than other people.'[30] In 1960 he told Lord Harewood: 'I was very ill for a year or so in the early days of the war in America. When the illness cleared, I knew quite definitely that my home did not lie there, that whatever the situation was, that I was a European, and so I came back.'[31] It is a mistake, however to imagine that Britten's geographical relocation marked a radical or immediate split in his relationship with Auden. He continued to hold the poet in high esteem, although his feelings about his 'American' opera were more ambivalent. Revisions which he began with Auden in 1941 were almost immediately abandoned, and writing to the American composer, Douglas Moore, Britten summed up the experience of composition in negative terms: 'I feel that I have learned lots about what not to write for the theatre.'[32]

One thing he may have learnt was not to be so dominated by his librettist. In a conversation with Donald Mitchell, 27 October 1990, Stephen Spender recalled some remarks made by Christopher Isherwood:

> Isherwood made a very revealing remark as a matter of fact, which I've been puzzling about ever since. I said something about Ben and he said, 'Well, Ben is like water in our hands. Ben is a very weak character and Wystan and I can do anything we like with him'.

> I think that Auden said he wrote to Ben after one of his operas a very praising letter but that Auden, considering himself a great expert on opera and music and everything – . . . had made a few criticisms, and the letter arrived in the envelope, torn up.[33]

However, Britten's later attitude towards the years he spent in America was not entirely negative. He wrote to David Rothman, 29 September 1942, that 'those three glorious years I spent in the States are becoming more & more dreamlike in quality – and a very beautiful dream it was too!'[34]

In his article 'The Origins, Evolution and Metamorphosis of *Paul Bunyan*: Auden's and Britten's "American" Opera', Donald Mitchell comments that the negative critical reception which *Paul Bunyan* received in 1941 may well have contributed to Britten's suspicion of, and hostility towards, analytical and critical interpretations of his work. Although, as Mitchell points out, there were also

---

30 LL, vol. 2, pp. 793–4.
31 LL, vol. 1, pp. 618–19.
32 24 June 1941; LL, vol. 2, p. 947.
33 LL, vol. 2, pp. 1338–9.
34 *Ibid.*, pp. 1084–5.

positive comments about the operetta, Britten was notoriously sensitive to criticism and censure. Many subsequent events – such as the establishment of the English Opera Group and later the Aldeburgh Festival, thereby providing Britten with a carefully chosen group of trusted collaborators and a 'protected' forum for performance – may be traced to Britten's fragility and self-doubt when faced with even the most constructive form of criticism.

One additional factor influencing Britten's original decision to travel to America may have been the potential offer of work on a film in Hollywood. A letter to Wulff Scherchen, 7 February 1939, hinted: '((((Shshshsssh . . . I may have an offer from Holywood [sic] for a film, but don't say a word))).'[35] He wrote again, ten days later: 'Hollywood seems a bit nearer – I've got an interview with the Producer on Monday.'[36] The promised commission did not materialise but Britten had high hopes for *Paul Bunyan*, writing to his sister, Beth: 'Wystan & my opera [sic] is settled for Broadway when we have done it.'[37] Although neither aspiration was achieved, such objectives surely influenced the actual composition of the opera. The fulfilment of the American Dream is intimately connected with success in Hollywood and it is interesting that at the end of *Paul Bunyan*, when Johnny Inkslinger is reconciled with Paul Bunyan, he is rewarded with an offer to go to Hollywood, such as Britten himself had desired. The Western Union messenger boy rides in on a bicycle, bearing a summons to Hollywood:

> *A telegram, a telegram,*
>   *A telegram from Hollywood.*
> *Inkslinger is the name;*
>   *And I think that the news is good.*

However, in the end Britten himself discarded his American optimism, ignoring the words of his own 'hero', 'America is what you choose to make it'. Liberated by his newly found love for Peter Pears, Britten turned his back on the American Dream and chose a different path; in so doing, he cut himself free from the burden of expectation placed upon him by the dominating, sometimes bullying, figure of Auden. In future, the struggle to fulfil his personal 'dreams' would take place on his native soil and, indeed, it was during the home-bound journey, aboard the liner *Axel Johnson*, that Britten and Pears made the first sketches of what was to become *Peter Grimes*. Yet, as analysis of his subsequent operas will reveal, Britten found it almost impossible to totally shut out the perceptive and persuasive voice of the older poet, whose words resonate with force throughout Britten's life and operas:

> *VOICE OF PAUL BUNYAN: You and I must go our own way;*
> *I have but one word to say:*
> *O remember, friends, that you*
> *Have the hardest task to do*

---

[35] LL, vol. 1, p. 610.
[36] *Ibid.*
[37] 19 October 1939, LL, vol. 2, p. 707.

> As at freedom's puzzled feet
> Yawn the gulfs of self-defeat;
> All but heroes are unnerved
> When life and love must be deserved.

Britten's eventual 'break' with Auden was presaged as early as 1936, with Auden's decision to fight in the Spanish Civil War. While Britten was deeply opposed to Fascism, he could condone no violent retaliation against it, and wrote in his diary, 1 December 1936: 'After dinner he tells me he's decided to go to Spain after Xmas and fight – I try to dissuade him, because what the Spanish Gov. might gain by his joining is nothing compared with the world's gain by his continuing to write; but no-one can make W. H. A. alter his mind.'[38] Yet despite his disapproval, he told John Pounder, 'one has enough respect for his integrity than to try & persuade him not to go'.[39]

This disagreement was an early sign of the irreparable differences of opinion which shortened their professional collaboration and eventually led to a definitive split in their personal relationship. However, despite the unbridgeable distance, literal and emotional, which subsequently separated the two men, Auden seems to have exerted an enduring influence throughout Britten's career. In an interview with Lord Harewood for the BBC in 1960, Britten remembered: 'I was very much influenced by Auden, not only in poetry but in life too, and politics, of course, came very strongly into our lives in the late thirties.'[40] Their respective ambitions and professed priorities may have increasingly diverged, but still one senses an innate, shared sense of purpose and intention. During the 1930s, that 'low dishonest decade', the prevailing atmosphere was one of political, social and moral upheaval. Auden had declared, 'Personally the kind of poetry I should like to write but can't is "the thoughts of a wise man in the speech of the common people" ',[41] a statement which is in echoed in Britten's own consciousness of his social responsibility: 'I want my music to be of use to people, to please them.'[42] Furthermore, in his 1935 essay, 'Psychology and Art Today', Auden set out a psychological account of the genesis of the artist and his place in society:

> You cannot tell people what to do, you can only tell them parables; and that is what art really is, particular stories of particular people and experiences, from which each according to his immediate and peculiar needs may draw his own conclusions . . .
>
> Poetry is not concerned with telling people what to do, but with extending our knowledge of good and evil, perhaps making the necessity for action more urgent and its nature more clear, but only leading us to the point where it is possible for us to make a rational and moral choice . . . one must disabuse people

---

[38] Donald Mitchell, *Britten and Auden in the Thirties: The Year 1936* (London: Faber & Faber, 1981), p. 87.

[39] LL, vol. 1, p. 465.

[40] *Ibid.*, p. 618.

[41] Mendelson, *The English Auden*, p. 360.

[42] Britten, *Aspen Award Speech 1963*, in LL, vol. 1, p. 66.

of the idea that poetry is primarily an escape from reality. We all need escape at times, just as we need food and sleep, and some escape poetry there must always be . . . one must show those who come to poetry for a message, for calendar thoughts, that they have come to the wrong door, that poetry may illuminate but it will not dictate.[43]

In the final scene of *Paul Bunyan*, Johnny Inkslinger calls upon Paul Bunyan to bless them all. Man has tamed the wilderness but we are reminded that the hardest task is ours: 'all but heroes are unnerved/When love and life must be deserved'. Bunyan's final rhetoric possibly looks ahead to the solemnity and introspection at the close of *Peter Grimes*:[44]

> PAUL BUNYAN:
> *Where the night becomes the day,*
> *Where the dream becomes the fact,*
> *I am the Eternal Guest,*
> *I am Way,*
> *I am Act.*
>
> PETER GRIMES:
> *What harbour shelters peace*
> *Away from tidal waves*
> *Away from storms!*
> *What harbour can embrace*
> *Terrors and tragedies?*
> *Her breast is harbour too –*
> *Where night is turned to day.*

Hel Helson alone remains inarticulate: lacking the power of reflection and self-knowledge, he wonders what will become of him, and America, when Paul Bunyan leaves.

In 1941, when he returned to England, Britten could not have been consciously aware of the range and significance of the choices which he would be forced to make in his personal and professional life; nor could he foresee how he would dramatise these choices in a series of operatic 'parables' that might provide an occasional or temporary 'escape', and which would seek to *illuminate* but never to *dictate*. The questions posed at the end of *Paul Bunyan* resonated throughout Britten's life, and were partially and creatively 'answered' in his operas; they remain as apposite for us all today as they were sixty years ago. Britten's 'rôle' as a

---

43 Mendelson, *The English Auden*, p. 341 and pp. 329–30. In 1927 the undergraduate Auden, rebelling against the ethic of public service, had written, 'All genuine poetry is in a sense the formation of private spheres out of a public chaos' ('Preface' to *Oxford Poetry* (Oxford: Basil Blackwell, 1977, p. v)). One might argue that Britten's operas were the formation of a public sphere out of a private chaos.

44 Milton Smith, the stage director of the original production recalls his 'attempt to get Auden to do something to give us a more rousing, patriotic *end*' (quoted in Mitchell, *Britten and Auden*, p. 107).

composer was not to explain or instruct but rather to liberate the listener, the performer and Britten himself into a future in which he or she could learn to choose a path of their own.

> All the others translate: the painter sketches
> A visible world to love or reject;
> Rummaging into his living, the poet fetches
> The images out that hurt and connect,
>
> From Life to Art by painstaking adaption,
> Relying on us to cover the rift;
> Only your notes are pure contraption,
> Only your song is an absolute gift.
>
> Pour out your presence, a delight cascading
> The falls of the knee and the weirs of the spine,
> Our climate of silence and doubt invading;
>
> You alone, alone, imaginary song,
> Are unable to say an existence is wrong,
> And pour out your forgiveness like a wine.[45]

---

[45] W. H. Auden, *The Composer*, December 1938.

3

Peter Grimes

I set out to study [the score] . . . and I came to the conclusion that there was absolutely not one thing about the Peter Grimes in the poem that related to Peter Grimes in the opera . . . [I]f there was a model on which Ben hung the character in the opera, it was on Crabbe himself.   Jon Vickers[1]

Who is Peter Grimes? In his article 'George Crabbe and Peter Grimes'[2] E. M. Forster identifies two men, distinguishing between Crabbe's harsh, dull and insensitive murderer, for whom no possibility of mercy intervenes, and Britten's 'misunderstood Byronic hero', 'sensitive, touched by pity, stung by remorse, and corrected by shame'. Crabbe's Grimes embodies the dark side of a morally weak society, which the poet satirises but does not judge, whereas Britten's Grimes is the victim of a cruel society, which is criticised and condemned. Forster's observations are penetrating but his divisions are too categorical and cannot accommodate the complexities of Britten's Grimes and his relationship to the society that rejects him.

Peter Pears, the first interpreter of the role, acknowledged the difficulty of 'defining' Peter Grimes:

> In the opera, the Borough is very much the same as Crabbe's Borough . . . Peter Grimes himself, on the other hand, is a more complicated character and considerably removed from the desperado of the poem . . . Grimes is not a hero nor is he an operatic villain. He is not a sadist nor a demonic character, and the music quite clearly shows that. He is very much of an ordinary weak person who, being at odds with the society in which he finds himself, tries to overcome it and, in doing so, offends against the conventional code, is classed by society as a criminal, and destroyed as such. There are plenty of Grimeses around, still I think![3]

Significantly, Pears suggests that Grimes has two 'identities', a dramatic persona and a musical persona, but his unequivocal interpretation is an inadequate response to the complexities of the opera. Moreover his sympathetic reading – he also states that 'it is clear that he was no murderer' – is undermined by contradictory interpretations proposed by Britten and Pears elsewhere. Thus their

---

[1] Jon Vickers, 'Jon Vickers on Peter Grimes', *Opera*, August 1984, vol. 35, no. 8, 835–43.

[2] E. M. Forster, 'George Crabbe and Peter Grimes', in *Two Cheers for Democracy* (London: Arnold, 1972), pp. 166–80. This essay was first given as a lecture at the 1948 Aldeburgh Festival.

[3] Peter Pears, 'Neither a Hero nor a Villain', *Radio Times*, 8 March 1946, 3.

vacillations, or deliberate misrepresentations, further complicate any attempt to unravel the knot of incompatible 'readings' of Grimes.

Pears draws attention to the conflict between the individual and society which is present in many Crabbe poems (and in nearly all of Britten's operas), explaining the destructive nature of Grimes's social alienation and so blaming the Borough for the tragedy which ensues. However, Britten's Grimes is repulsed by *and* attracted to the community in which he lives, and it is this unsettling dialectic between attraction and repulsion which informs many of the opera's dramatic tensions. Furthermore, Grimes is at war not only with the Borough but also with himself. His conformist longing for social acceptance, which he hopes to achieve through material success, conflicts with his violent and rebellious individual will, which finds expression in his more visionary aspirations. These contradictory desires might be considered to be manifestations of his conscious and subconscious ambitions, aspirations which are ultimately irreconcilable.

The composition of *Peter Grimes* involved the interaction of various personalities and ambitions and the resulting opera is an elaborate amalgam of the designs of Crabbe, the librettist Montagu Slater, Britten and Pears. As layers of text accumulated and were superimposed, so Grimes's identity fragmented. Furthermore, not only is Grimes a schizophrenic muddle but the Borough which destroys him is also redefined as a dualism by the restructuring of the text: the community are simultaneously guilty of neglecting their moral responsibility – 'We live and let live and look/ We keep our hands to ourselves' – and of appropriating the right to pursue and punish Grimes in order to satisfy their own lust for violence – 'Him who despises us/ We'll destroy'.

These ambiguities might be elucidated by tracing the history and process of composition as revealed by the extant drafts of text and score. The following analysis will attempt to demonstrate how, as Britten's dramatic and musical conceptions developed during the process of composition, the central focus of the opera was diverted from Crabbe's realistic representation of eighteenth-century society and turned ever more intensely upon the psychology of Peter Grimes himself, isolating him from his social and human environments. I shall begin with an examination of the importance of place and setting and continue with an analysis of Grimes's relationships with his father and the apprentice (and their ghosts), Ellen and the Borough. Many of the details from Crabbe's poem which had initially attracted Britten's interest were removed or realigned as the opera evolved, and these radical transformations obscured the motivation behind Grimes's actions, transferring the burden of explication from the verbal to the musical text. As features such as Grimes's father, the apprentice, and Ellen Orford's redemptive status were diminished to verbal shadows and represented musically, there was a gradual movement away from what was 'known' or stated in Crabbe's poem towards what was 'unknown' or articulated only in musical terms in Britten's opera.

In the above quotation Pears posits a possible reason for the opera's dramatic power, i.e. the identification of the audience with the protagonist. Hans Keller commented upon this: 'I should indeed go further than Pears and say that in each of us there is something of a Grimes, though most of us have outgrown or at least outwitted him sufficiently not to recognise him too consciously.'[4]

In this chapter, I shall explore how Britten's own identification with Crabbe's anti-hero influenced his operatic portrayal of Peter Grimes. Returning from America in 1942 to an England which was suspicious of the motives for his departure three years earlier, resentful of his success, and which criminalised pacifists and homosexuals alike, he may have shared Peter Grimes's sense of social insecurity and exclusion. Moreover, as Britten struggled to understand and accept his own sexuality he may have identified with Grimes's internalisation of society's oppression; more ominously, he may have recognised in Grimes's violence his own potential and repressed 'dark side'. In this way, his opera may represent an attempt to find a means of transforming problematic and potentially destructive emotions into a positive creative force. Through detailed analysis of the text and score, I shall explore how Britten attempted to mitigate the social and sexual violence implicit in Crabbe's 'Peter Grimes' through his music. In so doing I hope to unravel the tangled web of complex and often contradictory strands in which the voices of Crabbe, Slater, Britten and Pears intermingle, and from which the 'silenced' voices can never be wholly eradicated.

'To think of Crabbe is to think of England.'[5] So began the *Listener* article by E. M. Forster which Britten and Pears read while working in California in 1941. Forster's words fostered their latent homesickness for the England which they had left three years earlier and led them to seek out for themselves a volume of George Crabbe's poetry. Britten recalled: 'I did not know any of the poems of Crabbe at that time, but reading about him gave me such a feeling of nostalgia for Suffolk, where I had always lived, that I searched for a copy of his works, and made a beginning with "The Borough".'[6] The seeds of an opera based upon the story of Crabbe's brutal fisherman, Peter Grimes, extracted from *The Borough*, were quickly sown, as revealed by Britten's copy of Crabbe's complete works, which is inscribed with the following words by Peter Pears: 'I bought this book at a San Diego [underneath is written "Los Angeles"] bookseller in 1941 and from this we started work on the plans for making an opera out of "Peter Grimes".'[7] In a radio interview Pears commented: 'by the time we came back to London, the whole story of "Peter Grimes" as set in the opera was already shaped and it simply remained to call in a librettist to write the words.'[8] These early drafts would be

4   Hans Keller, 'Peter Grimes: The Story, the Music not Excluded', in Hans Keller and Donald Mitchell (eds.), *Benjamin Britten: A Commentary on His Works from a Group of Specialists* (London: Faber & Faber, 1952), pp. 111–24.

5   E. M. Forster, 'George Crabbe: The Poet and the Man', *The Listener*, 29 May 1941.

6   Benjamin Britten, 'Introduction', in Eric Crozier (ed.), *Benjamin Britten: Peter Grimes*, Sadler's Wells Opera Books, no. 3 (London, 1945), p. 7.

7   Britten's copy of *The Life and Works of the Revd. George Crabbe. Edited by his son, in one volume* (London: John-Murray, 1851) (BPL).

8   Peter Pears, 'Birth of an Opera', unedited tape (BPL), quoted in Philip Brett (ed.), *Benjamin Britten: Peter Grimes*, Cambridge Opera Handbook (Cambridge: CUP, 1983), p. 35.

radically altered during the composition of the opera but it is apparent that Pears's own contribution in these initial stages was considerable: 'while Ben Britten was writing *A Ceremony of Carols* and *Hymn to St Cecilia*, which he wrote on board this ship [the *Axel Johnson*, in March–April 1942] . . . I was planning the original shape of the *Peter Grimes* libretto.'[9] Furthermore, Crozier recalled that it was Pears who contributed many of the libretto's most memorable phrases,[10] and it is interesting to note that when Britten asked Christopher Isherwood to be his librettist he declined, replying: 'I don't see any possibility of collaborating with *you and Peter* [italics added] on the PETER GRIMES libretto.'[11] Following Isherwood's refusal Britten approached Montagu Slater whom he had met during the 1930s when they had collaborated on projects such as *Coal Face* at the GPO Film Unit. Britten had also composed incidental music for Slater's left-wing plays *Stay Down Miner* and *Easter 1916*. At first Britten seemed delighted with Slater's work, writing to Elizabeth Mayer: 'M. has taken to Grimes like a duck to water.'[12] He continues: 'I am actually down in the country staying for a few days with Montagu & Enid Slater, and working with M. hard on the libretto of Peter Grimes. It is going so well & I'm very keen on his whole attitude to the subject – Very simple, full of respect for Crabbe, and with real stage experience.'[13] He told Pears, 12 June 1942: 'The opera is going well – I am delighted with Montagu's attitude to it, & he's steaming ahead.'[14] However, this optimism was short-lived and Britten soon expressed his dissatisfaction to Pears: 'I am sure it isn't <u>fundamentally</u> hopeless, there are too many things I like about it . . . I see so clearly what kind of music I want to write for it . . . I'm beginning to feel that Montagu may not be the ideal librettist; but who? Wystan, well – there are the old objections.'[15] Britten disagreed with Slater's wish that *Peter Grimes* be an extension of his own work in the realist theatre and have a strong socialist sub-text. This discord was aggravated by Slater's working method. According to Eric Crozier, the first producer, Slater was a slow, cautious worker who was unable to respond quickly to Britten's demands.[16] The first typescript libretto is annotated with musical descriptions (aria, recitative, chorus etc.) revealing that from the earliest stages Britten had a clear perception of the opera's musical structure. Consequently he often forged ahead of his librettist, composing music for scenes which were only sketched or not written at all, and the words had to be rewritten to fit pre-existing music.[17] It seems that from the start Britten relied on the music rather than the text to convey the drama, and would sacrifice words without hesitation if they conflicted with the dramatic

---

9   Brett, 'Fiery visions', in *ibid.*, p. 47.
10   *Ibid.*, p. 61.
11   *Ibid.*, p. 35.
12   4 May 1942, LL, p. 1037.
13   5 June 1942, LL, p. 1059.
14   LL, p. 1065.
15   LL, p. 1124.
16   See Brett, *Benjamin Britten: Peter Grimes*, pp. 37–8.
17   Brett (*ibid.*, pp. 67–8), outlines several passages where text was rewritten or considerably adjusted after composition.

thoughts which had shaped his musical ideas.[18] There might be only a momentary link between words and music, although the two would ideally coincide at the opera's dramatic climaxes.

Britten's interest in Crabbe probably owed much to the poet's graphic descriptions of the landscape and inhabitants of his native Suffolk, and more particularly, Aldeburgh. Despite the antipathy which the people of the town frequently showed towards him, Crabbe drifted back to Aldeburgh throughout his life. Like the operatic Peter Grimes, he seems to have believed:

> *I am native, rooted here . . .*
> *By familiar fields,*
> *Marsh and sand,*
> *Ordinary streets,*
> *Prevailing wind . . .*
> *By the shut faces*
> *Of the Borough clans;*
> *And by the kindness*
> *Of a casual glance.*

Similarly, after three years in America, Britten was beginning to understand the veracity of Auden's words, 'an artist must live where he has roots',[19] for he would later declare: 'I am firmly rooted in this glorious county. And I proved this to myself when I once tried to live somewhere else.'[20]

Kenneth Green's preliminary sketches for the stage sets of *Peter Grimes* demonstrate Britten's need for a realistic and naturalistic locale, indicating the importance of the decor and stage movement to Britten. Green, himself a Suffolk

---

[18] Ronald Duncan, the librettist of Britten's next opera, *The Rape of Lucretia*, when asked by Britten to modify Slater's libretto, understood that his own text would be no more sacred than Slater's: 'I realised then that I was setting a precedent; and that the same kind of liberties, though less extensive would one day be taken with my own work' (Duncan, *Working with Britten*, p. 37). Indeed, Britten's sister, Beth, acknowledged that the best librettist for Britten would be 'someone who does not object to having his work altered' (Beth Britten, *My Brother Benjamin*, p. 185). However, Slater did not take this attitude and Crozier remembers one incident when the normally passive Slater, distraught at having the integrity of his text undermined, thumped the table, shouting 'but this is my work, this is my work'. In 1946 he published his own text separately as *'Peter Grimes' and Other Poems* (London: Bodley Head, 1946). His text is almost identical to the 1945 Boosey and Hawkes libretto. Brett suggests (in ' "Fiery visions" (and revisions) *Peter Grimes* in Progress', in Brett, *Benjamin Britten: Peter Grimes*, pp. 47–87) that the 1945 publication was set from an early version of the vocal score, and not from that used for the premiere in 1945. This idea is substantiated by Eric Crozier's working copy (BPL) which was used for the first production and which contains many handwritten additions, substitutions and corrections of the sort found in the 1961 text. These discrepancies can be explained by Slater's exclusion from many of the final discussions concerning last-minute changes which were necessitated by technical difficulties during rehearsals and by Britten's growing dissatisfaction with Slater's text. The 1979 libretto rectified those small errors which had remained in the 1961 edition.

[19] LL, p. 186.

[20] From a speech on being presented with the freedom of Lowestoft in 1951. Quoted in Eric Walter White, *Benjamin Britten: His Life and Operas* (London: Faber & Faber 1983), p. 112.

man, told Mitchell that although his finished designs bore little relation to his early sketches: 'He begs [sic] me to give some visual ideas about the look of the stage – just a rough idea! . . . Ben seemed helped by what visual vague scenery I conjured up.'[21] Significantly the earliest drafts in Britten's hand contain an indication of the physical setting which is accompanied by a basic but clear lay-out of the stage. Whereas Pears's earliest drafts emphasise the opposing forces in the drama,[22] Britten's first thoughts reveal his preoccupation with the theatrical dimension of the opera, which was a striking feature of the first production; as Brett remarked: 'Several eye-witnesses have told me that one of the most powerful effects of the [first] production was the almost claustrophobic atmosphere engendered by the small and crowded stage – a quality they missed in the Covent Garden production two years later.'[23] Britten appears to have considered the physical setting of *Peter Grimes* to be integral to the creation a specific dramatic atmosphere and in several of his later operas he would similarly concerned to define a literal or symbolic stage 'space'.

The nostalgic longing for the Suffolk coast felt by Crabbe, Grimes and Britten is characterised by a fascination with the power and magnificence of the sea. Crabbe wrote to Elizabeth Charter, 14 September 1818, that it was 'that first great object of my Admiration and indeed the first of my Notice. I was an Infant Worshipper of its Glory'.[24] In *The Borough* Crabbe evokes the comforting gentleness and the dangerous latent power of the sea, depicting its endless restlessness which reflects the patterns of human life and death:

> With ceaseless motion comes and goes the Tide,
> Flowing, it wills the Channel vast and wide;
> Then back to Sea, with strong majestic sweep
> It rolls, in ebb yet terrible and deep.   (*The Borough*, I, 37–40)[25]

Similarly, Britten indicated that his passion for the sea influenced the conception of *Peter Grimes*:

> For most of my life I have lived closely in touch with the sea. My parents' house
> in Lowestoft directly faced the sea, and my life as a child was coloured by the

---

[21] Quoted in Brett, *Benjamin Britten: Peter Grimes*, p. 42.

[22] The draft outline in Pears's hand (GB–ALb 2–9401375) contains the following diagram:

The Sea	v	The Earth
(The Incalculable – Uncontrolled)		(Secure, Unchanging)
cf war – violence		Peace etc.
Peter Grimes	v	Ellen Orford
	the boy	
Smugglers	Landlord	Churchgoers
	Sailors.	

[23] Brett, *Benjamin Britten: Peter Grimes*, p. 90.

[24] Quoted in Oliver F. Sigworth, *Nature's Sternest Painter: Five Essays on the Poetry of George Crabbe* (Tucson: University of Arizona Press, 1965), p. 93.

[25] George Crabbe, *The Borough* in *The Complete Poetical Works*, vol. 1, Norma Dalrymple-Champneys and Arthur Pollard (eds.) (Oxford: Clarendon Press, 1988), pp. 360–98. All subsequent references are to this edition.

fierce storms that sometimes drove ships on to our coast and ate away whole stretches of the neighbouring cliffs. In writing Peter Grimes, I wanted to express my awareness of the perpetual struggle of men and women whose livelihood depends on the sea.[26]

This struggle is effectively portrayed in Act 1, Scene 1 where the Borough defiantly assert the obstinate rhythms of their shanty song, ignoring the rhythmic swells of the sea, as depicted by the orchestra. However, Britten's words are to some extent misleading. The sea is more than just a literal backdrop for the action, and it is interesting that he was dissatisfied with stage representations which were too realistic in emphasis:

> We had a brilliant production by Tony Guthrie, but Ben didn't like it at all because the accent was thrown on the sea. Ben said, 'No, it's got nothing to do with the sea. It has to do with the people in the village.' Tony said, 'But Ben, the sea made the people what they were', and Ben replied, 'No, these people would be the same wherever they were.'[27]

Interlude I depicts a coastal dawn; above the rising tidal sweep of clarinet, harp and viola, a sustained and penetrating melody for violin and flute emphasises the pitch E, which has a crucial dramatic function in the opera. The gentle grace notes, F–E, introduce the semitone interval which, in its inverted major seventh and minor ninth forms, embodies the psychological tension of the opera.

Britten's sea is a metaphor for Grimes's subconscious, and this is most apparent in Act 2 where the storm at sea parallels the storm within him. Grimes freely embraces the spirit of the sea. It is a symbol of his loneliness but one which also contains intimations of rebirth. In the first scene of the opera the villagers sing, 'For us sea-dwellers this sea birth can be/ Death to our gardens of fertility', and the sea is both life and death for Grimes:

> *What is home?*
> *Calm as deep water.*
> *Where's my home?*
> *Deep in calm water.*
>
> *Water will drink my sorrows dry and the tide will turn.*

In *The Borough*, George Crabbe makes the mocking chastisements of the dead 'Father-Foe' the focus of Grimes's paranoia, and it is this factor which precipitates his insanity. At the door of Hell Grimes explains that it is his father who has brought him to disaster:

> My Father's Spirit – he who always tried
> To give me trouble, when he liv'd and died –
> When he was gone, he could not be content
> To see my Days in painful labour spent,

26 Britten, 'Introduction', in Crozier, *Peter Grimes*, p. 8.
27 Comments by Ande Anderson, who joined the Covent Garden staff in the late 1940s. Quoted in Brett, *Benjamin Britten: Peter Grimes*, p. 97.

> But would appoint his Meetings, and he made
> Me watch at these, and so neglect my Trade.
>
> (*The Borough*, XXII, 292–7)

The cycle of hostility, fear and guilt which characterises Grimes's relationship with his father possibly replicated Crabbe's own relationship with his father, which Forster describes as similarly troubled. A small town customs official who supplemented his salary by working as a fisherman, Crabbe's father was intelligent and well-read, and he passed on this literary enthusiasm to his children, but his frustration with his immediate environment provoked violent outbursts, exacerbated by alcohol, and Crabbe came to fear him.

Britten's copy of Crabbe's works is heavily annotated, and although it is not apparent when these annotations were made, the large number of markings against references to Peter's father suggests that the father–son relationship was an important factor in Grimes's psychology in the early stages. Pears explained: 'Initially we had a prologue in which Peter Grimes's father appeared on his death-bed, in which he solemnly cursed the boy – the young man – Grimes; but it became apparent fairly soon that this was not a very good idea and the prologue was reshaped by the time we arrived back in England.'[28] A draft scenario which Pears made on board the *Axel Johnson* during the voyage from America, in which he listed the musical numbers that would form the Prologue, confirms this:

No 1. Ellen + old Grimes waiting.
No 2. Enter Peter, drunk, is rude to Grimes, rebuked by Ellen, Old Grimes asks for silence.
No 3. Grimes' last speech + death.
No. 4. Duet (Peter maudlin, Ellen strong + loving).
No. 5. Entracte (The Sea) . . .
No. 11. Grimes' Apostrophe of Sea (appearance of old Grimes ghost?)[29]

There was evidently a strong association between Grimes's physical 'roots' – his father – and his spiritual 'roots' – the sea – and this is strengthened elsewhere in the sketches:

> *I have a father in the sea*
> *Scolding from tides, and it was he*
> *Who made the laws that we shall disobey.*[30]
>
> *Ghosts scene – Grimes monologue. The Sea calls him . . .*[31]

In order to emphasise the cycle of violence which afflicted successive generations of males in the drama, Britten and Pears originally intended to include scenes in which Grimes remembered episodes from his own childhood (as had appeared in Crabbe), thereby clarifying the desire–disgust dichotomy which

[28] In conversation with John Evans, in *Peter Grimes/Gloriana*, ENO Guide, p. 62.
[29] GB–ALb 2–9401377.
[30] GB–ALb 2–9401382.
[31] GB–ALb 2–9401375.

characterised Grimes's relationship with his own father and with his 'surrogate' sons, the apprentices. His father had shown him no love, only violence, and his treatment of the boys is shaped by this experience. Though touched by their vulnerability and innocence he is unable to articulate his empathy and, in his frustration, compassion rapidly turns to anger. A draft in Pears's hand records:

> *admits his youth hurts him, his innocence galls him, his uselessness maddens him. He had no father to love him, why should he? 'Prove yourself some use, not only pretty – work – not be only innocent – work do not stare; would you rather I loved you? You are sweet, young etc. – but you must love me, why do you not love me? Love me damn you.*[32]

This demand for love by an unlovable man resonates with sexual violence and homoeroticism, and continues in a draft of Act 2:

> *ELLEN: Peter tell me one thing, where*
> *Young stranger got his bruise and weals.*
> *PETER: Out of my true affection.*[33]

In the final version of the libretto Peter's reply is changed:

> *PETER: Out of the hurly burly.*

In the draft, Ellen is still sympathetic to Grimes although there is real evidence of his cruelty:

> *PETER: By God I'll beat it out of you*
> *Stand up (lash). Straighter (lash). I'll count two*
> *And then you'll jump to it. One . .*
> *Well? Two (The boy doesn't move. Then Peter lashes hard, twice.*
> *   He runs. Peter follows.)*
> *Your soul is mine*
> *Your body is the cat o' nine*
> *Tails' mincemeat. O! a pretty dish*
> *Smooth-skinned & young as she could wish*
> *Come cat! Up whiplash! Jump my son*
> *Jump (lash) jump (lash) jump, the dance is on.*[34]

The reference to the cat'o'nine tails is retained until a late stage, appearing in the typescript libretto. When Grimes abuses the boy in Act 2, Scene 2 he cries:

> *PETER: You sit there silently. Your eyes*
> *Are like old Ellen's womanly.*
> *You sit there yearning like a girl*
> *Whose face has the wrong tale to tell*
> *You sit there . . .*
> *. . . Will you move if the cat starts making love?*[35]

---

[32] GB–ALb 2–9401375.
[33] GB–ALb 2–9401384.
[34] GB–ALb 2–9401385.
[35] GB–ALb 2–9401387.

In contrast, Slater's portrayal of Grimes's relations with his apprentice was more prosaic:

> GRIMES: Lay off the blubbering. We can be
> Friends when the town's not standing by.
> Not happy youngster? . . .
> We shall sail. When we cast off,
> O we'll gulp the salt of life.
> While we round the point you'll shout
> To hide the terror in your heart.
> When the gunwale dips and waves
> Leap upon us from above,
> And the lonely seagulls cry
> You'll be frightened. So shall I.
> You'll discover by and by
> What this ends in is the sea.[36]

This pragmatic honesty is absent in the opera, replaced by Grimes's assertions that he will 'fish the sea dry'.

Grimes shows both cruelty and tenderness towards the boy, a mixture which stems from his identification with the child's suffering. Crabbe reveals how, in order to overcome what he perceives as his own lack of freedom, he deprives the apprentice of his, so initiating a degenerative cycle as the child repeats Grimes's actions:

> To prove his Freedom and assert the Man;
> And when the Parent check'd his impious Rage,
> How he curs'd the Tyranny of Age, – . . .
>
> He wanted some obedient boy to stand
> And bear the blow of his outrageous hand;
> And hop'd to find in some propitious hour
> A feeling Creature subject to his Power . . .
>
> Struck if he wept, and yet compell'd to weep, –
> The trembling Boy dropt down and strove to pray,
> Received a Blow and trembling turned away . . .
>
> Thus liv'd the Lad in Hunger, Peril, Pain,
> His tears despis'd, his Supplications vain:
> Compell'd by fear to lie, by need to steal.
>
> (*The Borough*, XXII, 23–5, 54–7, 82–4, 89–91)

The boy represents Grimes's younger self, and his presence confronts Grimes with his own former innocence.

Carpenter describes how, later in his life, Britten developed strong attachments to a series of boys – Piers Dunkerley, Robin Long, David Spenser, Humphrey Maud, Jonathan and Sam Gathorne-Hardy, David Hemmings and Roger Duncan

---

[36] Montagu Slater, *'Peter Grimes' and Other Poems*.

– which left him vulnerable to suspicion. Jonathan Gathorne-Hardy recalled: 'Ben was intensely, remorselessly competitive in an almost sadistic way playing games. When you were beaten by him at squash or tennis . . . you literally felt that he'd been "beating" you . . . In Grimes, I sometimes wonder whether the beating is more than a symbol.'[37] Interestingly Eric Crozier told Humphrey Carpenter that Britten had revealed to him that he had been raped by a schoolmaster: 'as if his sexual deviation had stemmed from that one incident – but nobody who knew him well could doubt that he was inherently and undeniably homosexual.'[38] In this way, Britten's behaviour and attitude might echo Grimes's ambivalent feelings for his apprentices.

In Act 2 of the opera Ellen sings:

> *Child you're not too young to know*
> *Where the roots of sorrow are*
> *Innocent you've learnt how near*
> *Life is to torture.*

Grimes is himself like a child who drifts between reality and fantasy. He subconsciously yearns for a lost innocence which, in his conscious state, he acknowledges will be destroyed by experience, and which can only be rediscovered in the watery oblivion of the sea. The fact that the apprentices die at sea reinforces Grimes's identification with their suffering: the patterns of life and death repeat themselves to the rhythms of the sea. When called to trial to explain their deaths, Crabbe's Grimes is unsympathetic and unrepentant:

> 'Yes! so it was,' said Peter, 'in his play,
> For he was idle both night and day;
> He climb'd the Main-mast and then fell below;' . . .
>
> He gave th'Account; profess'd, the Lad he lov'd,
> And kept his brazen Features all unmov'd.
> (*The Borough*, XXI, 108–10, 157–8)

In contrast, in a typescript version of the complete libretto the self-pitying Grimes is full of recriminations and excuses:

> GRIMES: *Have you ever been afraid of the fear*
> *Of a cringing child?*
> *Or known life being bound*
> *To a scared companion?*
> *Have you tried solitude*
> *Doubled by a shy one?*
> *When evening brings despair*
> *To your gaunt cabin*
> *And you launch your boat to find*
> *Comfort in fishing.*[39]

---

[37] HC, p. 223.
[38] HC, p. 20.
[39] GB–ALb 2–9401387.

However, hand-written alterations to the carbon copy of the libretto (which are reproduced in Slater's poem) suggest a more distant and less emotionally involved Grimes, who confides in a sympathetic Balstrode:

> GRIMES: *Picture what my life was like*
> *Tied to a child.*
> *Whose loneliness, despair*
> *Flooded the cabin.*
> *I launched my boat to find*
> *Comfort in fishing.*
> *Then the sea rose to a storm*
> *Over the gunwales*
> *And the child's silent reproach*
> *Turned to illness.*
> *And I watched*
> *Among fishing nets*
> *Alone, alone, alone*
> *With a childish death?*[40]

Grimes's isolation and aloofness are increased, a process which culminates in the final version of the text, where Grimes's actual relationship with the child is replaced by a symbolic connection:

> GRIMES: *Picture what that day was like*
> *The evil day.*
> *We strained into the wind*
> *Heavily laden,*
> *We plunged into the wave's*
> *Shuddering challenge*
> *Then the sea rose to a storm*
> *Over the boy's silent reproach*
> *Turned to illness.*
> *Then home*
> *Among fishing nets*
> *Alone, alone, alone*
> *With a childish death.*

Enid Slater revealed to Donald Mitchell that Slater had originally written a spoken part for the boy.[41] Slater's earliest drafts do contain text for the apprentice but it is clear from Pears's preliminary workings-out that this issue was a contentious one from the start. Pears had written (Act 2, Scene 2):

> *Ellen with boy – Singing to him old stories – (Boy is dumb learnt for 1st time). She pities him for not being able to speak – wants to take him to church.*[42]

---

[40] GB–ALb 2–9401388.
[41] Donald Mitchell, 'Montagu Slater (1902–56): Who was He?', in Brett, *Benjamin Britten: Peter Grimes*, pp. 39–40.
[42] GB–ALb 2–9401375.

Mitchell suggests that making the boy dumb would have propelled Grimes beyond anyone's sympathy. Perhaps more significantly it would have deprived the opera of its most symbolic utterance. In the Act 2 cliff-top scene, as the apprentice falls to his death, his piercing scream slides from c", a pitch frequently associated by Britten with innocence and purity. Grimes's own 'fall' is thus chillingly underlined as he literally descends down the cliff face after him.

Britten musically dramatises the relationship between Grimes and the child in the fourth instrumental interlude of the opera. Originally this interlude was entitled 'Boy's suffering' and was planned as a fugato movement. The final version is a passacaglia in which the incessant bass melody is derived from Grimes's melodic phrase 'God have mercy upon me' and the chorus's related melody, 'Grimes is at his exercise'. The counter-melody, played by the viola, represents the workhouse boy. As the melody expands and develops, Peter's mind wanders guiltily over his past actions. The boy is reduced from literal to symbolic status, becoming a manifestation of Peter's rebellious ambitions. As Grimes aspires to a more lofty future, the rising pitch and widening intervals suggest hope and optimism. Moving first to A major and then to E major, the increased rhythmic energy implies fulfilment. However, repeated dissonances between E and F infect the score and the inescapable and ever-present ground bass, together with the unshakeable repetitions of a low F, anchor Grimes firmly in the sordid reality of the present. As the variations continue the dissonances increase; there is no harmonic resolution at this stage and the interlude is interrupted by Grimes's melismatic 'Go there!', directed in rage at the trembling boy. At the end of the act, following the apprentice's death, the passacaglia theme is restated by the viola in C major, accompanied by shimmering celeste arpeggios which trace a major seventh descent, from B to C (Act 2, Fig. 72). The *pianissimo* repetitions of C in the final cadence suggest the boy's last breaths or the dying pulses of Grimes's hopes. The ultimate failure of Grimes's ambitions is revealed in the sixth musical interlude, where the passacaglia theme returns in its original and inverted forms but disintegrates as Grimes's will and strength fades. This is a musical translation of one of Crabbe's themes – the incongruity between aspiration and achievement as revealed by the failure of the individual to attain a happiness which had seemed tantalisingly possible.

By diminishing the literal intimacy between Grimes and the apprentice, Britten also reduced the connection between these 'sons' and Grimes's own father, a connection which was established in Crabbe's verse, where the ghosts of Peter's victims return to torment him.

> Now, from that day, whenever I began
> To dip my Net, there stood the hard Old Man –
> He and those Boys: I humbled me and pray'd
> They would be gone; – they heeded not, but stay'd:
> Nor could I turn, nor would the Boat go by,
> But gazing on the Spirits, there was I;
> They bade me leap to death, but I was loth to die:
> And every day, as sure as day arose,
> Would these three Spirits meet me ere the close;

> To hear and mark them daily was my doom,
> And 'Come,' they said, with weak, sad voices, 'come.'
> To row away with all my strength I try'd,
> But there were they, hard by me in the Tide,
> The three unbodied Forms – and 'Come,' still 'come,' they cried.
>
> (*The Borough*, XXII, 314–27)

These supernatural apparitions arise from Grimes's subconscious and precipitate his descent into insanity. Forster had declared that he would have 'starred the murdered apprentices' since Crabbe's preface makes clear that 'no feeble vision, no half-ghost, not the momentary glance of an unbodied being, nor the half-audible voice of an invisible one'[43] would be sufficient to turn his desensitised brute to remorse and shame. Slater had written:

> GRIMES: *Sometimes I see two devils in this hut.*
> *They're here now by the cramp under my heart –*
> *My father and the boy I had*
> *As prentice until you arrived.*
> *They sit here and their faces shine like flesh.*
> *Their mouths are open but I close my ears,*
> *We're by ourselves young prentice. Shall we*
> *Make a pact before they come?*[44]

The 1945 libretto suggests the actual presence of the murdered boys but in the 1961 text Grimes's visions are less specific:

> GRIMES: *Sometimes I see that boy here in this hut.*
> *He's there now, I can see him. He's there.* [1945]

> GRIMES: *Sometimes I see a face here in this hut.*
> *It's there now. I can see it. It is there.* [1961]

The ghosts do not appear on stage and are indicated only by musical reminiscences. The demons which torment Britten's Grimes arise from his inner anxieties and, as he possesses sufficient imagination to conjure up these visions from his guilty subconscious, it is not necessary for them to appear on stage. The final libretto of *Peter Grimes* deletes all references to Grimes's father and the ghostly hauntings, and diminishes the significance of Grimes's paternal and sexual feelings for his apprentices. Perhaps Britten feared that the explicit dramatisation of these features would suggest an identification which was too personal.[45] However, the presence of these themes in Crabbe's poem and the opera's early drafts establishes a dramatic momentum which resonates in Britten's later operas – *Billy Budd*, *The Turn of the Screw*, *A Midsummer Night's Dream*, *Owen Wingrave* and *Death in Venice* – where ambiguous father–son relationships, ghostly apparitions

---

[43]　Crabbe, *The Complete Poetical Works*, pp. 354–5.
[44]　GB–ALb 2–9401388 – this version incorporates pencil revisions to the typescript in Britten's hand.
[45]　Beth Britten's remarks are interesting in this context: 'we were a bit afraid of our father . . . My sister and I thought my father had funny habits' (quoted in HC, pp. 24–5).

connected with the repressed moral conscience of the subconscious mind, and the imaginative insight located in the world of dreams reappear.

Another consequence of the alterations made during the evolution of the libretto is that the Borough is more emphatically censured than in Crabbe and the conflict between the community and the outsider, Grimes, more starkly depicted. Britten establishes the estrangement of Grimes from the Borough in musical terms, by organising the harmonic structure of the opera around two contradic-tory tonal 'axes'. The music of the Borough is centred about the pitch B♭, with F and E♭ playing a subsidiary role, thereby creating a balanced key symmetry. Britten selected his individual characters from those whose stories are told by Crabbe in the 'Letters' which comprise *The Borough* – Abel Keene, Mrs Sedley, Ellen Orford – but in the opera they are most effective when they speak as a single unanimous voice (as, for example, in the passage following the judgment of Grimes in the Prologue; the outdoor fishing scene in Act 1, Scene 1; the round 'Old Joe has gone fishing'; the music following the church service in Act 2, Scene 1 when Grimes is condemned by Auntie, Boles and Keene; the scene in which Swallow and the mob find Peter's hut empty; and the Barn dance in Act 3, Scene 1).

Peter Grimes's music is centred about an axis A–E–B and this establishes a tritonal and semitonal conflict with the music of the Borough. The irreconcilable musical tensions between these two harmonic areas reflect the impossibility of Grimes ever being fully accepted by the community. The first words sung in the opera indicate this conflict: Grimes's name is sung by Hobson on the pitch A which clashes with Swallow's pompous opening orchestral motif in B♭. The long sustained A in the strings breaks down the rhythmic motion and reinforces the idea the Grimes disrupts the normal rhythm of life in the Borough.

The conflict between the two axes is strongly felt in the church scene in Act 2. Throughout the service, the harmonic tension is intensified by the conventional operatic procedure of using the background chorus to comment indirectly on the foreground conversation between Ellen and Peter. The ringing church bells, the first on B♭ and the second on E♭, disrupt the relaxed A major of the third orches-tral interlude, 'Sunday morning'. A loud B♭ pedal appears in the bass but this is immediately countered in the high woodwind by a trill on A, creating a grating semitonal dissonance. Ellen demonstrates her trust in Grimes, her music moving towards E major during her conversation with the apprentice boy; however, before long her D♯'s are enharmonically reinterpreted as E♭'s – she will prove unable to abandon her 'schoolhouse ways' and will bow to the pressure of the morality of the Borough. Yet, for the moment her indecision is unresolved. The refrain line in the quartet for four female voices at the end of the scene – 'Do we smile or do we weep or wait quietly till they sleep' – culminates on the chord F–A–B♭: the F resolves as the initial note of the following interlude, and the stri-dent B♭–A interval indicates Ellen's uncertainty.

Crabbe had not condemned the Borough and did not intend his poem to be interpreted as social criticism: 'From the title of this Poem, some persons, will, I fear, expect a political satire, – an attack upon corrupt principles in a general view, or upon the customs and manners of some particular place: of these things they will find nothing satirised, nothing related.'[46] His Peter is not a victim of social determinism but rather an independent youth whose rebellion against authority unleashes self-destructive forces within him. As his violent actions develop into a pattern of habit his moral nature is fixed and his isolation deepened:

> And as these Wrongs to greater numbers rose,
> The more he look'd on all Men as his Foes.
> (*The Borough*, XXII, 49–50)

However, Crabbe does suggest that Grimes's cruelty is no more evil than the Borough's casual acceptance of it:

> But none enquir'd how Peter us'd the Rope,
> Or what the Bruise, that made the Stripling stoop; . . .
>
> None reason'd thus – and some, on hearing Cries,
> Said calmly, 'Grimes is at his exercise.'
> (*The Borough*, XXII, 69–70, 77–8)

Slater, who portrayed Grimes as a man who was driven to violence principally by the injustices of the social system, wonderfully incorporated Crabbe's lines into his libretto, exposing the hypocrisy of the community. As Auntie, Boles and Keene sing 'Grimes is at his exercise', the chorus interjects:

> *Parson, lawyer, all at prayers!*
> *Now the church parade begins.*
> *Fresh beginning for fresh sins.*
> *Ogling with a pious gaze.*
> *Each one's at his exercise.*

Balstrode's efforts to halt the Borough's gossip – 'Let him be. Let us forget what slander can invent . . . When Borough gossips start somebody will suffer' – ironically lead to the community's wilful abdication of moral responsibility for the boy's welfare:

> *We live and let live,*
> *And look we keep our hands to ourselves.*

In an early draft[47] Britten had outlined a scene, later removed, where Grimes would be seen physically mistreating his apprentice, thereby exposing the falsity of his pleas of innocence in the subsequent scene. The initial inclusion of this scene further substantiates the belief that Grimes's brutality was an essential part of the early conception of his personality, despite the later denials of Pears (previously cited). The 1961 libretto contains the following additional text, which increases the element of doubt surrounding Grimes's culpability:

> *KEENE: Old Woman. You're far too ready*
> *To yell blue murder*

---

[46] Crabbe, *Complete Works*, vol. 1, p. 345.
[47] On the reverse of a letter to Elizabeth Mayer, 1 June 1942 (BPL).

Where's the body?
If people poke their noses into other's business –
No! They won't get me to help them –
They'll find there's merry hell to pay!
You just tell me where's the body?

The addition of the cries of the illegal posse – 'We despise', 'We'll destroy' – fully implicates the Borough in the deaths of Grimes and his apprentice.

The conflict between antagonism and desire which shapes Grimes's psyche, is evident in his ambivalent relationship with the Borough. His social ambition is at odds with his romantic dreams and as Britten emphasised his visionary or 'creative' characteristics, diminishing his brutality and coarseness, this discrepancy widened, as a comparison of the 1945 and 1961 libretto texts illustrates:

They listen to money	*They listen to money*
These Borough gossips	*These Borough gossips*
I listen to courage	*I have my visions*
And fiery visions.	*Fiery visions.*
They call me dreamer	*They call me dreamer*
Scoff at my knowledge	*Scoff at my dreams*
And my ambition	*And my ambition*
I'll find a way	*I'll find a way*
To change the Borough	*To answer the Borough*
I'll win them over.	*I'll win them over.*
[1945]	[1961]

Similarly in Act 2, Scene 2, Grimes is converted from a 'thinker' to a 'dreamer', from rationalist to romantic:

But thinking builds what	*But dreaming builds what*
thinking can disown.	*dreaming can disown.*
[1945]	[1961]

However, despite his disgust with the Borough, Grimes longs for acceptance and reconciliation. Britten illustrates this harmonically at moments when Grimes's music drifts towards to Borough's tonal axis, as in Act 1 when he asks for help in landing his catch, and when he attempts to explain to Balstrode the truth behind the apprentice's death. Peter's inner division is represented harmonically during the Act 2 church scene. Peter sings to Ellen that he will 'Buy us a home, buy us respect, buy us freedom from pain of grinning at gossip's tales', his desire for acceptance suggested by the key of his melody, F. In the next phrase the futility of this desire is revealed by the rise of his phrase to F♯ on the words 'Believe in me we shall be free!', which conflicts with the repeated F♮s in the chorus's phrase 'I believe in God the Father Almighty.' Ellen's gradual conversion to the Borough's side is suggested by her phrase 'We were mistaken to have dreamed', which is securely based on the B♭–F axis – where Peter joins her with his words 'So be it and God have mercy upon me!' Brett notes the effectiveness of the choral 'Amen' at this point: originally it was to have accompanied Ellen's 'We have failed', but by aligning it with Peter's words Britten emphasises Grimes's self-condemnation.[48]

In the final Act of the opera, Britten entirely detaches Grimes from human life and social conditions. His insistence upon Grimes's existentialism and social alienation conflicts with Slater's intention that Grimes should be reintegrated through his love for Ellen, and this dissimilarity is most apparent in their respective versions of the Act 3 'mad' scene. Crabbe had illustrated how, in his mad terror, Grimes desires the human contact he has shunned:

> Wild were his Dreams, and oft he rose in fright,
> Wak'd by his view of Horrors in the Night, – . . .
> And though he felt forsaken, griev'd at heart,
> To think he liv'd from all Mankind apart;
> Yet, if a Man approach'd, in terrors he would start.
>
> (*The Borough*, XXII, 225–31)

Slater's text, identical to the first typescript draft of the libretto, reads:

> PETER: Quietly. Here you are. You're home.
> This breakwater with splinters torn
> By winds, is where your father took
> You by the hand to this same boat
> Leaving your home for the same sea
> Where he died and you're going to die.
> Quietly here you are. You're home.
> You're not to blame that he went down.
> It was his weakness that let go.
> He was too weak. Were you to know?
> He was too weak, and so the sea
> Engulfed him, and you're going to die.
> VOICES: Peter Grimes. Peter Grimes.
> PETER: You shouters there – I've made it right.
> It was my conscience, my fate
> Got rid of him. If you who call
> Don't understand, old Swallow will.
> [second draft of libretto reads 'my father will']
> (Ellen comes in. His appearance startles her.)
> ELLEN: Peter!
> PETER: Was is you who called?
> I'm alone now as you foretold.
> I am alone. The argument
> Is finished and the money spent.
> The drinking over, wild oats sown.
> You hear them shouting? I'm alone.

[48] Brett writes: 'to have Peter literally take his note and words from out of the mouths of his oppressors was to get at the root of the matter: Grimes at this moment not only succumbs to them but also in his own mind becomes the monster he perceives they think him to be' (Brett, *Benjamin Britten: Peter Grimes*, p. 76).

ELLEN: The cries you hear are in your mind.
Hallucination.
VOICE, very near and loud: Peter Grimes.
PETER: You hear it?
ELLEN: No.
PETER: Will you also take
Away my smell and touch and taste?
You hear them call my name, the sky
Hears it, so do the stars, the sea.
(He shouts back at them.)
Peter Grimes. Peter Grimes. Peter Grimes. Peter Gr-i-i-mes.
VOICES: Peter Grimes.
PETER: Peter Grimes. Peter Grimes.
ELLEN, soothes and calms him: Your spasm's over now. The cool
Sea will tranquillise your soul.
Peter. I'm going to fetch Balstrode.
He'll help you to prepare your boat.
(Peter, let alone, sings in a tone almost like prolonged sobbing. The
    voices shouting 'Peter Grimes' can still be heard, but more distantly
    and more sweetly.)
PETER: Prentice forgive. I did not mean
That your need should give way to mine.
Young prentice come
Young prentice home.
Young prentice if your candle flame
Of little life dies in the dawn
Young prentice come.
Young prentice home.

In the final operatic text, Ellen does not literally appear during Grimes's delirious outburst in Act 3, but exists merely as a musical memory, a melodic echo in Grimes's fragmentary monologue. Grimes is too deranged to respond to any real-life Ellen and stands alone with his dreams and memories, hopes and fears. However, by diminishing her redemptive status Britten creates a more problematic Ellen, reducing her relevance in the drama, since there is little to connect her to Grimes's visionary aspirations and she can offer him no consolation when these dreams fail.

Slater's conviction that Ellen might 'save' Grimes may have arisen from Crabbe's description of the compassion which the women of Aldeburgh felt for Grimes:

> Follow'd and curs'd the groaning Man was led.
> Here when they saw him, whom they us'd to shun,
> A lost Man, so harrass'd and undone;
> Our gentle Females, ever prompt to feel,
> Perceiv'd Compassion on their Anger steal.
>
> (*The Borough*, XXII, 254–8)

It was Slater who insisted on the inclusion of the quartet for women's voices which closes Act 2, Scene 1:

the more I think about it the more I am convinced that it is simply the clue to Ellen's whole outlook and character and it should at all costs be the curtain line of the scene.

> Men are children when they strive
> We are mothers when they weep
> Schooling our own hearts to keep
> The bitter treasure of their love.

is Ellen's own summary of her own life and character.[49]

Britten, however, was determined to reduce Ellen's redemptive significance. For example, the 1945 version of her Act 2, Scene 1 aria resonates with genuine and personal optimism which was later replaced by more general sentiments:

Let this day then be to us	*Let this be a holiday*
Sun and sea and quietness	*Full of peace and quietness.*
While the treason of the waves	*While the treason of the waves*
Glitters like love's	*Glitters like love.*
[1945]	[1961]

Britten's music for this text begins in A major (Act 2, Fig. 11) and is later repeated in B major. Aligned with Grimes's tonal axis, it thus indicates Ellen's optimism, although her hopeful words are unsettled by the repeated B♭'s and E♭'s of the tolling bell. After discovering the bruises which Grimes has inflicted upon the child, her hopes give way to despondency: the Borough's tonality infects her melody which descends to her lowest pitch with the lines:

> *Storm and all its terrors are*
> *Nothing to the heart's despair*
> *After the storm will come sleep,*
> *Like ocean's deep, like ocean's deep.*

Additional dialogue between Ellen and Grimes in the 1961 libretto was also intended to demonstrate how Ellen becomes a focus for Grimes's frustration and anger, and the changes made to Grimes's aria 'What harbour shelters peace?' further diminished the intimacy between them. An early draft shows how originally this aria was addressed directly to the young apprentice:

> *GRIMES: Young stranger shall we sail beyond*
> *The borough streets, the timid land? . . .*
> *He stares out as if at the sea ghosts that haunt him*[50]

As the child's role was reduced Ellen became the focus for Grimes's dreams:

> *GRIMES: What harbour shelters peace?*
> *Away from tidal waves, away from storm*
> *What harbour can embrace*
> *Terror and tragedies?*

---

[49] Letter from Slater to Britten, 3 December 1944, quoted in Brett, *Benjamin Britten: Peter Grimes*, p. 63.
[50] GB–ALb 2–9401388.

*With her there'll be no quarrels,
*This time the mood will stay,
Her breast is harbour too
but they . . . but they[51]

In the carbon copy of the typescript libretto these lines are altered. Omitting the starred lines, Grimes sings:

A harbour evermore
Where night is turned to day.

Britten's music for this scene is related to the Grimes-Ellen duet which concludes the Prologue, and to Peter's 'confession' to Balstrode later in Act 1. Both passages illustrate Grimes's yearning for reconciliation, his search for a 'home', human or elemental. Grimes's desire for a 'shelter . . . away from tidal waves, away from storm' replicates the sentiments of his Act 1 aria (Fig. 41), where he had described to Balstrode how he and the apprentice 'plunged into the wave's shuddering challenge.' The rising minor ninth, which throughout the opera is associated with Peter's isolation and loneliness, is supported by a solo cello whose F–E sighs recall the 'sea' melody of Interlude 1. In the Prologue, the unaccompanied melodic lines of Grimes and Ellen are notated bitonally in enharmonically related keys: Ellen's E major triad shares a degree (G♯/A♭) with Peter's F minor. On the word 'truth' he abandons his wish for social acceptance and his music rises one semitone to E. The duet closes in E major, Britten's 'key of love', but the upwards minor ninth interval reveals the futility of their dreams [Example 4]. This interval returns during their argument in Act 2, with the lines 'Out of the hurly burly', 'Take away your hand!', 'Wrong to plan! Wrong to try! Wrong to live! Right to die!'[52]

Ultimately, just as Grimes's father had been eliminated from the text, the mother-substitute, Ellen, was also excluded. In an early version of the libretto, Ellen had cried 'Peter, come home!' but these words were later replaced by '. . . come away'. When Balstrode and Ellen finally enter, she sings:

ELLEN: Peter,
We've come to take you home,
O come home out of this dreadful night.

However, deprived of human attachments Grimes has become a symbol of isolation. He must submit to the black void of the night, the fog and the ocean, for he has no human roots and is bonded only with the watery wastes which beckon him.

Who is Grimes? Is Forster's assessment that, whereas Crabbe's Grimes is a man without sensitivity or remorse, Britten's Grimes is an imaginative 'artist'

---

[51] GB–ALb 2–9401388.

[52] Interestingly, when Peter sings to the apprentice of his plans to set up house with Ellen (Act 2, Scene 2) his melody traces a major ninth, E–F, an extension which retains an identifiable link with the earlier scenes but which represents a positive transformation of the musical meaning.

Example 4

tormented by the censure of the Borough and his own moral conscience, too simplistic? It is true that the former despondently and impotently casts his eyes downwards while the latter intermittently strives, defiantly and hopefully, to direct his gaze upwards to the heavens. Crabbe's evocation of the dull mud flats to which Peter retreats perfectly captures the mood of sullen depression which is a prelude to Grimes's madness:

> There hang his Head, and view the lazy Tide
> In its hot slimy Channel slowly glide; . . .
> How dull and hopeless he'll lie down and trace
> How sidelong Crabs had scrawled their crooked race;
> Or sadly listen to the tuneless cry
> Of fishing 'Gull' or clanging 'Golden-eye'; . . .
> He nurst the Feelings these dull Scenes produce,
> And lov'd to stop beside the opening Sluice;
> Where the small Stream, confin'd in narrow bound,
> Ran with a dull, unvaried, sad'ning sound;

Where all presented to the Eye or Ear,
Oppress'd the Soul! with Misery, Grief, and Fear.

(*The Borough*, XXII, 185–204)

In Act 2 of the opera, the aspiring words of Grimes's 'Great Bear and Pleiades' aria (Fig. 76) contrast starkly with the oppressive weight and absence of elevation in Crabbe's passage. The chorus anticipates Grimes's entry into *The Boar*, singing 'Mind that door' to a unison E, the pitch which subsequently dominates his melody as he searches for truth and love. A low pedal E clashes with the Borough's Eb's and Bb's in the upper registers, before the door bursts open and 'Grimes stands there, looking wild'. At this moment – the dramatic, musical and theatrical apex of the opera – it appears that Peter's creativity will defeat the hypocrisy and petty-mindedness of the Borough. Grimes temporarily transcends the practical mechanism of the plot, literally holding back both the storm which is raging outside and the malicious gossip of the Borough within. Furthermore, his aria also interrupts the musical momentum: the pedal notes which precede his entry suspend the rhythmic and harmonic motion, and the hypnotic repeated Es which begin each phrase anchor the melody to this pitch [Example 5]. A spread chord, spanning more than six octaves, which punctuates the vocal line, represents the star-scape which has transfixed Grimes and indicates the expanse of his vision. This scene, not in Crabbe, suggests that Britten envisaged a more 'universal' drama (exploring the 'Grimes' within us all), which co-existed with, but was not necessarily related to, the specifics of the story of Grimes's judgment and condemnation. In *Peter Grimes* this universal dimension is scarcely articulated in the verbal text and Britten relies on a few brief musical moments to clarify its significance. However, these moments are neither sufficiently sustained nor adequately reinforced through repetition to provide an enduring sense of redemption. In the 'Great Bear' aria the main melodic shape is a repeated descent from a high E, falling successively through C♯ major and C major before reaching the 'home' key, E. Despite the apparent harmonic consolation, the downwards motion of the melody is ominous and recalls the oppressive weight of Crabbe's bleak and negative vision. In the moments after Grimes's aria, the note E invades the vocal lines of the members of the Borough, before their sea-shanty succeeds in deflecting the music back to Eb. The entry of Ellen and Hobson with Grimes's new apprentice further 'darkens' the tonality which modulates to Eb minor and the Act concludes on this pitch with the ironic choral cry 'Home! Do you call that home!'

In the final scenes of the opera, Britten reinforces the pessimistic mood. Grimes's mad soliloquy begins with restatements of his own name accompanied by the dominant seventh chord which characterises his rootlessness, thus paralleling the opening moments of the Prologue, when Swallow calls him into the dock. The scene is a fractured reminiscence of verbal and melodic fragments from earlier in the opera which reiterate his frustrated yearning for resolution:

Steady! There you are! Nearly home!
What is home? Calm as deep water.
Where's my home? Deep in calm water . . .

Example 5 (a)

Example 5 (b)

Example 6

> Do you hear them all shouting my name?
> D'you hear them? D'you hear them?
> Old Davy Jones shall answer:
> Come home! come home! come home! come home!

As he sings 'Turn the skies back and begin again!', Grimes's melody descends through an E major scale resting on the pitch D♯, directly recalling his 'Great Bear' aria with its overtones of hope and redemption [Example 6]. However, Grimes's fantasy of rebirth is futile; the D♯ is undermined by the tuba's simultaneous E♭. The fog-horn's enharmonic interpretation falls a semitone to D, and the Borough posse interrupts, crying 'Peter Grimes!' Peter's frenzied repetitions of his own name, which are both an attempt to retain his own identity and to challenge the Borough with an unflinching mirror of their own moral weakness, conclude with a related falling phrase, but now the final semitone is notated E–E♭ and not E–D♯. The fog-horn's re-entry underlines Grimes's defeat. The leaping minor ninth intervals intensify the sense of his loneliness and despair; this time there is no Ellen to unite with him melodically. The final descent in this scene is notated C♭–B♭♭–A♭–F♭–E♭. This is an enharmonic realisation of Grimes's E major descent but one which, supported by a tuba E♭, stresses the Borough's tonal axis and emphasises Grimes's tragedy [Example 7].

At this point the music is silenced: the following text is spoken:

> BALSTRODE: Come on, I'll help you with the boat.
> ELLEN: No!
> BALSTRODE: Sail out till you lose sight of the Moot Hall, then sink the boat. D'you hear? Sink her. Good-bye Peter.

An anonymous critic writing in *The Times*, 15 June 1945, described this passage as 'a dangerous intrusion of an alien element'.[53]

---

[53] Quoted in Brett, *Benjamin Britten: Peter Grimes*, p. 92.

Example 7 (a)

Why does Britten silence his musical narrative at this point? Thus far, Grimes's potential has been disclosed not by his *words* or deeds but by his *musical* persona, and the cessation of this element represents an expressive decrescendo which complements the mood of utter hopelessness and confirms Grimes's failure. He has expressed his longing for the moment when 'night is turned to day', yet Britten declines the opportunity to reprise the 'utopian' music from the 'Great Bear' aria which would surely have suggested that, in submitting to the darkness of the night and the ocean, Grimes indeed finds a new 'light'. Instead, Britten depicts a more literal dawn and the sun rises on the Borough the following morning.

Example 7 (b)

   As the activities of everyday life resume, several questions remain unanswered. In the absence of unequivocal guilt, why does Grimes so passively accept his death? Why do none of the inhabitants of the Borough mention his suicide? All attempts in the opera to speak/sing out are frustrated. For example, when Grimes asks Balstrode 'Are you my conscience?', the retired Captain replies, 'Might as well try shout the storm down as to tell the obvious truth'. Similarly, in Act 2 Ellen entreats the apprentice to communicate his distress – 'John, what are you trying to hide?' – but her words are ironically undercut by the choral interjections of the rector and the congregation – 'O Lord open thou our lips, And our mouth shall show forth thy praise.' In this way the boy's silence is shown to be intimately connected to Grimes's real or perceived guilt. When the suspicion of the Borough falls upon Ellen, they urge her to 'Speak out in the name of the Lord!' but her honest attempts to win their sympathy by revealing the simple hopes she shared with Grimes are ineffectual and are met with mockery:

> *Ha-ha! Tried to be kind.*
> *Murder!*

The chorus's ridicule culminates in a sustained cry – 'Murder!' – which encapsulates the major harmonic and melodic tensions of the opera; the chord B♭–F–E♭–C (the Borough's axis) resolves to a unison A (Grimes's tonality), while the highest melodic line falls from B♭ to A, delineating the minor ninth interval which evokes Grimes's isolation.

By beginning the Prologue with Grimes's courtroom trial Britten had the opportunity to unequivocally settle the matter of Grimes's guilt. The Borough's verdict is that the boy died in 'accidental circumstances' but the essential issue is not one of guilt but of failure to conform. Grimes acknowledges that the speculation about him will continue:

> GRIMES: *Stand down you say. You wash your hands.*
> *The case goes on in people's minds*
> *Then charges that no court has made*
> *Will be shouted at my head.*
> *Bring the accusers into the hall.*
> *Let me thrust into their mouths,*
> *The truth itself, the simple truth.*

He yearns to answer the questions that are not asked, to shatter the 'open secret', to speak out or 'come out', simultaneously striving for respectability and personal integrity. Confronted with this silence, Grimes is driven first into isolation and then into insanity – his madness is associated with the creative freedom of his imagination, finding its outlet in the poetic sentiments of the lyrical outbursts which are incomprehensible to the Borough. Thus Grimes's heightened sensibility endows him with a vision which penetrates beyond the tangible yet forces him to dwell alone in a world of hallucination and imagination. Britten's opera replicates both the Borough's silence and Grimes's reaction to it, as it circumscribes the crucial issues and displaces them from the text to the music. Britten's musical expansions are therefore an attempt to deflect charges which are never articulated in the libretto and consequently the incongruity between the symbolic and actual dramas is intensified.

Grimes's eventual and inevitable 'fall' is graphically depicted in the cliff-top scene which ends Act 3, as the illegal posse, instigated by Mrs Sedley, approaches his hut. The chorus screeches Grimes's name, and the final three repetitions, separated by pauses, cadence forcefully with the progression B♭–F. However, these hysterical proclamations cannot 'fix' or constrain Grimes. The problem is that Grimes cannot be defined solely by his actions and words. The residue of his psyche is sited in the music; thus it is the musical score which must overcome the unsettling implications of the drama and text. Grimes is himself characterised by a dominant seventh chord (restated at the start of Interlude 6) which is never resolved, a perfect musical parallel for the psychological and dramatic irresolution of Britten's opera. The musical organisation of the opera attempts to persuade us of the psychological 'rightness' of the drama, but while Britten's Grimes is a man of the imagination, his death – in contrast to the deaths of the protagonists in Britten's later operas – is neither sacrificial nor redemptive, and the grandeur and seductiveness of his music is at odds with his neuroticism and failure. Desmond Shawe-Taylor noted in an early review of the opera:

> But is there not something shocking in the attempt to win our sympathies for a character simply because he is an outlaw and an enemy of society – and no more questions asked? What I am quite prepared . . . to believe is that the richness and dramatic power of Britten's music will enable us to ignore (for the time being) an adolescent conception of man and society which is in sober truth indefensible. In the theatre we may well be lulled into acquiescence; but at home, shall we not begin to wonder?[54]

The anomaly which Shawe-Taylor describes might have been exacerbated by the presence of Peter Pears in the title role. While his stage demeanour and vocal character invited a sympathetic reading of Grimes's psyche, sufficient traces of Crabbe's brutal murderer remained to unsettle the audience. One critic commented that 'the musical personality of Grimes, devised for Pears, cannot be made to fit the character of the libretto'.[55] Similarly, Frank Howes, writing in *The Times*, 8 June 1945, believed that while Pears 'commanded all the vocal resources required for a great and exacting part . . . he was not completely convincing as a sadist'.

Before the first performance there had been much dissent at Sadlers Wells when Pears was chosen for the title role, since he was considered to have insufficient stage experience and to lack a mode of 'heroic' operatic projection. Britten, however, was adamant that Pears should sing the part of Grimes. Pears himself clarified Britten's views: 'He always felt that a singer's personality had to be right for his part. That was why he was so careful in his own casting and was dubious about some choices in houses or productions over which he had no control. In general, he was chary of big voices – the important thing was that the voice had to express character.'[56] Britten reinforced this opinion: 'The singers must, of course, have good voices, but these should be used to interpret the music and not for self-glorification.'[57] He wrote to Pears, 18 November 1943: 'It was heaven to hear your voice, & to know you're feeling better. Practise hard & get the golden box back in its proper working order again. Something goes wrong with my life when that's not functioning properly'[58] and again, 11 February 1944: 'I'm writing some lovely things for you to sing – I write every note with your heavenly voice in my head.'[59] Clearly the role was shaped by Britten's artistic and emotional response to

[54] Desmond Shawe-Taylor, 'Peter Grimes', in *New Statesman and Nation*, 8 June 1945.
[55] Andrew Porter, quoted in ENO Opera Guide, p. 13.
[56] Peter Pears in Blyth, *Remembering Britten*, p. 20.
[57] Blyth, *Remembering Britten*, p. 14.
[58] LL, p. 1165.
[59] LL, p. 1187.

Pears's voice which inspired, embodied and could communicate Grimes's 'character'. A cast list dated 1 June 1942 reveals that originally the role of Grimes was conceived as a baritone part and was only later changed to a tenor. This change introduced an element of tension which would grow as composition progressed. As Ferrucio Bonavia observed, in *The Daily Telegraph*, 8 June 1945: 'Peter is played by the tenor, the protagonist in most opera, but he does not and is not meant to engage very deeply our sympathies.' Audience discomfort arises from the discrepancy between the dramatic character and the musical character of Peter Grimes, an inconsistency which was insurmountable and perhaps even essential to Britten's conception of the part. He admired the performance of William Morton in a Canadian production of the opera precisely because the singer sustained both sides of Grimes's personality: 'This young singer has a voice of just the right timbre. It was not too heavy, which makes the character simply a sadist, nor was it too lyric, which makes it a boring opera about a sentimental poet *manqué*; but it had, as it should, the elements of both.'[60]

Jon Vickers[61] has identified those musical characteristics of the part of Grimes which he believes were deliberately shaped to exploit the peculiar registral and timbral qualities of Pears's voice, stressing in particular the emphasis given to the pitch E, a pitch which is notoriously troublesome for tenors as it lies across the conventional break in the voice, the *passagio*. In his own performance Vickers attempted a new and personal interpretation, one which sought to portray Grimes's cruelty and brutality more emphatically, and it is interesting to compare the recorded performances of Vickers and Pears at three of the opera's musical and dramatic climaxes – 'What harbour shelters peace?', 'The Great Bear and Pleiades' and the Act 3 'mad' monologue.

In 'What harbour shelters peace?' the overall tone quality of Vickers's voice is rougher, even brasher, than Pears's more lyrical and 'sophisticated' timbre. The projection is less even and smooth: for example, there is more dynamic variety, the tone colour is altered in response to the text, portamento between notes and swells through individual pitches evoke the unpredictability and wildness of Grimes, and the words are more forcefully articulated with vowel sounds distorted and exaggerated. In contrast, Pears's singing is more refined and controlled. The tone is cleaner, softer and less 'open'. The rhythms are more precise and consequently the phrases in Grimes's lower register are not lost in the surge of the orchestral storm. The vowel sounds are standardised to facilitate a smoother vocal line which does not convey the fisherman's crudeness and brutality.

Elsewhere Vickers, while highlighting Grimes's roughness, does not neglect his visionary qualities. This is particularly notable in 'The Great Bear and Pleiades' where the two aspects of Grimes's personality are defined by the use of opposing vocal colours. Vickers described this technique to Loppert: 'I actually use one kind

---

60 Blyth, *Remembering Britten*, p. 13. This comment contradicts Pears's statement cited earlier in this chapter.
61 John Vickers, *Opera*, August 1984.

of voice for the inner Grimes, and another for the outer Grimes . . . I used a veiled quality in the 'mezza voce' for a very distinct dramatic purpose: it's something contained, there's a veil over it, there's confusion, there's injury . . . I believe that the writing was designed really so that the extrovert and the introvert are very clearly defined in the vocal line.'[62] As previously described, the structure of the aria is determined by three phrases which begin with repeated high E's and are followed by a scalic descent. For the first of these, 'Breathing solemnity in the deep night', Vickers dwells on the quavers of 'deep night' emphasising the profundity of his internal depths which are complemented by the 'strangeness' of the harmonic change to C# major at this point. Forcefully he asks, 'Who can decipher in storm or starlight the written character of a friendly fate?', reaching the moment of greatest intensity at the last two words. The second descent, 'As the sky turns the world for us to change', is sung less emotively; the words intimate that Grimes may break free from fate, and the corresponding move to C major (Britten's key of purity and 'innocence') supplies a moment of tonal relief and clarity after the harmonic obscurities of the preceding phrase. The final phrase is 'Who, who, who, who, who can turn skies back and begin again?' The repeated 'who' is articulated ever more fiercely, as the pitch wavers under the emotional strain. As the music descends through E major Vickers recalls his opening tone colour. The circular patterns of natural and human life are thereby enhanced by harmony, melody and timbre in Vickers's performance. His interpretation may be less musically accurate than Pears's – his pitch is less consistent, and his rhythms are free and fluctuating – but his singing has a dramatic intensity and variety which Pears lacks.

Pears's performance is more deliberately 'visionary'. Words and melody flow with greater elision and evenness as Pears takes fewer breaths and standardises his pronunciation. (He even goes so far as to roll the 'r' in 'Breathing', a classical gesture which is surely out of keeping with Grimes's background.) There is less variety of tone colour and tempo – the first descent on 'deep night' contains none of the piquant bitter-sweetness with which Vickers imbues the line – and although his interpretation is generally faster, the 'animato' passage is slower and more inhibited. The final phrase is more faithful to Britten's *tranquillo* marking, and is tender and reflective rather than disturbed. However, by focusing exclusively on the 'artist' in Grimes, Pears provides little timbral variety and this dilutes both the harmonic and dramatic effectiveness of the final bars.

Contrast is again a feature of Vickers's mad scene. He begins slowly and delib-erately, as if Grimes cannot connect his visions and thoughts into a coherent whole. The reminiscence, 'Turn the skies back and begin again', wonderfully recalls the timbre of the earlier statement – the E major tonality reinforcing the

---

[62] *Ibid.*, p. 842. In a review of Vickers's performance in *Musical Times*, September 1975, vol. 116, p. 811, Patricia Howard did not detect this dual characterisation. She noted that Vickers rendered: 'magic passages as inarticulate raving – an intensely dramatic experience but musically a limited one. We are not asked to believe in Grimes's visions, only in his madness.'

idea that Grimes will never break free, either from the Borough's persecution or from his own nature and fate. The inaccuracy of Vickers's pitch does have one unfortunate consequence: the line, addressed to Ellen, 'my hope is held by you' rises on the last syllable to F♯, a pitch associated with Grimes's tonal area. However, Vickers sings this note considerably under pitch and thus loses the contrast with the succeeding phrase, 'if you leave me alone', which rises to F♮, a pitch associated with Grimes's defeat by the Borough.

Pears's monologue lacks the energy and urgency of Vickers's. Despite the lyrical beauty of the vocal line, his Grimes sounds merely bewildered and listless. From a purely musical perspective his performance may be more aurally soothing and satisfying but Vickers's interpretation is dramatically more affecting.[63]

To what extent did Britten identify with Grimes's predicament and fear his failure? Grimes is both the 'criminal' condemned by a hypocritical and oppressive society and the artist whose creativity estranges him from 'normal life'. Some critics have suggested that Grimes's drama is an encoded projection of Britten's own experience, interpreting the opera as a disguised and flawed endeavour to win compassion and sympathy for the homosexual community.[64] Indeed Britten wrote to Elizabeth Mayer that the opera was becoming so topical as to be 'unbearable in spots'.[65] In contrast, Edmund Wilson proposed that Britten's pacifism was the major motivating force in the opera: '*Peter Grimes* is the whole of bombing, machine-gunning, mining, torpedoing, ambushing humanity, which talks about a guaranteed standard of living yet does nothing but wreck its own works, degrade or pervert its own moral life and reduce itself to starvation.'[66] These critics are seeking to ascertain who is speaking, for whom, and why, but perhaps Britten did not intend to speak for any single 'minority' group; in this way *Peter Grimes* should not be considered as a public manifesto but rather as a private letter in which Britten musically re-examined his inner anxieties.

Ronald Duncan's observations suggest similarities between Britten and his protagonist:

A reluctant homosexual, a man in flight from himself, who often punished others for the sin he felt he'd committed himself . . .

No man had more charm, could be more generous or kind – as I should

63 One of the most recent interpretations of Peter Grimes is that by Philip Langridge (ENO 1993/4 season). In a private letter, cited above, Langridge suggested that: 'Now that P.P. [sic] is no longer with us, Ben's music has become like any other composer's music, and can be performed by anyone with the ability to sing sensitively. One must always understand what the composer is saying and then expressing [sic] that with one's own voice.' However, Langridge's own performance emphasised Grimes's tragedy and suffering, suggesting that Pears's interpretation, so crucial to Britten's perception, may not be easy to discard.
64 See Brett, 'Britten and Grimes', in *Benjamin Britten: Peter Grimes*, pp. 180–9.
65 LL, p. 1211.
66 Edmund Wilson, 'London in Midsummer', in *Europe without Baedeker* (London: Secker and Warburg, 1948), p. 130.

know; but behind that mask was another person, a sadist, psychologically crip-
pled and bent . . .

Ben was one of the most tortured people I have ever known: he was on the
rack, the rack of his own making. He was tortured; he was the torturer. He had
compassion for others, none for himself.[67]

Indeed, Britten described the empathy which he and Pears felt for Grimes: 'A
central feeling for us was that of the individual against the crowd; with ironic
overtones for our own situation. As conscientious objectors we were out of it . . .
this feeling led us to make Grimes a character of vision and conflict, the tortured
idealist he is, rather than the villain he was in Crabbe.'[68] However, Pears denied
that there was a homosexual subtext in *Peter Grimes*: 'the queerness is unimpor-
tant & doesn't really exist in the music . . . so it mustn't do so in the words. P.G. is
an introspective, an artist, a neurotic, his real problem is expression,
self-expression.'[69] Pears may have unintentionally identified the central point –
that for Britten the problem was not one of 'expression' but of 'self-expression'.
Grimes is not persecuted because he has murdered his apprentice but because he
is 'different', and it is Britten's inner awareness of his own 'difference' that the
music may attempt to articulate – to 'thrust into their mouths, The truth itself, the
simple truth'. The silencing of the music in the final scene of *Peter Grimes* indicates the failure of such an endeavour at this stage. Britten retreats into silence, as
Grimes finds comfort in oblivion, thereby removing the element of choice and
self-determination. Is this a sign of personal or artistic weakness? Writing in *Time
and Tide*, 14 June 1945, Philip Hope-Wallace criticised this silence or absence: 'it
just fails to make explicit enough either in music or drama its essential and difficult 'hidden' theme of its hero's divided nature . . . the inner nature of the man and
his motives – a wonderful subject for music – have very largely to be accepted on
trust. In short, this hero remains curiously negative and the conflict of his divided
heart is not disclosed.'[70] However, in the final scene of *Peter Grimes*, the chorus
quote directly from Crabbe:

> In ceaseless motion come and goes the tide.
> Flowing, it fills the channel vast and wide;
> Then back to Sea, with strong majestic sweep
> It rolls, in ebb yet terrible and deep:

(The Borough, I, 37–40)

The sense of regeneration, as 'night is turned to day' and life resumes among the
inhabitants of the Borough, suggests that the search for truth will be resumed.

[67] Duncan, *Working with Britten*, pp. 28, 145, 159.
[68] HC, p. 203.
[69] HC, pp. 199–200.
[70] Quoted in Brett, *Benjamin Britten: Peter Grimes*, p. 94.

4

The Rape of Lucretia

If she is adulterous, why is she praised? If chaste, why was she put to death?

St Augustine[1]

The myth of *The Rape of Lucretia* tells of the rape of the beautiful, chaste Lucretia by Tarquinius, the son of the Etruscan King who rules over the Romans. At a soldiers' camp outside Rome Lucretia's husband, Collatinus, extols the virtue and purity of his wife. Tarquinius, incensed and incited by this boasting, rides that night to Collatinus's house and attacks Lucretia. Stricken with shame she sends a messenger to her husband. On his arrival she publicly exposes Tarquinius's crime after which, fearing that she has brought dishonour upon Collatinus's good name, she commits suicide. In some versions of the story, which has been retold by diverse writers including St Augustine, Ovid, Livy, Shakespeare, Sidney, Lee, Heywood and Ponsard, Lucretia's death acts as a catalyst for a Roman rebellion against the Etruscan oppressors.

The subject was brought to Britten's notice by Eric Crozier, who had attended a production of *Le Viol de Lucrèce* by the French dramatist, André Obey, during the 1930s. He presented a copy of this text to Britten in 1944. *The Rape of Lucretia* (1946), composed for eight singers and twelve instrumentalists, was Britten's first 'chamber opera' and marked a radical stylistic shift from the rich orchestral palette and melodic romanticism of *Peter Grimes*. However, a degree of continuity was assured by the involvement of many of those who had worked with Britten on *Grimes*; Crozier was again the producer, and the cast included four singers from the original *Grimes* production – Peter Pears, Joan Cross, Owen Brannigan and Edmund Donlevy. Crozier has suggested[2] that the intimate nature of the subject required an intensification and clarity which could only be achieved in a small-scale format, but more practical issues may also have influenced Britten's decision to abandon 'grand opera' for 'chamber opera'. Reducing the scale of the production vastly lessened the financial liability of the project, which was initially funded by John and Audrey Christie at Glyndebourne, and made a subsequent tour of the provinces more feasible (although the poor reception of *Lucretia* later led Christie to withdraw his support). The first signs are evident that Britten was

---

[1] St Augustine, *Concerning the City of God against the Pagans*, trans. H. Bettenson (Harmondsworth: Penguin, 1974), p. 30.

[2] Eric Crozier (ed.), *The Rape of Lucretia* (London: Bodley Head, 1948), pp. 55–60.

beginning to gather around him an elite coterie of personally selected performers and artists, a process which subsequently led to the founding of the English Opera Group and the Aldeburgh Festival in 1948. The use of a small, hand-picked cast and technical team, rehearsing intensely over a considerable period of time, may have enabled Britten to exercise almost total control over the production in a way which was not possible in the more public arenas of Sadlers Wells or Covent Garden, where various and conflicting interests might vie for supremacy.

The librettist of *The Rape of Lucretia* was Ronald Duncan, a left-wing poet and playwright whom Britten had met in the 1930s. He had composed a *Pacifist March* for the Peace Pledge Union which Duncan and his wife, Rose Marie, had been instrumental in establishing, and had supplied incidental music for Duncan's play *This Way to the Tomb*, first staged in 1945. It was to Duncan that Britten had turned when problems arose with Slater's libretto for *Peter Grimes*, and evidently he was encouraged by this collaboration: 'Montagu agreed to the new mad-scene, & I kept your part in it fairly quiet, altho I murmured that you helped us abit! [sic] Actually your work in that omens well for our future work together, I think.'[3] Initially their work progressed well, Britten writing to Pears: 'I am very fond & impressed by Ronnie – & we are discussing the opera hard. I think we can make Lucretia into a lovely piece.'[4] Statements by both men appear to confirm this optimistic impression. In a Foreword printed in the original vocal score Britten wrote that the ' "working together" of the poet and composer . . . seems to be one of the secrets of writing a good opera . . . The composer and poet should at all stages be working together in the closest contact, from the most preliminary stages right up to the first night. It was thus in the case of "The Rape of Lucretia" '.[5] Similarly Duncan remembered: 'we had written *Lucretia* working closely together, almost at one desk, each influenced by the other, I willing to add a line or a verse to suit the flow of his music, and he equally able and anxious to make the most of any musical opportunity when the librettist accidentally or deliberately gave him one.'[6]

However, closer examination of the opera suggests that the tensions and disharmony that had characterised Britten's collaboration with Slater, also tempered his relationship with Duncan. For example, Duncan, a renowned 'philanderer', seems instinctively to have empathised with the masculine power and virility of Tarquinius. In contrast, Britten's music suggests that he found little to attract, or even interest, him in this character, and that he identified more closely with Lucretia herself, although he was perhaps less interested in her as an individual and more as a site for tension between desire and violence. She is, like Peter Grimes, a victim of social tyranny, oppressed by the community that defines her, and the internalisation of this oppression fosters the inner guilt which

---

3   Britten to Duncan, 24 February 1945, LL, vol. 2, p. 1243.
4   6 August 1945, LL, vol. 2., p. 1277.
5   Quoted in DH, p. 117.
6   Duncan, *Working with Britten*, p. 64. 'Working together' may imply that the meaning of the work evolved in the course of the working process, rather than being pre-established.

prompts her to take her own life. Although an integrated member of her society, she is forced to live as an 'outsider', elevated and separated by her chastity and purity to a position of unearthly respect. In the same way that Grimes's isolation from the Borough is engendered by contradictory forces within him – i.e. his creative individualism versus his brutality and violence – so the physical beauty which affirms Lucretia's virtue resonates with darker, antagonistic undertones. Her virtue and beauty co-exist in a complex and unstable alliance which finds dramatic expression in her compulsion to confess, a preoccupation which is not wholly explicable in terms of the narrative. In *Peter Grimes* the repressive silence which drives Grimes to his death persists to the final bars of the score; although, in contrast, Lucretia does find a public voice, this speaking out fails to heal her private shame, and neither text nor music clarify the nature or extent of her guilt. Britten appears to have been unable to resolve these tensions and to have attempted to effect a conclusion by the imposition of an anachronistic, and morally inappropriate, Christian frame. Duncan was harshly criticised for the weakness of this framing device but the libretto drafts confirm his assertion that it was Britten who proposed the inclusion of a Christian epilogue which was intended to verify the redemptive nature of Lucretia's death.

The notion of the composer and poet 'at all stages . . . working together in the closest contact' is thus undermined by the evidence of the opera drafts and completed text and score.[7] While Britten effectively characterises the action sequences in the narrative – the soldiers' revelry, Tarquinius's ride to Rome, the servants' linen song – at the moments when Duncan's libretto reaches its expressive climaxes, Britten's music disengages itself from the text. He silences the score's emotional power and refocuses the music's expressive force in order to articulate, often through the voices of Peter Pears and Joan Cross who took the parts of Male

---

7 The vocal score is inscribed 'Libretto after André Obey's play *Le Viol de Lucrèce*'. Duncan and Britten did reproduce some features of Obey's text, such as the Male and Female Chorus who provide objective commentary on the action and participate in the actual presentation of the drama. However, Duncan's text probably owes more to Shakespeare's poem *The Rape of Lucrece*. Although he insisted (in 'How *The Rape of Lucretia* Became an Opera', *Shakespeare Quarterly*, no. 1, Summer 1947, 95–9) that he had not intentionally reread Shakespeare's version of the myth, he admitted that he had been subconsciously influenced by his familiarity with Shakespeare's poem. The acknowledgement to Obey was included when the threat of a plagiarism case arose, as the following letter from Britten to Duncan, 31 May 1946, reveals: 'I've seen Heinsheimer [of Boosey & Hawkes] who saw the French author Society chap in Paris, and Roth, who'd had your agents letter – & thrashed out again this Obey business. He's certainly got us stymied – because of the Droits Morales, & because the work is <u>written</u>. You & I know how little it owes to him, but there are coincidences which to a court of law would seem obvious. Anyhow two things to me seem clear – (i) that we must <u>avoid</u> a court case; I personally would prefer to give up any little money I might earn over the piece than to waste time, energy, money in court. (ii) that the performance <u>cannot</u> be postponed. We have got a first-rate company together on good-will, & if that failed they'll never come again. The experimental character of the work makes the difference – if it were just another opera or even a new song, we could postpone or substitute another work – which we can't in this case . . . I generally think that Obey is not being exactly helpful over the matter; but he has too many weapons, & after all he can't be expected to like us very much!' (RD).

and Female Chorus respectively, his personal response to the myth. Britten's willingness to tolerate the opera's hasty and unsatisfactory resolution suggests that his engagement with the drama was less intense than in *Peter Grimes*. While some features of the original subject, and Duncan's reworking of it, attracted him, other factors – the fact that the protagonist was female, the lack of an obvious part for Peter Pears, the verbosity of Duncan's text – perhaps militated against a more sustained emotional involvement. His relative lack of interest is further substantiated by his reluctance to collaborate with Duncan again. Preliminary discussions concerning possible future operatic projects (including *The Canterbury Tales*, *Letters to William* based on *Mansfield Park*, and *Abelard and Heloise*) were all subsequently abandoned. Duncan's sense of rejection led to an estrangement between him and Britten, and partially accounts for the bitter tone of some of his later autobiographical writings.

In an article, 'The Problems of a Librettist: Is Opera Emotionally Immature?', Duncan described *The Rape of Lucretia* as a continuation of the dramatisation of the conflict between the Individual and Society which Britten had begun in *Peter Grimes*: 'But the real reason why we settled for this subject besides its universality . . . was that it echoed our inner obsessions. Do not misunderstand me. I mean the subject made the same link with Britten as *Grimes* did; but here in *Lucretia*, the individual is personified by Lucretia whose virtuous personality is persecuted, raped, by Tarquinius, who symbolises Society.'[8] True, this element probably attracted Britten's interest; but as in *Peter Grimes* where it was the depiction of Grimes's individual psychology which had absorbed his creative energies, so in Lucretia it was the inner tensions of the protagonist herself which his music most particularly sought to express. In contrast to Grimes, Lucretia is not an oppressed exile and consequently her internal anxieties receive more explicit attention than her conflict with Roman society. As the social ethics are predefined, the moral discussions are more focused and there are none of Grimes's melodramatic outbursts.

The text and score of *Peter Grimes* had been scattered with the Borough's literal attempts to construct Grimes's identity through the repetition of his name: in the Prologue Swallow calls out 'Peter Grimes' as Grimes climbs into the dock, the first of the namings which culminate in the hysterical cries of the posse in the final Act. Grimes's self-naming in his 'mad scene' is partially an attempt to reappropriate his identity from his oppressors. Lucretia's identity is similarly defined by a society which classifies her as beautiful and chaste, attributes which confirm Collatinus's status and power and uphold the social structures. However, beauty and chastity prove dubiously compatible, and thus a complex and dangerous dialectic between innocence, complicity and guilt is generated. Britten was later to re-explore a similar tension in *Billy Budd*, *The Turn of the Screw* and *Death in Venice*.

The melodic motif which is associated with Lucretia's name, and which

---

8   Ronald Duncan, 'The Problems of a Librettist: Is Opera Emotionally Immature?', *The Composer*, no. 23, Spring 1967, 6–9.

Example 8

symbolises her status as both an object of adulation and a destructive temptress, dominates the fabric of the musical score.[9] Although Lucretia does not actually appear on stage until the second scene, Tarquinius introduces her name motif at the start of Act 1, in a toast to her chastity and beauty (Fig. 18), initiating some elaborate counterpoint in the key which is consistently identified with Lucretia, B minor [Example 8]. Even at this early stage in the drama, her name incites both awe and violence. The music immediately returns to the masculine tonal area of Bb minor (Fig. 19), as stabbing quintuplets based on her name motif, played by high flute and oboe, penetrate the accompaniment to Junius's complaint, 'I'm sick of that name'. The motif persists in the accompaniment throughout the opening scene, underpinning Junius's jealous outburst in which he reviles Collatinus's virtuous wife as a 'cruel jewel'. It returns at the opera's dramatically sensitive moments; for example, it reappears in C minor as Tarquinius bids Lucretia good-night (Fig. 96). Likewise, the motif's minor third permeates Lucia's contemplation of the fragile beauty of the flowers which she and Bianca are arranging (Act 2, Fig. 63), implying a comparability with the sleeping Lucretia. In this scene the purity of the orchids inflames Lucretia's sense of shame and guilt and her fragmentary cries, which stylistically recall Peter Grimes's mad monologue, culminate in the bitter, ironic phrase, "For all men love the chaste Lucretia", set to her 'name motif' in the 'male' key of C minor (Act 2, Fig. 74). In this way, the music reinforces the effects of oppressive social conditioning upon Lucretia.

Roman society as depicted by Duncan is characterised by a rigid division between male and female groups: men and women are portrayed as co-dependent units defined by their respective competitiveness and collectiveness, and also by the degree of their sexual awareness. Recalling the binary tonal opposition of *Peter Grimes*, Britten's score opposes male and female through a simple conflict of two harmonic 'axes', which simultaneously defines the formal structure of the opera and provides opportunities for local and more general musical expression. The male characters are broadly associated with an axis of flat keys, C minor–Eb–G minor–Bb, while the female characters are identified more closely with a 'sharp' axis, C♯ minor–E–G–B. For example, the opening scene (which takes place in the soldiers' camp outside Rome) is centred about the 'flat' axis, and the chord which accompanies the Male Chorus's narration of the political and personal history of Tarquinius Superbus is a minor ninth, C–Eb–G–Bb–Db. The Interlude between Scenes 1 and 2, which depicts Tarquinius's ride to Rome, alternates between Eb

---

[9]   Significantly, the libretto sketches show that Duncan initially preferred the spelling 'Lucrece', after Shakespeare and Obey, while Britten favoured 'Lucretia', presumably for its greater singability.

major and C major, initiating the movement from a male to a female environment. Scene 2 takes place in Lucretia's house; the E♭ harmony which accompanies the Female Chorus's description of the ladies who sit sewing and spinning is inflected with repeated C♭'s, which are enharmonically reinterpreted as B♮, the dominant of E. This new key is established with Lucretia's entry (Fig. 58): her scalic melody is based upon a mode on E and rises repeatedly to this pitch. E major is fully established with the entry of Bianca (Fig. 68).

Exploiting a subject which is inherently misogynist, Duncan's libretto emphasises the male-female opposition in the drama. For example, in the opening scene he condemns the inconstancy of women:

> JUNIUS: *Love, like wine, spills easily as blood . . .*
> TARQUINIUS: *And husbands are broken bottles.*
> MALE CHORUS: *Last night some generals rode back to Rome*
> *To see if their wives were chaste.*
> JUNIUS: *Maria was unmasked at a masked ball.*
> TARQUINIUS: *Celia was not found at all,*
> *Flavius is still searching for her!*
> JUNIUS: *And Maximus found his wife Donata*
> *Had been served by some Sicilian actor!*
> TARQUINIUS: *Sophia's silver chastity belt*
> *Was worn by her coachman – as a collar!*
> JUNIUS: *There Leda lay after a midnight bout,*
> *Too drunk to give a clear account.*
> TARQUINIUS: *Patricia lay naked with a negro.*
> *She told Junius she'd been having a massage!*

The libretto drafts suggest that the more extreme chauvinism in the text was reduced as the opera progressed. For example, Lucia was transformed from a flirtatious lady-in-waiting to a more innocent maiden, her reaction to Tarquinius's presence, "Before this man a woman knows she is a woman", being altered to the indignant words, "How can he dare to seek shelter from Lucretia?" Similarly, the Act 2 Interlude had originally painted a stereotypical portrait of male and female:

> MALE CHORUS: *Like a great pine tree man*
> *Stands in the wind of woman's love;*
> *And reaches for the light,*
> *From his roots of night;*
> *His limbs lean into her suppleness,*
> *His loins anoint her smoothness*
> *As he climbs towards the sun*
> *Seeking the womb luminous*
> *From which he came from; thus*
> *With his passion poised like a dart*
> *At the heart of woman*
> *Man becomes a god*
> *Making himself again*
> *In the dark loins of pain.*
>   *Taking thus, he gives,*

Giving thus, he lives.
FEMALE CHORUS: As an unending river
Woman flows for ever
Slaking the fierce thirst of man
With her love generous as water.
Man from her own muscles torn,
Man from her own thighs is born.
Man her child, man her master.
Man the thirst, she the river
Flowing on and never
Being of herself, but always of the river
Flowing to the thirst of man she gives.
Yielding thus, she takes
Taking thus, she lives.[10]

These lines were apparently replaced at Britten's request by lines which he supplied himself and which are found in the sources on a single sheet in Britten's hand, headed 'Ronnie':

Here, tho' this scene deceives
Spirit invincible
Love's unassailable
All this is endless
Crucifixion for him.
Nothing impure survives,
All passion perishes
Virtue has one desire
To let its blood flow
Back to the wound of Christ.
She whom the world denys [sic]
Mary Mother of God,
Help us to lift this sin
Which is our nature
& is the Cross to him.

She whom the world denies
Mary most chaste & pure,
Help us to find your love
Which is his Spirit
Flowing to us from Him.

Britten's insistence upon this textual alteration, together with the evidence of his score, suggests that he was less interested in simplistic divisions between man and woman, and more stimulated by the complex relationship between Tarquinius and Lucretia which dramatised the subtle and ambiguous tensions between the 'seducer' and 'seduced'. For example, Tarquinius is introduced musically immediately after the opening Chorus Refrain, as the Front Cloth rises to reveal a soldiers' camp outside Rome (Fig. 11). The key is a weighty, masculine G

---

10 GB–ALb 2–9100355. This passage is much worked out in Duncan's notebooks.

minor but the fleeting harp flourish associated with Tarquinius, which traces a stepwise third in B minor and stubbornly persists at this pitch throughout the Male Chorus's aria, unambiguously links his fate with that of Lucretia.

In contrast to Britten's response to the source narrative, Duncan's autobiographical writings frankly testify to his own identification with Tarquinius's masculine virility:

> Rose Marie had invited Petra to stay with us . . . I did not close my eyes all night: I lay there knowing she was weeping. I ached to receive those tears . . . My impulse was to emulate Tarquinius and steal through the silent hall. I began to realise that whatever I wrote, I eventually lived.[11]
>
> . . . as for my sexual frustration, which was now temporarily fixed on my cousin, I took steps to relieve that too . . . My room was on the ground floor: hers somewhere above me. Emulating Tarquinius, I mounted the stairs, then paused to take my bearings.[12]

In the opera, as Tarquinius creeps through Lucretia's house, Britten harnesses the expressive properties of the percussion section to depict the assailant's tense energy, recalling the rhythmic patterns of his ride to Rome. This passage foreshadows the explosive, sprung rhythms of Aschenbach's Dionysian dream in *Death in Venice,* where the violence latent in sexual desire is similarly unleashed. However, in contrast to the tense atmosphere which precedes Tarquinius's assault upon Lucretia, the musical representation of the rape itself – Duncan's dramatic climax – is peculiarly muted. As Tarquinius arrives at Lucretia's bed the solo harp repeats a *pianissimo* octave B three times, harmonically complementing the stage action, but Britten makes no attempt to complement the implicit violence of the rape with any musical violence. Tarquinius is deprived of his potency, emasculated by the musical discourse as Britten focuses the score's expressive power on the representation of Lucretia herself. Tarquinius mounts Lucretia's bed and a slow, sombre, unaccompanied quartet commences (Act 2, Fig. 42).

---

[11] Ronald Duncan, *How to Make Enemies* (London: Rupert Hart-Davis, 1968), p. 146.

[12] Ronald Duncan, *All Men are Islands* (London: Rupert Hart-Davis, 1964), p. 55. Duncan describes one particular passage in the libretto which was derived from a personal experience during the composition of the opera, when Marion Stein was residing with Pears and Britten at their St Johns Wood High Street flat: 'I thought I might take a cup of tea into Marion. Her bedroom was next to the kitchen. Noiselessly I opened her door not unaware that I was enacting Tarquinius' stealthy walk through the sleeping house towards Lucretia's bed. Marion did not wake . . . I picked up a pencil and just described what I saw before me:

> She sleeps as a rose
> Upon the night
> And light as a lily
> Her eyelids lie over her dreaming eyes
> As they rake the hallows and drag the deep
> For the sunken treasures of heavy sleep
> Thus sleeps Lucretia.

Then I tiptoed out of the room and put the lullaby on Ben's piano' (Duncan, *Working with Britten*, p. 71).

See how the centaur mounts the sky,
And serves the sun with all its seed of stars.
Now the great river underneath the ground
Flows through Lucretia, and Tarquinius is drowned.[13]

After the rape Duncan implies that Tarquinius's suffering is the greater, that he is the 'victim', an agent of Fate who is destroyed by the power of female beauty:

TARQUINIUS: I hold the knife
But bleed.
Though I have won
I'm lost.
Give me my soul
Again
In your veins sleep
My rest.

During the attack, Tarquinius's obsessive repetitions of Lucretia's name infiltrate the orchestral texture (Act 2, Fig. 38). Lucretia struggles to remain 'beyond your reach' but she is trapped by the social definition of the morally ambiguous beauty which is embodied in her name:

LUCRETIA: What peace can passion find? . . .
If beauty leads to this, beauty is sin!

Her words echo Shakespeare's disbelief in the existence of unequivocal innocence – 'But no perfection is so absolute/ That some impurity doth not pollute'[14] – and later she clarifies her potential culpability:

Women bring to every man
the same defection;
Even their love's debauched
By vanity or flattery.
Flowers alone are chaste.
Let their pureness show my grief
To hide my shame
and be my wreath!

Lucretia's beauty and virtue form an uneasy union, as likely to incite lust as to inspire goodness.[15] Her physical beauty is both an unconscious sign of her inner

---

13 This passage reinforces the identification of Lucretia with the potent, fertile forces of the river. In Act 1 (Fig. 54), during the Male Chorus's narration as Tarquinius crosses the Tiber on his ride to Rome, Lucretia's name motif forms an asymmetrical five-note pattern on the flute which mimics the lapping motion of the water. The crossing culminates with an impassioned melisma upon Lucretia's name.

14 Shakespeare: *The Rape of Lucrece* (lines 853–4) in George Wyndham (ed.), *The Poems of Shakespeare* (London: Senate, 1994), pp. 43–112. All subsequent references are to this edition.

15 In Shakespeare's poem it is Lucretia's chastity more than her beauty which arouses Tarquin, since Tarquin rides to Rome to seek a woman he has never seen, impassioned by word of her

purity and a conscious blush upon her virtue, the agent of its own destruction and responsible for the moral corruption of others. In the opening scene of the opera, Junius, whose wife has been unfaithful, argues that beauty and virtue are not equitable:

> TARQUINIUS: But Lucretia's virtuous.
> JUNIUS: Virtue in women is a lack of opportunity.
> TARQUINIUS: Lucretia's chaste as she is beautiful.
> JUNIUS: Women are chaste when they are not tempted.
> Lucretia's beautiful but she's not chaste
> Women are all whores by nature.

Similarly Tarquinius, enraged by Collatinus's boasts about his wife's virtue, later sings:

> Loveliness is never chaste;
> If not enjoyed, it is just waste!
> Wake up, Lucretia!

This scene is Tarquinius's most lyrical (Grimes-like?) outburst, half-meditative, half-ecstatic (Act 2, Fig. 22). There is no violence or guilt implicit in this music: Tarquinius responds unconsciously and instinctively both to Lucretia's virtue (C major) and to her beauty (E major). The Female Chorus's C major phrase, 'Thus sleeps Lucretia', alternates with Tarquinius's passionate E major melody which climaxes on the word 'Loveliness', proclaimed on a high E. With the word 'chaste', a D♮ directs the harmony back towards C major. Tarquinius entreats Lucretia to awaken with a gentle, scalic phrase in C major but gradually, intoxicated by her image, his physical desire escalates and the harmony returns to E major:

> As blood red rubies set in ebony;
> Her lips illumine,
> The black lake of night
> To wake Lucretia with a kiss
> Would put Tarquinius asleep awhile.

As he kisses her, the Female Chorus recites on a monotone E (Act 2, Fig. 26):

> Her lips receive Tarquinius,
> She dreaming of Collatinus
> And desiring him draws Tarquinius
> And wakes to kiss again and . . .

---

chastity alone. Duncan's own suspicion that chastity was at least partially responsible for its own violation undoubtedly informed his libretto. When his wife, Rose Marie, converted to Catholicism he reacted: 'Chastity was a religion in which I did not like treading. I began to suffer from erotic hallucinations, vulnerability and a sense of being persecuted' (Duncan, *How to Make Enemies*, p. 238). 'Ghandi had talked a lot to me about chastity and the need of being unattached to the senses. I now found that chastity itself can be a kind of perverse sensual gratification' (*ibid.*, p. 297).

Peter Grimes's dreams had raised him to heroic stature but Lucretia's dreams merely betray her, as Tarquinius's desire becomes her crime (Act 2, Fig. 32):

> *TARQUINIUS: Yet the linnet in your eyes*
> *Lifts with desire*
> *And the cherries of your lips*
> *Are wet with wanting*
> *Can you deny your blood's dumb pleading?*

At the heart of *The Rape of Lucretia* is a complex dialectic between a series of opposites: violator/violated, beauty/virtue, ignorance/complicity and guilt/innocence. Is Lucretia a violated innocent or the helpless victim of her own repressed desires? Are these desires active or passive, conscious or subconscious? Duncan was apparently eager to imply Lucretia's complicity in her violation; he makes desire the subject of Lucretia's aria after the spinning quartet in Act 1, Scene 1, and the drafts indicate that this passage was originally more overtly physical:

How cruel men are	*How cruel men are*
To teach us love	*To teach us love*
They wake us from	*They wake us from*
frigidity	*The sleep of youth*
Into the sleep of passion.	*Into the dream of passion*
Then ride away	*Then ride away*
While we still burn.	*While we still burn.*
How cruel men are	*How cruel men are*
To teach us love.	*To teach us love.*
[Draft[16]]	[1946 libretto]

Shakespeare and Obey had provided a justification for Lucretia's surrender by relating Tarquinius's threat that, if she should refuse to submit to him, he would entwine the dead, naked bodies of Lucretia and her most base slave, announcing to all Rome that he had killed them after thus finding them. Duncan omits this episode and, recalling Obey's inference that Tarquinius is 'a large fire which is rousing you, the wind of your yearning', hints that her submission illustrates her suppressed passion. The Male Chorus describes Tarquinius as 'panther agile, panther virile' and, when Tarquinius awakens her, Lucretia sings:

> *In the forest of my dreams*
> *You have always been the tiger.*

Britten's score suggests that he is less concerned with the degree of Lucretia's personal complicity and more interested in exploring the subtle interactions between desire and violence, love and sin. Lucretia's first musical phrase – 'Collatinus! Whenever we are made to part, We live within each others hearts, Both waiting, each wanting.' – is a modally inflected rising scale which strives towards E. As previously described, in *The Rape of Lucretia*, harmony centred about E is associated with a specifically female environment; but in *Peter Grimes*

---

16 GB–ALb 2–9100355.

the pitch E had been identified with Grimes's creativity, with love and sexuality, and the resonances of these earlier associations linger in *Lucretia*. When the Female Chorus describes Lucretia's reception of Tarquinius (Act 1, Fig. 92) her music fluctuates between C minor and E major/minor, indicating the intrusion of an alien masculine element in a female environment and also anticipating the sexual experience to come. This is clarified in Tarquinius's E major aria, sung over the body of the sleeping Lucretia (Act 2, Fig. 22), where the identification of Lucretia with the related pitches E and B musically complements the verbal ambiguity concerning her sexual complicity and possible guilt.

In *Peter Grimes*, Grimes's undefined, subconscious desires find practical expression in his yearnings for material and creative success, but in *Lucretia* Britten makes no attempt to depict the sublimation of physical desire into art. Shakespeare had described the elusive perfection of Lucretia's beauty and virtue which corrupts the observer by stimulating an obsessive but futile craving for possession:

> O happiness enjoy'd but of a few!
> And if possess'd as soon decayed and done
> As is the morning silver-melting dew
> Against the golden splendour of the sun!
> An expired date, cancell'd ere well begun . . .
> What win I, if I gain the thing I seek?
> A dream, a breath, a froth of fleeting joy.   [lines 22–6, 211–12]

Likewise, Duncan describes Lucia's reflections on the transient beauty of the rose:

> *These roses which in scarlet sleep*
> *Dream in tight buds of when*
> *   They'll be open*
> *   Be wanton*
> *With the winds and rain and then*
> *   be broken,*
> *   and quite forgotten.*

Duncan briefly implies that Tarquinius's physical longing might be transferred to an aesthetic realm, sublimating his lust which thus becomes a symbol of man's eternal quest for the human beauty which is a visual representation of 'truth':

> *TARQUINIUS AND JUNIUS:*
> *If men were honest*
> *They would all admit*
> *That all their life*
> *Was one long search,*
> *A pilgrimage to a pair of eyes,*
> *In which there lies*
> *   a reflection greater than the image,*
> *   a perfection which is love's brief mirage.*

In *Billy Budd* and *Death in Venice* Britten responded to the texts' inferences that the perfection which is defiled by human touch might be immortalised in art, but in *Lucretia* he shows no inclination to transform Tarquinius, in the manner of Peter Grimes, Captain Vere, or Gustave von Aschenbach, from violator to visionary. Lucretia's death is not redeemed through art; but Britten evidently believed that an additional frame of reference was required to alleviate the moral ambiguity of her suicide.

Writing in *Time and Tide*, 12 October 1946, William Glock observed: 'By the twisting of character the normal historical ending is made impossible. Yet some kind of epilogue is certainly needed. One cannot finish with Lucretia's death.' Why not? Many contradictory readings of her death may be invoked but perhaps no single interpretation is satisfactory. Lucretia's suicide is presented as a personal and social purgation or sacrifice but one that neither confirms nor eradicates the intimations of her guilt. The imposition of a Christian framework on the libretto of *The Rape of Lucretia* is an attempt, but one which is historically and morally flawed, to ensure a redemptive interpretation by unequivocally equating Lucretia's suffering and death with Christ's Crucifixion.[17] Duncan recalled that it was Britten who had insisted that such a framework was necessary:

> 'I've got an impossible problem for you: from your point of view the opera is dramatically complete with Lucretia's death and the finale of epitaphs sung over her body, but I've discovered that musically its not finished. I want to write a final piece beyond the curtain to frame the entire work.' . . .
>
> 'The only way, I said eventually, would be to give the chorus some universal comment on the entire tragedy to frame it dramatically . . . This will mean making the chorus take up their position as commentators outside and beyond the tragedy itself. Perhaps reverting to the position as Christians again.' . . .
>
> 'Now I see why you insisted on making them Christians. It gives them a definite point of view from which they can objectify the pagan tragedy.'[18]

Duncan supplied the following text to imply that Lucretia's rape by Tarquinius symbolises a perennial violation by humanity:

> *FEMALE CHORUS:*
> *Is it all? Is all this suffering and pain,*
> *Is this in vain?*
> *Does this old world grow old*
> *In sin alone?*
> *Can we attain*
> *nothing*
> *But wider oceans of our own tears?*
> *And it, can it gain nothing*
> *But drier deserts of forgotten years?*
> *For this did I*
> *See with my undying eye*
> *His warm blood spill*
> *Upon that hill*

---

17 Christian imagery was present, but was less didactic, in Shakespeare's and Obey's versions of the myths.

18 Duncan, *Working with Britten*, pp. 75–6.

> *And dry upon that Cross?*
> *Is this all loss?*
> *Are we lost?*
> *Answer us?*
> *Or let us*
> *die in our wilderness. Is it all? Is this it all?*
> *MALE CHORUS:*
> *It is not all. Though our nature's still as frail*
> *And we still fall,*
> *And that great crowd's no less*
> *Along that road,*
> *endless and uphill;*
> *yet now*
> *He bears our sin and does not fall*
> *And He, carrying all*
> *turns round*
> *Stoned with our doubt and then forgives us all.*
> *For us did He*
> *live with such humility;*
> *For us did He*
> *die that we*
> *might live, and He forgive*
> *Wounds that we make*
> *and scars that we are.*
> *In His Passion*
> *Is our hope*
> *Jesus Christ, Saviour. He is all! He is all!*

The music for the Male Chorus moves towards B major and reintroduces the pulsing rhythm associated with Lucretia's death, thereby recalling her suicide and transforming it from an act which illustrates an human tragedy to one which implies a symbolic redemption.

The Christian dimension of the opera is established primarily in a unison passage for the Chorus which punctuates the opening of each Act and concludes Act 2. The first statement of this passage is introduced by the Female Chorus (Act 1, Fig. 7):

> *FEMALE CHORUS:*
> *This Rome has still five hundred years to wait*
> *Before Christ's birth and death from which Time fled*
> *To you with hands across its eyes. But here*
> *Other wounds are made, yet still His blood is shed.*
> *MALE AND FEMALE CHORUS:*
> *While we as two observers stand between*
> *This present audience and that scene;*
> *We'll view these human passions and these years*
> *Through eyes which once have wept with Christ's own tears.*[19]

[19] Originally these lines were less specifically Christian: *Whilst we as two observers stand*

This refrain was sung in the first production by Peter Pears and Joan Cross, and occupies a structural position in Act 1 identical to that of the Grimes-Ellen duet which had closed the Prologue in *Peter Grimes*. Whereas in *Grimes* the duet's harmonic impulse towards E major symbolised the yearning of Peter and Ellen for truth or human love, in *Lucretia*, the refrain's C major melody complements the text's striving for a universal, specifically Christian form of love [Example 9]. At this stage, it is not supported by stable C major harmony but is underpinned by an unresolved dominant pedal, an irresolution which clarifies the opera's large-scale musical and dramatic goal. Furthermore, the tonal purity of the melody is polluted by the inclusion of chromatic pitches which push the melody towards a mixolydian mode on the dominant, G. When this melody is reprised in Act 2, Scene 1 it has digressed further from its intended harmonic path; the key is A major, the dominant pedal of which is E, a pitch identified both with Lucretia and with Tarquinius's desire. In the Epilogue, the refrain returns to its original pitch but is now accompanied by a tonic C pedal which harmonically affirms the Christian morality of the text. However, an element of doubt persists: this pedal enters on a weak rhythmic beat and fades to *pianissimo* in the final bars. As the curtain falls the rhythmic throb of Lucretia's suicide motif trembles in the lowest registers – the unsettling implications arising from her death cannot be entirely nullified.

Critical assessments of the Christian frame were hostile, and the responsibility for the failure of this element was attributed principally to Duncan. Ernest Newman wrote: 'Here [in the epilogue] his pity, or love for easy effect, seems to me to have got the better of his dramatic sense: [in] lines like these at the end of an opera on the subject of Lucretia . . . – which have no real connection with what has been occupying us until then, Mr Duncan comes closest . . . to poetic and dramatic pinchbeck!'[20] One problem is that Roman and Christian standards are basically irreconcilable. For the Romans the issue of Lucretia's guilt is rendered irrelevant, since she judges herself according to the standards dictated by social convention and law. However, the Christian notion of conscience hypothesises a subconscious guilt which suggests that Lucretia's suicide was not evidence of her innocence but a tacit confession of her essential corruption. Furthermore, according to Christian doctrine her act is a mortal sin which cannot be 'redemptive'.

Duncan has described how originally it was intended that the opera should dramatise Collatinus's growing understanding of the nature of love, as brought

---

between/ This present audience and that scene/ Outside of the mad calvacade of Time/ We'll guard the permanent and sing in rime (GB–ALb 2–9100355).

[20] Ernest Newman, *Sunday Times*, 28 July 1946. Newman's comments were typical. Cecil Gray, *The Observer*, 14 July 1946, remarked: 'there are moments when it is difficult to reconcile the simple brutal story of ancient Rome with the superstructure of sententious neo-Catholic moralising imparted by the chorus!', while W. J. Turner judged, in *The Spectator*, 6 September 1946: 'The utter irrelevance of this six-hundred year later chorus with its feeble historical mutterings and frequently tasteless and always banal comments destroys Mr Britten's opera irrevocably.'

Example 9 (a)

about by Lucretia's death. Collatinus's first soliloquy on 'love' occurs in Act 1 (Fig. 30), the C minor tonality revealing the extent of his ignorance:

> Those who love create
> Fetters which liberate.
> Those who love destroy
> Their solitude.
> Their love is only joy
> Those who love defeat
> Time, which is Death's deceit,
> Those who love defy.
> Death's slow revenge.
> Their love is all despair.

Interestingly, the bass line of this aria alternates between B♮ and G: B♮ is the leading note in C minor but is also the pitch most specifically identified with Lucretia herself, and the resulting strident dissonances between melody and harmony act as a commentary upon the emotional distance between Lucretia and her husband.

Following Lucretia's confession Collatinus reveals a new profundity (Act 2, Fig. 92):

Example 9 (b)

> *If spirit's not given, there is no need of shame.*
> *Lust is all taking – in that there's shame*
> *What Tarquinius has taken*
> > *Can be forgotten;*
> *What Lucretia has given*
> > *Can be forgiven.*

The ascending chordal accompaniment played by the woodwind and harp, in B major, reverses the descending motion of Lucretia's own musical confession (Act 2, Fig. 81, discussed below), implying hope and resolution. Yet, ironically, Collatinus's forgiveness unwittingly necessitates her death, as Duncan's notes explain: 'Collatinus [sic] gesture of forgiveness Commentators both warn him not to forgive they are too late consequently the added remorse (caused by C's forgiveness) causes L to kill herself.'[21] Collatinus's B major passage resolves to E (Fig. 95) at the start of passacaglia, which was originally designed to conclude the opera (and which recalls the passacaglia in Interlude 4 of *Peter Grimes* which had musically dramatised Grimes's relationship with his apprentice). Collatinus

---

[21] Microfilm X24 (BPL).

kneels over Lucretia's dead body, just as Tarquinius had leaned over her sleeping form, a visual and dramatic association which is complemented musically by the shared harmonic centre:

> *This dead hand lets fall*
> *All that my heart held when full*
> *When it played like a fountain, prodigal*
> > *With love liberal,*
> > *Wasteful.*
> *So brief is beauty,*
> *Is this it all? It is all!*

In an unambiguous E major, one by one the characters join him above a calm ostinato bass. This ostinato figure unites Tarquinius and Lucretia, consisting of the scalic motif associated with Tarquinius and the staccato minor third demi-semi-quavers which accompany her suicide.

Duncan's original plan for the opera's ending is revealed in the sources:

> ?Collatinus kills himself
> > ?No, a trio with Collatinus, and Commentators lifting whole tragedy to universality, can love die? does beauty perish? the whole ending as triumph of Love rc Collatinus? A canzone.[22]

He later described Britten's opposition to these ideas:

> Ben had suggested that every character should have an epitaph to sing over Lucretia's body which he intended to set as a scene to bring the opera to an end.
> > At this point I could not tell whether I was writing the libretto or whether it was writing me.[23]

The climax of this section is reached in a unison passage which juxtaposes a C major melody with E major harmony, a musical 'stalemate' which perfectly embodies the ambivalence of the text (Act 2, Fig. 100):

> *How is it possible that she*
> *Being so pure should die!*
> *How is it possible that we*
> *Grieving for her should live?*

In the final bars, the antagonism between the various elements persists; the harmony is left unresolved, suspended between E major and C♯ minor.

In some versions of the myth Collatinus's emotional maturity has social and political repercussions, as Lucretia's rape is used as a pretext to liberate Rome from the Etruscans. For example, in Shakespeare's poem Lucretia becomes a symbol of a violated Rome as a political dimension is conferred on her personal privacy:

> *Her house is sack'd, her quiet interrupted,*
> *Her mansion batter'd by the enemy,*

22 *Ibid.*
23 Duncan, *Working with Britten*, p. 75.

Her sacred temple spotted, spoil'd, corrupted,
Grossly engirt with daring infamy.   [lines 1170–3]

Duncan alludes to the threat of social unrest at the start of Act 2, Scene 1 but Britten shows little interest in developing this consequence of the rape.

It is perhaps significant to note that in *The Rape of Lucretia* Britten employs a musical refrain which is not implied by textual repetition and one which inverts the tonal direction of the Christian refrain, thereby undermining its moral authority. The following four passages are reprised to identical music in Act 1 (Figs. 25 and 54) and Act 2 (Figs. 42 and 91):

1) *Oh my God with what agility does jealousy jump into a small heart*
And fit till it fills it, then breaks that heart.
Lucretia.

2) *Now stallion and rider wake the sleep of water*
Disturbing its cool dream with flank and shoulder
Tarquinius knows no fear, he's across, he's heading here!
Lucretia!

3) *See how the rampant centaur mounts the sky*
And serves the sun with all its seeds of stars.
Now the great river underneath the ground
Flows through Lucretia and Tarquinius is drowned.

4) *O my love our love was too rare*
For life to tolerate or Fate forbear from soiling
For me this shame, for you this sorrow.

These passionate words trace the opera's 'alternative' narrative, one which contrasts with the cool solemnity of the Christian refrain, and reveal how Collatinus's immature complacency incites and is shattered by Tarquinius's jealousy and violent desire, an experience which provides the stage characters and the audience with a more profound comprehension of love and loss. This move towards knowledge is complemented by the harmonic progression of the musical repetitions. In the first passage, the Male Chorus describes Junius's jealousy in B♭ minor and the passage culminates with Lucretia's 'name motif' in this key. The second passage, in C minor, accompanies Tarquinius's crossing of the river as he travels to Lucretia's house and climaxes with a free and impassioned melisma on her name; this is linked to the third statement which depicts the actual rape. The final repetition contains the text of Lucretia's confession: her words reveal her sense of shame but do not clarify the extent of, or reasons for, her complicity or guilt. Her musical phrase, which resolves onto a monotone B, is accompanied by a shimmering string texture which cadences on an unresolved major seventh chord on B, and inspires Collatinus's words of forgiveness and understanding which were at one stage intended to conclude the dramatic argument of the opera.

It is Lucretia's confession, not her rape, which is the climax of the opera, a climax which is essentially musical and not verbal. Her powerful entry in Act 2, Scene 2 is wordless, the dramatic expressivity being sited solely in the score, as

Duncan acknowledged: 'At the beginning of the work I found I was underesti-
mating the power of music to express precise emotion and characterisations, but
later relied on its contribution to the actual statement of the drama. The most
successful example of this, I think, is in Lucretia's unsung aria when she enters to
make her confession to Collatinus. In such places music can be more coherent
and lucid than language.'[24] The ponderous, off-beat quavers in the bass mock her
and her onlookers with their satirical reference to Tarquinius's journey to her bed,
while the cor anglais stutters fragments of her 'name motif' in B minor in a futile
attempt to preserve her identity [Example 10]. With Collatinus's entry and his
words of forgiveness (Act 2, Fig. 82) the cor anglais melody briefly expands,
supported by a pedal B, before returning to the first of two repetitions of her
entrance music. In this musical passage Britten suspends the forward momentum
of the plot and briefly opens a window on an alternative dialectic, one which is
ever-present but elusive. As Britten's music inextricably interlocks the musical
motifs of the two protagonists it reveals the interdependent relationship between
Tarquinius and Lucretia, an interaction which exposes the ambiguous and unstable
balance between beauty, virtue and desire which is at the core of the drama.

    Britten had originally planned to follow this verbal silencing with a musical
silence: 'Ben had told me that he wanted me to write a soliloquy for Lucretia
before she kills herself. "Forget about me", he said, "I shan't even try to set it. It
can be spoken. After all, I've written the music for her final entrance without
words. Now it's your turn." '[25] In the event, Britten introduces Lucretia's actual
words with a contra-motion scale in B minor, setting her text on a monotone low
B, recalling her phrases when she awakens after the rape:

> LUCRETIA:If it were all a dream
> Then waking would be less a nightmare.
> LUCIA: Did you sleep well?
> LUCRETIA: As heavy as death.

Perhaps Britten feared that a musical silence at this point would revive the mood
of despair and hopelessness, and the accompanying concept of victimisation,
which had dominated the spoken ending of Act 3 of Peter Grimes.

    In contrast to Peter Grimes, Lucretia does not passively admit her guilt and
submit to society's demand for silence. Her confession and death are not private
and unremarked but are thrust into the public domain.[26] She shatters her
self-imposed silence and throws open the door of her private closet. Her
self-violation might be interpreted as a repetition of Tarquinius's rape, as an
attempt to assert the sexual identity which she is denied by the society whose

---

[24] Ibid., p. 62.
[25] Ibid., p. 74.
[26] Shakespeare had indicated the danger latent in such an act of public disclosure. He depicts
Brutus as a 'dumb' fool who covers discretion with a coat of folly. Duncan introduces a
similar theme:
> JUNIUS: God knows it's never safe to speak one's mind in Rome,
> But now every whore has the Emperor's ear.

Example 10

equilibrium depends upon the worship of her purity. In this way, her suicide is not sacrificial, submissive or redemptive but is defiant and rebellious. Although this alternative interpretation is undermined by the Christian epilogue, it cannot be entirely erased: there is therefore an uneasy tension between antagonistic arguments which are raised in the verbal text and which are not satisfactorily resolved in the musical score.

*

The issues raised by St Augustine, and quoted at the opening of this chapter, hover
in permanent suspension above *The Rape of Lucretia* but the essential questions
are never articulated: Why does Lucretia die? Is her suicide an act of wilful
self-destruction or a passive surrender to oppressive social forces? Is her death the
ultimate sign of her innocence or confirmation of her guilt? The silent rhetoric
associated with her death prevents these issues from being openly discussed and,
as in *Peter Grimes*, the result is confusion and ambiguity. Grimes is technically
guilty yet musically innocent, whereas Lucretia is morally innocent but dramatically guilty. Shakespeare had considered this ambivalence:

> 'To kill myself', quoth she, 'alack what were it,
> But with my body my poor soul's pollution?'   [lines 1156–7]

> 'What is the quality of my offence,
> Being constrain'd with dreadful circumstance?
> May my pure mind with the foul act dispense
> My low-declinéd honour to advance?
> May any terms acquit me from this chance?
> The poisoned fountain clears itself again;
> And why not I from this compelled stain?'   [lines 1702–8]

Britten's Lucretia sings:

> *Even great love's too frail*
> *To bear the weight of shadows.*
> *Now I'll be forever chaste,*
> *[She stabs herself]*
> *With only death to ravish me.*
> *See, how my wanton blood*
> *Washes my shame away!*
> *[She dies].*

In the libretto, her suicide is presented, with some musical support, as a religious
sacrifice, a striving for purification which repeats Peter Grimes's act of voluntary
drowning. However, neither human nor divine love can wash away the blemish
which stains her beauty and virtue. Neither Grimes nor Lucretia can differentiate
between shame and guilt; Lucretia learns that no water is deep enough to drown
her shame or to obliterate the rumours. At the heart of the myth of Lucretia's rape
is the violent theme of the destruction and the destructive nature of virtue and
beauty and, in spite of the Christian frame which attempts to contain and transform this violence, Lucretia's suicide redeems neither her nor the society which
demands it.

Why did Britten abandon his original idea that the opera should conclude with
a threnody over the dead body of Lucretia? Moreover, why did he reject Duncan's
idea that the opera should dramatise the 'triumph of Love', particularly as his
inclusion of an 'alternative' musical refrain which complements this subtext
suggests that this interpretation initially appealed to him? Had he developed these
'solutions' Lucretia might have recovered her identity from the 'society' which

defined her as chaste, and her death might have freed her from the social constraints imposed upon her. Thus, the myth would have been revealed as a tragedy of inhibited passion which breaks social constraints, a passion which is repressed from both within and without:[27]

> *MALE CHORUS: All tyrants fall though tyranny persists*
> *Though crowds disperse the mob is never less.*
> *For violence is the fear within us all*
> *And tragedy the measurement of man.*

These words, originally sung by Peter Pears, offered Britten a perfect invitation to consider this interpretation, but he chose to ignore the verbal 'bait'. He avoided an exploration of the fear within himself and focused on the opera's Christian dimension, which universalised Lucretia's experience but reduced the potency of his personal identification with her suffering. However, as Lucretia herself acknowledges, 'What I have spoken never can be forgotten.' The result is that, as in *Peter Grimes*, there are effectively two dramas – the violence of the rape and the passivity of the Christian frame – which co-exist in an unstable and unsatisfactory alliance. At times the score illuminates the alternative reading of the drama which intermittently rises to disturb the Christianised surface, but the music, weakened by its multiple duties, cannot fully redeem the inherent ambiguities of the subject or the weaknesses of Duncan's text, and the final lines of the libretto can only hint at the myth's latent but undeveloped potential:

> *Since Time commenced or Life began*
> *Great Love has been defiled by Fate or Man.*
> *Now with worn words and these brief notes we try*
> *To harness song to human tragedy.*

---

[27] Alternatively, Lucretia need not have died at all. Interestingly in Britten's next stage work, the comic opera *Albert Herring*, the protagonist also defies social convention and oppression but is rewarded with a newly discovered personal integrity and social inclusion.

5

Albert Herring

Who knows, who can tell, what grim struggle raged in the Rose-king's soul between the powers of good and evil; with what headlong attacks, stratagems, and temptations Satan beset that timid and virgin heart; what suggestions, images, and desires the Evil One conjured up, to compass the ruin of that elect soul?   Guy de Maupassant, *Le Rosier de Madame Husson*[1]

In his article 'Character and Caricature in *Albert Herring*',[2] Philip Brett describes *Albert Herring* as a 'parable of oppression', a label which suggests that the opera is a further examination of the dramatic conflict between social oppression and self-repression, liberation and defeat which lay at the heart of *Peter Grimes* and *The Rape of Lucretia*. Based upon Guy de Maupassant's short story, *Le Rosier de Madame Husson*, in many ways it does appear to be a comic companion piece to *Lucretia*. It was composed for the newly formed English Opera Group and premiered at Glyndebourne on 20 June 1947 by the same singers and instrumentalists who had performed *Lucretia* in the preceding year. Furthermore, the Suffolk setting and the satirical presentation of a hypocritical ruling elite recall the landscape and social milieu of *Grimes*.[3]

The librettist of *Albert Herring* was Eric Crozier, who had himself suggested the subject to Britten. Crozier had little writing experience and must have been as surprised to find himself promoted from adviser/producer to librettist as Britten's previous collaborator, Ronald Duncan, was to find himself rejected after what he considered to be his successful partnership with Britten on *The Rape of Lucretia*. Duncan describes how he and Britten had discussed and begun to develop ideas for future operatic projects:

> While we were rehearsing *Lucretia* John Christie invited Ben and me to write a new opera which he promised to present the following year. Ben agreed and said that he wanted to write a comedy. This put *Abelard* [*Abelard and Heloise*] out of the question and since the new piece was to be a chamber opera the *Canterbury*

[1] Guy de Maupassant, *Madame Husson's Rose-King* (*Le Rosier de Madame Husson*) (London: J. M. Dent and Sons Ltd, 1977), pp. 89–90. All subsequent references are to this edition and are given in parentheses in the text.
[2] Philip Brett, 'Character and Caricature in *Albert Herring*', *Musical Times*, October 1986, 545–7.
[3] Britten's use of self-parody and self-quotation means that the score of *Albert Herring* is liberally scattered with textual and musical references to *Grimes* and *Lucretia*.

Tales wasn't suitable either. And during Lucretia rehearsals he had decided that he wanted to write a work for Kathleen Ferrier. It was Joan Cross who eventually produced a subject for us by suggesting *Mansfield Park*.[4]

When rumours reached Duncan that Britten had begun working with Crozier on *Abelard and Heloise* he wrote asking for an explanation: 'Ben's reply was that there was no truth in the story that he was writing *Abelard* with Crozier. Even then he did not have the guts to say he was writing something else, though when *Albert Herring* was finished he naievely [sic] asked if he could play it to me, which he did when I was in London.'[5] The damage to their relationship was not fully repaired until near the end of Britten's life.

Having witnessed the unpredictability of Britten's professional relationships, and the unheralded demise of his two predecessors, Crozier remained wary despite the close friendship which developed between him and Britten. He told Humphrey Carpenter that Britten:

> always had a particular favourite, somebody whose confidence mattered a great deal to him, and upon whom he would lavish affection and admiration in the most genuine fashion, while at the same time foreseeing with a grim kind of enjoyment the day when that special friend would be cast off . . . Just before Christmas one year during that period [the late forties] a parcel arrived marked FRAGILE . . . 'Who is it from?' I asked. He handed the picture to me with a curious expression of distaste mixed with embarrassment. 'Monty Slater,' he replied. 'One of my "corpses" '. Then, with a queer kind of pleasure, he went on: 'You'll be one too, one day.'[6]

As the atmosphere among the members and performers of the English Opera Group became more insular and exclusive, resentment grew. Joan Cross recalled: 'I think it is fair to say that Benjamin Britten liked in those days to write for the voices and personalities of singers he knew well . . . It was like a family reunion when singers and orchestra, stage and music staff reassembled for rehearsals on the new piece.'[7] Not everyone involved in the production was happy with this 'family atmosphere'. Years later, Frederick Ashton, who was invited to choreograph the opera, later told Keith Grant, then manager of the English Opera Group, that 'Ben and his friends behaved impossibly during *Albert Herring*, and that he [Ashton] really felt quite vexed by their cliqueishness – he used to say, "I never liked coterie art." '[8] Joan Cross confirmed this impression, disliking the way

---

4 Duncan, *Working with Britten*, pp. 142–3. In the draft notes for *Working with Britten* Duncan writes: 'He had said he wanted to write a comedy or two or three one act comedies which might somehow be linked together: Eventually we settled on *The Canterbury Tales* and decided on selecting three, using the pilgrims as a link through an overture and two interludes and an epilogue. We drafted out a synopsis and later I started to write a libretto basing the first part on the *Nun's Tale*' (RD).

5 Draft notes for *Working with Britten* (RD).

6 HC, p. 243.

7 Joan Cross, *Aldeburgh Festival Programme Booklet*, 1962.

8 HC, p. 251.

in which 'Eric and Peter and Ben sort of gathered together against us . . . He [Pears] was standing behind Ben, and if Ben didn't approve of anything, Peter put the words in his mouth.'[9] Following the Glyndebourne production of *Albert Herring*, John Christie, disappointed by the low financial returns of the *Lucretia* tour, refused to support another potentially loss-making English Opera Group tour. This provided Britten and Pears with the opportunity to break decisively with Glyndebourne and to redefine the priorities of the English Opera Group. The result was the founding of the Aldeburgh Festival in the following year which opened with a performance of *Albert Herring* by the company.

The cliquish atmosphere of *Albert Herring* was intensified by Crozier's transposition of Maupassant's French tale to a rural East Suffolk setting which was modelled on the small towns and villages around Aldeburgh. In addition, Britten's score indulged in caricature of some of the actual inhabitants of these villages as well as of his own family and friends.[10] There were naturally fewer opportunities for lyrical expansion within the comic genre and it was probably this factor, combined with the patronising tone of much of the text, that contributed to the opera's negative critical reception. While some observers admired Britten's technical facility, effective characterisation and ingenious orchestration, the opera was generally perceived as superficial and condescending, as 'a charade'[11] or 'hardly an opera . . . rather a play with an extremely animated musical surface'.[12]

There was considerable disapproval of Crozier's text which was judged to be brash and vulgar. For example, Ernest Newman declared that there was a danger of 'a first class opera talent going partly to waste because of a failure to find the right libretto'.[13] Ronald Duncan was particularly disparaging: 'I was distressed to find de Maupassant's sophistication translated to a church-bazaar parochialism.'[14] Crozier's prosaic style could not have been more different from the verbose rhetoric of Duncan's *Lucretia* libretto. He defended his libretto for *Albert Herring* in a Preface to the original publication:

> A librettist is a craftsman working for an artist. He may also be an artist himself, but in writing an opera his main job is not to write as a poet does, compressing thought and emotion into an inevitable and unchangeable pattern of words: it is to provide the composer with words, ideas, emotions and actions that are all

9   *Ibid.* Elizabeth Sweeting, who was on the Glyndebourne staff during this period substantiated Cross's suspicions that Pears was responsible for aggravating the tension.

10 For example, Albert was named after a grocer from Tunstall near Snape. Britten's sister Beth describes: 'Ben really let himself go in the brilliant characterisation of the roles. He modelled Lady Billows on my mother-in-law, with exaggeration of course, but Cuckoo liked to think herself the Queen Bee of the village and was a terrible snob. Ben threatened to call the schoolmistress Miss Welford, but I dissuaded him and he called her Miss Wordsworth instead' (*My Brother Benjamin*, pp. 189–90).

11 Frank Howes, *The Times*, 21 June 1947.

12 William Glock, *Time and Tide*, 28 June 1947.

13 Ernest Newman, *Sunday Times*, 29 June 1947.

14 Autobiographical drafts (RD).

true to character and true in style, and yet infinitely capable of being modified and reshaped to musical ends. Composer and author are working with the same aim, the expression of drama, character and emotion through the fusion of words and music – but the words are only part of a whole whose architectural shape must be determined by musical laws. The librettist must remember that he is writing to be sung, not to be read from the printed page . . . This is not poetry. It is a simple form of verse written and rewritten to meet a particular situation. Its highest ambition is to serve the composer's intention sincerely, neatly and well.[15]

After his problematic partnerships with Slater and Duncan, Britten must have welcomed Crozier's flexible attitude and readiness to alter his text in accordance with the composer's demands.[16] While Crozier's libretto has little purely poetic merit, its style is unassuming and unaffected and the text is not cluttered with overt symbolism or personal rhetoric. The composer is freed from any obligations to a pre-established interpretation of the subject which might conflict which his personal reading of the drama and there is less sense that the text and score are striving towards contradictory ends. It is perhaps in the moments of more expansive musical lyricism that we should look for possible evidence of a more profound 'meaning', one which might transcend the distractions of the comic surface. Indeed, the dramatic eloquence of the reflective musical passages in Britten's score is in some ways intensified by the rapid burlesque of the surrounding farce as related by Crozier.

In *Albert Herring* Britten reinterprets the experience of one who, like Peter Grimes and Lucretia, suffers the anxieties and dilemmas of internal and external oppression, and who must choose between rebellious individualism or socially conditioned repression. In contrast to the tragic experiences of Grimes and Lucretia, Albert's attempt at 'liberation' appears to have a positive conclusion. However, closer analysis reveals that the ostensible balance between personal integrity and social integration which Albert achieves at the end of Britten's comedy is as illusory or ambivalent as the anguished 'resolutions' of his first two operas. Furthermore, the absence of any obvious conflict between librettist and composer, text and score, does not necessarily mean that Britten's score unambiguously and openly expresses his own response to the drama. Although the alterations to Maupassant's short story and the musical intensification of these events go some way towards disclosing his own reading, the unanswered questions which had destabilised *Grimes* and *Lucretia* resurface and are rearticulated in *Albert Herring*, and the comic context is unable to entirely eradicate these ambiguities and tensions. Is Albert virtuous/innocent? What *is* the 'experience' which liberates him from maternal/social domination? Is his personal liberation genuine and will his rebellion bring about lasting and meaningful social transformations?

---

[15] Eric Crozier, 'Preface' to *Albert Herring*, quoted in DH, pp. 137–8.
[16] Crozier later collaborated with Britten on the librettos of *Billy Budd*, *The Little Sweep* and *Saint Nicolas*.

*

In Maupassant's short story, *Le Rosier de Madame Husson*, the restriction of his protagonist's individual freedom by oppressive social conventions has a tragic outcome. Crozier and Britten retain Maupassant's essential plot but make a number of subtle and illuminating changes, not least the substitution of a comic conclusion for the original's pessimistic denouement. In the opera, Loxford's social 'elite' are depicted in far greater detail than in Maupassant's story, as Britten and Crozier emphasise the pettiness and hypocrisy of its members through the words and stage actions of their characters.[17] However, the most radical transformation is that of Albert himself, the role which was taken by Peter Pears in the first production. He is less naive and foolish than Isidore, and the reasons for, and nature of, his rebellion are consequently more complex. The result of these alterations is that a simple account of suffocating provincialism and rebellious over-indulgence is potentially transformed into a complex dramatisation of the nature of virtue and innocence, in which personal integrity defeats sexual repression. The protagonist, previously imprisoned by life-denying maternal and social forces, wins his imaginative and practical freedom and is liberated into a world of creative and physical experience.

In *Albert Herring* the local benefactress, Lady Billows, has offered a prize of £25 to be given to a chosen 'May Queen' as an encouragement to virtue. In the absence of a suitably chaste village girl to receive the prize, a 'May King', Albert Herring, is nominated. On the day of the crowning ceremony the opera's two young lovers, Sid and Nancy, lace Albert's lemonade with rum. After his chastity and virtue have been extolled by Lady Billows, he is called upon to make a speech, but the now inebriated Albert can only stammer and hiccough in reply. Later that night, Albert overhears Sid and Nancy sympathetically discussing his domination by his mother and he decides to break away. Following his disappearance, his orange-blossom crown is discovered in the gutter, muddy and squashed, and Mrs Herring is convinced he has been killed. During the elaborate mourning threnody which the characters sing for the dead May King, Albert himself creeps in and explains that he has merely been on a drinking spree, gaining a taste of the worldly experience which has so far been denied him. He counters his mother's reproaches by blaming her for bringing him up too puritanically, and throws away his orange blossom crown in an act of defiance, encouraged in his new spirit of self-assertion by the support of Sid and Nancy.

At the start of the opera the sources of Albert's oppression are clearly defined: Albert is literally 'imprisoned' within his mother's shop and metaphorically oppressed by the labels imposed upon him by Loxford society. In his individual musical portraits Britten employs pastiche and caricature to underline the shallowness of his characters' ostentatious moralising but the very real menace latent in their collective bigotry is most powerful portrayed in the large-scale choruses

---

[17] In Maupassant's story the tale of the Rose-King's escapade is revealed indirectly, related to the narrator by an old friend who lives in Gisors where the events took place, and whose manner and actions embody the deadening claustrophobia of provincial life.

and set pieces, which recall the Borough's ensembles in *Peter Grimes*. Furthermore, the harmonic tension between B♭ and E♭, which are associated with Loxford's shallowness and hypocrisy, and E, which implies freedom, self-honesty and love, replicates the tonal dramatisation of the conflict between the individual and society previously established in *Grimes*. For example, in the opening scene, Florence, required by Lady Billows to gather evidence of the moral corruption of the young inhabitants of Loxford, despairs (Act 1, Fig. 7):

> FLORENCE: *One lifetime, one brain,*
> *One pair of hands are all too few for Lady B.*
> *Each day some new idea makes new demands*
> *Upon her sense of charity.*

The E major inflections of her vocal line imply her desire for escape, and conflict with the low E♭ and B♭ bass pedals which represent the tyranny and bigotry of her employer. As her confidence grows, the pedals rise to B♮ and E♮ thus complementing her melody (Fig. 8), before ultimately forcing it to return to E♭ (Fig. 9). Her final words are:

> *But oh! But oh!*
> *Sometimes I wish . . .*

Her phrase climbs chromatically and culminates with an expressive minor ninth leap from D♯ to E, a rise which implies resolution in E major and, recalling this interval's expressive force in *Peter Grimes*, suggests the intensity of her craving for freedom. The instrumental 'play-out' begins with *marcatissimo* E major chords but the futility of her dream is made apparent with the entrance of the members of the Loxford committee.

Drawing upon Maupassant's description of Madame Husson's 'deep instinctive horror of vice and especially of that form of vice to which the Church refers as the lust of the flesh' (p. 83), Crozier emphasises Lady Billows's abhorrence of sexuality, or the open display of sexuality, in the opening pages of the libretto:

> FLORENCE: *Doctor Jessop's midwife mustn't touch illegitimates*
>   . . .
> *Advert in chemist's window is indecent.*

The C major key of the aria (Act 1, Fig. 17), in which she declares her intention to honour a May-Queen, reveals her determination to 'purify' Loxford, but the impossibility of this mission is perhaps suggested by her acknowledgement that she 'Must make virtue attractive, exciting, desirable for young people', a phrase centred on E major, the key of sexual temptation and fulfilment.

Loxford society equates virtue unequivocally with sexual abstinence, recalling the self-delusive misconceptions of Maupassant's characters who are unshakable in their belief in Isidore's purity: 'Undoubtedly, Isidore was an instance of exceptional, conspicuous, impregnable virtue. No one, not the most sceptical, the most incredulous of mankind, could venture to suspect Isidore of the smallest infringement of any moral law whatever . . . He was perfection; a pearl of purity' (p. 85), ' "What do you wish to reward, Madame Husson? Virtue, I take it, virtue pure and simple. In that case, what does it matter to you whether its exponent be male or female? Virtue is eternal, and knows neither country nor sex. Virtue is simply virtue" ' (p. 86). However, like the red blush of beauty which stains the whiteness of Lucretia's virtue, Isidore's naivety threatens to betray him: 'He was so quick to blush at loose words, ribald jests, and unseemly allusions, that Dr Barbesol nick-named him the thermometer of modesty. Was he ignorant, or was he not? some of the neighbours slyly wondered. What was the cause of this emotion that so perturbed the son of Virginie, the greengrocer's widow?' (p. 85). In contrast to Isidore whose innocence has not been tested by the temptations of knowledge, it is evident in the libretto that Albert is not ignorant and that he fully understands his ridiculers' *double entendres*. However, the inhabitants of Loxford persist in their self-delusion. In Act 1 the Vicar sings (Act 1, Fig. 39):

> *Virtue*
> *Says Holy Writ,*
> *Is – Virtue.*
> *Grace abounding*
> *Whensoever*
> *Wheresoever*
> *Howsoever*
> *It exists.*
> *Rarer than rubies, pearls, amethyst*
> *Richer than wealth, wisdom, righteousness!*
> *Is Albert virtuous?*
> *Yes? Or no?*
> *That is all we need to know.*

The B♭ harmony, ponderous rhythm and thick, homophonic texture of this passage illuminate the society's unimaginative short-sightedness. The answer to the Vicar's question is that Albert *is* virtuous but only because he has not yet been granted the freedom to act unvirtuously. In the closing bars of the passage, Lady Billows asks 'Albert . . . what's his name?', to which the others reply 'Herr-ing', the two syllables of his naming effecting a resolution in B♭ major.

Peter Grimes's insistence that unsubstantiated rumour and gossip are respon-sible for his social alienation – 'The case goes on in people's minds/ Then charges that no court has made/ Will be shouted at my head' – are echoed in Maupassant's text which clarifies the role played by rumour in the formation of social reputa-tion: 'Not one emerged spotless from this rigorous inquisition. Francoise ques-tioned every one, the neighbours, the tradesmen, the school master, the school sisters, and accepted even the most insignificant rumours. No girl on earth entirely escapes the tattling tongues of gossips. In the whole neighbourhood not a single girl could be found whom the breath of scandal had not touched' (p. 84).

Loxford's desire to mould and control Albert's identity and destiny by eradi-cating his natural instincts is revealed when he is suggested for the May King acco-lade. As his name is proposed by Superintendent Budd the instrumental accompaniment is enriched and there is a subtle harmonic shift to E major. The other characters, initially amazed at this suggestion, cry 'Albert Herring', their phrase rising through an arpeggio of E, perhaps hinting at their subconscious awareness of Albert's latent desires. Likewise, at the end of the committee's deliberations concerning Albert's suitability, Lady Billows recites on a monotone E:

> *Either we abandon the festival or . . .*

She is interrupted by Budd's restatement of his 'Albert Herring' motif accompanied by a rising glissando played by the solo cello at the top of its range, spanning E–E, but once again the musical intimations of Albert's 'true' identity are ignored.

Albert's name and identity are most powerfully appropriated and defined by the Loxfordians in the May King 'hymn of praise' which is sung in his honour at the crowning ceremony. At the start of Act 2 Miss Wordsworth gathers the unruly children to practise this song (Act 2, Fig. 8). The E major tonality of this passage suggests their subconscious identification with Albert's latent, and as yet unacknowledged, desires, an impression which is strengthened by the children's greedy anticipation of the feast to come. Significantly, when they finally perform their set piece, E major is replaced by B♭ major [Example 11]; their behaviour is perhaps tempered by the presence of the Loxford committee (Act 2, Fig. 32):

> *Glory to our new May King!*
> *Albert, hail! All hail! we Sing.*
> *Every voice cries out rejoice!*
> *In happy song both loud and long!*

Albert's response to this adulation is complex. Initially, returning in high spirits from the feast, he proudly recalls their praise (Act 2, Fig. 63), elaborately decorating the hymn's melody:

> *Albert the Good! Long may he reign.*
> *To be re-elected, and re-selected, and re-expected,*
> *And resurrected again, and again, and again, and again, again,*
>   *again . . .*

However, as his dissatisfaction with the limitations of his life-style increase, so does his anger. While the upper echelons of Loxford society revere Albert as an unrealistic paragon of virtue, the children, Sid and Nancy ridicule his simplemindedness and his domination by Mrs Herring, a representation he later angrily rejects as equally false (Act 2, Fig. 89):

> *Nancy pities me – Sid laughs – others snigger*
> *At my simplicity – offer me buns*
> *To stay in my cage – parade*
> *Me around as their Whiteheaded Boy –*
>
> *Albert the Good! Albert who Should!*
> *Albert who Hasn't and Wouldn't if he Could!*
> *Albert the Meek! Albert the Sheep!*
> *Mrs Herring's Guinea-Pig!*
> *Mrs Herring's Tillypig!*
> *Mrs Herring's – Prig!*

Example 11

The animated tempo of this reprise, the dissonant harmony and the aggressive texture of the string and percussion accompaniment contribute to the mood of blatant and unapologetic defiance.

During the Act 2 crowning ceremony, Lady Billow's centrally located E♭ aria (Act 2 preceding Fig. 28) underlines her position as the dominant force of oppression and reveals the extent of the threat to Albert's self-validity. Her preposterous cries – 'Britons! Rule the deep!' – incite patriotic responses from the crowd of

Example 12

onlookers who are drawn into her E♭ tonality (Fig. 31). Albert's first entry (laden with an enormous bag of turnips) in Act 1, Scene 2 (Fig. 67) had suggested the weight of the subordination which he bears, the E♭ tonality, the low register and the heavy, deliberate rhythmic movement enhancing the claustrophobic atmosphere. Now, when he is called upon to give a speech of thanks, Albert rises 'slowly and miserably', the harmony modulating to a funereal B♭ minor, a sinister permutation of Loxford's harmonic centre. Repetitions of the May King motif infiltrate the orchestral texture as Albert's energy is slowly drained away by Loxford's moral restrictiveness. He gathers himself as if to speak but loses his nerve, finally stuttering on a monotone B♭ which holds him captive [Example 12]:

> *Er . . .*
> *Thank you . . . very much!*

This is the first of two expressive silences in the opera, the second occurring at the end of Act 2, when Albert is called upon to confess his 'crimes'. Initially the observers sympathise with Albert's shyness but they quickly lose interest in his afflictions and return to triumphant self-congratulation, the B♭ minor tonality swept aside by a retrograde version of the 'May-King' motif in a heroic B♭ major (Act 2, Fig. 44):

> *Albert the Good!*
> *Long may he reign!*
> *To be re-elected*
> *Again and again!*

The first signs of Albert's potential defiance are evident in Act 1 when, moved by Sid and Nancy's sincere displays of affection, he begins to doubt the wisdom of his mother's insistence upon abstinence (Fig. 76):

> *ALBERT: I wonder is he*
> *Right when he says*
> *I miss all the fun*
> *Because of Mum?*
>
> *Yes! Mum's uncommon keen*
> *About the need*

> *Of living chaste and clean*
> *In word and deed –*
> *For what?*

Although at this point in the opera he is unable to decide upon a course of action, his dissatisfaction is unambiguously registered and the seeds of defiance are sown:

> *ALBERT: It seems as clear as clear can be that Sid's ideas*
> *Are very much too crude for Mother to approve.*
> *And yet I'd really like to try that kind of life*
> *And see how it compares with serving customers.*

Albert's confusion is evoked by the melodic indecision of his vocal phrases, which are supported by a sustained pedal B, implying a forth-coming but as yet unfulfilled resolution in E. His vocal line fluctuates between C and E, and the word 'Mother' is intoned on B♭, subtly challenging the bass pedal.

Albert's domination by his mother features more significantly in the libretto than in Maupassant's text. Albert's disaffection initially finds expression in a surprisingly self-assertive outburst (Act 1, Fig. 92) which contrasts markedly with Isidore's passivity and meekness:

> *ALBERT: You shut me up in the shop all day!*
> *MUM: The wicked ingratitude of it! You'll pay*
> *For this, my boy.*
> *ALBERT: I'm sick and tired*
> *Of being ordered about –*
> *MUM: You little liar!*
> *I won't stand here and be attacked*
> *By a kid who wants his bottom smacked!*
> *Go up to bed and shut that door*
> *And don't you dare come down before*
> *You're ready to say sorry. Go on!*
> *You devil!*

Following his return from his nocturnal exploits, Albert unequivocally blames his mother for his actions, reciting on B♭:

> *ALBERT: You know what drove me . . .*
> *You know how I could . . .*
> *It was all because*
> *You squashed me down and reined me in,*
> *Did up my instincts with safety-pins,*
> *Kept me wrapped in cotton wool,*
> *Measured my life with a twelve-inch rule, –*
> *Protected me with such devotion*
> *My only way-out was a wild explosion!*

In Maupassant's short story it is during the festive celebrations that Isidore develops a taste for the alcohol which is responsible for his eventual degradation. Similarly, Albert's mutinous outbreak is ostensibly the result of the excessive quantities of potent lemonade punch which he has consumed. However, in reality the lemonade serves a more symbolic function. Albert's feelings are primarily aroused, not by alcohol, but by the love which he observes between Sid and Nancy, and it is perhaps significant that it is they who are responsible for lacing the lemonade with rum. In his article, 'Wagner, Britten and Innocence',[18] Lewis Jones describes how Britten complements this temptation musically by quoting the 'Tristan chord' from *Tristan and Isolde* at this point. Wagner's chord had originally marked the moment when his frustrated and inarticulate lovers share a mystical potion; in this way, their unexpressed desire was made musically explicit. The frustrated passion which resonated in Wagner's chord offered Britten an effective parallel in his own work.

Elaborating subtle insinuations in Maupassant's text, Crozier's libretto consistently emphasises the erotic potential of food and drink, insinuating that Albert's gluttonous over-indulgence may be a substitute gratification for his real 'hunger'. Maupassant had written: 'He was experiencing for the first time the delight of filling himself with good things . . . He only stopped eating long enough to raise his glass to his lips, and he kept it there as long as possible, enjoying the flavour at his leisure. He sat in silence, feeling a little guilty because of a drop of wine that had fallen on his white coat' (pp. 88–9). Isidore returns to his mother's shop, drunken and surfeited: 'The close air of the room was heavy with the strong vegetable odours, cabbages, and onions, mingled with the sweet, penetrating smell of strawberries, and the delicate, elusive fragrance of a basket of peaches. The Rose-king seized a peach, and took a large bite out of it, although his skin was as tight as a drum. Then, utterly beside himself with joy, he suddenly broke into a dance' (p. 89). Crozier intensifies the sexual symbolism of the peach in Act 1, Scene 2, as Sid flirts with Nancy in Albert's shop (Fig. 70):

> SID: *There's no need to worry! Have a nice peach?*
> NANCY: *Ooh! May I really?*
> ALBERT: *Those are sixpence each! –*
> SID: *Take two – I'll stand the damage . . .*
> NANCY: *I shan't eat them now.*
> *They're so ripe they might splash.*
> SID: *You can bring them tonight*
> *And we'll each take a bite,*
> *To flavour our kisses*
> *With a dash of peach bitters.*
> NANCY: *That sounds just delicious –*

The slow, seductive, rising arpeggio which accompanies Sid's invitation looks forward to the exotic sexually charged timbre of similar musical passages in *The Turn of the Screw*, *Owen Wingrave* and *Death in Venice*. In *Albert Herring* the peach becomes a symbol of uninhibited sexuality. At the end of Act 3 the newly

---

[18] Lewis Jones, 'Wagner, Britten and Innocence', in *Silence and Music* (Sussex: The Book Guild, 1992), pp. 75–80.

liberated Albert takes a basket of peaches and offers it to the children, in an act which recalls their early theft of 'Edenic' apples from his shop:

> ALBERT: Have a nice peach . . . ? Go on! Help yourselves!
> There's plenty for everyone! Put some more in your pockets!

Albert's words counter the Vicar's Act 1 aria which has served to incite the Loxford committee's moral indignation and horror at the 'evil' harboured within their community. Accompanied by a B♭ minor 'vamp' bar, they sing (Fig. 32):

> VICAR: Oh, bitter, bitter is the fruit
> Sprung from the seed of sin:
> It feeds on poison at the root
> And cankers all within.
>
> MAYOR: How sad to see a decent town
> Lose its good name and sink
> Slowly, slowly, slowly down
> And hover on the brink.

Albert eventually makes his decision to escape in Act 2, Scene 2. As he considers the choices before him, his waverings between freedom and repression are represented harmonically by the conflict between B♭–E♭ and E. This process begins in the preceding instrumental interlude and is varied in application. The expressive conflict may occur as a bitonal opposition between melody and harmony (Act 2, Fig. 60) or may be contained within a single melodic phrase (Act 2, Fig. 66). Both melody and harmony respond flexibly to Albert's words; for example, when Albert sings:

> It's your little Albert,
> Your sugar plum of a prodigal son,
> Clean as a whistle, Sound as a drum,
> From his Coronation.

This E major melody is supported by a C pedal, thereby suggesting the gap between his true identity and his socially conditioned self.

Following Albert's recollections, in E♭, of his crowning by Lady Billows, he speculates on the 'miraculous', potent effects of the lemonade which he consumed (Act 2, Fig. 72):

> Wonder how it's made?
> Nancy knows, I suppose
> Nancy will know
> Pretty name, Nancy!

His repetitions of Nancy's name centre on the pitch E, and are supported by an E pedal which is sustained in his subsequent aria (Fig. 74), the words of which suggest his sexual awakening:

> Why did she stare
> Each time I looked at her?
> Why was she watching

Whenever I turned of a sudden?
Nancy!
Why did she blush
Catching my eye as she passed?
What made her stammer
When speaking to me in that manner?
Nancy? Nancy?
No, she belongs to Sid, not me.

This passage [Example 13] is Albert's equivalent of Peter Grimes's 'Great Bear' aria: each of his phrases commences on a sustained E and the entire aria is supported by a pedal E (Act 2, Figs. 74–6). Grimes's cry 'Who, who, who can turn the skies back again?' is echoed in Albert's urgent implorings on E, 'Nancy? Nancy?' He does not look to the heavens for transcendental fulfilment but seeks a more human communion on earth. However, the final line, which traces a descending E major triad, discloses the inevitable frustration of his ambitions, for Nancy's blushes spring not from desire but from her guilt at having laced Albert's lemonade. His confusion is apparent in his response to Sid and Nancy's sympathetic restatement of the May-King motif in the following scene. The E major tonality of his phrase – 'Heaven helps those who help themselves. Help myself!' reveals his new confidence but is immediately contradicted by his angry cries, in B♭ (Act 2, Fig. 86):

O go, Go! Go away! and leave me alone
With doubts and terrors you have never known!

Albert's ultimate determination to resolve his moral dilemma is accompanied by a decisive modulation to E. The transformation begins with his agitated recitation (Act 2, Fig. 92):

But when, but when,
Shall I dare, and dare again?
How shall I screw my courage up
To do what should be done by everyone?

A toss of his prize coin, musically represented by a sweeping glissando on oboe and harp, will decide his fate: as the coin lands, the tremolo E played by the double bass indicates the inevitability of the outcome. As he looks at the coin 'grimly', slowly alternating timbres and harmonies – a unison C played by the horn and bassoon, and an E♭ triad sounded by the strings – unambiguously illustrate the choice before him.

Incarcerated by his mother's suffocating love, Albert has been unable to make the transition from childhood to adulthood, from innocence to experience, from ignorance to knowledge. Literally entrapped by his mother's embrace and symbolically restricted by his public reputation, Albert is forced to observe life from behind the glass of his mother's shop window. He complains that they 'make speeches at me like I was stuffed instead of flesh and blood', and Nancy comments that, 'It does seem wrong to show him off to everyone like a sort of plaster saint.' Effectively Albert is condemned to a 'living death', unable to develop his natural

Example 13

imaginative or physical desires. Similarly, when Isidore accepts his Rose-crown he is reminded: 'that all the rest of your life to your dying day must be in accordance with the promise of this auspicious beginning . . . you enter into a solemn engagement with your town, with all of us to maintain until the end of your days the admirable example of your youthful purity' (pp. 87–8). Evidently the citizens of Gisors would prefer a dead but pure Isidore to one who is 'tainted' by life's experiences. Indeed, his failure to heed their warning results in tragedy: 'He was not fit to be touched by a rag-picker. Nothing was left of his immaculate suit of white duck but a mass of rags, stained grey and yellow, greasy, muddy, tattered, and vile. He stank of the gutter and every form of degradation' (p. 91). Discovered thus Isidore subsequently dies of *delirium tremens*, his passing unremarked and unmourned by the village which had honoured him.

The inhabitants of Loxford are similarly obsessed with Albert 'the icon of virginity' and uninterested in Albert 'the man'. Lady Billows insists that the manhunt tracks him down 'dead or alive'. How then does Albert avoid Isidore's fate? In fact the Loxford worthies mistakenly believe that Albert *has* died, and the musical climax of *Albert Herring* is the threnody sung in his memory. They mourn him as one who as achieved salvation by rejecting his sexuality, sacrificing his own life in order to uphold society's moral code.[19] The solemn religious atmosphere contributes to their beatification of Albert as a sacred 'relic', as they sing in unison (Act 3, Fig. 51):

> ALL: In the midst of life is Death.
> Death awaits us one and all.
> Death attends our smallest step,
> Silent, swift and merciful.

The expressive implications of Bb minor and Bb major are now fully disclosed: there is a gradual modulation from the minor to major mode as the insincerity of the characters' religious solemnity is exposed – they are more concerned to perpetuate the myth of Albert's purity than to genuinely grieve his death.

The static nature of this passage contrasts with the relentless rhythmic pace of their music so far: time is 'frozen' as Albert's life-clock is stopped. 'Time' is a recurring symbol in the libretto. In the opening scene the Loxford busybodies are obsessed with time:

> MAYOR: It's just on half-past ten. We're very punctual by that
>   clock. . . .
> VICAR: As you will –
> [The clock strikes the half-hour]
> SUPERINTENDENT: Ten seconds fast, I make that.
> MAYOR: No, you're slow! Exactly right by mine.

This preoccupation with punctuality contrasts with Sid and Nancy's understanding and acceptance of the natural rhythms of life:

> SID: Come along, darling, come follow me quick!
> Time is racing us round the clock –
> Ticking and tocking our evening away.
> BOTH: Which we've hoped for
> And longed for all day.
> Hurry to work and hurry to play,
> Youth must hurry at headlong pace,

---

[19] Ironically, part of the Rose-King's prize is Foxe's *Book of Martyrs*.

> *Seizing and squeezing the pleasures of life*
> *In a cheerful and fearful embrace . . .*
> *BOTH: Time is a glutton, Time is a thief,*
> *Youth must challenge him as he flies,*
> *Catching and snatching its dreams of delight*
> *Between eight and eleven at night!*

To partake in life Albert must literally step out of 'time' and disappear into the night. As early as Act 1, Scene 2 he sings 'Oh, maybe soon I'll have the chance to get away. And golly! It's about time.' If the events of his nocturnal escapade are not fully explained this is perhaps because they take place in another dimension or 'space', one which in some way transcends the Loxford environment. Albert's experience therefore parallels that of Grimes and Lucretia, who similarly struggle for self-realisation in a world free from mundane hypocrisies and oppression. However, whereas Britten's first two protagonists aspire to restore their personal integrity in the after-life, Albert is not seeking divine consummation but desires a more earthly fulfilment. Indeed, Sid sings during the threnody:

> *The grave's a fine and private place*
> *But horribly cold and horribly chaste,*
> *And not attractive to my taste.*

Albert's decision to escape is as irreversible as the suicides of Grimes and Lucretia, but is essentially a decision to join life not to evade it:

> *ALBERT: The tide will turn, the sun will set*
> *While I stand here and hesitate.*
> *The clock begins its rusty whirr,*
> *Catches its breath to strike the hour*
> *And offers me a final choice*
> *That must be answered No or Yes . . .*
> *Well, you've gone and done it now!*
> *It's very plain*
> *You've burnt your boats*
> *And can't go back again.*

Albert's re-entrance in the final scene restarts time, which has been suspended during the threnody. The mourners' angry response to the exposure of their self-delusions recalls the self-defensive aggressiveness of the Borough in *Peter Grimes*:

> *OTHERS: We must persist*
> *And insist*
> *On the truth –*
> *However bad it is . . .*
> *The truth! At once! Tell us the whole truth!*
> *And nothing but the truth . . . !*

Their unison cry is supported by pounding E♭ chords which are reminiscent of the posse's music in Act 3 of *Peter Grimes*. Called upon to 'confess', Albert initially remains silent, answering his accuser's questions with nods and shakes of his head, before defiantly relating his grim tale and shattering their complacency. As he begins to speak the sustained *fortissimo* E♭ of the crowd's final 'truth' is undermined by a *pianissimo* viola entry on E (Act 3, Fig. 63) which introduces a brief reprise of the rhythmic pedal from his Act 2 aria sung in praise of Nancy. His confession is characterised by recitations on E, supported by a stable pedal E in the bass, which rise in pitch and intensity as his anger and confidence grow. His rebellion gathers unstoppable momentum and he draws his oppressors to his own tonal area, their horrified cries – 'This is revolting! Stop! Stop! Stop!' – puncturing the texture with accented unison E's. The passage climaxes with an impassioned outburst, tethered to a high E in a manner which recalls Peter Grimes's contempt for the Borough (Act 3, Fig. 67):

> *ALBERT: You wanted the truth! Do you want some more?*
> *Or will that do as a general sample*
> *Of a night that was a nightmare example*
> *Of drunkenness, dirt and worse . . . ?*

The audience might well reply that we do require 'some more': for while it is evident that Albert has been transformed by his experiences, the opera reveals neither what these experiences were nor where they will lead him.[20] Eric Walter White criticised the swift and over-simplistic conclusion: 'when the curtain falls, one does not feel that the experience gained in the course of this or any other drinking bout would have been sufficient to free him from the shackles of his painful inhibitions . . . Albert Herring, one suspects, lived down the momentary scandal of his May Day intoxication and became a respected citizen of Loxford.'[21] However, White places too literal an emphasis on Albert's 'May Day intoxication'. It is not alcohol which is responsible for Albert's rebellion but passion, for Sid and Nancy have laced his lemonade not with rum but with love. At the end of the opera, those characters who have retained their essential integrity – the children, Sid and Nancy – welcome back Albert, who has now recovered his own identity:

> *ALL: Albert's come*
> *Back to stay*
> *Better for his holiday!*
> *Let's all say*

---

[20] Carpenter informs that Crozier wrote a sequel to *Albert Herring* entitled *Albert in Later Life*, originally intended for inclusion in Faber's *Tribute to Britten on his Fiftieth Birthday*. The story describes how, following the death of his mother, Albert leaves Loxford and finds employment in a Lowestoft hotel where he blackmails the owner. His later jobs include working for a clergyman who has a penchant for curly haired youths, and whom he also blackmails, and selling erotic literature. He becomes romantically entangled with Cissy Woodger, who is now an operatic diva and attempts to 'dispose' of her by setting fire to the theatre in which she is performing. Unfortunately for Albert she survives, marries him, and they return to Loxford where it seems she will bully him as mercilessly as his mother had done. Anthony Gishford, the collection's editor, told Crozier that although the tale entertained him: 'I am afraid that the voice of caution warns me against using a story [about] blackmail, pederasty, pornography and arson' (HC, p. 421).

[21] White, *Benjamin Britten*, pp. 155–6.

> *Hip-hip-hooray!*
> *Good luck to him, anyway!*

'Innocence', mistakenly identified with sexual inexperience, is now rejected and replaced with a 'knowledge' which establishes an equilibrium between independence of spirit and some degree of social integration. The problem is that this 'knowledge' or experience is never openly articulated in either the text or score of *Albert Herring*.

Isidore's tragedy occurs because he accepts society's image of himself and is unable to change the pattern of his behaviour: 'washed and lectured and locked up', he appears 'penitent and ashamed', but he soon reappears 'reeling against the walls . . . drunk, hopelessly drunk' (p. 91). In contrast, there are few clues at the conclusion of *Albert Herring* to indicate how Albert's newly acquired self-validity will affect his own, and society's, behaviour. If Britten's opera is to be more than an escapist comedy it must strive for something beyond conspicuous caricature and condescension, and suggest a more profound and sustainable transformation. Yet in the final moments of the opera the characters ranged against Albert revert to stereotype: Lady Billows *et al.* express exaggerated outrage and disgust, while the children recommence their teasing. Following his mother's tearful exit (Act 3, Fig. 74) the music returns to E♭: Albert is not permitted to indulge his desires since Nancy's congratulatory kiss is met with a suspicious warning from Sid, 'Hi! that's my girl!', declaimed on a B♭ arpeggio. The tone is light-hearted but Albert is still an 'outsider', exiled by one social group and not fully accepted by the other. His final gesture of rebellion – he tosses aside his orange-blossom crown crying 'Good riddance!' – is superficial and ineffectual, and Britten's music underlines the dramatic indeterminacy, the score cadencing in G major, the central point between the opera's two expressive centres, B♭ and E.

In *Albert Herring* Britten evidently sought an alternative resolution to the passive internalisation of social oppression which destroys the protagonists of *Grimes* and *Lucretia*, where rebellion and self-validity are found only in the after-life. However, despite the comic conclusion of *Albert Herring* there remains an ambivalence which recalls the tension in the two earlier operas between the desire to exercise freewill and the wish for social integration. The one unambiguous element in the opera is the sincerity and constancy of the love between Sid and Nancy, a love which is unashamedly physical and sensuous. The natural, unaffected lyricism of their music implies a celebration of physical passion but the presence and effect of their love is only intermittently felt, and is absent from the opera's hasty concluding scene. However, it is possible this passion finds creative expression beyond the confines of the text and score of *Albert Herring*. Following the completion of the opera Britten's next composition was the *Canticle I: My Beloved is Mine and I am His*, which was premiered by Pears and Britten in November 1947. The text is adapted from the *Song of Solomon* which interestingly had been alluded to in passing in Act 1, Scene 1 of *Albert Herring*:

> MISS WORDSWORTH and VICAR:
> *'And lo! the winter is past, the rain is over and gone,*

The flowers appear on the earth!'
VICAR: Solomon's Song, you know!

The *Canticle* is a celebration and glorification of sexual passion, the text of which suggests a potential solution to the mystery of Albert's experience:

If all those glittering monarchs, that command the servile quarters of
    this earthly ball
Should tender in exchange their shares of land
I would not change my fortunes for them all!
Their wealth is but a counter to my coin:
The world's but theirs;
But my beloved's mine.
Not time, nor place, nor chance, nor death
Can bow my least desires, unto the least remove.
He's firmly mine by blood, I his by vow
He's mine by faith, and I am his by love.
He's mine by water, I am his by wine:
Thus I my best-beloved's am, Thus he is mine . . .
He gives me wealth:
I give him all my vows:
I give him songs:
He gives me length of days.
With wreaths of grace he crowns my longing brows
And I his temples with a crown of praise
Which he accepts: an everlasting sign
That I my best-beloved's am, that he is mine.

Michael Wilcox[22] attempts to locate a specifically homosexual 'meaning' in *Albert Herring*. His interpretation of the opera identifies secret homosexual symbols in Crozier's text: for example, whistling, rattling keys and jingling bells, even *Swan Vesta* matches are imbued with potential erotic 'significance'. Wilcox goes as far as to suggest that 'Campsey Ash', where Albert's crushed wreathed is found, is an anagram of 'Yes! A.H.'s Camp!' These details, while they make mildly entertaining reading, are in practice far too limiting and reductive.

Wilcox endeavours to unlock the 'meaning' of *Albert Herring* but when he turns the key he finds only that Albert is camp. In contrast, the words of the *Song of Solomon* offer a more profound and fruitful reading. The verse revives the images of fecundity and fertility which characterise the libretto of *Albert Herring*, and suggests that physical love and beauty, as appreciated and experienced by Sid and Nancy, will transform and sustain Albert.

---

[22] Michael Wilcox, *Outlines: Benjamin Britten* (Somerset: Absolute Press, 1997), pp. 37–44.

6

The Little Sweep

How I wish that I could save you!
I would hide you far away
From the tyrants who enslave you
And torment you day by day!

Eric Crozier, Rowan's Song, The Little Sweep

. . . don't worry, and remember there are lovely things in the world still –
children, boys, sunshine, the sea, Mozart, you and me –

Peter Pears to Benjamin Britten[1]

In the weeks that followed the first Aldeburgh Festival, Britten's diary was more
crowded than ever. After a series of exhausting concerts, including performances
in England and Europe with the English Opera Group and the official première of
his cantata *Saint Nicholas*, Britten began work in earnest on what he referred to as
'the Spring piece'[2] – a choral symphony which had been commissioned several
years earlier by Koussevitzky. In addition, he received a request from David
Webster at Covent Garden, for a new, large-scale opera for the Festival of Britain
in 1951. However, these multiple pressures began to have a negative effect on
Britten's health. During a hectic recital tour in Holland with Peter Pears, in
December 1948, Britten suffered from a debilitating stomach complaint and,
diagnosed with nervous exhaustion, was ordered to take three months absolute
rest. He was suspected of having a stomach ulcer, and although an x-ray revealed
nothing, he remained exhausted and depressed in the early months of 1949.

A three-week holiday in Italy with Pears temporarily restored his mood and
energy, but upon his return to Britain, he found that he still felt drained and
dispirited. However, by March 1949 he had apparently recovered sufficiently to
contemplate another tour of America with Pears. The *Spring Symphony*, with
which he had struggled for some months, was now complete; but before it could
be scored, Britten had to turn his attention to the need for a new opera for the
second Aldeburgh Festival which was now only a few weeks away.

The Little Sweep was the first opera to be created specifically for the Aldeburgh
Festival. Set in Suffolk in 1810, it tells the story of how the children at Iken Hall
meet Sam, a pitiful sweep-boy, and rescue him from his bullying master, Black

---

[1]   Undated letter (late 1948, early 1949?); HC, p. 272.
[2]   Letter to Erwin Stein, 24 August 1948; HC, p. 270.

Bob. Eric Crozier, the librettist, recalls that for two years he and Britten had contemplated a chamber opera for children:

> I can recall the exact spot where Ben and I first discussed writing a stage work for children to perform – an almost empty ski-lift coming down one afternoon from the slopes for Zermatt . . . At that time (early February 1947) we could not think of a story, but eighteen months or so later, after the success of the first Aldeburgh Festival, the idea came up again as a distinct possibility for next summer.[3]

Several possible stories were considered and rejected, including Arthur Ransome's *Swallows and Amazons*. A letter from Crozier to Britten dating from this time (dated simply 'Wednesday') reads:

> My dear Ben,
>   Here is one kind of idea of a story for the children's opera. I have tried to think of something that puts the children-characters in a critical situation, with responsibility for much organisation and practical work, and finally they over-come considerable dangers by their own efforts. Is it too much of an adventure story?
>   At any rate, it gives us something to work from, and we can either discard it, modify it or use it!
>   With love,
>   Eric[4]

Crozier's first idea was for a plot about a family of musical children who are trans-fixed by the rehearsals of their elders (members of the local operatic society) in anticipation of the arrival of a visiting professional opera company. The pro-fessional company's eventual performance is in fact dreadful, and the local music master, Jack Tennison, agrees to compose the music for the children's own opera. The story of this opera was to be the tale of Jennifer and Tom who have been kept apart by Tom's father, the villainous Mr Bell. The children and Mrs Massey (Jennifer's sympathetic mother) must save Jennifer and Tom from Mr Bell's evil plans.

During early discussions and developments, it was Britten himself who remembered the child chimney-sweep who is depicted in two of William Blake's lyric poems, *Songs of Innocence and Songs of Experience*, upon which Crozier's final libretto was based.[5] Writing in the 1981 Buxton Festival Programme, Crozier declared:

> When he was about three, Benjamin Britten took part in a dramatic version of 'The Water Babies' at the Sparrow's Nest Theatre – his first contact with the stage. His mother played Mrs Do-as-you-would-be-done-by. Much later in life,

---

3   *Ibid.*, p. 273.
4   GB–ALb 2–9500472.
5   Blake's verse was later to inspire Britten's *Songs and Proverbs of William Blake* for baritone and piano (1965), a cycle which includes a setting of 'The Chimney Sweeper'. The published score announces that the words were 'selected by Peter Pears' from *Proverbs of Hell, Songs of Experience and Auguries of Innocence*.

on the occasion of receiving the freedom of Lowestoft in that same Sparrow's Nest Theatre, Britten recalled his struggle to memorise the lines he had to speak as Tom.

In Kingsley's Tale, Tom (Sam . . .?) is a little sweep boy who runs away to escape the bullying of his master Mr Grimes (!); he falls into the water (just like the two apprentices . . .?) and is transformed into a water baby. A charming photo exists of the small curly haired Britten sitting on his mother's lap with eleven other water-baby children around him.

The memory of childhood must, you will say, have prompted 'The Little Sweep' – yet curiously enough Britten never mentioned it to me. As early as Autumn 1946 I suggested that we might plan an opera for children, thinking of my two small daughters who were then at nursery school – but neither of us could think of a subject. Two years went by. We collaborated in writing 'Albert Herring' and the cantata 'Saint Nicolas', we founded the English Opera Group and then the Aldeburgh Festival, and still we had no subject. Then, one morning at Aldeburgh, Britten mentioned a chimney-sweeper's boy – not Kingsley's, but the hero of William Blake's two lyrical poems, 'When My Mother Died I was Very Young' and 'A Black Thing Among the Snow, Crying 'Weep! Weep!' in Notes of Woe'. And there we were . . . before evening we had sketched out the action, the characters, and the locale.

The Little Sweep forms part of the stage entertainment for the young, *Let's Make an Opera*. The first part of this entertainment is a play in which the writing and rehearsal of an opera is presented; the second part is the opera itself, *The Little Sweep*. Crozier outlined the original scenario:

> Our 'entertainment for young people' fell into three parts: (1) an expository first part about a group of enthusiasts banding together to write their own opera, (2) a musical rehearsal for the audience, and (3) 'The Little Sweep', the opera itself, in three scenes. After the exuberant first performances at Aldeburgh and elsewhere, Britten came (not unnaturally) to dislike the introductory play. What composer would not dislike having his music prefaced by a semi-didactic exposition in prose-dialogue? We made various attempts at rewriting but the problem remained (and perhaps remains) insoluble.[6]

A draft scenario[7] makes no mention of the Suffolk setting, the action taking place instead in the Jordan family home. Crozier's cast list reveals that his characters were broadly conceived as stereotypes: for example, Nanny was to be 'elderly, harsh, unimaginative'; Jenny, the young Scottish housemaid was more 'sympathetic'. As they worked on the opera, Britten and Crozier relocated the drama to a local setting, one which they knew well – Iken Hall near Snape, the home of the Spring-Rice family. The children in the opera were given the names of Fidelity

6 Eric Crozier, Buxton Festival Programme. Another aspect of the opera which is not guaranteed to be wholly successful, particularly today, is the involvement of the audience in several set-piece songs, which are rehearsed beforehand. Although the experience of rehearsing and performance these songs can be enriching and exciting, there remains a danger that the creators will seem to be patronising their audience. *The Little Sweep* was extensively revised by Britten in 1965.

7 GB–ALb 2–9104591: draft scenario, headed 'Sweep! Sweep'.

Cranbrook's five children, the Gathorne-Hardys, together with two cousins, Jonathan and Samuel, whose parents had a house near Aldeburgh.[8]

The time-scale for completion of the opera was short but despite this pressure and the necessarily rapid pace of composition, Britten seemed to find great pleasure in the task. Crozier remembers: 'he went about with a beaming smile . . . Time was short: so he composed all day and did the scoring each evening.'[9] Britten himself wrote to Pears, 8 April 1949: 'not stopping to think what I'm doing or how it is – because I have to deliver some of the score on Monday to Erwin! I think anyhow that it's gay enough, altho' [sic] possibly not very distinguished – and also it's easy, which is something!'[10] He also noted that this was the first opera he had composed in which Pears had not played a major part in conception, creation and performance: 'It's funny writing an opera without you in it – don't really like it much, I confess, but I'll admit that it makes my vocal demands less extravagant.'[11]

Crozier's text for *The Little Sweep* has a somewhat dated even Dickensian quality: the brutality of 'sullen, oafish' Black Bob and pitiful Sam's wretchedness and unquestioning acceptance of his bleak impoverishment are presented in rather simplistic terms in what is an occasionally mawkish and over-sentimental libretto.

It has been suggested that the opera (which is scored for a small ensemble of solo string quartet, four hands at one piano and percussion) could be considered a 'happy sequel' to *Peter Grimes*. Tragic or violent events are reinterpreted within a more benevolent framework and have a harmless outcome. For example, in the first scene of *The Little Sweep*, in what seems almost to be a replay of the hut scene in *Peter Grimes*, Sam is forced to strip off his clothes and to climb the chimney. In the 'Children's Shanty', in an effort to free Sam who is stuck fast up the chimney, the children pull on the rope which dangles from the flue and 'with a loud scream Sam falls down the chimney and lies flat in the hearth':

> *CHILDREN: Ooooohh!*
> *TWINS & SOPHIE: You've killed him!*
> *[The children anxiously surround Sam and lift him up]*

In contrast to the deathly drop which kills Grimes's unfortunate apprentice, Sam suffers no adverse consequences as a result of his 'fall'. Indeed, it might be suggested that Peter Grimes's apprentice has at last been given a voice and an opportunity to taste freedom. However, the resonances of *Peter Grimes* contained within *The Little Sweep* are more varied and complex than such a straightforward, one-dimensional interpretation of the opera's narrative suggests. Such a reading

---

8   In the Foreword to the opera, Crozier commented, 'We chose Iken Hall for the setting because it was a large rambling farmhouse on a lonely stretch of the river Alde where occasionally we went to visit friends: we took our children ready-made from the sons, daughters and nephews of other friends living in Great Glemham. To them, we added a quintet of professional singers.'

9   HC, p. 275.

10 *Ibid.*, pp. 274–5.

11 *Ibid.*, p. 275.

Example 14

overlooks both the ambiguity latent in Britten's earlier opera and the contradictions and cruelty implicit in Blake's original poems: these dark ambivalences potentially linger in *The Little Sweep*:

> When my mother died I was very young,
> And my father sold me while yet my tongue
> Could scarcely cry weep weep weep weep,
> So your chimneys I sweep & in soot I sleep.[12]

A powerful image in Blake's verses, and one that is replicated in Crozier's text, is the symbolic opposition of black and white:

> Theres little Tom Dacre, who cried when his head
> That curl'd like a lambs back, was shav'd, so I said.
> Hush Tom never mind it, for when your head's bare,
> You know that the soot cannot spoil your white hair.

Britten represents this dramatic conflict with a harmonic dissonance, the semitone. With the opening bars of the opera, the audience's first cry of 'Sweep!' powerfully foregrounds the tension between C♮ and C♯, both harmonically and melodically [Example 14]. This dissonance might be interpreted as the representing the equivocal, antagonistic relationship between 'innocence' and 'experience' which both Blake's poetry and Britten's operas explore.[13] Thus when Sam first appears at Iken,

---

12 William Blake, *Songs of Innocence and of Experience* (London: The Folio Society, 1992). All subsequent references are to this edition.

13 Peter Evans suggests that the ground basses and other ostinatos that abound in *The Little Sweep* 'afford a particularly straightforward means of charting the free against the fixed' (Peter Evans, *The Music of Benjamin Britten* (Oxford: Oxford University Press, 1996), p. 267). Evans describes the semitonal clashes resulting from the rhythmic dislocation of the

Example 15

Rowan, the nursery-maid to the Crome cousins, describes his abject, pitiful appearance, the falling sevenths of her melody and the quiet dissonance between E♮ and E♭ stressing the poignancy of his plight (Fig. 6) [Example 15]:

> *Small and white and stained with tears,*
> *Wrapped in scarecrow rages and patches,*
> *Faint with terror, full of fears,*
> *Wretched child whom sorrow catches.*

audience's regular lines and the overlapping repetitions of the accompanying ground in this opening chorus as the 'nightmarish *idée fixe* of Sam's employment' (p. 268).

'Small and white', Sam is yet to be touched by life's painful experiences, but when he is later forced to climb the chimney, his whiteness is sullied and his innocence lost. Black Bob and his son, Clem, threaten Sam and lift him to the mouth of the chimney to catch the first climbing rung (No. 3 Duet):

> BLACK BOB AND CLEM:
> Now, little white boy!
> Shiver-with fright boy!
> Scared-in the-night boy!
> Time for your climb! . . .
> BLACK BOB [shouting]
> Scrape the flue clean, or I'll roast you alive!
> [Sam's legs hurriedly disappear up the flue]
> When he comes back, boy!
> He'll be a black boy!
> Scraper-and-sack boy!
> Crawl-through-a-crack boy!
> A chimbley stack boy!
> Covered with grime!

The nursery is left empty and the only evidence that Sam is up the chimney is the portentous rope dangling in the hearth. At this point (Fig. 13) Rowan's melody, described above, is recalled: the slower tempo, the percussion timbre coloured by bass drum and gong, and the *ppp* dynamic of this ten-bar passage evoke a sense of affecting desolation as Sammy is left alone in the narrow chimney. Above a sustained A minor chord, a *dolce* solo violin melody traces two opposing tonal areas, alternating between the underpinning A minor tonality, A–C, and a five-note scalic ascent on D♭ (D♭–E♭–F–G♭–A♭). The sorrowful falling major seventh interval which closes the phrase, and which echoes in repetition into the silence, emphasises this dramatic and expressive conflict between C and C♯ (D♭).

The libretto drafts suggest that the threads linking *The Little Sweep* and *Peter Grimes* were originally even more transparent: for example, in Scene Two on the third page of the draft scenario[14] the children discover a piece of paper while playing in the trunk:

> GAY [turning the paper round, and reading]: At Crow's Nest Farm last Monday, a boy aged ten was trapped in a narrow flue while sweeping the chimneys. The sweepmaster declared the boy was only shamming and lit a straw fire in the heart to 'smoke him out'. An hour later, when a hole was broken in the flue, the boy was found to be dead . . .
>   At yesterday's inquest, a verdict was returned of Death by Misadventure . . .
>   The dead boy's master was sternly cautioned and the coroner warned him to take better care of his boys in future.

The echoes of the Borough's sinister cry, 'Accidental circumstances' are strong and we are reminded of the lawyer Swallow's advice to Grimes, 'do not get

14 GB–ALb 2–9104591.

another boy apprentice. Get a fisherman to help you – big enough to stand up for himself'. Similarly, in Scene 3 of the draft libretto young Johnnie recites a news-flash from the *Newcastle Chronicle*, 5 November 1825, which relates that 'A ruffian named Jones was sentenced this week to six months' imprisonment for cruelty to his eight-year old apprentice'.

Humphrey Carpenter suggests that in some ways *The Little Sweep* inverts the narrative of *Peter Grimes* and represents 'the story of lost innocence [is] now put into reverse'.[15] It is true that after his bath, a literal and symbolic cleansing, Sam is represented to the audience as a transformed figure, gleaming white:

> *AUDIENCE:*
> *She washes and rinses*
> *And scrubs willy nilly*
> *Till poor Sammy winces*
> *But shines like a lily!*
> *And now Sam is gleaming*
> *Like snow in the sun*
> *While Rowan stands beaming*
> *To see her work done.*
> *So all who were frightened*
> *When Sam was benighted,*
> *Please see how he's whitened*
> *And show you're delighted!*
> *CHILDREN AND ROWAN:*
> *O Sammy is whiter*
> *Than swans as they fly,*
> *O Sammy is brighter*
> *Than stars in the sky!*

The second audience song, performed while Sam undergoes this off-stage ritual 'purification', also looks back to *Albert Herring*. Loxford, in the words of Lady Billows, has been 'soiled' and 'despoiled'; only Albert is 'clean as new mown hay' and worthy of being crowned May King as his mother looks on:

> *MUM: Yes, he does look a treat in his white suit,*
> *I couldn't help feeling proud of him too.*

Albert later sullies his 'whiteness' and 'purity', over-excitedly stimulated by the rum which has laced his lemonade:

> *ALBERT: Mum! MUM! Yoo-hoo!*
> *It's your little Albert!*
> *Your sugar-plum*
> *Of a prodigal son –*
> *Clean as a whistle,*
> *Sound as a drum*
> *Home from his Coronat-i-um!*

---

[15] HC, p. 275.

The third scene of *The Little Sweep* opens with the children's cheerful cries – 'Morning, Sammy! Lovely weather/ For our journey home together!' It seems that a sparkling innocence has been regained, as the children announce with delight, 'Morning, Sammy! You look splendid/ Now your sweeping-days are ended!' However, as Carpenter observes,[16] this scene recalls a similar moment in *The Rape of Lucretia*, after innocence has been violated:

> LUCIA AND BIANCA:
> *Oh! What a lovely day!*
> LUCIA:
> *Look how the energetic sun*
> *Drags the sluggard dawn from bed,*
> *And flings the windows wide upon the world.*
> LUCIA AND BIANCA:
> *Oh! What a lovely morning!*

Indeed, earlier in *The Little Sweep*, a poignant ambivalence is introduced when, in Scene 2, the children and Rowan question Sam about his unhappy and distressing past; as Rowan helps him into his new, clean clothes the children cast a transitory glance at the pathos and sorrows of adulthood:

> CHILDREN, ROWAN and SAM:
> *O where is the home*
> *Where your life was gay?*
> *O where is the home*
> *That you love, poor boy?*
> *Home is a hundred miles away.*
> *How shall I laugh and play?*

The final line is repeated at the close of each of the three stanzas; and we wonder whether, even if he is 'liberated' or 'saved', Sam's sullied 'innocence' and faith can truly be restored.

It is Rowan's aria (No. 8) 'Far along the frozen river' which most powerfully explores the delicate and difficult transition and relationship between adulthood and childhood. Sung by a character who seems literally and emotionally caught between the two worlds, it is perhaps the only number in the opera which could satisfactorily find a place in an 'adult' opera, for its depth of feeling is the most explicit statement of the compassion which is one of the central themes of the opera. In this aria, less importance is given to figuration as a means of delineating character, and there is a much wider range of vocal styles and textures than in the opera's other numbers.[17]

---

16 *Ibid.*, p. 276.
17 *The Little Sweep* mimics Britten's technique in *Albert Herring* of establishing and distinguishing character through a series of contrasting melodic lines and accompaniment patterns, many of which parody or pastiche traditional genres or styles. For example, in the Quartet (No. 2) a hasty, rising scale of D major culminating on a dry E♭ chord announces the arrival of Miss Baggott, whose angular melodic shapes and abrupt rhythmic patterns immediately establish her as an officious, bossy 'domestic ogre'. In contrast, the Sweeps adopt

Rowan's opening declamatory phrases – 'Run, poor sweepboy! Run much faster!' – retain the A major key signature of preceding Trio (in which the Sweeps and Miss Baggott relish the punishments that they have in store for Sam), but the dislocating harmonies of the underpinning chords, the wide-ranging dynamics and the pauses which interrupt each phrase, bring the Trio's dramatic momentum to a shuddering halt. The aria's main motive, a brief scalic figure encompassing a tone and a semitone, expands to culminate with a falling octave on the pitch E♮, and it is this pitch to which Rowan's melody repeated returns (Fig. 24), subtly challenged by the E♭'s which colour the accompanying figuration.

The opposition of E♮ and E♭ continues in the central agitated section (Fig. 25); as this motive is developed, this dissonance and the astringent clash of C♮ and C♯ become more assertive. Rowan's soaring melodic line reinforces these dissonances, as she imagines that Sam will inevitably suffer the fate of Grimes's apprentices [Example 16]:

> Run, poor boy! O do not slacken!
> Black Bob follows swift behind.
> See his angry features blacken!
> Rage and fury make him blind.

Her hopes that she might 'save' Sam from his fate, recall the hopes of Ellen Orford, aspirations that are sadly revealed to be delusory:

> CHORUS: But when you came, I
> Said, Now this is where we
> Make a new start. Every day
> I pray it may be so . . .
> PETER: My only hope depends on you.
> If you – take it away – what's left?
> ELLEN: Were we mistaken when we schemed
> To solve your life by lonely toil? . . .
> Were we mistaken when we dreamed
> That we'd come through and all be well?

Similarly, in Rowan's lyrical lines the semitonal juxtapositions of the opening section linger, and despite the optimism of her words, the mood is one of resignation and regret. The children's echoes of Rowan's phrases soften the strained atmosphere, but their proposed 'solutions' to Sam's sufferings and their resolve to end his plight cannot silence the dissonant reverberations. The semitone which has undermined the aria's tranquillity is now inverted in the harmony, forming a series of sustained sevenths in the bass, thereby ensuring that the doubts concerning Sam's fate linger, despite the apparent optimism of the opera's final scene.

Britten had auditioned the children for *The Little Sweep* himself, and he

'dignified attitudes', delineated by a solemn, stately phrases sung in unison, supported by a heavy bass accompaniment and *marcato* bass drum trills. Between these passages, the tender rising and falling curves of Rowan's melody announce her compassion and humanity.

Example 16

attended as many rehearsals as possible. He wrote to Pears: 'We went . . . to Ipswich & heard 37 children for the opera! . . . Some, happily, very promising, & one poppet of a tough small boy!'[18] Basil Coleman, the producer, observed that 'There was always added excitement when he joined us, as he and the children responded so well to each other.'[19] Others also noted that a change appeared to come over Britten in the presence of children: 'It was almost a return to his own youth but a kind of idealized image of himself at the age of ten or twelve, the gay, attractive, charming young Lowestoft boy . . . It was like a flirtation that he carried on with any child he met, particularly young boys, trying to dazzle then and astonish them by his virtuosity and his charms, making them his undying friends.'[20] Similarly, Briony Duncan, the daughter of Ronald Duncan, remarked that when he was in the company of children 'he was just so like a little boy'; and David Spenser (who played the part of Harry in the original production of *Albert*

18 Undated letter (Spring 1949); HC, p. 277.
19 HC, p. 277.
20 Eric Crozier, HC, p. 344.

Herring) confirmed this: 'He had this way of entering into one's world'.[21] Certainly Britten's 'adoption' of a series of children – including Piers Dunkerley, Roger Duncan, the young basque boy whom he brought to Snape in 1937, Robin 'Nipper' Long, David Hemmings, Humphrey Maud, Jonathan Gathorne-Hardy among others – suggests that Britten may at times have preferred the world of children to the adult world.[22]

Certainly, *The Little Sweep* exceeds the boundaries of its genre and explores the complex and sometimes painful transition and interaction between the worlds of the adult and the child. In many ways, the opera repeats the cheerful comedy of *Albert Herring*, yet Sam's suffering also recalls the cruelty and violence perpetrated on children by Britten's other protagonists, Peter Grimes, Claggart, Peter Quint and Miss Jessel, the Wingrave family. For example, the Trio for Miss Baggott, Black Bob and Clem looks ahead to Claggart's gratuitous and ambiguous public humiliation and 'shaming' of the young Novice in *Billy Budd*:

> *Wait until we catch him; we'll whip him till he howls!*
> *We'll teach him to run off and leave his duty!*
> *Chain him up and kennel him; keep him with the fowl!*
> *And mortify his pride, the little beauty!*[23]

Moreover, *The Little Sweep* may also look ahead to the children's precocity and propensity to cruelty in *The Turn of the Screw*, such as during their boisterous games in 'The Window' scene:

> *MILES AND FLORA:*
> *Tom, Tom, the piper's son*
> *Stole a pig and away he run.*
> *Pig was eat and Tom was beat,*
> *Tom ran howling down the street.*

Such ambivalence and tension may be partially illuminated by an exploration of the Blake poems that originally stimulated Britten's and Crozier's conception of *The Little Sweep*. Essentially self-taught, passionate and imaginative, Blake began writing his own poetry at the age of thirteen, often composing in his head as he walked about the streets of London and undertook long expeditions to the surrounding country villages (as they then were) of Dulwich and Islington. It was

---

21 *Ibid*, p. 345.

22 John Drummond noted that at a party in the 1960s, after a Britten-Pears recital which was televised by the BBC, 'there were two children, a boy and a girl, about fourteen and twelve, and Ben obviously didn't want to speak to anyone else, and he sat down in the corner and talked to them – absolutely at his ease, absolutely relaxed, having a really serious conversation with these two kids. And then he turned and looked at the room, and a kind of frown came over his face as the world had to be confronted again', HC, p. 345.

23 The harmonic colour of these phrases is also interesting. The short scalic motive in the vocal lines is expanded, through D, culminating with an octave leap on the pitch E on the word 'beauty'; repetition places this phrase securely in A major. This presages Claggart's ambivalent response to Billy's 'beauty' in *Billy Budd*, and also anticipates Rowan's representation of Sam's inner 'goodness' in her succeeding aria.

during such ramblings and wanderings that he began to have the visions of angels which were later elaborated into a prophetic philosophy which was partly religious and partly artistic. Blake's system of beliefs challenged many conventional ideas concerning education and sexual morality, for he promulgated a libertarian view of the world in which everything that lives should be considered 'holy'.

It was a typical Blakean device that some of his more profoundly subversive and eccentric ideas should be contained in a work that was purportedly addressed to children; for Blake conceived the *Songs of Innocence and Songs of Experience* as belonging to the popular, contemporary genre of illustrated children's books and hymnals which had a long eighteenth-century tradition.[24] Part One, the *Songs of Innocence*, is set safely within the sunlit world of the children's nursery or idyllic garden; it depicts ideas of joy, comfort, tenderness and parental or divine security, although not exclusively so. In contrast, the *Songs of Experience* destabilise this tradition; the poems of Part Two explore themes of cruelty and injustice within a more hallucinatory, twilight version of the same landscape, characterised by shadows, nightmares, dark forests and menacing city streets.

Blake's extraordinary, and seductive, achievement in the *Songs*, is that he is able to embrace a children's mode in such a way that it produces a wholly 'adult' series of poems: for the cycle develops a complex and mature vision of human nature which questions many fundamental ideas about love, freedom, justice, cruelty and God. The naïve simplicity of much of the verse and imagery paradoxically contains a continual stream of questioning doubts, provocations, and ambiguous symbolism.

Superficially, Blake appears to have arranged his verses into a pattern of 'answering' poems, which employ similar or identical images and phrases, and which move from contentment and joy to sorrow and anger. However, in addition to the juxtapositions between the two parts of the *Songs*, there are also contraries and uncertainties within the poems. For example, intimations of anxiety and unease emerge to disturb the peaceful simplicity of innocence; likewise the terror, dread and anguish of experience may reveal glimpses of transcendence and release.

Thus the controlling theme of the *Songs* – expressed succinctly by its subtitle, 'Two Contrary States of the Human Soul' – is not a conventional juxtaposition of opposites but something more dynamic, mystical and ultimately disturbing. Richard Holmes[25] suggests that this darkening and intensification of mood between the two parts reflects Blake's own inner life, his spiritual quest and perhaps his marriage to Catherine Boucher, the beautiful young daughter of a market-gardener whom Blake had taught to read and prepare his artistic materials. Perhaps a similar emotional narrative is contained within Britten's opera, forming part of an on-going exploration of the precarious and sometimes dangerous interaction between the worlds of the adult and the child.

---

[24] Such books included Anna Barbauld's *Hymns in Prose for Children* (1781) and Mary Wollstonecraft's *Original Stories from Real Life* (1791).

[25] Richard Holmes, 'Introduction' to Blake, *Songs of Innocence and of Experience*, p. xi.

Composed as a 'children's opera', *The Little Sweep* may appear to present a world which is secure, comforting and sometimes naïve. The creators' prefatory remarks state: 'It will be easily seen that professional or very gifted amateurs are needed to play the grown-up parts and also the part of Juliet (provided, of course, that she can look convincingly youthful). It is essential that real children should play the children's parts – the boys with unbroken voices who shouldn't be scared of using their chest voices.' Yet, in depicting an ideal of childhood simplicity – and encouraging the audience to partake in that ideal, quite literally through their participation in the audience songs – the opera may in fact encourage or guide us to turn and re-examine the ambiguous boundaries between our own childhood and our supposed maturity. In so doing it may alert us to the possible darkness which resides within the light:

> Because I was happy upon the heath.
> And smil'd among the winters snow:
> They clothed me in the clothes of death.
> And taught me to sing the notes of woe.
>
> And because I am happy. & dance & sing.
> They think they have done me no injury:
> And are gone to praise God & his Priest & King
> Who make up a heaven of our misery.[26]

---

[26] Blake, 'The Chimney Sweeper', *Songs of Experience.*

7

Billy Budd

Beyond the communication of the sentence, what took place at this interview
was never known.   Herman Melville[1]

Psychology has split and shattered the idea of a 'Person', and has shown that
there is something incalculable in each of us, which may at any moment rise to
the surface and destroy our normal balance.   E. M. Forster[2]

In his first three operas, Britten had exploited the dramatic ambiguities latent in
the source narratives, but for his next opera he went further, selecting a text,
Herman Melville's novella *Billy Budd, Sailor*, which intentionally cultivated an
aura of mystery and inconclusiveness and which had at its core an essential indeterminacy of form and theme which the original author had deliberately
emphasised: 'The symmetry of form attainable in pure fiction cannot so readily be
achieved in a narration essentially having less to do with fable than with fact . . .
hence the conclusion of such a narration is apt to be less finished than an architectural finial . . . Truth uncompromisingly told will always have its ragged edges' (p.
405).[3] The undefined homoerotic sub-currents latent in Melville's text disrupt his
equivocal narrative with 'gaps' or 'mysteries' which might positively invite
musical interpretation or embellishment. It is perhaps surprising, therefore, that
Britten's operatic reading of Melville displays evidence of an attempt to
'de-eroticise' the text and to impose a dramatic and psychological unity on
Melville's 'ragged' form, principally by reducing the original text's narrative
multiplicity and by establishing a conceptual frame in the form of a retrospective
Prologue and Epilogue. However, perhaps less unexpectedly, the musical score
frequently injects the very innuendo and uncertainty which the libretto seeks to
eradicate.

---

[1] Herman Melville, *Billy Budd, Sailor and Other Stories* (Harmondsworth: Penguin, 1985), p.
     391. All subsequent references are to this edition and are given in parentheses in the text.
[2] E. M. Forster, 'What I Believe', in *Two Cheers for Democracy* (London: Arnold, 1938), p. 65.
[3] The issue of inconclusiveness is ironically emphasised by the fact that there is no definitive
     version of Melville's text. During the last years of his life Melville had made substantial revi-
     sions which remained incomplete at the time of his death in 1891. The novella was first
     published in 1924. In 1962 Harrison Hayford and Morton M. Seatts Jnr published *Billy
     Budd, Sailor: Reading Text and Genetic Text, Edited from the Manuscript with Introduction
     and Notes* (Chicago: University of Chicago Press, 1962) which attempted to correct a
     number of minor textual discrepancies.

Britten's structural and thematic decisions may have been motivated by the fact that *Billy Budd* marked his return to a more 'public' performance platform. In contrast to the chamber-operas *Lucretia* and *Herring*, which were designed for presentation by the sympathetic members of the English Opera Group, *Billy Budd*, whose rich melodic lyricism recalls the 'grand' operatic style[4] of *Peter Grimes*, was commissioned for the 1951 Festival of Britain and was premiered at Covent Garden on 1 December 1951.

The librettist of *Billy Budd* was E. M. Forster. Britten had first met Forster in 1937, through W. H. Auden and Christopher Isherwood, whose play, *The Ascent of F6* (for which Britten had composed the incidental music), was favourably reviewed by Forster when it was published in 1936. Moreover, Forster had indirectly influenced the composition of *Peter Grimes*, for it had been his essay on George Crabbe which had acquainted Britten with Crabbe's poem *The Borough*; he was later invited to present a lecture on Crabbe at the inaugural Aldeburgh Festival in 1949, at which *Albert Herring*, dedicated to Forster, was performed.

Ronald Duncan was astonished by Britten's decision to collaborate with Forster: 'When Britten turned to E. M. Forster in 1951 for a libretto for Billy Budd, I was amazed at his selection. I knew he admired Forster's novels; a taste I did not share; I knew Forster had no experience of music, of libretti writing, and I suspected little ear for music, either. I realised that Britten had sympathy for Forster as a man, but thought that insufficient to make him a suitable collaborator.'[5] Britten's 'sympathy for Forster as a man' was possibly kindled by the understated homoerotic subtexts of Forster's own novels which, together with Forster's appreciative criticism of Melville,[6] may have engendered Britten's hopes that he had at last found a librettist whose beliefs and ambitions were in accord with his own. Crozier revealed that it was Britten himself who proposed an opera on *Billy Budd*,[7] and his intense enthusiasm for, and commitment to, a project which presented considerable operatic problems – the all male cast, the fact that the action was narrowly confined on board ship, and the 'hero's' paralytic stammer – suggest that his engagement with the drama was profound.[8]

---

4   Although the general expansiveness and lyrical mood of *Budd* does recall *Grimes*, the intervallic contours of the former are more confined and the tonal and motivic interconnections more dense.

5   Duncan, *Working with Britten*, pp. 111–12.

6   For example, E. M. Forster, *Aspects of the Novel* (London: Arnold, 1937), pp. 181–2.

7   In 'Staging First Productions' (in DH), Crozier writes: 'It was not Forster, though, who suggested *Billy Budd*: it was Britten' (p. 31). Britten's memory of how the text was chosen is slightly different: 'We each suggested subjects, nearly settling on the Suffolk story Margaret Catchpole, but not quite. Who brought up the idea of *Billy Budd* no one can quite remember; it was probably telepathic and simultaneous' ('Some Notes About Forster and Music' in Oliver Stallybrass (ed.), *Aspects of E. M. Forster – Essays and Recollections Written for His 90th Birthday* (London: Edward Arnold, 1969), p. 85). Possibly both he and Forster were influenced by familiarity with a new edition of the text, published in 1947 with an introduction by William Plomer (a future Britten librettist), which was reviewed by Forster for the BBC.

8   When the opera was complete, Britten played the score through to the producer, Basil

Despite Britten's optimism, it seems inevitable that tensions and disagree-
ments would arise, as Forster was a homosexual of very different persuasion from
Britten. It was Eric Crozier, acting initially as Forster's dramatic consultant and
later as co-librettist, who almost found himself immediately acting as intermediary between composer and writer. Crozier, whose practical involvement and
emotional commitment to the subject were less intense than that of Britten or
Forster, wrote to his wife, Nancy Evans, in March 1949:

> Something is worrying him [Britten], spoiling his temper, jamming his work,
> and throwing his tummy out of gear. I can't make out what is the cause . . . I
> begin to suspect, that he does not really want to do Billy as an opera but feels that
> he cannot withdraw now that Morgan and I are so earnestly at work . . . It is
> worrying . . . and the long hours that Morgan and I are spending cloistered
> together seem almost to make him a little jealous.[9]

and again a few days later:

> I was right in my guess about Ben's wretchedness. He was going through a
> period of revulsion against *Billy Budd*, from a misunderstanding about the
> purpose of the story, and he wanted to give the whole thing up. But now he has
> come through and he sees that his feeling was muddled, and with that change
> everything has improved.[10]

Crozier does not specify what this 'misunderstanding' was but one of the
fundamental disparities between Britten's and Forster's readings of Melville
appears to have centred on the identification of the 'hero' of the novella. Forster
wrote in detail about this in *The Griffin* magazine in 1951:

> Each adaptor has his own problems. Ours has been how to make Billy, rather
> than Vere the hero. Melville must have intended this: he called the story *Billy
> Budd*, and unless there is strong evidence to the contrary one may assume that
> an author calls his story after the chief character . . . But I also think that Melville
> got muddled and that, particularly in the trial scene his respect for authority and
> discipline deflected him. How odiously Vere comes out in the trial scene. At first
> he stays in the witness-box, as he should, then he constitutes himself both
> counsel for the prosecution and judge, and never stops lecturing the court until
> the boy is sentenced to death . . . His unseemly harangue arises, I think, from
> Melville's wavering attitude towards an impeccable commander, a superior
> philosopher, and a British aristocrat. Every now and then he doused Billy's light
> and felt that Vere, being well-educated and just, must shine like a star . . . We

---

Coleman, who remembers: 'Britten half sang all the vocal parts, giving a vivid idea of the
characterizations he had in mind . . . [as] the terrible events of the story developed, Britten
became more and more immersed in them himself. At the finish he was exhausted, physically and emotionally. It was very apparent how much the work meant to him' (HC, p. 298);
Britten told the Harewoods, to whom the opera was dedicated: 'It is by far the biggest, & I
think the best, piece I've written for some time' (*ibid.*).

9   Eric and Nancy Crozier, *After Long Pursuit*, unpublished autobiographical typescript,
    quoted in HC, pp. 283–4.
10 *Ibid.*

(Eric Crozier and I) have, you see, plumped for Billy as a hero and for Claggart as naturally depraved, and we have ventured to tidy up Vere. Adaptors have to tidy up. Creators needn't and sometimes shouldn't.[11]

Forster attributes to Melville a confusion and vacillation which was perhaps more accurately his own.

Britten's alternative interpretation was more precise. In a 1960 radio interview he identified the focal character: 'Billy always attracted me, of course, the radiant young figure; I felt there was going to be quite an opportunity for writing nice dark music for Claggart; but I must admit that Vere, who has what seems to me the main moral problem of the whole work, round [him] the drama was going to centre.'[12] One might expect the roles of Billy, Claggart and Vere to be assigned to a tenor, bass and baritone respectively, but Crozier explained that Britten immediately envisaged the part of Vere for the tenor: 'Most composers, I am certain, would have allocated the tenor role to the innocent young hero Billy: Britten took it for granted that it must go to Melville's wise and thoughtful naval commander, Vere, who would be sung by Peter Pears.'[13] Pears described the part: 'Vere is torn between his duty, which is to uphold the law, and his recognition of Billy's essential innocence, between his duty, which means that Billy will be hanged, and his Christian conscience which tells him "Thou shalt not kill".'[14] However, in the opera Vere's dilemma is never so straightforward. The modifications made to Melville's pragmatic Captain transform Vere into a complex and unstable web of antagonistic impulses and energies (in the manner of Peter Grimes). Pears's unreadiness to acknowledge the complexities of the part recalls his over-simplification of Grimes's character. For example, in an interview in the gay newspaper, *Advocate*, Pears described a discussion at the Metropolitan Museum in New York in which he had taken part in 1978: 'A girl got up and said, 'I read the other day that Vere is just a faggot.' That sort of attitude is so puny and vulgar, and totally beside the point. Melville is too vast a figure to talk like that. And I don't know that we know how far Melville himself was an active homosexual. It's too easy, to read in a diary full of warmth about a handsome sailor and to think that he went to bed with him and all the rest of it.'[15]

It might be suggested that the psychologies in conflict in *Peter Grimes* have been resurrected by Britten in *Billy Budd*; now, they are no longer located in the divided mind of a single man but are separated and sited in two antagonistic characters. In this way, Claggart might be seen to represent 'Grimes the violent fisherman', whereas Vere stands for 'Grimes the visionary dreamer'. Billy, essentially silent and passive, thus re-enacts the role of the violated apprentice, but possesses

---

[11] E. M. Forster, in *The Griffin*, vol. 1, 1951, 4–6.

[12] HC, p. 287.

[13] *Ibid.*, p. 282. We can only speculate as to whether the opera would have been radically different had Pears been young enough to sing the part of Billy.

[14] Quoted in Headington, *Peter Pears*, pp. 164–5.

[15] Peter Pears, interview with Stephen Greco, published 12 July 1979, quoted in Headington, *Peter Pears*, p. 287.

Lucretia's capacity for redemption. Understandably, Britten may have been reluctant to resuscitate the 'dark' side of his own psyche which had been deliberately submerged in *Peter Grimes*, and which was now symbolised by Claggart's presence; instead, his musical energy was channelled into the effort of sustaining his creative *alter ego*, Captain Vere. Thus, despite the reputed attempts of Forster and Britten to 'tidy up' Melville, the complex ambiguities of *Billy Budd, Sailor* could not be wholly obliterated from the opera and unsettling echoes of the source linger in both the libretto and the score.

The process of revision involved making three major alterations to Melville's tale: in the operatic version of events Vere does not die immediately after Billy's death but lives to an old age; through the use of a framing Prologue and Epilogue he becomes the narrator of his own tale, and is thereby credited with narrative authority; and his words at the trial are reversed with those of his officers, subtly shifting the burden of responsibility for Billy's death.

Initially Forster was reluctant to incorporate a framing device into the libretto. He wrote to Britten, 20 December 1948:

> I like the idea of a chorus, shanties etc., provided it is at the level of the half-informed Greek chorus, which was always making mistakes. The well-informed commentator, the person or personages outside time, would not here be suitable. At least that is my first reaction, so I do not altogether agree with the three of you – formidable thought. But the idea is all new to me, and I may change when I have thought more about it.[16]

Evidently he was persuaded by Britten, Crozier and Pears to change his mind, as a near-finalised text for the Prologue was enclosed with a letter from Forster to Crozier, dated 27 January 1949. At the end of the enclosure, a note was added:

> *N.B. In the story Vere dies soon after. But had better live on.*[17]

The five-scene synopsis which dates from January 1949 refers to a Prologue and Epilogue:

> *Vere is left alone on the quarter-deck, and the light gradually closes in around him till he resumes his function as chorus, and brings the action to an end with an Epilogue.*[18]

The libretto begins with the elderly Vere's recollections of the tragic events of his past:

> *I am an old man who has experienced much.*

His words are preceded by an instrumental passage which establishes the terms of the opera's dramatic dialectic by harmonic means [Example 17]. A lyrical, rocking

16 Quoted in E. M. Forster, *Selected Letters*, vol. 2 (Glasgow: Wilkins and Son Co., 1985), p. 235.
17 E. M. Forster Collection, King's College, Cambridge.
18 GB–ALb 2–01051593.

Example 17

melody played by the *pianissimo* strings, evoking the gentle undulation of the waves, dissonantly juxtaposes the pitches B♮ and B♭; at this stage neither pitch is confirmed as the tonic or the harmonic goal of the work but as the opera progresses the association of B♭ with the forces of conformity and repression and B♮ with freedom and rebellion is established.[19] B♮ is quickly affiliated with dramatically or morally disruptive motives such as Billy's stutter (Fig. 2).[20] Moreover, in

---

[19] In *Billy Budd* (Cambridge: CUP, 1993), Mervyn Cooke proposes that B♭ symbolises reconciliation and salvation, supporting his argument by pointing to the resolution in B♭ in the final bars of score. This reading is only applicable if one considers the opera to have an affirmative resolution: given the identification of B♭ with the forces of oppression in *Peter Grimes* and *Albert Herring*, it seems more likely that B♭ carries more sinister implications.

[20] Other examples include the impressment of the three new recruits (Act 1, Fig. 23), and Billy's mortal blow (Act 2, Fig. 20) which are underpinned by penetrating pedal B's.

an opera in which timbre appears to be as important an expressive element as harmony, the 'colour' of the motifs associated with the three main characters is also clearly determined: Vere is identified with the indefinite softness of the strings, whereas Claggart is characterised by the abrasive raspings of the trombones and lower brass instruments located on a 'flat' axis B♭–F. Billy's energy and optimism is musically rendered by the bright liveliness of arpeggios played by the trumpets and upper woodwind in the 'sharp' keys of A and E major.[21] As the Prologue continues, Vere shatters the calm air of detachment with a flamboyant, melismatic outburst. His mood turns to anguish and remorse, as he poses the questions which define the dramatic conflict:

> VERE: O what have I done? Confusion, so much is confusion. I have tried to guide others rightly, but I have been lost on the infinite sea. Who has blessed me? Who saved me?

Vere is the opera's central consciousness, the narrator and the source of moral truth, yet his personality and vision are never fully exposed. As he sings the phrase 'infinite sea', the melodic dissonance B–B♭ is pungently sounded: the sea embodies the eternal flux of human emotion and experience which cannot console man with unequivocal moral hierarchies. As Vere returns to more objective recollections, the Prologue closes in B♭, but the opposition of B♭/B♮ persists in the following scene, and throughout the opera.

For example, Act 1, Scene 1 opens in B minor, although conflict is insinuated by the presence of a dissonant oboe A♯ in the second bar (this pitch can be accommodated within the B minor mode but also enharmonically implies B♭). The sailors' cry 'O heave! O heave away' (Fig. 5) unites them in their oppression and foreshadows Billy's unintentionally seditious farewell to his former ship, The Rights O'Man (Fig. 33). The Bosun attempts to deflect the focus of his crew's unity from dissension to submission, compelling them towards B♭ with the work-cry 'Sway' (Fig. 11), a phrase whose integrative force becomes apparent during the pursuit of the French frigate in Act 2, Scene 1 (Fig. 12).

The sea mists which hinder Vere's comprehension also obscure the audience's understanding of events and, in spite of the initial aim of Crozier and Forster to accurately and realistically present the details of naval life, the sea and the ship remain purely metaphoric in the opera.[22] Forster appears to have had some worries about the sea setting: 'I will not recall you to the sea. Much as I love it, I

Similarly, the officers' discussions (Act 1, Fig. 67) of the mutiny at the Nore, Claggart's role in preventing mutinous insurgences upon The Indomitable (Fig. 70), and the Novice's tempting of Billy (Fig. 117) are harmonised in B minor.

[21] In contrast to the frugal instrumental forces required in Lucretia and Herring, Britten employed an extremely large orchestra in Billy Budd, scoring the work to include four flutes, four trumpets and six percussionists.

[22] The source material details the considerable historical research undertaken by Crozier and Forster; for example, a letter from Forster to Crozier states: 'I think we might well go down to Portsmouth some time next month, but we must find out first when the Victory is visible. I hear there is a young fellow at Trinity who specialises in Naval History. As soon as we have definite questions to ask him, I might visit him. I also went to the University Library to see if

believe that you ought to postpone it until you can create an old-man's sea. Anyhow much later in your career.'[23] Britten does in fact create an 'old man's sea' but it is a seascape which is situated almost entirely in the mind of Captain Vere. John Piper recalled his designs for the sets for *Billy Budd*: 'We must never lose sight of the fact that the whole thing is taking place in Vere's mind, and is being recalled by him.'[24] Furthermore, the producer Basil Coleman noted that the mists which descend at the start of Act 2 are 'a mist of doubt and fear in the mind of Vere when he is about to close with Claggart'.[25] Vere sings:

> *Disappointment, vexation everywhere – creeping over everything, confusing everyone. Confusion without and within.*
> *Oh, for the light, the light of clear Heaven, to separate evil from good!*

A more realistic representation of life at sea, or an account of the rigid rules required to sustain the isolated floating community 'lost' on the morally void sea, might have explained the forces which compel Vere to act as he does, thereby clarifying the power of social conformity and the need to the uphold the authoritative practices which maintain social cohesion and stability, and which lessen the need for personal moral responsibility. Indeed, at Billy's trial Melville establishes Vere's awareness of his duties as 'King' – i.e. upholder of God's laws – on board the *Indomitable*, which must override 'Nature' – i.e. his instinctive desires. Earlier in the novella, Melville relates:

> Feeling that unless quick action was taken on it, the deed of the foretopman, so soon as it should be known on the gun decks, would tend to awaken any slumbering embers of the Nore among the crew, a sense of the urgency of the case overruled in Captain Vere every other consideration . . . Accordingly a drumhead court was summarily convened, he electing the individuals composing it: the first lieutenant, the captain of marines, and the sailing master. (p. 381)

Moreover, Melville's Vere equates the 'measured forms' necessary in his naval life with the coherence of artistic form, in a passage ironically at odds with the author's own practice: ' "with mankind", he would say, "forms, measured forms, are everything; and this is the import couched in the story of Orpheus with his lyre spellbinding with wild denizens of the wood" ' (p. 404). Vere, the unimaginative and inflexible law-maker, cannot comprehend the flux of experience which is life, and which the genuine artist creatively reshapes into artistic 'truth'.

The removal of these passages from the opera means that the conflict in *Billy Budd* no longer takes place between the individual and the 'community' but is fought entirely in Vere's own mind. Consequently, there is little suggestion in the

it has any more . . . naval drawings' (27 January 1949, Eric Crozier's transcript of his correspondence with Forster 1948–69 (EMF)).

23 Undated letter from Forster to Britten (EMF).

24 John Piper, '*Billy Budd* on the Stage: An Early Discussion between Producer and Designer', *Tempo*, Autumn (1951), 21.

25 Quoted in Joe K. Law, 'We Have Ventured to Tidy Up Vere', *Twentieth Century Literature*, 31 (1986), 296–314.

opera that Vere's refusal to save Billy might arise from, or be partially justified by, the social pressures upon him. Originally it was intended that during Billy's trial Vere should interrupt the court with his speculations. Following Melville's example, in the 1949 January–March draft the drumhead court turns to Vere for guidance and he frankly admits his bafflement:

> VERE: My friends I am as bewildered as you are I cannot lead you . . . If indeed there is a mystery of iniquity may there be not a mystery of goodness – deeper still, too deep for the vision of men. If Claggart were evil and this boy – save for that fatal defect, that stammer – were good, if he were perfect, what then? Where then do we stand? We are cooped in this little cabin on a ship which floats upon a great sea, the sea is but part of the world, the world itself but a speck in space, infinity surrounds us. Before what tribunal do we stand if we destroy goodness?
> 1ST LIEUTENANT: Do you mean we should acquit Budd sir?
> Vere: [after a pause] No . . . No. If he is to be condemned, it must be here. If his blood is to be on another's head, let it be on mine. If his innocence –
> 1ST L.: Sir, he's not innocent. Promising seaman we agree, pleasant enough lad, and struck in a fit of temper, but he's done it.
> VERE: Mr. Redburn, he's innocent, but these things lie too deep. They are a private trouble with which I should not have raised in the light. Pronounce your verdict.[26]

After the sentencing Vere had lamented:

> Justice and mercy! Justice and mercy! Ah the age long conflict between them, and oh it was the only conflict here. Then could my soul be at peace. I have seen the . . . flames of hell open, and the strength of heaven strike them down, and I am obliged to chose [sic]. The choice has been made on earth, a boy has transgressed earth's laws and will die, but in the heaven, in the heights and depths ah what?
> I could have saved him. At the price of my honour, perhaps of my life, and of my ship's safety, it could have been done. I could have rescued him from the snare. I could have rescued goodness. O beauty, o handsomeness, o goodness, how will you pardon me? I too have betrayed you. Will you ever forgive me? Will you ever understand? How shall I tell him? Until I see him I cannot know. I must not too closely consider these mysteries. As mysteries let them remain. I serve the King and my course is laid out for me. I must pursue it, inflexibly. Honour, tradition, the safety of my ship, the exigencies of war compell [sic] me. Poor lad! May God grant him strength.[27]

However, in the final libretto Vere remains silent at the trial, aloof from the proceedings of the court and unresponsive to Billy's desperate pleading:

> VERE: I have told you all I have seen. I have no more to say . . .
> OFFICERS: Sir, before we decide, join us, help us with your knowledge and wisdom. Grant us your guidance.
> VERE: No. Do not ask me. I cannot.
> OFFICERS: Sir, we need you as always.
> VERE: No. Pronounce your verdict . . .
> BILLY: I'd have died for you, save me! . . . Save me!

26 GB–ALb 2–01051594.
27 GB–ALb 2–01051594.

The element of self-doubt which troubles Vere is crossed through in Britten's copy of the draft and replacement text is inserted, some of which is contained on a supplementary sheet in Britten's own hand:

> *I accept their verdict: Death is the penalty for those who break the laws of earth. And I who am king of this fragment of earth of this floating monarchy, have exacted death. But I have seen the divine judgment of heaven; I've seen iniquity overthrown. Cooped in this narrow cabin I have beheld the mystery of goodness, and I am afraid. Before what tribunal do I stand if I destroy goodness? The angel of God has struck, & the angel must hang – through me. Beauty, handsomeness, goodness, it is for me to destroy you.*

Alongside the excised passage[28] is written 'Epilogue?' – the question of Vere's 'guilt' was thus temporarily postponed.

Vere's silence separates his internal anguish from the tensions of the life on board ship. For example, the potent sense of sexual frustration which is latent in Melville's description of fraternal life and military activity on *The Bellipotent* is noticeably absent from the seamen's shanties and the portrayal of *The Indomitable*'s futile pursuit of the French frigate at the start of Act 2 of the opera. In this way, Melville's insinuation that Vere relies on naval discipline and procedures as a means of avoiding a confrontation with his own conscience is not effectively presented in the opera, and these episodes are in danger of becoming a distraction, albeit a musically attractive one, from the 'real' drama which takes place within Vere's psyche.

This internal drama is literally embodied in the forms of John Claggart, the master-at-arms, and Billy Budd, the new recruit. Melville's portrait of Claggart is shrouded in obscurity and shadows: 'His portrait I shall essay but never hit . . . Nothing was known of his former life . . . these were circumstances which in the dearth of exact knowledge as to his true antecedents opened to the invidious a vague field for unfavorable surmise' (pp. 342–3). He labels Claggart's 'peculiarity' 'Natural depravity: a depravity according to nature' (p. 353), an equivocal term which might imply that Claggart's 'depravity' transgresses the laws of nature or alternatively that it is itself 'natural'. His office of master-at-arms aligns him with the forces of hypocrisy and oppression, and he is overwhelmed with self-pity, self-hatred, paranoia and guilt: 'a nature like Claggart's, surcharged with energy as such natures almost invariably are, what recourse is left to it but to recoil upon itself' (p. 356), 'this, like a subterranean fire, was eating its way deeper and deeper into him' (p. 367).

The tension between Claggart and Billy is symbolised by a series of harmonic dissonances: B♭–B and F–E, the opera's primary centres of tonal conflict. For example, in Act 1, Scene 3 (Fig. 98) Claggart's interruption of the fight between Billy and Squeak is accompanied by an emphatic B♭ played by the trombones, tuba and timpani as he forcefully restores discipline among the agitated crew. However, perpetual instability is harmonically implied by Britten's use of

---

[28]   The passage is excised from GB–ALb 2–01051594.

bitonality, the orchestral accompaniment being in the key of F minor, while the seamen's shanty is notated in E major (Fig. 103). Billy's potential both to weaken Claggart's professional authority and to fracture his personal impenetrability is harmonically embodied in the challenge which Billy's E major tonality poses to Claggart's F minor, the two keys being enharmonically related by the shared third degree G♯/A♭,[29] a threat which is emphatically demonstrated in Claggart's Act 1 monologue.[30]

Forster seemed anxious to remain faithful to Melville's portrayal of Claggart. Describing his progress on the libretto to Trilling,[31] Forster declared that 'Claggart came easy – natural depravity, not evil, being the guide'. He elaborated his intentions in *The Griffin*: 'Claggart is less of a problem. Melville's hint of 'natural depravity' has to be followed. Claggart gets no kick out of evil as Iago did, he is not an arch-devil, though Vere and Billy may mistake him for one.'[32] In Claggart's Act 1 aria Forster depicts Billy as a light which has pierced Claggart's shield of darkness and which, having illuminated his depravity, cannot be extinguished:

> CLAGGART: *But alas, alas! the light shines in the darkness, and the darkness comprehends it and suffers. O beauty, O handsomeness, goodness! would that I had never seen you.*[33]

However, he was disappointed with Britten's music for this aria: 'It is my most important piece of writing and I did not, at my first hearings, feel it sufficiently important musically . . . I want passion – love constricted, perverted, poisoned, but nevertheless flowing down its agonising channel; a sexual discharge gone evil. Not soggy depression or growling resolve.'[34] Despite the unsubtle and overwhelmingly bleak ambience of this aria, Britten does musically embody the antagonistic forces struggling for control of Claggart's psyche. The danger latent in

---

[29] Britten had exploited the dramatic potential of an identical enharmonic relationship in *Peter Grimes*.

[30] The reverse is also true: for instance after the 'tempting scene' Billy's deluded self-confidence is undermined by insinuations of Claggart's descending fourth motif and F minor tonality (Fig. 126).

[31] Forster to Trilling, 16 April 1949, *Selected Letters*, vol. 2, p. 236.

[32] Forster, *The Griffin*. In the draft libretto of January-March 1949, Vere had himself highlighted the unfathomable mystery of Claggart's 'depravity': *VERE: The question is beyond me too. The only person who could answer it is – there [points], and he will never speak. He is tongue tied for ever. We are concerned not with the dead man's motives but with his death. Even if the motives were foul, even if he did desire to destroy handsomeness beauty and goodness, we must ignore them. Their* [sic] *is a mystery here, whose veil no one can lift. Maybe it is the mystery of iniquity* (GB–ALb 2–01051594).

[33] Significantly, it is this 'clear light' which Vere craves to illuminate his moral path through the mists of confusion. He sings (Act 1, Fig. 62) 'O God grant me light to guide us all!', and again (Act 2, Fig. 50), 'O for the light, the light of clear Heaven.'

[34] Forster to Britten, dated 'Tuesday' (early December 1950?) in *Selected Letters*, vol. 2, p. 242. Crozier shared Forster's dissatisfaction, believing that Claggart had become a: 'boring, black-masked villain, not a tormented individual who is driven into evil by some kind of inadequacy in his nature. I felt that Britten wasn't sufficiently interested in Claggart; he was interested in Vere' (HC, p. 291).

Billy's beauty is suggested by the A major key signature (Fig. 105) and Billy's tonal axis is literally sustained in the first part of the aria, by a woodwind ostinato which accompanies Claggart's despairing cries. Self-pity later gives way to fatalism, as Claggart's melody moves towards F minor (Fig. 109):

> *So may it be! So may it be! O beauty, O handsomeness, goodness, you are surely in my power tonight. Nothing can defend you!*

Yet Melville's Claggart had not entirely lacked the potential for love: 'Then would Claggart look like the man of sorrows. Yes, and sometimes the melancholy expression would have in it a touch of soft yearning, as if Claggart could have even loved Billy but for fate and ban' (p. 365); and the music now returns to A major as Forster and Britten strive to depict Claggart's comprehension of the love which he has lost (Fig. 110):

> *For what hope remains if love can escape? If love still lives and grows strong where I cannot enter, what hope is there in my own dark world for me?*

The passage ends, after a general pause, with Claggart's vow to destroy Billy. Why does Claggart wish to eradicate Billy? Billy may be the 'beauty' which lights up Claggart's moral 'ugliness'; alternatively, it may be that by inspiring Claggart's homosexual desires he deepens Claggart's self-loathing and thus must be obliterated. By corrupting Billy, he may hope to drag him down from the heavens into his own depraved underworld.

In Melville's text considerable sexual imagery is attached to Billy: nicknamed 'Beauty' and 'Baby' he is 'the jewel of 'em', 'the flower of [the] flock'. His beauty is not unambiguous and he introduces, unconsciously, an erotic element into an environment dependent upon its repression: 'in aspect he looked even younger than he really was, owing to a lingering adolescent expression in the as yet smooth face all but feminine in purity of natural complexion but where, thanks to his seagoing, the lily was quite suppressed and the rose had some ado visibly to flush through the tan' (p. 328). The conflict between the red and white in Billy's complexion recalls the red stain of complicity which mars Lucretia's white virtue, and Albert's white coronation dress which is deflowered with splashes of red wine. In a line of Melville's novella, retained in the opera, Claggart warns Vere of the danger latent in Billy's beauty: 'You have but noted his fair cheek. A mantrap may be under the ruddy-tipped daisies' (p. 372). In the opera Claggart's accusation is effective: like a dart of self-knowledge it shatters Vere's confident B major protests (Act 2, Fig. 43):

> *Nay, you're mistaken. Your police have deceived you. Don't come to me with so foggy a tale. That's the young fellow I get good reports of.*

The mists of insecurity, suspicion and irresolution are reinstated.

Billy's beauty, like Lucretia's, acts both as a magnet for peace and harmony – 'a virtue went out of him, sugaring the sour ones' (p. 325) – and as a catalyst for revolution. Melville reveals: 'what it was that had first moved him [Claggart] against Billy, [was] his significant personal beauty' (p. 355). Yet it is Billy's innocence, born of an ignorance which protects him from the torments of self-knowledge, which Claggart most fears, suspects and detests: 'little or no sharpness of faculty or any trace of the wisdom of the serpent, nor yet quite a dove, he possessed that kind and degree of intelligence going along with the unconventional rectitude of a sound human creature, one to whom not yet has been proffered the questionable apple of knowledge' (p. 330). Claggart's destructive self-knowledge is deepened by the challenge posed by Billy's apparent innocence: 'One person excepted, the master-at-arms was perhaps the only man in the ship intellectually capable of adequately appreciating the moral phenomenon presented in Billy Budd. And the insight intensified his passion, which assuming various secret forms within him, at times assumed that of cynical disdain, disdain of innocence – to be nothing more than innocent!' (pp. 355–6). In the manner of Lucretia, Billy's ignorance appears self-complacent and his innocence remains untried, leading Melville to comment that 'innocence was his blinder' (p. 366). Billy's wilful passivity, or pseudo-innocence, is just as destructive as Claggart's active viciousness; both characters consciously submit to and indulge in a comforting fatalism, a similarity which Melville emphasises at the moment of their respective deaths. The absence of mechanical ejaculation and *rigor mortis* at Billy's hanging implies a symbolic castration and echoes Melville's portrayal of the dead Claggart: 'The spare form flexibly acquiesced, but inertly. It was like handling a dead snake' (p. 377).

In contrast to Melville's complex portrait, the operatic Billy is less a 'real' character than a symbol, a saintly or seraph-like saviour for Vere. For example, following Claggart's accusations against Billy, Vere descends into a trough of self-doubt and pessimism. His entreaty 'O for the light, the clear light of Heaven' (Act 2, Fig. 50), is set in Billy's key, E major. The extended orchestral passage which concludes this scene consists of a sequential repetition which traces a step-wise ascent from B♭ to E (Fig. 52), thereby depicting the uplifting, restorative effect of Billy's love upon Vere's moral conscience, and enabling Vere to temporarily resolve his ethical dilemmas in the subsequent scene.

Britten and Forster emphasise the 'divine' element in Billy's character, exploiting and expanding the astrological and celestial imagery in Melville's text. References such as 'the Handsome Sailor . . . [was] . . . like Aldebaran among the lesser lights of his constellation . . . A superb figure, tossed up by the horns of Taurus against the thunderous sky' (p. 321), blend with Vere's nickname, Starry Vere – bestowed upon him because 'at times he would betray a certain dreaminess of mood' (p. 339) – and intensify Vere's identification with Billy. Melville had described the motivation behind Vere's promotion of Billy to the mizzentop: 'he had thought of recommending him to the executive officer for promotion to a place that would more frequently bring him under his own observation' (p. 372). Vere's desire to transform and neutralise Billy's beauty is finally realised when Billy is raised and hanged from the yard-arm of the ship. The transcendent image of Billy's ascent to heaven recalls the visionary language of Peter Grimes's 'Great Bear and Pleiades' aria, while the lowering of his body into the sea is reminiscent, like Claggart's watery burial, of Grimes's death.

The sanctifying of Billy was not Forster's original intention. In *The Griffin* he declared:

> Billy's primacy granted, he must not be pathetic, and he must not be emasculated. Here again we have to hunt for the right hint. Some critics, while accepting him as a hero, have noted his almost feminine beauty and the suggestion of his gentle birth . . . and the absence of sexual convulsion at his hanging has persuaded them that Melville intends him as a priest-like saviour, a blameless fool. They can make out a case. But the hints of masculinity seem stronger. 'Belted Billy' belongs to adolescent roughness, to the watches of Queequeg and Jack Chase, and John Marr . . . whom the world can easily trap and destroy, but who are, in the precise meaning of the word, men.

Billy's hanging is indeed redolent with Christian symbolism, but while the temptation to portray Billy's death as a Christ-like sacrifice which 'saves' Vere and his fellow crew members was evidently difficult to resist, Forster ultimately rejected this reading. In *Aspects of the Novel* he had written: 'The story of the Fall always fascinates me as a play ground, but I cannot find any profound meaning in it, because of my 'liberal' view of human nature: I cannot believe in a state of original innocence, still less in a lapse from it, and I am always minimising the conception and the extent of Sin and the sinfulness of sex.'[35] He warned Britten that: 'Melville, I believe, was trying to do what I've tried to do. It is a difficult thing to attempt, and even he has failed; the ordinary loveable (and hateable) human beings connected with immensities through the tricks of art. Billy is our Saviour, yet he is Billy, not Christ or Orion. I believe that your music may effect the connection better than our words.'[36] In fact, in the opera Billy becomes less physical and more spiritual, a process which culminates in the closing pages of the score. As he awaits death, Billy experiences a 'Grimes-like' moment of vision, revealed in the ballad 'Billy in the Darbies' (the text being taken from Melville's 'false' account at the conclusion of the novella):

> *Look! through the port comes the moonshine astray.*

In this gently lilting aria, Billy's words are characterised by passive acceptance and self-sacrifice. As Billy sings of the Fate which has shaped his destiny, Claggart's rumbling trombone chords are restated, although their menace is countered by Billy's climactic cry 'Starry Vere, God bless him' which rises to a high E. In a B♭ passage which appears to confirm his defeat, Billy bids farewell to his shipmates. However, he has 'sighted the far-shining sail that's not fate', and his melody repeatedly cadences in A major, the key of love and salvation. In this way, an originally subversive feature of the text is incorporated into the harmony of the whole, and textual irony is replaced by musical seductiveness.

The simplification of Claggart and Billy were not the only examples of the efforts of Britten and Forster to 'sanitise' Melville's text. The removal of the

---

[35] Forster, *Aspects of the Novel*, p. 181.
[36] Forster to Britten, 20 December 1948, *Selected Letters*, vol. 2, p. 235.

physical attraction latent in the relationships between Melville's characters was matched by the corresponding excision of physical violence from the text. This is most noticeable in the presentation of the flogging of the Novice in Act 1, which in contrast to Melville's text, takes place off-stage, unwitnessed by the men. A detailed five-scene draft synopsis, dating from January 1949, reveals that origi- nally this event was to have been directly dramatised:

> Vere is joined by his other officers (Sailing Master, Ratcliffe and six others), the marines are marched into place below and across the quarterdeck, a gang of seamen brings a square grating to which the offender is lashed, the ship's corporal stands ready with the whip, and all the crew stands to watch the scourging.[37]

Crozier reveals that in August 1949 Britten requested that the flogging episode be removed and replaced with a more lyrical episode.[38]

Britten and Forster cultivate an atmosphere of spite and pettiness which is not present in Melville. Whereas in the novella the Novice is flogged for irresponsibly contravening naval rules, in the opera he has committed no such misdemeanour:

> [The hoisting crews run swiftly off stage. The Novice slips as he runs, and falls.]
> BOSUN: You again, you novice! That's done for you! I'll teach you!
> NOVICE: I didn't mean to slip, sir. I can't do anything right here . . .
> BOSUN: Take this man away, and list him for twenty strokes. See it's done at once.

There are interesting echoes of Peter Grimes's threat (ultimately deleted) to his apprentice in the Bosun's warning:

> BOSUN: Don't you answer an officer back. You take care. I've me eye on you. You need a taste of the cat.

Vere's responsibility for the atmosphere of gratuitous malice was to be lessened by the inclusion of a passage in which:

> Vere expresses abhorrence of flogging for trivial offences, but realises that it is the only way of keeping discipline on a man-of-war whose crew contains a large proportion of impressed men.

This was later crossed through and, like Grimes's violent behaviour, the flogging was simply removed from view.

The undercurrents of violent, sexual tension are partially explained by the claustrophobic, closeted atmosphere on board ship, which gives rise to male bonding among the crew. Unable to express their 'love' for one another, their emotions are transmuted into violence. Britten's insistence that the flogging be removed from the stage action perhaps suggests that he felt in some way impli- cated in this process.

Humphrey Carpenter has proposed that the behind-the-scenes flogging was linked in Britten's mind to the memory of the physical punishment – and as

---

[37] GB–ALb 2–01051593.
[38] DH, p. 32.

Crozier suggests, sexual abuse – endured during his schooldays at South Lodge.[39] Certainly there is little to account for the Novice's 'shame' after his beating:

> FRIEND: *The pain'll soon pass.*
> NOVICE: *The shame'll never pass.*

What is this 'shame'? The only other reference to humiliation in the opera occurs in Act 1, Scene 2 when the Sailing Master remembers the *Nore* Mutiny:

> *Oh, the Nore, the Nore!*
> *The shame of it, the shame, the shame . . .*
> *I remember, I remember.*
> *I served there, those days are clear in my mind.*
> *I saw the disgrace and the sorrow.*

However, the congruence between mutiny and sexuality is weaker in the libretto than in Melville, and the significance of this reference is never fully unexplained.

Interestingly, Forster was dissatisfied with Britten's music for the Novice's dirge which follows his flogging:

> Ben has played us most of the first act of Billy – it should run to 40 minutes. I have had my first difference of opinion with him – over the dirge for the novice. He has done dry contra-puntal stuff, no doubt originally excellent from the musician's point of view, but not at all appropriate for mine. I shall want a big discussion when the act is finished.[40]

The 'dry contrapuntal stuff' which Forster refers to is in fact a sinuous, lyrical melody rendered by the seductive tones of the saxophone. The F-based tonality reinforces Forster's very specific association of the Novice's experience and actions with 'Fate', as disclosed in the 'Librettist's note on the Dirge Libretto' which was inserted in the three-act draft libretto, January–March 1949:

> *Intended to convey not only that the men were lost but <u>where</u>: – the infinite sea. First of four references to such a plight: the next being Vere's after trial: the next Billy's solution when he sights the sail of love which isn't Fate: the last Vere's in the Epilogue when he sees what Billy's shown him.*
> *Intended – apart from these high matters – to show the sea's round and almost <u>in</u> the boat . . . I'd thought of the dirge in strongly defined stanzas of increasing length each ending in a recognisable refrain. That there would be contrapuntality hadn't occurred to me.*

Strengthening this connection between the Novice and Fate, the saxophone melody returns in its original and in an inverted form, in the tempting scene as the Novice wonders (Fig. 111):

> *Oh, why was I ever born? Why? It's fate, it's fate. I've no choice. Everything's fate. There's no end to it, and may God forgive me.*

---

[39] HC, p. 289.
[40] Undated letter (4 Crabbe Street, Aldeburgh: Sunday, April 1950?) from Forster to Bob Buckingham (EMF).

The characters cannot stray from the path dictated by a hostile Fate. After Billy has struck Claggart, Vere cries out 'Fated boy, what have you done?' and Billy later acknowledges the role of Fate in his tragedy:

> But I had to strike down that Jemmy-Legs – it's fate. And Captain Vere had to strike me down – Fate.

In the final scene, Vere, 'lost on the infinite sea', almost submits to the overwhelming tide of destiny, as the haunting saxophone melody of the dirge returns. However, Billy's vision of the 'far-shining sail' rescues the Captain. In this way, the Novice's dirge represented for Forster the defeated element in the conflict between Fate and Love which he had striven to depict in the libretto, a reading he believed was true to Melville's conceptions: 'Melville believed in Fate, but he kept seeing out of the corner of his eye a white sail beating up against the storm. Doom is fixed, the trap clicked, the body splashed, the fish nibbled. But he kept seeing the obstinate white sail.'[41]

By 'silencing' the erotic and violent undertones of Melville's narrative, Forster and Britten increase the obscurity of a text already permeated with silences or 'gaps'. Melville's novella abounds with self-referential, literal, symbolic and metaphoric silences, with 'mysteries' which are never fully explained. The most obvious of these is Billy's stutter, which is not just a physical defect and a symbol of a moral flaw but also represents the inability of all the characters to express the 'unspeakable' elements in the drama, most specifically 'homosexuality' and 'mutiny'.

There is an obvious *double entendre* between 'mutiny' and 'homosexuality' in Melville's *Billy Budd, Sailor*. Mutinous and homoerotic inclinations are symbols of latent rebellion against conventional authority: neither word can be spoken yet both are unquestionably present in the text. For example, after revealing the mutinous feelings experienced by some of the impressed men Melville continues by describing the effect which Billy's presence has on the crew of *The Bellipotent*: 'something about him provoked an ambiguous smile in one or two harder faces amongst the blue jackets' (p. 329). When Claggart alludes to the recent mutiny at the *Nore* during his interview with Vere, the Captain is 'indignant at the purposed allusion' (p. 370); similarly, when Vere informs his men of the impending execution of Billy: 'The word *mutiny* was not named in what he said' (p. 394). In contrast, the opera is more explicit: in Act 1, Scene 2 Vere tells his officers:

> Great danger, great danger. There is a word which we scarcely dare speak, yet at moments it has to be spoken. Mutiny.

Likewise, Vere responds defiantly to Claggart's insinuations about Billy's mutinous activities in Act 2, Scene 1:

> VERE: Mutiny? Mutiny? I'm not scared by your words. Your evidence for this?

Before his confrontation with Claggart, in an episode not present in the original novella, Billy swears allegiance to his Captain:

41 Forster, in *The Griffin*.

BILLY: I'd serve you well, indeed I would. You'd be safe with me. You could trust your boat to me. Couldn't find a better coxswain – that's to say, I'll look after you my best. I'd die for you – so would they all.

Vere's confident defence of Billy against Claggart's false accusations, together with the bright optimism of Billy's leaping arpeggios, played by the horn, reduces the social divide between the Captain and his sailor, unites them in friendship, and weakens the reading that Billy is a threat to Vere's position as upholder of social discipline on the ship. It is consequently more difficult to justify Vere's eventual refusal to prevent Billy's execution. Indeed, the reasons that Melville's Vere cites in order to justify the necessity of the execution to his wavering officers – excuses which in fact break both the spirit and the letter of naval law – are omitted in the opera.

In Britten's *Billy Budd*, with the threat to Vere's naval authority removed – and given the identification between mutiny and sexuality in Melville – it seems that it is solely Billy's potential to expose Vere's sexual vulnerability which necessitates the young sailor's destruction; for Billy's execution ensures that Vere's illicit desire remains repressed. Significantly, following Billy's death, Melville emphasises Vere's upright masculinity – 'Captain Vere . . . stood erectly as a musket in the ship-armorer's rack' (p. 400) – the very feature which had been lacking in Billy and Claggart.

Billy's stammer is associated with a 'feminine' blemish – 'like the beautiful woman in one of Hawthorne's minor tales, there was just one thing amiss about him' (p. 331). The identification of his impediment with moral weakness is made explicit in the libretto Prologue:

VERE: Much good has been shown to me and much evil, and the good has never been perfect. There is always some flaw in it, some defect, some imperfection in the divine image, some fault in the angelic song, some stammer in the divine speech. So that the Devil still has something to do with every human consignment to this planet of earth.

In Melville, Billy's stammer surfaces 'under sudden provocation of strong heart-feeling'. This is directly dramatised in the opera, when Billy is silenced by his 'defect' at moments of embarrassment, anger, astonishment and frustration. The climactic moment occurs when he is accused by Claggart of inciting the ship to mutiny. Transfixed and mesmerised by the phenomenal effect of Claggart's eyes, those 'lights of human intelligence' in which he recognises, if not under-stands, the profundity of Claggart's 'depravity', Billy strikes out: 'Could I have used my tongue I would not have struck him. But he foully lied to my face and in the presence of my captain, and I had to say something, and I could only say it with a blow, God help me' (p. 383). Melville had written: 'But for the adequate comprehending of Claggart by a normal nature these hints are insufficient. To pass from a normal nature to him one must cross 'the deadly space between'. And this is best done by indirection' (p. 352). In his enforced silence, Billy crosses this 'deadly space' with an equally deadly blow, which is supported by a penetrating *fortissimo* B♮ pedal bass (Act 2, Fig. 70).

It is in the 'closeted' interview between Billy and Vere that the silence is most penetrating. Melville ensured that the secrets of this locked room remained undisclosed and Britten musically represents this episode with a wordless, sustained harmonic progression, usually referred to as the 'interview chords'. These kaleidoscopic harmonies are the opera's own 'stammer'. The silencing of the verbal and vocal discourse introduces a gap in sound, in communication and in meaning and initiates an articulative crisis which the listener is challenged to overcome. Wayne Koestenbaum has explored the phenomena of vocal schism, writing:

> The tendency of a diva's voice to break down makes queer people feel at home ... In crisis the vocal organ calls attention to its schism, narrates its own history, and reveals to the queer subject that voice or identity is always torn in half, broken, dispossessed ...
>
> Vocal crisis is a form of communication ... the moment when queer meanings of opera begin to speak – because at the moment of vulnerability and breakdown, the diva proves that seamless singing has been masquerade, and now her cracked, decayed, raucous, and undisguised self is coming out ...
>
> In [the diva's] interruption I hear the imagined nature of homosexuality as a rip in meaning, in coherence, in cultural systems, in vocal consistency. Homosexuality isn't intrinsically an interruption; but society has characterised it as a break and a schism, and gay people, who are molded in the image of crisis and emergency, who are associated with 'crisis' ... may begin to identify with crisis and hear the interrupted voice as our echo.[42]

Indeed, some musicologists have identified the chordal 'interruption' in *Billy Budd* as being representative of a homosexual crisis, and have analysed the tonal progression of the chord sequence to support the hypothesis that the passage provides an affirmative vision of sexual love [Example 18].

The 'interview chords' are frequently analysed as a large-scale resolution in F major, although Clifford Hindley rejects this reading and suggests that they outline a plagal cadence, F–C, which resembles the Amen cadence 'So be it'.[43] Certainly, the chords do harmonise successive tones of a mode on F which might imply an expressive solution to the hypothetical equation (Claggart = F) + (Billy = A/A♭ – i.e. enharmonic G♯, E major third degree) + (Vere = C) =? Thus, Donald Mitchell has written that the chords are 'the true musical realisation of the ultimate passions involved, when, in Melville's words, "two of great Nature's nobler order embrace".'[44] Likewise, Philip Brett argues that they 'suggest that in Platonic terms, the love of Ideal Beauty can lead to wisdom, knowledge and forgiveness; and that in Christian terms, goodness and love have the power to forgive. This moment of unalloyed optimism is perhaps the crux of the opera.'[45] Clifford

---

[42] Koestenbaum, *The Queen's Throat*, pp. 126–8.

[43] Clifford Hindley, 'Britten's *Billy Budd*: The "Interview Chords" Again', *Musical Quarterly*, Spring 1994, vol. 78, no. 1, 99–126.

[44] Donald Mitchell, *Music Survey* 4, 1952, quoted in HC, p. 295.

[45] Philip Brett, 'Salvation at Sea', in Christopher Palmer (ed.), *The Britten Companion* (London: Faber & Faber, 1984), p. 142.

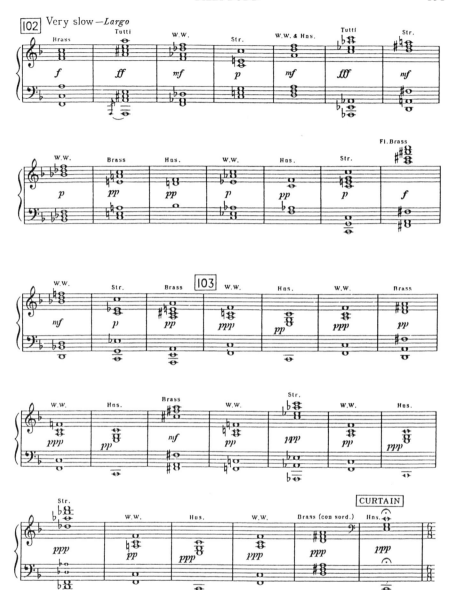

Example 18

Hindley goes further still, proposing that the passage symbolises 'a positive and indeed idealised form of homosexual love . . . implicit in the relationship between Billy and Vere'.[46]

In some ways it is appropriate that a purely musical episode should symbolise

[46] Clifford Hindley, 'Love and Salvation in Britten's *Billy Budd*', in *Music and Letters*, August 1989, 363–81.

sexual freedom and acceptance, since in the novella it is Billy's power of song that spreads harmony and contentment among the crew. Though uneducated, Billy is not uncreative but 'like the illiterate nightingale was sometimes the composer of his own song' (p. 330). The melodies of his aria 'Billy Budd King of the birds!' (Act 1, Fig. 31) repeatedly rise to a high E, foreshadowing his eulogistic praise of 'Starry Vere' (Fig. 58). Furthermore, in Melville's text Billy's final blessing of Captain Vere is linked with his gift of song: 'delivered in the clear melody of a singing bird on the point of launching from the twig' (p. 400). In Act 1, Scene 2 of the opera, Vere interprets the singing of his men as a sign of their contentedness:

> VERE: *And listen to them singing below decks. Where there is happiness there cannot be harm. We owe so much to them – some torn from their homes.*

However, it is also through song that the sailors express their discontent, their work cry 'O Heave! O Heave away!' echoing the melody of Billy's unintentionally subversive farewell to his former ship, *The Rights O'Man*. This melody resurfaces in the mutinous murmurs of the crew after Billy's death.

If 'song' in the opera is an agent of both harmony and rebellion, then Britten's passage of purely musical discourse might similarly embody both the highest and the lowest of human aspirations. In this way, the equation F+A♭+C might indicate the potent unification of Claggart's violent passion, symbolised by a F minor triad with a missing fifth (e.g. Fig. 36), with Vere's spiritual compassion, located in the deflected pitch C with which he is identified.[47] The radiant, sonic canvas of extensive dynamic range and colour thus encompasses an entire spectrum of human experience and emotion. Although the 'interview chords' are linked to the dark trombone harmonies which symbolise Claggart's blackness – for example, Claggart's description of Billy as 'a find in a thousand' (Act 1, Fig. 29), his reference to Billy's dazzling necktie (Act 1, Fig. 55), his odious compliment 'handsomely done' (Act 1, Fig. 101), and his betrayal of Billy (Act 2, Figs. 5 and 38) – they also reappear at restorative moments in the opera, such as at Billy's final farewell to *The Indomitable* and his blessing of Captain Vere. Therefore, there is no unequivocal reason why the chords should symbolise the realisation of 'an idealised form of homosexual love'. Indeed, their affinity with Claggart's trombone chords, which reverberate with evil intent (see also the orchestral passage preceding the trial scene (Act 2, Fig. 80) and the trial itself (Fig. 88)), would seem to undermine this reading.

It is possible that the interview chords are not primarily an intellectual exposition of the opera's essential conflict, conveniently realised and resolved as an harmonic progression, but should be experienced as an instinctive, physical and dramatic event whose power is emotional rather than rational. In this way, they

---

47 This interpretation is reinforced by the musical events of the trial scene. As the officers pronounce the verdict and sentence Vere's monotone C utterances – 'Pronounce your verdict . . . I accept your verdict', are accompanied by Claggart's 'fifth-less' triad, thus musically replicating Claggart's aria (Act 1, Fig. 110): *I, John Claggart, Master-at-Arms on board the Indomitable, have you in my power, and I will destroy you.*

are concerned less with 'meaning' and more with 'expression'; they 'speak' to us but wordlessly and in a language that we cannot consciously decipher. In performance, the observer is confronted only with emptiness which, inspired by the sonic kaleidoscope which reverberates in this space, his own creative imagination is invited to fill. This is the most powerful dramatic moment in the opera but paradoxically it is the one moment that will not reveal the opera's 'meaning'. Britten appears to have followed Vere's advice – 'I must not too closely consider these mysteries. As mysteries let them remain'.

Therefore, in spite of the affirmative readings of this passage cited above, the dilemma concerning the apportioning of guilt and innocence persists. Melville had commented on the apparent reversal of guilt and innocence in his tale: 'In the jugglery of circumstances preceding and attending the event on board the *Bellipotent*, and in the light of that martial code whereby it was formally to be judged, innocence and guilt personified in Claggart and Budd in effect changed places' (p. 380). In the opera the respective innocence and guilt of Billy and Claggart is not in doubt: instead, it is Vere, the tale's narrator, racked by his conscience, whom the audience judges. Vere himself brings about this change of emphasis. After Billy has struck his deadly blow, Melville's Captain remarks: 'Struck dead by an angel of God! Yet the angel must hang!' (p. 378). In contrast, in the opera Vere is immediately thrown into moral chaos:

> VERE: *The mists have cleared. O terror! what do I see? Scylla and Charybdis, the straits of Hell. I sight them too late – I see all the mists concealed. Beauty, handsomeness, goodness coming to trial. How can I condemn him? How can I save him? My heart's broken, my life's broken. It is not his trial, it is mine, mine. It is I whom the devil awaits.*

His words and melody are scattered with fragmented allusions to the verbal and musical motifs of Billy, Claggart and the Novice, and the passage fluctuates between the opera's tonal centres. What is the reason for Vere's self-condemnation, which is restated in identical form after the trial? Owing to the suppression of Vere's voice in the trial scene, his tormented sense of responsibility seems out of proportion with the actual operatic events. Forster was troubled by this issue of culpability and wrote to Lionel Trilling during the early stages of work on the libretto:

Why is it Vere's touch on Billy's shoulder that precipitates the blow?[48]

Is it the confrontation with Claggart's evil or with Vere's compassion which renders Billy inarticulate and initiates the tragedy? The ambiguity arises because if Vere is to be 'saved' by Billy he must experience self-doubt, yet to ensure the audience is sympathetic towards Vere, he must not be depicted as culpable.

Forster attempted to resolve the problem in the Epilogue, where he diminished Vere's liability and clarified Billy's role as 'saviour'. In Britten's copy of the March 1949 draft the following handwritten text precedes the Epilogue:

---

48 Forster to Trilling, 16 April 1949, *Selected Letters*, vol. 2, p. 236.

> *Epilogue – starting with partial repetition of Prologue. Vere realises that there was another choice.* For I could have saved him: ought to have saved him. He knew it – even his ship mates knew it, tho' earthly law silenced them. By the heavenly laws I have erred, if heaven never passes into action.

Forster's copy includes the lines:

> VERE: *God has blessed me and also admonished me . . . By the heavenly laws I have erred, and if Heaven never passes into action, what meaning remains in our lives, how do we escape from Fate? I have erred, but pardon has come to me, and the wisdom that passes understanding.*

On 8 August 1951 he wrote to Britten:

> *Billy's last cry is insoluble . . . it was compassion, comprehension, love. Only Vere understood it and it has the supernatural force inherent in something which only one person understands . . . Since we have to use words, Starry Vere seems better than Captain Vere, but the really wrong word is God: who but Billy at such a moment could bless.*[49]

The final Epilogue text reads:

> VERE: *For I could have saved him. He knew it, even his shipmates knew it, though the earthly laws silenced them. O what have I done? But he has saved me, and blessed me, and the love that passes understanding has come to me. I was lost on the infinite sea, but I've sighted a sail in the storm, the far-shining sail, and I'm content. I've seen where she's bound for. There's a land where she'll anchor forever.*

Possibly taking his cue from Plomer who, in a 1943 essay on Melville had remarked that for Melville romantic companionship between men was 'a fleeting memory of a visionary ideal which offered some compensation to a lonely heart in a terrifying world', Forster ignores Melville's ambivalent close and imposes his own conclusive reading.

Melville's ending is shrouded in uncertainty. He writes: 'But though properly the story ends with his life, something in the way of sequel will not be amiss. Three brief chapters will suffice' (p. 405). There follows an account of Vere's death in battle which has occurred shortly after Billy's execution, a 'false' newspaper account, and the ballad 'Billy in the Darbies'. The vision is negative: the reader is left with only deception and death. Claggart is destroyed by his distorted self-loathing love, Billy by his self-destructive beauty and Vere by his self-deluded authority. However, Forster seems unwilling to concede to this pessimism. Commenting upon Plomer's criticism of Melville, he declared: 'It centres on the central warmth and on the bonfire in the heart and on the Milk of Paradise. Possessed of these, we can flourish and endure and understand. Not all is lost. All cannot be lost. The hero hangs dead from the yard arm, dead irredeemably and not in any heaven, dead as a doornail, dead as Antigone, and he has given us life.'[50] The significance of the decision to allow Vere to survive into old age is now

---

[49]　Forster to Britten (EMF).
[50]　Forster, in *The Griffin*.

apparent, for in the novella Billy does *not* save Vere; this reading is specific to the opera and is made central by the framing device of the Prologue and Epilogue.

It is the love between men, not that between Man and God, which sustains Forster's overwhelming optimistic vision:

> no form of Christianity and no alternative to Christianity will bring peace to the world or integrity to the individual; no 'change of heart' will occur. And yet we need not despair, indeed, we cannot despair; the evidence of history shows us that men have always insisted on behaving creatively under the shadow of the sword . . .
>
> Where do I start? With personal relationships. Here is something comparatively solid in a world of violence and cruelty.[51]

He clarified his beliefs in a letter to Bob Buckingham, 7 February 1952: 'Do you remember the passage in Act IV after the Darbies where he ends, 'I'm strong, and I'll stay strong, and that's all and that's enough'? It's immensely important to the opera and to my view of things, and, I think, to Melville's' (EMF). The passage to which Forster refers occurs in the closing moments of the opera:

> BILLY: *We are both in sore trouble, him and me, with great need for strength, and my trouble's soon ending, so I can't help him any longer . . . Don't matter now being hanged, or being forgotten and caught in the weeds. Don't matter now. I'm strong, and I know it, and I'll stay strong, and that's all and that's enough.*

This passage (Act 2, Fig. 117) is set by Britten to a reprise of the interview chords, temporarily inferring their redemptive significance although this reading is undermined in the closing moments of the opera.

Forster had already attempted to dramatise the reciprocation of love and salvation, in his novel *Maurice*, which remained unpublished until 1972. Maurice, like Billy, is child-like and ignorant, 'not doused with imagination', 'part brutal, part ideal', and resists initiation into the world of knowledge:

> He had lost the precocious clearness of the child which transfigures and explains the universe, offering answers of miraculous insight and beauty . . . Maurice forgot he had ever been sexless, and realised in maturity how just and clear the sensation of his earliest days must have been. He had sunk far below them now, for he was descending the Valley of Life . . . he longed to be a little boy again, and to stroll half awake forever by the colourless sea.[52]

His dream of an ideal friend – 'He could die for such a friend, he would allow such a friend to die for him; they would make any sacrifice for each other, and count the world nothing' (p. 26) – echoes Billy's desire:

> BILLY: *Starry I'll follow you . . .*
> *Follow thro' darkness, never you fear . . .*

---

[51] Forster, 'What I Believe'. In his 'Commonplace Book' Forster recorded: 'two people putting each other into salvation is the only theme I find worthwhile. No rescuer and rescued, not the alternating performance of good turns, but it takes two to make a Hero.'

[52] E. M. Forster, *Maurice* (Harmondsworth: Penguin, 1972), pp. 25–30. All subsequent references are to this edition and are given in parentheses in the text.

> *I'd die to save you, ask for to die . . .*
> *I'll follow you all I can, follow you for ever!*

Similarly, Maurice's striking of the man on the train directly parallels Billy's assault upon Claggart.

Initially the love of Clive Durham for Maurice is presented as the love of a man of intellect and imagination for a companion in whose beautiful body he locates an essential integrity of spirit, and it is thus an enactment of Forster's homosexual ideal. However, Forster was unable to sustain his confident vision and the destructive forces inherent in homosexuality are symbolised by the 'gaps' in his text. The most notable of these is the 'crack in the floor' in the psychiatrist's surgery which, like Billy's stutter, represents the homosexual 'flaw' in Maurice's psyche, and symbolises the internal and social fragmentation which he shares with Claggart: 'By pleasuring the body Maurice had confirmed – that very word was used in the final verdict – he had confirmed his spirit in its perversion, cut himself off from the congregation of normal man' (p. 187). In spite of Forster's assurances that the relationship between Maurice and Alec Scudder will be permanent, Maurice remains convinced that 'the situation was disgusting – of that he was certain, and indeed never wavered till the end of his life.' His ending is idealistic, a fictional escape to the 'greenwood' ('the land where she'll anchor forever'), which supplies the fortunate conclusion not attainable in life. Forster acknowledged the weakness of the close in his 'Terminal Note': 'A happy ending was imperative. I shouldn't have bothered to write otherwise. I was determined that in fiction anyway two men should fall in love and remain in it for the ever and ever that fiction allows' (p. 218). This definitive resolution is a rejection of Melville's 'ragged' form, and foreshadows Forster's subsequent 'tidying up' of *Billy Budd, Sailor*. Thus, in both Forster's novel and Britten's opera there is evidence of an attempt to transform homosexual love into a form of 'truth', religious, spiritual or artistic.

Forster's collaboration with Britten appears to have given him great spiritual and creative solace and satisfaction:

> You and I have both put into it something which lies deeper than artistic creation, and something which we both understand. It could never have got there but for both of us. I hope to live and write on it in the future, but this opera is my Nunc Dimittis, in that it dismisses me peacefully, and convinces me I have achieved.[53]

On one level, Britten appeared similarly satisfied with the results of their partnership:

> Apart from the great pleasure it has been, it has been the greatest honour to have collaborated with you, my dear. It was always one of my wildest dreams to work with E.M.F. – and it is often difficult to realise that it has happened. Anyhow, one thing I am certain of – and that's this; whatever the quality of the music, and it seems people will quarrel about that for some time to come, I think you and

53   Forster to Britten, 9 December 1951, *Selected Letters*, vol. 2, p. 246.

Eric have written comparably the finest libretto ever. For wisdom, tenderness, and dignity of language it has no equals.[54]

Yet, Britten seems to have sensed that Forster was preoccupied with his own quest for resolution, and that he failed to recognise the full potential of the opera's musical discourse, neglecting the expressive power of concordance and contradiction between the verbal and musical strands. He told Erwin Stein that when Forster had first heard the whole of *Billy Budd*, at Crag House in September 1951, he made 'no comment *at all*, not even of disapproval! He doesn't seem to be able to grasp it at all – or really interested in the musical side of the opera. Still, I must be grateful for a wonderful libretto.'[55]

Forster may have placed his trust in the conciliatory power of human, earthly love but the persistent tensions in the musical score imply that Britten did not share his faith that 'Love' or 'Goodness' would inevitably prevail. His evident need for further reassurance is suggested by the composition which immediately followed *Billy Budd*, and which was in fact Britten's only work before his next opera, *Gloriana*. This work was *Canticle II: Abraham and Isaac*. Possibly taking his lead from Melville's suggestion that in the closeted interview Vere '. . . may in the end have Billy to his heart, even as Abraham may have caught young Isaac on the brink of resolutely offering him up in obedience to the exacting behest' (p. 392), in this *Canticle*, Britten dramatises the removal of the threat to mortal innocence (characterised on Britten's own Decca recording by the voice of an adolescent boy on the verge of breaking) through divine intervention, thus establishing an irrefutable ethical frame which is absent in *Billy Budd*.

The score of *Billy Budd* confirms the doubts which Britten shares with Vere. In the final scene of Act 2 the harmonic progression from B♭ to E (Act 2, Fig. 50) which had symbolised Billy's spiritual potential, is reversed. The substantial orchestral introduction to this scene begins with a low pedal E (Act 2, Fig. 123). Billy's presence and influence are further emphasised by a chordal sequence initiated by Vere's entry (Fig. 128), which harmonises successive pitches of the E major triad, and so recalls the mood and effect of 'interview chords'. The passage climaxes (Fig. 130) with an E major chord with an added C (Vere's pitch?), which accompanies the First Lieutenant's recitation of the Articles of War. As Billy is hung, E minor pervades the musical fabric – as the crew echo Billy's salutation, 'Starry Vere, God bless you', their thoughts are with the victim and not his dedicatee. The 'Heave' melody from Act 1 is restated, now supported by an imposing E–B ostinato, as the sailors hover on the verge of mutiny. Once more 'sound' is more potent than 'word' as the sailors utter a non-verbal cry, 'ur'. However, the officers extinguish the rising rebellious fervour by deflecting the harmony towards B♭. Initially this pitch is notated enharmonically, as a Lydian A♯, but is ultimately transformed into B♭ by the force of the officers orders 'Down! Down!' The mood of defeat is stressed by the emphatic pedal B♭ (Fig. 139) which concludes the scene and which persists in the Epilogue.

---

[54] Britten to Forster, 7 December 1957 (EMF).
[55] HC, p. 298.

Example 19

The opening words of the Epilogue recall Peter Grimes's search for a haven where 'night is turned to day':

VERE: We committed his body to the deep. The sea-fowl enshadowed him with their wings, their harsh cries were his requiem. But the ship passed on under light airs towards the rose of dawn, and soon it was full day in its clearness and strength.

Punctuating Vere's anxious cries 'I could have saved him', bitonal chords under-line his ineradicable doubts. As he openly voices his torment, 'Oh, What have I done?' (Fig. 142), his melody moves to B minor and Billy's fanfare motif is reiter-ated. Vere's stubborn silence and his refusal to save Billy are unjustifiable and appear ultimately to imply the defeat of 'love' by 'authority'. The phrase which verbally clarifies Forster's optimistic vision – 'I've seen where she's bound for. There's a land where she'll anchor forever' – is undermined musically by the final resolution in B♭, the key of conformity and repression. However, ambiguity persists, as at this precise moment the melodic motifs of both Billy and Claggart are restated [Example 19]. Vere's monologue descends and dissolves, coming to rest on D, the one pitch shared by the B minor and B♭ major triads which had first been opposed in the opening bars of the Prologue. Britten had struggled to musi-cally characterise Vere as a man who could overcome external and internal oppression and find consolation in peace, goodness and love. However, at the end of the opera self-knowledge exists but salvation remains elusive.

8

Gloriana

The blood flew through his veins in vigorous vitality; he ran and tilted with the sprightliest; and then suddenly health would ebb away from him, and the pale boy would lie for hours in his chamber, obscurely melancholy, with a Virgil in his hand.
Lytton Strachey, Elizabeth and Essex[1]

> *I love, and yet am forced to seem to hate;*
> *I am, and am not; freeze, and yet I burn;*
> *Since from my other self I turn.*
> William Plomer, Gloriana, 'The Queen's Dilemma', Act 3

Britten's first four operas had been characterised by the persistent presence of an unarticulated drama which ran parallel to the ostensible 'plot' and which at various times complemented or contradicted the discernible stage action. The tension generated by this 'shadow' drama pervaded the verbal and musical discourses and complicated the relationship between the text and score. It might be simplistically defined as a conflict between external and internal forces or between social duty and personal inclination, and it found powerful outward expression in the schizophrenic dislocation in the psyches of Britten's protagonists, of the kind described in the above quotations.

In Britten's next opera, *Gloriana*, this conflict between public and private worlds informed every dimension of the opera, from the nature of the commission and conception, to the performance and critical reception of the work at a gala premiere at Covent Garden on 8 June 1953. It was an essential feature of the source text and was complicated by Strachey's personal identification (discussed below) with the inner lives and tragic experience of his characters, an identification reminiscent of Britten's own sense of personal implication in his previous operas. The antagonistic forces in *Gloriana* influenced not only the theme and characterisation but were also an important factor in the structural organisation

---

[1] Lytton Strachey, *Elizabeth and Essex: A Tragic History* (London: Chatto and Windus, 1932), p. 4. All subsequent references are to this edition and are given in parentheses in the text. In Britten's copy of Lytton Strachey's text this passage is annotated with a single vertical pencil line. Philip Reed suggests that the absence of any other annotations might indicate that a different copy, now missing, was used by Britten and Plomer during the writing of the libretto. (See Philip Reed, 'The Creative Evolution of *Gloriana*', in Paul Banks (ed.), *Britten's 'Gloriana': Essays and Sources* (Woodbridge: The Boydell Press, 1993), pp. 17–47).

of the opera. The unease and imbalance which pervade *Gloriana*, together with the opera's controversial performance history, confirm the complexity of the challenge had Britten set himself, i.e. to reconcile his public responsibilities and ambitions with his need for private fulfilment. In this way, it might be suggested that Britten's experience of composing this Coronation opera was a partial re-enactment of the tragic experience of Gloriana herself.

The subject of Britten's new opera was proposed by George Harewood in May 1952, during a holiday in Gargallen with Britten and Pears. While discussing 'nationalist opera' they were unable to name an English equivalent to such nationalist works as Smetana's *The Bartered Bride*, Mussourgsky's *Boris Godunov* or Verdi's *Aida*, and it was suggested that Britten should write one himself:

> The next 3 or 4 hours were spent discussing a period – the Merrie England of the Tudors or Elizabethans? – and a subject – Henry VIII? too obvious, and an unattractive hero. Queen Elizabeth? highly appropriate! what about a national opera in time for next year's Coronation? We talked into the night, agreed that Lytton Strachey's *Elizabeth and Essex*, which I had recently read, would make a good starting point, and then started to face the difficulties.[2]

Harewood began dividing Strachey's text into operatic scenes and William Plomer was asked to act as librettist.

Plomer was a friend of E. M. Forster and a peripheral member of the Bloomsbury Group.[3] In 1948 he had been invited to present a lecture on Edward Fitzgerald at the inaugural Aldeburgh Festival and shortly afterwards wrote to Britten: 'I do just want to thank you again very much indeed for allowing me to join in the Festival, & for all your kindness: and to say how immensely I enjoyed every moment of Aldeburgh – particularly *Albert Herring*.'[4] A friendship developed between the two men and in August 1951, when Britten required a librettist for a children's opera he was planning based upon Beatrix Potter's *The Tale of Mr Tod*, he approached Plomer, sending him a sketch of the basic plan of the opera – six scenes with suggestions as to how it might be staged. Plomer replied:

> My dear Ben,
> Yes, I have been familiarizing myself with Mr Tod – it is intensely dramatic, &

2   George Harewood, *The Tongs and the Bones: The Memoirs of Lord Harewood* (London: Weidenfield and Nicolson, 1981), pp. 134–5.
3   Plomer had met Strachey at a Tavistock Square party in 1931, an event he describes in his *Autobiography*: 'Strachey was then still in his forties, but his beard and spectacles made him look older. They seemed to create a certain distance between him and others. About Strachey's eyelids, as he looked out through the windows of his spectacles over the quickset hedge of his beard, there was a suggestion of world-weariness: he had in fact just two more years to live. To me he did not seem like a man in early middle-age, and although his beard made him look older than he was, I did not think of him in terms of a sum of years but as an intelligence alert and busy behind the appendage of hair and the glass outworks. A glint came into his eyes, the brain was on the move as swiftly as a bat, with something of the radar-like sensitivity of a bat, and when he spoke it was sometimes in the voice of a bat' (William Plomer, *An Autobiography* (London: Cape, 1975), p. 250).
4   Plomer to Britten, 10 June 1948 (BPL).

I am delighted that you are going to use it & that you feel I may be able to help you. Your outline seems to me excellent – it can no doubt be modified if necessary & in due course . . . I feel a good deal of diffidence about my ability to provide what you need, so I must sustain myself with the comforting knowledge that you believe I can![5]

Although these plans were later abandoned, Britten was evidently encouraged by his preliminary work with Plomer, for on returning from his continental holiday he wrote 'it is imperative that I see you; about what I can only explain, when I see you'.[6]

He explained his plans for *Gloriana* when they met in March 1952 and although Plomer was initially wary about accepting Britten's proposal, he later agreed.[7] Imogen Holst describes how they were forced to work at a tremendous pace in order to complete the opera in time for the premiere which was less than a year away.[8] In a radical departure from his previous method, Britten did not wait for Plomer to complete a typescript libretto but began composing the score immediately, working from densely annotated drafts and frequently altering the text without consulting his librettist. On 14 September he invited Plomer to Aldeburgh: 'because I have had to make drastic changes in the form of this part . . . & I hope and pray you'll approve . . . In the meantime I'll go ahead and hope we can sort out any difficulties later' (BPL). Their progress suffered a set-back when Plomer fell ill in November. Britten continued working on Act 3, composing songs for which Plomer had not yet written the text. He requested a reply for Essex to the Queen's decree that he must go to Ireland and when Plomer's text arrived, replied: 'the lovely Essex speech . . . fits what I'd planned (& even sketched in!) like a glove. A lovely case of thought transference! The other bits are fine also although I haven't actually fitted them in yet.'[9] This implies that Britten was concerned less with the specific words used and more with the ideas expressed. His correspondence with Plomer, both during and after their collaboration, suggests that he found Plomer to be a sympathetic and flexible colleague who, despite his inexperience, could write fluently for music and who was willing to alter his text in response to Britten's requests.[10]

[5]   Plomer to Britten, 26 August 1951 (BPL). The project was abandoned after difficulties arose concerning the copyright of Potter's tale and an alternative subject, *Tycho the Vegan* – a science-fiction story – was proposed. The essential shape of this opera was settled on 14 March 1952 and Plomer began drafting the text, as a letter of 22 March reveals: 'My dear Ben, I was delighted to get your letter, & to hear that you had been enjoying yourselves, & thinking about *Tycho the Vegan*. I enclose with this a Prologue – my only fair copy of it – for you to see whether you like the tone & manner of it' (BPL). However, this project was also discontinued when work on *Gloriana* commenced.

[6]   Britten to Plomer, 27 April 1952 (BPL).

[7]   George Harewood recalls that it was decided that if Plomer declined to write the *Gloriana* libretto, Britten was willing to consider working with Ronald Duncan, although he insisted that in such circumstances Harewood should act as a neutral assistant and intermediary. (Revealed in a private communication to Philip Reed, quoted in Banks, *'Gloriana'*, pp. 18–19.)

[8]   Imogen Holst, 'Working for Britten', *Musical Times*, vol. 118, February 1977, 202–6.

[9]   Britten to Plomer, 23 November 1952, quoted in Banks, *'Gloriana'*, p. 37.

[10] For example, he wrote to Plomer, 23 July 1953: 'It has been an enormous success, from the

Despite this, there is some evidence that once again Britten's intentions may have deviated from those of his librettist. Plomer – like Britten, Forster and Strachey – was a homosexual, but although he had read *Maurice* in 1932 (writing that if only he had read it at seventeen years of age 'it would have been something to steer by'[11]), when Forster's *The Life to Come and Other Stories* was published in 1972 he professed 'a strong incuriosity about the stories and no keenness to read them'.[12] Likewise, he regarded the autobiography of his friend Joe Ackerley, *My Father and Myself*, as 'a book that should never have been written, let alone published'. Plomer preferred to keep his life and art entirely separate:

> You're quite right to suggest that homosexual overtones or undertones are present in my writings, and I hasten to say that any general view of my writings – and my life – should take notice of them. Although, as we know, it is now possible and customary to be much more candid than it was when I was young, I never feel that candour is a constant necessity, if only because people who keep telling one all about themselves, in print or viva voce, are apt to be unduly self-centred, to assume that what is important to them will seem so to others, and therefore to be extremely boring. I think that blatant homosexuality, like other forms of blatancy, can be tiresome and uncivilised.[13]

The subtly different priorities of the composer and librettist may have contributed to the incongruity between the external and internal dramas present in the opera, as most powerfully personified by the figure of Elizabeth herself.

Although the actual composition of the opera progressed comparatively smoothly, behind the scenes discontent was growing. Before commencing *Gloriana*, Britten had begun work with Myfanwy Piper on a new chamber opera for the English Opera Group which had been commissioned for the Biennale Festival in Venice, based on Henry James's novel *The Turn of the Screw*. The members of the English Opera Group, who relied on Britten for repertory, were now angered by the postponement of this project and the mood of disaffection was intensified by in-fighting among members of the Aldeburgh clique. Ironically, this artistic community depended upon Britten for its existence and continuation in much the same way that the stability of the Elizabethan court and state hung entirely on the figure of Gloriana. Just as Elizabeth's bestowal of preference and privilege was fickle and unpredictable, so Britten's friends and colleagues could find themselves inexplicably ignored or ostracised. Joan Cross

---

box office, having on average beaten all other operas there this season. I expect that you, like me, have felt abit [sic] kicked around over it – perhaps more than me, because I'm abit more used to the jungle! But the savageness of the wild beasts is always a shock. The fact remains that I've loved working with you, my dear, and that you've produced a most wonderful libretto, that it is impossible for me adequately to express my gratitude for – Please let us sometime work together again – no hurry – just don't forget me' (BPL). Britten and Plomer did indeed collaborate again, on Britten's three church parables.

11 Plomer, p. 447.
12 *Ibid.*
13 *Ibid.*

recalled: 'He just used people and he finished with them, and that was that',[14] and Dame Janet Baker declared 'to be with him was a bit like being with the Queen'.[15]

Furthermore, while these tensions escalated in private, an altogether more public dissatisfaction was fermenting. Britten had insisted that *Gloriana* be made 'in some way official, not quite commanded but at least accepted as part of the celebrations'[16] and Lord Harewood had contacted his cousin, Sir Alan Lascelles, the Queen's private secretary, to ask for her approval, which was quickly granted. This action inevitably thrust the project into the public arena, exposing Britten to critical scrutiny more brutal than the sympathetic understanding he had previously enjoyed in the protective environment of Aldeburgh. The reasons for Britten's professed determination to have *Gloriana* officially sanctioned are not clear but may have been motivated by a need for the recognition which he believed had been denied him, for Michael Tippett disclosed that Britten had once confessed 'I would be a Court composer, but for my pacifism and homosexuality'.[17]

In fact, many leading figures of the social and cultural Establishment were angered by the apparent preferment bestowed upon Britten, even suggesting that there was a homosexual conspiracy in the art world.[18] *Billy Budd* had been commissioned for the 1951 Festival of Britain and there was considerable resentment that Britten had been once again been chosen to compose an opera for a national celebration. Furthermore, Ninette de Valois, upset that a separate dance gala had not been commissioned for the Royal Ballet, clashed with Britten over the quantity and status of the dance scenes in *Gloriana*, and challenged his appointment of John Cranko as choreographer. Hostilities intensified when on 1 June 1952 Britten was made a Companion of Honour in anticipation of the forthcoming performance. The publication that year of *Benjamin Britten: A Commentary on His Works from a Group of Specialists*, edited by Donald Mitchell and Hans Keller,[19] undoubted fuelled the animosity. The rather eulogistic tone of the book was attacked by critics such as Robin Mayhead and Peter Tranchell who denounced what they considered to be 'incoherent verbiage' and hysterical 'hero-worship'.[20]

---

[14] HC, p. 321.

[15] *Ibid.*, p. 464. In *New Statesman*, 13 June 1953, Desmond Shawe-Taylor, in what was otherwise a relatively favourable review of *Gloriana*, made a pointed reference to this similarity: 'For this royally commissioned opera the composer has had recourse to yet another librettist, William Plomer – his sixth, if we count the collaboration of Auden in the forgotten *Paul Bunyan*. This Tudor fickleness provides welcome evidences of discontent; nevertheless, if solid masterpieces are to be achieved, it is time to settle down. Can we look for a Catherine Parr in Plomer . . .?'

[16] See Harewood, *The Tongs and the Bones*, p. 135.

[17] HC, p. 194.

[18] For example, when Britten was offered the musical directorship of Covent Garden, William Walton is reputed to have complained: 'There are enough buggers in the place already, it's time it was stopped' (HC, p. 313).

[19] Keller and Mitchell, *Benjamin Britten: A Commentary on His Works from a Group of Specialists* (London: Faber & Faber, 1952).

[20] Robin Mayhead, 'The Case of Benjamin Britten', *Scrutiny*, vol. XIX, no. 3, Spring 1953, and

The premiere of *Gloriana* has been hyperbolically described as 'one of the great disasters of operatic history'.[21] The audience was divided into two factions, consisting of an Establishment element which hoped that the opera would confirm their hopes that the coronation of Queen Elizabeth II would herald a new period of spiritual, social and cultural revival,[22] and a potentially fractious musicological contingent eagerly awaiting the opportunity to judge Britten's latest operatic offering. Inevitably, Britten could not satisfy the demands of both these groups. The 'gala' audience – who had little experience of, or liking for, opera or 'modern music' – were bored by the long pageant scenes which Britten had designed specifically to satisfy their ceremonial expectations, while the 'critical' audience attacked these scenes as dramatically irrelevant.[23] The formal structure of the opera was arranged to alternate between 'public' and 'private' scenes, but the result was that the dramatic flow was disrupted, thereby increasing the episodic feel of the work and making consistent characterisation difficult to achieve.

Ernest Newman's comments in the *Sunday Times*, 14 June 1953, were typical: 'The bulk of the music is hardly more than pastiche, sometimes very clever pastiche, sometimes not so clever . . . In general the music seems to me to fall far below what we have come to expect from a composer of Mr Britten's gifts.' Plomer was also attacked and judged to possess 'insufficient theatrical experience to unite convincingly the elements of ceremonial pageant with the psychologically complex relationship between the aging, but still imperious Elizabeth I and the dashing young Earl of Essex'.[24] Most censures of the opera, including a long-running correspondence in *The Times*, focused not upon the actual music but upon the 'unsuitable' subject matter which was deemed insulting to the new Queen Elizabeth II. Recent reviewers have attempted to account for this; for example, Rodney Milnes, in his review of Opera North's 1993 production, observed: 'It cannot have been simply because the subject was 'disrespectful'; one of the problems of the piece is that the public scenes not only threaten to overwhelm the private concerns, but lay on flattery of the monarchy with a trowel whose capaciousness might have made even Disraeli blush . . . I suspect that one aspect of the piece that stuck in people's throats . . . was the relationship between an old woman and a young man.'[25] Britten had set himself an almost impossible challenge, to achieve a satisfactory compromise between artistic integrity and

---

Peter Tranchell, 'Britten and the Brittenites', *Music and Letters*, April 1953.

[21] Harewood, *The Tongs and the Bones*, p. 138.

[22] Plomer recalled that the prospect of a 'new Elizabethan age' had been raised during a meeting he had had with the Queen Mother and Princess Margaret (see Banks, '*Gloriana*', p. 27). In *Elizabeth and Essex* Strachey describes the original Elizabethan Renaissance: 'Essex and Raleigh – young, bold, coloured, brilliantly personal – sprang forward and filled the scene of public action. It was the same in every other field of national energy: the snows of the germinating winter had melted, and the wonderful spring of Elizabethan culture burst into life' (p. 8).

[23] These ceremonial scenes demonstrate Britten's consummate technical skill but there is little sense of any real engagement on Britten's part.

[24] Edmund Tracey, 'London Music', *Musical Times*, vol. 107, January 1954, 36–7.

[25] Rodney Milnes, *The Times*, 20 December 1993.

public duty, as he revealed in a letter to Plomer, 11 May 1952: 'My feelings at the moment are that I want the opera to be crystal-clear, with lovely pageantry . . . but linked by a strong story about the Queen & Essex – strong & simple. A tall order, but I think we can do it!'[26]

Peter Pears appears to have anticipated the conflict of interest which Britten experienced. From the start Pears was unenthusiastic about a project which he justly feared would interrupt his forthcoming concert tour with Britten: 'Peter had taken up a glum position over the whole thing, hating the cancellations, disliking the disturbance of his routine, the official nature of the affair, the risk involved in the venture into international waters, and perhaps too of playing a young, ardent lover, in the shape of Essex, which Ben of course planned to write for him. He preferred to sing Cecil, let Ben find another Essex!'[27] After the critical storm had broken, Britten told Harewood that he had 'received a broadside from Peter – did not the reception confirm his worst fears? Should they not in future stick to the public that wanted them, the loyal Aldeburgh friends, and not get mixed up with something that was none of their concern? Ben was in the mood to take his advice.'[28] When Pears threatened to withdraw, the bass, Boris Christoff, was proposed for the part but Britten refused to consider this option: '[he] wanted Pears for Essex, and he was accustomed to getting his own way.'[29] Pears's later comments reveal his discomfort with some dimensions of Essex's character: 'I adored the lute songs, of course, and there are two wonderful duets with Elizabeth, but I think that in many ways in the rest of the part I was wrongly cast. I'm not sure but I think somebody else should have done it rather than me.'[30] By taking the part of Essex, Pears now found himself cast in a 'Billy Budd-like' role – as the young 'innocent' whose beauty inspires both love and hatred and who must be sacrificed on the altar of public responsibility. In Britten's previous opera, Pears had communicated the moral dilemma of the ultimately redeemed 'sacrificer', Captain Vere, and in the next, The Turn of the Screw, he would take a Claggart-like part, as Peter Quint, dramatising the destructive dimension of love. It is as if Britten was exploring, through Pears's voice, all possible denouements of the dialectic between repression and desire.

If Pears found the part of Essex uninviting, it may have been because Britten's creative energies were focused on Gloriana herself, with the result that the characterisation of Essex was weakened. Strachey had maintained a balance between the unpredictability of his nature and behaviour and the sincerity of his devotion to the Queen, but in the opera the number of 'private' scenes where this affection could be depicted was reduced and Essex can appear merely petulant and quarrelsome. The two sides of his personality are not synthesised and he is given no arias or monologues to explain his motivation.

---

26 Quoted in Banks, 'Gloriana', p. 20.
27 Harewood, The Tongs and the Bones, p. 136.
28 HC, p. 327.
29 Harewood, The Tongs and the Bones, p. 136.
30 ENO Opera Guide, no. 24, p. 68.

Indeed, many of the criticisms of *Gloriana* focused on the deficiencies of the characterisation: 'it was probable that [Britten's] heart was not in the enterprise. Nor can his poet's have been; for his characters are lifeless – puppets and not men and women.'[31] The problem sprang partly from the fact that the complex inter-weaving of personalities in Strachey's text, which was crucial in explaining the motivation of his characters, had to be simplified in the opera in order to accom-modate the required amount of festive pageantry. Plomer had suggested that J. E. Neale's history *Queen Elizabeth I* should be used as a 'sort of corrective to Lytton Strachey'.[32] While Neale's text may have clarified the historical context of the opera, in his concern for factual simplicity and verisimilitude, Plomer overlooked the very feature of Strachey's text which probably attracted Britten; for Strachey's *Elizabeth and Essex* is not a history at all, but a dramatic biography which intri-cately fuses fact and fiction, and which reveals Strachey's own emotional involve-ment in his characters' tragic experience.[33]

Strachey's biographer, Michael Holroyd, describes how: 'At times he [Strachey] appeared . . . to enter a world of imagination, so that it became difficult to disentangle what was real from fantasy.'[34] Strachey was mesmerised by the two principal characters, their tormented romance arousing memories of his own youthful love affairs which mingled with his present-day infatuations, particu-larly his obsession with Roger Senhouse. His depiction of the aging Elizabeth's passion for Essex focuses on the unbridgeable age gap between them and, strangely, echoes Melville's description of Billy Budd:

> It was plain to all – the handsome, charming youth, with his open manner, his boyish spirits, his words and looks of adoration, and his tall figure, and his exquisite hands, and the auburn hair on his head, that bent so gently down-wards, had fascinated Elizabeth. The new star, rising with extraordinary swift-ness, was suddenly seen to be shining alone in the firmament. She was fifty-three, and he was not yet twenty: a dangerous concatenation of ages. (p. 5)

Age's obsession with the innocence and redemptive potential of Youth preoccu-pied Strachey, who at this stage in his life was suffering from a debilitating sense of sterility and loss of creative confidence. This was a theme that Britten had already dramatised and which would find its most explicit expression in *Death in Venice*.

Holroyd proposes that Strachey's probing of Elizabeth's neuroses aggravated

31 Richard Capell, *The Daily Telegraph*, 13 June 1953.
32 Plomer to Britten, 8 May 1952 (BPL).
33 *Elizabeth and Essex* is a 'new biography' of the type described by Virginia Woolf, whose own novel *Orlando* is a similar blend of truth and fantasy. Strachey's text is a search for 'self' as much as an account of the historical 'facts' as Maynard Keynes observed: 'You seem, on the whole, to imagine yourself as Elizabeth, but I see from the pictures that it is Essex whom you have got up as yourself. I expect you managed to get the best of both worlds' (letter from Keynes to Strachey, 3 December 1928, quoted in Michael Holroyd, 'A Daring Experiment – An Introduction to *Elizabeth and Essex*', in *Peter Grimes and Gloriana: ENO Guide* (London: John Calder, 1983), p. 77).
34 Michael Holroyd, *Lytton Strachey: The New Biography* (New York: Farrar, Strauss and Giroux, 1994), p. 595.

his own nervous ailments. His health was adversely affected by his emotional instability and his struggle to finish his text, and he wrote to Senhouse, 19 April 1928: 'At the moment I am almost dead with exhaustion from this fearful tussle with the Old Hag.'[35] He identified with the psychosomatic nature of the illnesses suffered by both Elizabeth and Essex, which he had described: 'Early in February, Essex took to his bed. The Queen came to visit him; he seemed to recover after so signal an act of favour; and then once more was prostrate. The nature of his ailment was dubious: was he sulking or was he really ill? Perhaps he was both' (pp. 127–8). Significantly, Strachey implies that Elizabeth's emotional paranoia and hysterical ailments were rooted in the sexual imbalances in her constitution:

> Though her serious illnesses were few, a long succession of minor maladies, a host of morbid symptoms, held her contemporaries in alarmed suspense . . . Probably the solution of the riddle . . . was that most of her ailments were of hysterical origin. That iron structure was prey to nerves. The hazards and anxieties in which she passed her life would have been enough in themselves to shake the health of the most vigorous; but it so happened that, in Elizabeth's case, there was a special cause for a neurotic condition: her sexual organisation was seriously warped. (pp. 19–20)

Strachey's biography is notable for its emphasis on the sexual irregularities of his subjects and for the Freudian reading which he proposes as an explanation for Elizabeth's sexual neurosis:

> After making careful inquiries, Feria had come to the conclusion, he told King Philip, that Elizabeth would have no children . . . The crude story of a physical malformation may well have had its origin in a subtler, and yet no less vital, fact. In such matters the mind is as potent as the body. A deeply seated repugnance to the crucial act of intercourse may produce, when the possibility of it approaches, a condition of hysterical convulsion, accompanied, in certain cases, by intense pain. Everything points to the conclusion that such – the result of the profound psychological disturbances of her childhood – was the state of Elizabeth. (p. 24)

In *Gloriana*, Plomer hints at the connection between Elizabeth's physical and mental peculiarities in Essex's cry of outrage:

> *Her conditions are as crooked as her carcase!*

Holroyd probably exaggerates the extent of Strachey's identification with his character, implying that by living 'inside' Elizabeth, he emerged with some of her warped sexual characteristics. However, Strachey clearly empathised with the Queen's sexual anxieties and sought to express these in terms of the public-private tensions which shaped her personality and behaviour, and which he characterised as the 'male' and 'female' sides of her divided nature:

> She was a woman – ah, yes! a fascinating woman! – but then, was she not also a virgin, and old? But immediately another flood of feeling swept upwards and

---

[35] *Ibid.*

engulfed her; she towered; she was something more – she knew it; what was it? Was she a man? She gazed at the little beings around her, and smiled to think that, though she might be their Mistress in one sense, in another it could never be so – that the very reverse might almost be said to be the case. She had read of Hercules and Hylas, and she might have fancied herself, in some half-conscious day-dream, possessed of something of that pagan masculinity. (p. 28)

Similarly, Plomer and Britten juxtaposed these antagonistic elements, which culminate with the cry of the four conspirators in Act 2:

> *Oh see what comes of being ruled*
> *By a King in a farthingale.*

Likewise, the Queen's lines following the second lute song which has aroused her personal affection – 'I am a woman, Though I be a Queen, And still a woman, Though I be a Prince' – have a lyrical, 'feminine' quality which contrasts with the more 'masculine' style of the subsequent 'Soliloquy and Prayer' in which she accepts the burdens of state and acknowledges the human cost:

> *If life were love and love were true,*
> *Then I could love thee through and through!*
> *But God gave me a sceptre,*
> *The burden and the glory –*
> *I must not lay them down:*
> *I live and reign a virgin,*
> *Will die in honour*
> *Leave a refulgent crown!*
> *O God, my King, sole ruler of the world,*
> *That pulled me from a prison to a palace*
> *To be a sovereign Princess*
> *And to rule the people of England: . . .*
> *O maintain in this weak woman the heart of a man!*

Although the harmonic palette of *Gloriana* is more varied than in Britten's previous operas – bright 'ceremonial' keys (C, D, G and F major) characterise the 'public' scenes – key symbolism, and more particularly the localised juxtaposition of dissonant pitches, continues to have an important dramatic function. The oppressive burden of public responsibility is represented by the key area E♭–B♭–F,[36] while Elizabeth's creative spirit and private desires, united in her love for Essex, are symbolised by E–B–A,[37] thereby reproducing the harmonic dialectic

---

[36] See, for example, Raleigh's pompous aria which is underpinned by a series of B♭ pedals, and Cecil's 'Song of Government'.

[37] Significant examples of this identification include Essex's phrases (particularly the line 'Follower of a dream' after the second lute song, which is recited on a high E), and Penelope Rich's melody in the Act 2 conspirators' quartet which is similarly centred about E (Act 2, Fig. K): *Call on the stars above/ To give us one great hour/ And the force to shape our fate/ I with the power of love/ You with the love of power/ We can seize the reigns of state.* Interestingly, as their dreams are transformed into a determined intention to usurp the throne, the music modulates to E♭ (Act 2, Fig. N).

of Britten's preceding operas. For example, the Queen's first entry is harmonised in a secure E♭ major, and her melodic phrases decisively confirm this tonality. However, even at this early stage disruptive elements are present in the form of an invasive B♮ in the opening accompaniment gesture, and the tonally irregular C♭ which penetrates her vocal line and the choral refrain 'Rivals for a lady's favour'. This C♭ pitch (an enharmonic B♮) returns in a more explicitly sinister context in Act 3.

The public worship and iconographic idolatry of the Virgin Queen had clarified her function as a source of peace, harmony and creativity among her subjects. Strachey had described how Elizabeth exploited her 'feminine' indecisiveness in order to maintain a fragile peace, at home and abroad, in which the artistic inspiration of her subjects could flourish:

> A deep instinct made it impossible for her to come to a fixed determination upon any subject whatever . . . Only a woman could have shuffled so shamelessly, only a woman could have abandoned with such unscrupulous completeness the last shreds not only of consistency, but of dignity, honour, and common decency, in order to escape the appalling necessity of having, really and truly to make up her mind . . . A decision meant war . . . It was not that she was much disturbed by the cruelty of war – she was far from sentimental; she hated it for the best of all reasons – its wastefulness. Her thrift was spiritual as well as material, and the harvest that she gathered in was the Great Age, to which, though its supreme glories were achieved under her successor, her name was given. (pp. 11–14)

The opening scenes of the opera introduce the Queen as a deliverer of peace, as she effects a rapprochement between Essex and his rival, Mountjoy, in an 'Ensemble of Reconciliation'. Essex sings:

> *The wisdom of the Queen hath made us brothers.*

and the chorus of adulation – 'Thanks we now give to our great Queen . . . Long may she keep this realm/ From war and war's alarms' – initiates the first full statement of the hymn of praise [Example 20]:

> *Green leaves are we.*
> *Red rose our golden Queen,*
> *O crownèd rose among the leaves so green.*

All music in *Gloriana* essentially derives from the Queen's presence and these idolatrous phrases are echoed melodically and rhythmically throughout the score.[38] The bright major key, the falling sixths and rising sevenths, and the swaying freedom of the 5/4 rhythm evoke the motion of the bowing homage of the crowd. The harp which accompanies the first brief hint of this chorus (Act 1, Fig. M) looks forward to the lute accompaniment of Essex's songs which Gloriana similarly inspires.

---

[38] For example, see Essex's 'A favour now for every fool!' (Act 1, Fig. N), the accompaniment to the Queen's Act 1 entry, the phrase 'Good Frances do not weep' which occurs after Lady's Essex humiliation by the Queen, and the Act 3 'Prelude and Verdict'.

Example 20

Paradoxically, it is through her symbolic status as a Virgin Queen that Elizabeth's 'fertile' influence is most potently effective. Neale had recounted Elizabeth I's 1563 parliamentary speech in which she set out her intention to remain unmarried, and it is to this speech that Plomer's libretto alludes at the opening of the Norwich masque scene:

they may have a greater or wiser prince, but they shall never have a prince more loving.

Similarly in her first dialogue with Cecil, Elizabeth sings:

> *Hark, sir! This ring*
> *I had at my crowning:*
> *With it I wedded*
> *Myself to the realm.*
> *My comfort hath been*
> *That my people are happy.*

The melody of the final two lines traces the 'Green leaves' shape. However, at significant moments in this aria, the neutral G major tonality gives way to the relative minor, E minor, such as when Elizabeth declares 'Love's better than fear'. Similarly, Cecil's shallow words 'O Princess, whom your people love' are accompanied by sustained E major triads which seem to undermine the verbal message.

The Queen's private persona is revealed in her duets with Essex, most powerfully in the lute songs in Act 1. Essex's sudden entry in Act 1, Scene 2 shatters the harmonic and dramatic confidence of Cecil and Elizabeth who have resolved to 'watch and wait' on a unison E♭ (Act 1, Fig. K). The psychological instability which Essex's arrival initiates is musically represented by bitonal musical notation – while Elizabeth's music continues to be notated in Cecil's F major, Essex's lines are set in B major – a device which Britten had previously exploited for dramatic effect in *Peter Grimes* and *Billy Budd*. The optimism and exuberance of Essex's cry 'Queen of my life', which contrasts with the crest-fallen mood of the repetition of this phrase in Act 2 (Fig. G), quickly diverts Elizabeth from her cares. The C♭ and E♭ which conclude her melody and the bass accompaniment respectively are translated to B♮ and D♯, as the music modulates to E major for Essex's first lute song, 'Quick music is best'. However, Essex's lively, bright melody is dogged by a persistent and weighty pedal E♭ which subverts the superficial gaiety of the song. Essex struggles to escape from this oppressive burden, dragging his melody up a semitone for the second verse but the insistent pedal obstinately follows him, rising now to E.

Essex's self-revelation continues in the second lute song, 'Happy were he', a setting of a poem by the original Earl of Essex, Robert Devereux, which Strachey had included in his text [Example 21]:

> To be away from all this – and for ever! Away from the glory and the struggle – to be back at home, a boy again at Chartley – to escape irrevocably into the prolonged innocence of solitude and dreams! With a play upon his own name – half-smiling, half melancholy – he wrote some lines in which memory and premonition came together to give a strange pathos to the simple words –
>
> > *Happy were he could finish forth his fate*
> > *In some unhaunted desert, where, obscure*
> > *From all society, from love and hate*
> > *Of worldly folk, there should he sleep secure,*
> > *Then wake again, and yield God ever praise;*
> > *Content with hip, with haws, and brambleberry;*
> > *In contemplation, passing still his days,*
> > *And change of holy thought to keep him merry:*
> > *Who, when he dies, his tomb might be the bush*
> > *Where harmless Robin resteth with the thrush:*
> > *– Happy were he!* (p. 105)

Elizabeth has requested 'a dream, a mood, an air/ To spirit us both away'. Her inner tension is musically signified by the juxtaposition of harmonically unrelated chords in a progression which closes with two plagal cadences (E♭–B♭ followed by A–E). Indeed, after the rapid action of the opening scenes of the opera and the rhythmic vitality of the first lute song, the contemplative mood of Essex's 'Brambleberry Song' does seem to suspend time and translate the lovers to a 'far-off place' away from the 'cares of state'. It establishes an other-worldly mood of mystery which recalls the still unreality of Peter Grimes's 'Great Bear' aria. The free melodic expansiveness and rhythmic repose is never recapitulated in the opera, for the dream cannot be sustained – indeed, the inaccessibility of the dream world may in part account for its attractiveness. The C minor key signature of this song (the relative minor of E♭) exposes the deceptiveness of its sentiments, and the

6. Second Lute Song. ESSEX, later QUEEN ELIZABETH.

Example 21

subsequent duet for Elizabeth and Essex confirms that the progress of time cannot be halted, nor youth regained:

ELIZABETH: O heretofore	ESSEX: What solace more
Though ringed with foes,	Can I disclose?
I only bled with arrows of the spring.	Better than tears the faithfulness I
	bring,
My sense was only wounded by the rose	What my heart holds, only thy heart
	knows:
And I too then could sing:	And I too now can sing:
But years decline and go:	Are tears a sign to show
Video et taceo!	That we shall reap but as we sow?

These words of self-knowledge, which explicitly link creativity with love, are poignantly echoed in Act 3, Scene 1 where the strains of the lute song are heard once more as Essex, returning from Ireland, bursts in upon the half-dressed Queen:

QUEEN: Dear name I have loved,	ESSEX: Oh, put back the clock
Oh, use it no more!	To the birth of our hope!
The time and the name	The chime as it rang
Now belong to the past:	Told the hour when you gave
They belong to the young,	Of your grace, when I sang,
And the echoes are mute:	When my heart was the lute:
Happy were we!	Happy were we!

The uneasy balance which Gloriana maintains between her public and private selves is undermined when she is confronted with evidence of Essex's treachery. Her dilemma is similar to Vere's predicament in *Billy Budd*: should she pardon the seditious Essex to satisfy her own desires and risk undermining the fragile stability of her kingdom, or should she sacrifice him in the interests of social and political security? However, whereas Budd is essentially blameless, Essex is guilty of treason. Moreover, Vere is redeemed by Billy's loving forgiveness; in contrast, should Gloriana condemn Essex, then she will have only her public role to sustain her.

Just as Captain Vere's position as 'King' aboard *The Indomitable* bestows upon him the right to administer the 'law', so Elizabeth as Queen, or 'Prince', has the power to forgive or condemn. Strachey hints at the divine nature of her jurisprudence: 'Men felt, when they came near her, that they were in a superhuman presence. No reverence was too great for such a divinity' (p. 26). However, while Vere's status is never in doubt, Essex later challenges Elizabeth's position: ' "Doth God require it? Is it impiety not to do it? What, cannot princes err? Cannot subjects receive wrong? Is an earthly power or authority infinite? Pardon me, pardon me, my good Lord, I can never subscribe to these principles" ' (p. 177).

In *Billy Budd* Britten had eliminated Melville's account of Vere's self-interrogation when called upon to judge Billy. Britten's Vere remains silent and he accepts the judgement of his officers. In contrast, *Gloriana* reproduces the deliberations and hesitations which Strachey had described:

To abolish, in a moment, the immediate miserable past – to be reconciled once more; to regain, with a new rapture, the old happiness – what was there to prevent? Nothing, surely; she had the power for such an act; she could assert her will – extend her royal pardon; after a short eclipse, he would be with her again; not a voice would be raised against; . . . and so would not all be well? It was indeed a heavenly vision, and she allowed herself to float deliciously down the stream of her desires. But not for long. She could not dwell indefinitely among imaginations; . . . She saw plainly that she could never trust him. And yet, after all, might she not take the risk? (pp. 256–6)

Britten musically dramatises her search for a solution in a series of scenes in which subtle dissonant harmonic relationships symbolise her anguish and doubt.

Her hesitations contrast with the unequivocal declamations of her councillors in Act 3, Scene 3, the 'Prelude and Verdict', which is harmonised in a 'governmental' E♭ major:

> COUNCILLORS: *Essex is guilty and condemned to die! . . .*
> CECIL: *She may delay once more,*
> *And spare his life.*
> RALEIGH AND COUNCILLORS: *Never! Essex can she not forgive!*
> ALL: *Essex is guilty and condemned to die!*
> QUEEN: *Let me hear the verdict.*
> *Are you all agreed?*
> CECIL: *May it please you Majesty,*
> *The verdict was unanimous.*
> RALEIGH: *After trial the court has found*
> *The Earl of Essex guilty of treason.*
> COUNCILLORS: *Guilty of treason and condemned to die! . . .*
> RALEIGH: *(proffering the death warrant) Only awaits your royal hand*
> *To ratify his doom.*
> QUEEN: *I will not sign it now!*
> *I will consider it!*

Cecil warns of the dangers of the Queen's evasion of the responsibilities of her office and her actual entry (Act 3, Fig. C) appears to vindicate his fears. Her appearance is anticipated by a subtle twist from E♭ to E♮ in the choral confirmation of Essex's condemnation, and is characterised by a violent dissonance between a G major woodwind triad (incorporating B♮) and a bass B♭ which lingers and begins to undermine Gloriana's resolve. However, at this point she remains defiant, resisting the power of the unison instrumental B♭ which accompanies her refusal to sign the warrant.

Cecil's anxiety is indicated in the following number, 'Cecil's Warning'. He slyly attempts to influence Elizabeth by situating his appeal in her own key at this point, G major, but his cunning is disclosed by the abrasive repeated B♭ pizzicato chords which punctuate the aria, and which act as a subtle but constant reminder of her public duties. The rising dramatic and harmonic tension ignites Elizabeth's anger and she dismisses her Council. As Cecil and Raleigh exit the dissonances intensify, the semitonal conflation of B♭ and B♮ expanding to incorporate the enharmonically related pitches A♯ and C♭, which are continually reinterpreted as

Gloriana subjects herself to profound psychological self-scrutiny in 'The Queen's Dilemma' [Example 22].

In this scene, the bass A♯ challenges the alien B♭'s which colour Elizabeth's vocal line, a juxtaposition which musically embodies her inner divisions:

> *I grieve, yet dare not show my discontent;*
> *I love, and yet am forced to seem to hate;*
> *I am, and am not; freeze, and yet I burn;*
> *Since from my other self I turn.*

The first libretto draft for this number had emphasised Elizabeth's sense of culpability:

> *While Robin lives, I cannot live.*
> *He tried to be too great.*
> *I am in part to blame:*
> *I let him be too great.*
> *Happy were we!* [39]

The dissonance is reversed in the following scenes: as Mountjoy, Lady Essex and Penelope Rich enter to plead for leniency for Essex, the timpani A♯ which closes the 'Queen's Dilemma' reverts to B♭, and this pitch consistently disturbs the A minor/major entreaties of the former conspirators. (The tonality is a reference to their tender scenes in Act 2). The softness and gentle flexibility of Lady Essex's A major implorings are abruptly curtailed by the timpani's intrusive B♭ at the Queen's recitative-like rejoinder:

> *Harken, it is a Prince who speaks.*
> *A Prince set upon a stage*
> *Alone, in the sight of all the world;*
> *Alone, and must not fail.*

Elizabeth, affected by the purity and sincerity of Lady Essex's love for her husband and children, empathises with her femininity and adopts her A-based tonality as she sings, 'Frances, a woman speaks . . . Your children, Frances, will be safe'. However, these motions towards forgiveness are swept aside with the majestic entry of Lady Rich.

The F♯ major key signature of 'Lady Rich's Pleading' might suggest that Elizabeth has freed herself from the fetters of state. However, disharmony is not expunged – B♭ changes once more to A♯ which, in the form of a tense semitonal rocking motif, underscores the Queen's increasingly agitated interjections. As Penelope's melody recalls the 'Queen's Dilemma' (Act 3, Fig. M) the significance of the key signature becomes apparent: Elizabeth's dialogue with Lady Rich is merely an extension of her former self-questioning. The voice which now harasses her is the voice of her 'other self'. The climax is reached with Lady Rich's appeal to the Queen's 'Love', declaimed on a piercing, high B♭ which rises to B♮ with the words, 'God forgive you' (sung to a falling fifth motif, B–E). Such an appeal is

[39] GB–ALb 2–9200295.

Example 22

intolerable to Elizabeth as it reminds her of the love which she has rejected and betrayed, and immediately she declares that she will sign the death warrant. As the Epilogue commences Lady Rich's screeching glissando descent from a top C reminds us of the apprentice's deathly scream in *Peter Grimes* – by sanctioning Essex's death the Queen has destroyed her youthful, innocent 'other self'.

In the matter of Essex's trial and judgment, Strachey's text echoes the ethical confusion present in *Billy Budd*: 'In the present case there was no doubt whatever of the technical guilt of the accused . . . The real question at issue – the precise nature of the Earl's motives – was indeed a complicated and obscure one' (pp. 245–8). An interesting paradox is evident: Billy, who is essentially 'innocent', is condemned by Vere without hesitation, whereas the fate of Essex, whose seditious intentions undoubtedly threaten both Elizabeth's personal safety and the stability of her realm, is held in the balance until the last possible moment. This is partly a result of the insubstantiality of the operatic Essex's psychological portrait and dramatic role. Strachey had portrayed a powerful personality: 'His mind was made up of extremes, and his temper was devoid of balance. He rushed from opposite to opposite; he allowed the strangest contradictions to take root together, and grow up side by side, in his heart. He loved and hated – he was a devoted servant and an angry rebel – all at once' (p. 248). However, in the opera Essex's rebellious and loving impulses are both diminished, and his dramatic potential as either a traitor or lover is not fully explored. Whereas Strachey provides copious details of the rebellious winds which gather force during Essex's incarceration (recalling the potential mutiny among the crew of *The Indomitable* in *Billy Budd* following the condemnation and hanging of Billy), Britten only briefly alludes to this at the opening of Act 3. Similarly, the consummate expression of his love – the second lute song – is affecting and sincere at its original rendition, but is insufficient to establish the existence of a genuine love between Essex and Elizabeth.

In *Gloriana* there is no song of salvation to match 'Billy in the Darbies' and Essex is not permitted a vision of the 'far-shining sail'. Indeed, in *Elizabeth and Essex* his final moments are characterised by a violence and despair which contrast radically with Billy's spiritual repose:

> During the ordeal of the trial Essex had been bold, dignified, and self-possessed; but now, back in the Tower, he was seized by a violent revulsion; anguish and horror overpowered his mind. A puritan clergyman, who had been sent to minister to him, took the opportunity to agitate his conscience and fill his imagination with the fear of hell. He completely collapsed. Self-reliance – self-respect – were swept away in a flood of bitter lamentations. (p. 253)

Consequently, Essex's death cannot 'save' Elizabeth. Indeed, at this stage in the opera he has practically 'disappeared' from the drama and the fragmented restatements of his lute song by the Queen in her dying moments affirm the impression that the Essex she is recalling is not a 'real' character at all but merely a symbol of Elizabeth's frustrated and repressed 'other life'. Thus his actual fate matters less than her own psychological balance; she objects not only to his weaknesses and treachery but because he arouses the desire which she covets but mistrusts, which she has repressed and now regrets is lost:

> Was the whole history of their relations, then, one long infamous deception? Was it all bitterness and blindness? Had he perhaps truly loved her once? – Once! But the past was over, and time was inexorable. Every moment widened the desperate abyss between them. Such dreams were utter folly. She preferred not to look in her looking-glass – why should she? There was no need; she was very well aware without that of what had happened to her. She was a miserable old woman of sixty-seven. She recognised the truth – the whole truth – at last. (p. 257)

Elizabeth's insistence upon her public duty is a displacement of her psychological stress, and it is her guilty '*self*', as opposed to the guilty *Essex* that she wishes to destroy. By signing the death warrant, she suppresses this 'other self' but, in contrast to Vere, Elizabeth cannot entirely eliminate her sense of self-betrayal. This is powerfully dramatised in the final moments of the opera. Plomer had originally intended to conclude the opera with the climactic signing of the death warrant and it was Britten who suggested a slow fade-out, with a spotlight on the Queen, suggestive of her death:

> I've had a big idea about the end of the opera, which I'll hint at, only, now. After the great discussion, & the deputations about Essex's execution, & the signing of the Warrant – could we make a quite unrealistic slow fade out of the Queen? Like this. Signing of warrent [sic]. Take lights down except for a spot on Elizabeth. Then, so as to suggest her mind is on Essex, play an orchestral version of the 'Bramblebury' [sic] song, while people come & hand her documents to sign, consult her on matters – to which she replies automatically or not at all. Then finally, perhaps one might suggest she's dying; some doctor tells her to go to bed – she won't, but continues to stand there gauntly, like some majestic fowl, & slow fade of all lights to show the end. Could you think about this?[40]

The use of spoken text in this scene was criticised: 'just as the music was at last taking charge of things and building up to a magnificent climax, we were suddenly brought down to earth with a bump by a spate of spoken words.'[41] However, the silencing of the melodic discourse at this point – in a manner reminiscent of Balstrode's spoken words at the conclusion of *Peter Grimes* – is dramatically appropriate since it realistically represents Gloriana's declining physical state, symbolises her creative sterility and signals her admission of defeat. The instrumental quotations of fragments of lute song (and the E major harmony) undermine the sentiments of her words:

> *I count it the glory of my crown that I have reigned with your love, and there is no jewel that I prefer before that jewel. Neither do I desire to live longer than that I may see your prosperity; and that's my desire.*

The song's gentle phrases are bizarrely distorted and extended, and the unstable and protracted delivery of its melodic and harmonic strains indicates the transformation of this initially whimsical 'conceit', or 'melting song', into a bleak vision of truth or death. There is no betrayal of youth or corruption of innocence, and no sacrificial seraph at hand to illuminate the path to salvation. Without Essex's love to sustain her Elizabeth cannot, in contrast to Vere, don the mask of office once more. Her psyche fractures, her public persona detaching from her emotional and creative self, and death seems inevitable.

The dissolution of the musical and verbal discourse in the closing bars of

---

40 Britten to Plomer, 24 July 1952 (BPL). Plomer replied: 'I like <u>very much</u> your suggestions about the final scene' (Plomer to Britten, 2 August 1952 (BPL)).
41 Stanley Bayliss, 'Not a Great Britten', *Daily Mail*, 10 June 1953. It was also considered that the inclusion of a series of unidentified figures at this stage was confusing for the audience, and irrelevant to the psychological denouement, and for the 1966 Sadlers Wells revival Britten removed these ghostly apparitions.

Gloriana recalls the fragmented delusions of Peter Grimes's mad soliloquy, and implies a heightened state of self-awareness. The self-knowledge which Elizabeth and Essex have achieved has led them, like Grimes, to silence and solitude, as Strachey had described: 'Essex made no appeal. Of what use would be a cry for mercy? Elizabeth would listen to nothing, if she was deaf to her own heart. The end came in silence: and at last he understood' (p. 260), 'So it had come to this! It was all too clear – her inordinate triumph had only brought her to solitude and ruin. She sat alone, amid emptiness and ashes, bereft of the one thing in the world that was worth having. And she herself, with her own hand, had cast it from her, had destroyed it' (p. 276).

Both Peter Grimes and Elizabeth ultimately concede to the forces of conformity and the price they pay for this submission is silence. Denied the fulfilment of their 'visionary' aspirations, they are also deprived of the creative voice through which they can communicate this vision. In contrast to *Billy Budd*, the conclusion of *Gloriana* is pessimistic – as Strachey had implied, there can be no creative transcendence for Elizabeth 'could not dwell indefinitely among imaginations'. She cannot escape to 'some unhaunted desert', a 'greenwood' or a 'land where she'll anchor for ever'. In her dying moments, Elizabeth accepts the only love available to her – the love of her subjects – and she has only the muted echoes of their public hymn of praise to console her.

Britten appears to have identified with the sexually and emotionally unfulfilled Queen; only in Act 3, as the drama is focused entirely in the mind of Elizabeth, does his music lyrically expand and intensify. However, in the final bars, with no Pears to sing for him, Britten's music degenerates into silence. Furthermore, the opera contains warnings of the danger of even momentarily allowing the mask of respectability to slip. Gloriana's grotesque appearance in Lady's Essex's ill-fitting dress exposes her to public humiliation and ridicule: this was the potential consequence of submitting to one's desires.

Lord Harewood has proposed that *Gloriana* marked a crisis point in Britten's career. Indeed, it might be suggested that the inner demons which have destroyed Elizabeth, and which Vere faced and defeated, symbolise the choices which every 'artist', including Britten, must make:

> I have little doubt that the initial public and critical failure of *Gloriana* was a turning-point for Ben. It shut him in on himself and he became even more private. He had made a great public gesture and the public had, so to speak, rejected him. He had risked writing for other than 'his' audience . . . he was determined not to take that kind of risk in future . . . Every creative artist who goes before the public takes something private with him, something vulnerable that can be crushed and wounded, only with Ben it turned out sometimes to have been too private to risk.[42]

---

[42] Harewood, *The Tongs and the Bones*, p. 148.

9

The Turn of the Screw

There is ... no eligible absolute of the wrong; it remains relative to fifty other elements, a matter of appreciation, speculation, imagination – these things moreover quite exactly in the light of the spectator's, the critic's, the reader's experience. Only make the reader's general vision of evil intense enough, I said to myself – and that is already a charming job – and his own experience, his own imagination, his own sympathy ... will supply him quite sufficiently with all the particulars. Make him think the evil, make him think it for himself, and you are released from weak specifications.

Henry James, 'Preface' to *The Turn of the Screw*[1]

MILES: *'You see – I am bad. I am bad, aren't I?'*
Act 1, Scene 8, Myfanwy Piper, *The Turn of the Screw*

There is a silence at the centre of Henry James's *The Turn of the Screw* which stubbornly refuses to be filled. Each twist of the plot drags the reader deeper into the narrative maze and moral quagmire. Each step and detail tantalises with the promise of explanation and resolution, yet each turn of the screw is not a movement towards 'meaning' but a further evasion of definition. The reader reaches the end of the narrative frustrated and exhausted by the ethical battle within: the promised revelation is never supplied and the text retains its secrets.

James's silence may be the silence which is 'everything', an infinite panorama of all possibilities. Alternatively, it may represent the 'unknowable'. Throughout the novella knowledge is assumed but unarticulated, and Douglas, the narrator of James's Prologue, warns: ' "The story won't tell," said Douglas; "not in any literal, vulgar way".'[2]

The text abounds with unread, unsent and diverted letters, self-referential symbols in a novella which is itself an untitled 'letter' whose story has been kept secret for twenty years.[3] For example, the Governess confronts Miles about the theft of her letter to his guardian:

1 Henry James, 'Preface to *The Aspern Papers; The Turn of the Screw; The Liar; The Two Faces*' in *The Art of the Novel* (London: Scribner's, 1934), pp. 169–77.
2 Henry James, *The Turn of the Screw and the Aspern Papers* (Hertfordshire: Wordsworth Editions, 1993), p. 6. All subsequent references are to this edition and are given in parentheses in the text.
3 See Shoshana Felman, 'Turning the Screw of Interpretation', in *Literature and Psycholanalysis: The Question of Reading Otherwise* (Baltimore: John Hopkins University

'You opened the letter?'
'I opened it.'
'And you found nothing!' (p. 124)

In his 'Preface', James suggests that his silence is an emptiness, a 'nothingness', and that his novella is merely a *jeu d'esprit* in which he manipulates the reader's literary and moral sensibilities. It is: 'a piece of ingenuity pure and simple, of cold artistic calculation, an *amusette* to catch those not easily caught . . . There is not only from beginning to end of the matter not an inch of expatiation, but my values are all positively blank.'

If James intended *The Turn of the Screw* to be a 'trap', then it is one which generations of critics have fallen into. Since its original publication, in serialised form in the American journal *Collier's Weekly* in 1898, James's story of the corruption of two 'innocents' by unspecified forces of 'evil' has generated an extraordinary amount of critical literature and been at the centre of a relentless, and continuing, sometimes acrimonious debate. The four main issues of contention are the 'reality' of the ghosts, the reliability of the Governess, the integrity of the children's innocence and the exact nature of their contamination by the ghosts, Peter Quint and Miss Jessel. The opposing critical factions can broadly be described as the 'literalists', who include Leon Edel, Allen Tate and Robert Heilman, and the 'Freudians', led by Edmund Wilson. Wilson's 1952 article 'The Ambiguity in Henry James',[4] in which he suggests that James's Governess is a classic psycho-neurotic Freudian case study, provoked a fierce reaction from opposing critics and initiated the on-going battle between 'scientific' and 'imaginative' readings of the narrative.

It was this complex and problematic text which Britten selected to be the subject of his sixth opera. He may have been aware of the contemporary controversy surrounding the text since he originally intended to call the opera *The Tower and The Lake*, a title loaded with Freudian overtones. Superficially, it is easy to imagine why James's novella attracted him. Its ingredients include a pair of 'innocent' and uninitiated children of the apprentice-Lucretia-Albert-Budd type, who are threatened and apparently destroyed by corruptive forces represented by two ghosts, Peter Quint and Miss Jessel, of the Grimes-Tarquinius-Claggart model. Refereeing this battle between good and evil is the Governess who, like Vere and Gloriana, occupies a morally ambiguous middle ground between the forces of purity and depravity. She is tormented by self-doubt, suspicious of her own motives and fearful of her own culpability in the ensuing tragedy.

It was surely this absence of moral absolutes which most strongly appealed to Britten. James had provided him with a pre-established unstable ethical field, where both the questions and the answers were shrouded in mists of uncertainty. James's literary evasions might set a precedent for, or even justify, the elusiveness

Press, 1982) pp. 94–207, for an examination of the silences in James's text, focusing on the symbol of the unread letter and the ambiguous association of 'seeing' and 'knowing'.

4   Edmund Wilson, 'The Ambiguity in Henry James', in *The Triple Thinkers* (Harmondsworth: Penguin, 1962), pp. 102–50.

of Britten's own dramatic and musical meaning. Furthermore, the emptiness at the core of the novella might have seemed to positively invite theatrical and musical fulfilment, since gesture, voice, melody and harmony might proffer explanation without destroying the indefinition upon which the text's emotional power relies. Indeed, Britten does 'fill' some of the gaps in James's text: for example, his decision that the ghosts should sing (which they surely must if they are to be musically and dramatically effective) inevitably makes them more 'real'. However, elsewhere the music increases James's ambiguity: by assigning two roles to one singer, or by the use of motivic and melodic association, Britten's score intensifies our actual experience of a psychological instability which James could only suggest.

James's silence may also have seemed to Britten to be a literary equivalent of the private, inner space to which he longed to withdraw after the disastrous public reception of *Gloriana* in the previous year. The critics' sadistic delight at the relative failure of this opera led Peter Pears to urge Britten to abandon the public arena and the 'grand opera' format, and to retreat to the 'safe-haven' of Aldeburgh. In Act 1, Scene 2, 'The Welcome', the Governess sings 'Bly, I begin to love you . . . For Bly is now my home', and later, 'I too am home. Alone, tranquil and serene.'

She mistakenly believes that Bly is a haven where she will be protected from life's dangers. Her words recall Peter Grimes's desire to 'buy us a home', a phrase echoed by Ellen when she tells the apprentice 'Peter will take you home.' The Borough's outrage – 'Home? Do you call that a home?' – anticipates Grimes's own disillusionment in the final scene, when he realises, 'What is home? Calm as deep water. Where's my home? Deep as calm water . . . ' Perhaps for Britten, home or 'calm water' was to be found away from prying eyes in a quiet refuge on the Suffolk coast.

Britten had first became acquainted with Henry James's *The Turn of the Screw* in 1932. He noted in his diary, 1 June: 'Also listen to wireless . . . – a wonderful, impressive but terribly eerie & scary play "The Turn of the Screw" by Henry James.'[5] In January 1933 he read the novella for himself and the seeds were sown for an opera which would come to fruition twenty years later. It appears that initially a film version of the opera was considered. Eric Crozier told Humphrey Carpenter that following the successful production of *Peter Grimes*, Gabriel Pascal, the film producer, had approached Britten with the idea of making an opera film, and that Britten now resurrected this idea as a useful way of raising funds for the English Opera Group: 'We hadn't got any particular subject at that time. It was simply that we felt we could get support from Michael Bacon [a film producer], who was interested in us.'[6]

According to Myfanwy Piper, it was she who was responsible for proposing James's text as a suitable subject. After witnessing the 1952 English Opera Group

5   LL, vol. 1, p. 254.
6   HC, p. 331.

film of *The Tales of Hoffmann*, which she disliked: 'I remember meeting Peter in the foyer and saying "If Ben's got to do a film, why doesn't he look at *The Turn of the Screw*?" And because we were all busy, no more was said. And then some time later Ben was casting about for something to do, and Peter said he'd just reread *The Turn of the Screw*, and he remembered that I'd suggested it.'[7] Piper may be over-estimating the extent of her influence; her enthusiasm, and that of Pears, may merely have reignited Britten's former interest in James's novella. Clearly James's work kept resurfacing during discussions, and in 1953 Basil Douglas, once a flatmate of Pears and now the English Opera Group Manager, travelled to Venice to negotiate a commission for an opera to be performed at the Biennale Festival. Upon his return preliminary work on *The Turn of the Screw* was begun but progress was interrupted, much to the annoyance of the English Opera Group and Pears, by the composition of *Gloriana*.

Following the completion and performance of Britten's coronation opera work resumed on the libretto of *The Turn of the Screw*. Despite his apparent satisfaction with his previous librettist, William Plomer, Britten did not ask him to write the text for his new work but turned instead to the inexperienced Myfanwy Piper.[8] The partnership began informally: 'Ben said to me: "Would you try to think of a way it [*The Turn of the Screw*] might be done and then we might get someone in to write it." . . . So I worked out a possible way, and then we began to work on it together, and there seemed no reason to ask anyone else.'[9] The Pipers had been close friends of Britten and Pears for some time: John Piper had designed the scenery and costumes for each of Britten's operas since *Lucretias* and *Herrings* had observed the composition and rehearsal of these works at close hand. She told Carpenter:

> I think he turned to me because, with the Lucretias and Herrings and the various things which John and I had been through with Ben, he often talked to us about the words. He'd say 'What am I to do here?' I don't like this', and I was very much aware of the kind of things he didn't like. So although I hadn't got any qualifications for writing a libretto, it didn't disturb me . . . [he was] very easy to work with, because he knew what he wanted – he was quite definite.[10]

---

7   *Ibid.* When Carpenter asked Piper why she thought James's story might interest Britten, she
    replied: 'I knew he was interested in the effect of adult, or bad, ideas on the innocence of chil-
    dren. I also thought it was densely musical prose which would suit his work' (p. 337).
8   Perhaps Plomer was reluctant to expose himself to further critical onslaughts of the kind
    which had followed *Gloriana*. Moreover, he professed to dislike Henry James. However, he
    did monitor the progress of the opera, writing to Britten, 1 December 1953: 'I feel immense
    curiosity . . . about the way *The Turn of the Screw* is shaping . . . I have written a word or two
    to Myfanwy partly because she said she wanted to know what I thought & partly in the hope
    of drawing her attention to the task that ought to be, it seems, more in hand than it is' (BPL).
    Britten did continue his partnership with Plomer, the latter introducing Britten to Japanese
    Nō drama, which he witnessed while travelling in the Far East, and writing the librettos for
    Britten's three church parables which were modelled on this form.
9   HC, p. 332.
10 *Ibid.*

Britten evidently sought to dispel any doubts Piper may have had, for she wrote to him: 'And thank you for being so encouraging about the Screw. I feel very much more confident than I did a few weeks ago.'[11] However, some practical obstacles did arise since Piper found that her family commitments (she had four small children) made sustained work on the libretto difficult. Discussions deemed necessary were conducted by post but Britten appears to have been satisfied with these arrangements in the early stages: 'So far there are not many alterations in the words to suggest – nothing that cannot be done by writing. The best plan seems to be for me to go on working and writing the suggestions of changes daily (or telephoning if they are urgent) and when it seems to need your actual presence I will write to you suggesting it and hope you may be able to fit it in.'[12] In fact, the enforced distance between composer and librettist may have been partially liberating for, as the drafts of the libretto reveal, Britten was able to make alterations and additions to the text as he desired, changes which Piper was happy to allow.

Another potentially more serious problem also surfaced at this time: the debilitating pain in Britten's right shoulder, which had troubled him for some time, now recurred. Bursitis was diagnosed and complete rest ordered. Carpenter notes that although Britten was able to write with his left arm he showed no inclination to begin composition of the score, and concludes from this that Britten's physical illness provided a welcome excuse to delay a confrontation with James's complex moral issues. One might go further and suggest that the bursitis, or at least the degree to which it affected Britten's creative energies, was reminiscent of one of Gloriana's hysterical ailments, to which she willingly submitted in order to avoid her internal conflicts. Carpenter further observes that it was at this time that the Home Secretary, Sir David Maxwell-Fyfe, initiated a police investigation into homosexual activity in Britain which resulted in the arrest, prosecution and imprisonment of a number of prominent public figures.[13] Britten was himself interviewed and although no action was taken against him it is possible that this public scrutiny of his private life aggravated his persecution complex and contributed to his reluctance to undertake a musical expression of a text which was laden with sexual, homosexual and pederastic undertones. Whatever the reasons for the delay, Britten did not begin composition until 30 March 1954, when the premiere was just five months away.

The formal structure of *The Turn of the Screw* – a cinematic sequence of sixteen short scenes separated by instrumental interludes – articulates the passing of time which is conveyed in the novella by 'gaps' in the narrative. The stage play, *The Innocents*, which Piper saw after beginning the libretto, had confined the action to a single day, a compression she disliked: 'The innocents took elements out of the story & rewrote and telescoped other elements in order to compress the action and the scene into one place and one time. By doing it they entirely lost the

---

[11] Piper to Britten, 4 November 1952 (BPL).
[12] Britten to Piper, March 1953, quoted in DH, p. 10.
[13] See HC, pp. 333–5.

pervasive atmosphere which is the whole point.'[14] James's 'gaps' are filled in the opera by a series of orchestral variations on the 'screw theme' which is presented after the Prologue. The open-ended variation form – ever-changing permutations which increase in intensity through repetition and elaboration – musically embodies the turns of the dramatic screw. A small amount of material generates the melodic, harmonic and rhythmic fabric of the opera, matching James's atmosphere of single-minded obsession. The fact of the 'idea' at the centre of the text is the only 'constant', since the expression of this idea is unstable and equivocal. Similarly, the transformations of the 'screw theme' are always identifiable but never identical.[15]

The 'screw theme' is formed from the twelve pitches of the chromatic scale [Example 23]. Analysis has focused on Britten's use of melodic serialism, but the significance of the theme lies not in its twelve-tone features but in its melodic character and shape (although the use of twelve equal pitches is appropriate as it suggests both a liberating freedom from conventional tonal rules and, as the twelve pitches accumulate in the 'Theme', the destructive freedom which results when total dissonance erupts into unfocused anarchy). The pitches are arranged to imply a cycle of fifths, a traditional method of harmonic organisation which always ends where it has begun. The fifth interval is itself an important melodic motif which persistently infiltrates orchestral and vocal lines, and which is specifically identified with the questions 'What is it?', 'Who is it?' In this way, the melodic fifth, or inverted fourth, is associated with unanswered questions and undisclosed knowledge.

Furthermore, the harmonic structure of the 'screw theme' elucidates the large-scale tonal plan of the opera. When the twelve pitches are arranged scalically the first six notes imply A major (the Governess's tonal area), while the last six suggest a pentatonic hexachord on A♭ (Quint's harmonic colour), the two areas being linked by the enharmonically shared pitch G♯/A♭. Starting from the Governess's A-based tonality in Act 1, Scene 1, the opera progresses methodically through her pitches, each harmonic step representing her increasing self-knowledge. By the conclusion of Act 1, she comprehends the challenge which faces her, and the Act closes in A♭. Act 2 reverses this modulation, beginning in an emphatic A♭, and descending through a series of 'black note' keys, reaching A in the final scene. Any implication of dramatic 'resolution' afforded by this harmonic destination is undermined by the events which we have witnessed. The harmonic structure is supported melodically by the restatements of the 'screw theme' in its original form: after the initial presentation of the theme in A, as the Governess travels to Bly, the theme reappears at the end of Act 1 (Fig. 87) in A♭, when both Quint and the Governess beckon to Miles. Quint's ascendancy at this point is reaffirmed at

---

14 Piper's 'Notebook' (BPL).

15 Britten's musical variations mimic the literary search for resolution. Furthermore, it could be suggested that the 'search' in *The Turn of the Screw* is a microcosm of Britten's long-term search for artistic and personal truth, which he articulated musically and dramatically in his operas. In this way, each successive opera is a further twist of the expressive screw.

Example 23

the opening of Act 2 (Fig. 20), when the theme is repeated in A♭ during the ghosts' 'Colloquy'. The final statement unfolds gradually in the last scene (Act 2, Fig. 121).

One of the first problems which Britten and Piper had to confront was the issue of the 'reality' of the ghosts. Henry James's fascination with the supernatural was not surprising given his family's interest in spiritualism. His brother, William James, was an active psychical researcher and member of the *Society for Psychical Research*, the reports of which appear to have provided James with the framework and some of the details of his tale. However, this family obsession with the occult need not mean that James intended his ghostly apparitions to be objective presences, and Freudian interpreters can draw upon the evidence that William James was also an influential psychologist, while their sister, Alice, suffered from depression and neurosis of the kind they ascribe to James's Governess.

Those seeking the answer in James's 'Preface' to the 1908 New York edition will be disappointed. James writes:

Recorded and attested ghosts are in other words as little expressive, as little dramatic, above all, as little continuous and conscious and responsive, as is consistent with their taking the trouble ... to appear at all ... I had to decide ...

between having my apparitions correct and having my story 'good' – that is producing the impression of the dreadful, my designed horror . . . They would be agents in fact; there would be laid on them the dire duty of causing the situation to reek with the air of Evil . . .

That is to say, I recognise again, that Peter Quint and Miss Jessel are not 'ghosts' at all, as we now know the ghost, but goblins, elves, imps, demons as loosely constructed as those of the old trials for witchcraft.[16]

He seems to be have been less concerned with the ghosts' 'actuality' than with the extent and nature of the evil evoked by their potential presence:

The essence of the matter was the villainy of motive in the evoked predatory creatures . . . Portentous evil – how was I to save that, as an intention on the part of my demon-spirits, from the drop, the comparative vulgarity, inevitably attending, throughout the whole range of possible brief illustration, the offered example, the imputed vice, the cited act, the limited deplorable presentable instance? . . . If my bad things, for *The Turn of the Screw*, I felt, should succumb to this danger, if they shouldn't seem sufficiently bad, there would be nothing for me but to hang my artistic head lower than I had ever known occasion to do.

Britten apparently made an early decision that the ghosts did exist. Lord Harewood remembers: 'Ben and I argued about the haunting; had it to be explicit, or could it be the product of the governess's paranoia – she was convinced that something was wrong, but was it really? I insisted on ambivalence, he on the need for the composer to make a decision – and he had taken one: that the haunting was real.'[17] In fact Britten went beyond an insistence that the ghosts were real and 'was determined that they should sing – and sing words (no nice anonymous, supernatural humming or groaning'.[18] His decision was made partly in response to dramatic and theatrical considerations. If the operatic ghosts were to have an effective stage relationship with each other and with the children, then musical communication between them was essential. However, there was also an expressive dimension to this issue. In some ways, Quint's relationship with Miles seems to take over where Peter Grimes's relationship with the apprentice boy had left off: Quint's voice, which beckons to Miles from an unexplained and shadowy world characterised by liberation and fulfilment, is like the voice of Grimes calling from the depths of the ocean where he has finally found freedom from the oppressive restrictions of the Borough.[19] The two parts were designed for the same singer, and through Peter Pears they become one voice, a voice which sings a song of promise, possibility and potentiality which we might define as 'love'. If Quint's song carries more ominous resonances, we might hear these as the echo of Claggart's tortured soul, as he too was banished to a dark, underwater wilderness but one which was not illuminated by the light of the imagination.

16 James, 'Preface', in *The Art of the Novel*, pp. 169–77.
17 HC, p. 338.
18 Myfanwy Piper, 'Writing for Britten', DH, p. 9.
19 This identification between the two characters is intensified by John Piper's sketches for Quint, which closely resemble photographs of Pears playing the part of Grimes.

Excluding the Prologue, Quint's presence is first intimated musically in Interlude 3 which precedes the 'Tower' scene where he appears before the Governess. The free-flowing flute arabesques suggest his unfettered spirit and imaginative creativity. Significantly, when the clarinet joins the flute (Act 1, Fig. 20) these flourishes repeatedly cadence with a falling fifth, B♭–E♭, a motif which later shapes the Governess's distraught cries 'They are lost! lost! lost! lost!' (Fig. 70), her melody characterised by falling glissandi and the accompaniment coloured by Quint's celeste and gong timbre.

It is in Scene 8, 'At Night', that Quint's voice is finally heard [Example 24]. The preceding interlude confirms his musical persona, which is characterised by unrestrained melodic ornamentation, upward-sweeping expansive arpeggios, pentatonic 'black note' harmony, and exotic orchestral colours which exploit the expressive timbres of the harp and percussion instruments. However, it is the celeste that heralds his song in Scene 8 which is established as *his* instrument. There is only one previous instance of Britten using the celeste operatically – it had accompanied the apprentice's fatal cliff fall in *Peter Grimes*. Britten overturns the conventional 'heavenly' connotations of the instrument, and identifies its ethereal tones with the idea of a 'fall', perhaps a 'sexual fall'. His inversion of the natural musical order may be ironic yet thereby Britten is also able to intimate that the impulses which motivate 'corrupters' such as Grimes and Quint may be of pure or spiritual origin. There is no denying the beauty and seductiveness of Quint's melodies, and Britten may be implying that 'love' is essentially good even if society decrees that paedophilia is not.

Quint's nocturnal appeal to Miles was inspired by Peter Pears's performance of an unaccompanied twelfth-century motet by Perotin, *Beata Viscera*, in a Suffolk church. The scene is one of unearthly beauty and mysterious seductive power, in which the Governess's frantic activity in the preceding scenes is halted by this moment of timeless reflection. All of Quint's entries begin with or centre about the pitch E♭, a feature which Miles, and later Flora, imitate when they respond to Quint's call – 'Secrets, O secrets!' (Fig. 77), 'I'm here, O I'm here' (Figs. 73 and 80). (Quint's Act 2 aria 'I seek a friend' (Fig. 16) also contains much recitation on E♭). The chord cluster B♭/D♭/E♭, which accompanies his lyrical outpourings, is used throughout the opera to indicate his presence or influence.[20] The stepwise pitches of Quint's melody outline a rising or falling fourth interval, thereby 'filling in' the 'who is it?' motif. In this way, his song may be the 'solution' to the unanswered questions in the text: however, Miles alone is responsive to the meaning which is incarnate in this voice, a voice which for Britten was inseparable from the voice of his own lover.

It is interesting to compare the performances of Peter Pears and David Hemmings on the original 1955 Decca recording, conducted by Britten, with a more recent

---

[20] For example, in Act 1, Scene 2 the children's 'adult' bows are illustrated by sweeping harp arpeggios; similarly in Act 2, Scene 3 Miss Jessel's lamentations are accompanied by Quint's harp cluster and his flute arabesques.

SCENE VIII. **At Night**. *Nachts.*

Example 24

version by Philip Langridge and Sam Pay (Collins 70302). Throughout the scene, Pears's tone is well-centred and controlled, not ghostly and ethereal but poised and sure, a 'living' voice singing to a living boy. Each pitch of the elaborate runs is clearly and smoothly articulated; each phrase commences with a freely held opening note and concludes with a gentle *ritenuto*, subtly implying his manipulative power over Miles. Hemmings's replies are eager and excited. He answers confidently and loudly, and his tone has a roughness and vitality with suggests his willing compliance and trust.

In contrast, Langridge emphasises the other-worldly aspects of Quint's nature. His opening phrases are more distant and less forceful, and his vocal arabesques float rapidly over the pitches. The overall tempo is faster than Pears's version, and Langridge takes fewer liberties with the rhythmic structure. As he sings 'I am King Midas' the pace accelerates: in contrast to Pears, who deliberately varies the delivery of his phrases thereby suggesting a multitude of promises, Langridge rushes through the scene. Although this does imply Quint's energy and determination, it also makes him appear more aggressive and distances him from his youthful listener. Sam Pay's responses are quieter and less exuberant than Hemmings's enthusiastic cries. His tone is less 'natural' and his voice has the asexual quality of the trained choirboy. His communion with Quint is therefore less intense and his enchantment more equivocal.

The adult–child relationship which is curtailed by the death of the youth in *Peter Grimes* (and *Billy Budd*), is similarly unfulfilled at the close of *The Turn of the Screw*. Quint's longing for a 'friend' echoes Forster's use of this term to describe the relationship between Billy Budd and Captain Vere, as well as that between Maurice and Alex Scudder in *Maurice*,[21] and also anticipates Oberon's partnership with Puck in Britten's subsequent opera, *A Midsummer Night's Dream*:

> QUINT: I need a friend –
> Obedient to follow where I lead,
> Slick as a juggler's mate to catch my thought,
> Proud, curious, agile, he shall feed
> My mounting power.

The identification between the two pairs is strengthened by Britten's re-employment of Quint's celeste timbre and E♭–centred melody in association with Oberon.

Some critics have complained that Piper's lines for the ghosts, and their

---

21 The term also appears in the Prologue duet between Grimes and Ellen in *Peter Grimes*, which concludes:
> My/Your voice out of the pain,
> Is like a hand
> That I/you can feel and know:
> Here is a friend.

In the final scene of *The Turn of the Screw* the Governess sings 'I stay as your friend, I stay as your friend.'

relationship with the children, is too explicit. For example, Colin Mason objected: '[Mrs Piper] had occasionally been insensitive to some of Henry James's silences and reticences, without the one conceivable justification of using a definitive interpretation of them. The unhappiest example is the last scene of Act 1, in which the episode with Miles on the lawn at night is expanded into a quartet in which the relationship between the children and the ghosts is made crudely explicit, and yet no more intelligible.'[22] Similarly, in *The Times*, 16 September 1954, a reviewer described the ghosts as 'two too solid stage villains', while Martin Cooper considered that they 'appear too often . . . and say too much.'[23] Despite Britten's insistence that the ghosts were 'real', Piper's stage directions – such as her indication in the 'Lake Scene' that 'Flora silently and deliberately turns round to face the audience away from Miss Jessel', and the instruction in Act 2, Scene 4 that Quint listens 'unseen' to Miles's 'Malo Song' – do reinstate some of James's ambiguity and allow for the possible interpretation that the ghosts are merely projections of the Governess's subconscious. Moreover, by a process of melodic identification and repetition Britten is able to suggest that Quint is indeed the Governess's 'other voice' or 'other self': Quint's melodies are obviously a more forceful and imaginative elaboration of her weaker vocal motifs and thus their voices and personalities are inextricably linked.

James's novella contains many instances of cross-identification between the Governess and the ghosts. For example, Mrs Grose describes the former Governess: 'She was also young and pretty – almost as young and pretty, miss, even as you' (pp. 18–19).

Likewise, after catching a glimpse of Quint through the mirror-like window: 'It was confusedly present to me that I ought to place myself where he had stood. I did so; I applied my face to the pane and looked, as he had looked, into the room . . . She saw me as I had seen my own visitant . . . I gave her something of the shock that I had received' (pp. 31–2), 'I remember sinking down at the foot of the staircase – recalling that it was exactly where, more than a month before, in the darkness of night and just so bowed with evil things, I had seen the spectre of the most horrible of women' (p. 86). Britten seizes upon James's insinuations and musically implies that the two sides of the Governess's schizophrenic psyche have separated and are located in her own voice and that of Quint. In *Billy Budd* Vere and Claggart had re-enacted the battle between Peter Grimes's irreconcilable brutal and visionary natures; in *Gloriana*, Elizabeth had struggled to defeat her rebelliousness, which was embodied in the seditious Essex. Now the Governess faces her own 'other self' in the form of Quint.

Britten illustrates the Governess's self-delusion by the use of a melodic phrase – 'the identity theme' – which first occurs in Act 1, Scene 1 (Fig. 3) [Example 25]:

22 Colin Mason, in *The Guardian*, 15 September 1954.
23 *The Telegraph*, 15 September 1954. Britten may have been sensitive to some of these attacks as Basil Coleman's 1956 production reduced the objective reality of the ghosts. *The Times* described this later production, 27 September 1956: 'In the first scene of the second act, where rather dubiously the ghosts become solid flesh, they no longer act so physically and their colloquy remains in the world of shadow.'

Example 25

> GOVERNESS: Whatever happens it is I,
> I must decide.
> A strange world for a stranger's sake.
> O why, why did I come?

The melody is accompanied by a striking textural change and closes with a long dramatic pause. Harmonically it superimposes the opera's opposing tonal areas A–E and Ab–Eb. The repetitions of this theme act as an index of her comprehension of her purpose, progress and ultimate failure. For example, as she is introduced to her new pupils (Fig. 9) the solo violin plays a tentative version of this theme; later in Scene 5, 'The Window', Mrs Grose's cry 'Is there no end to his dreadful ways?' initiates a more extensive orchestral elaboration (Fig. 44) which culminates with the Governess's realisation (Fig. 46):

> But I see it now, I must protect the children . . .
> See what I see, know what I know, that they may see and know nothing.

Here her phrase is accompanied by a slow rising scale which delineates first her harmonic area, and then Quint's, and her melody closes on an ambiguous D♯ (Eb?) which unites the two tonalities. In the closing moments of Act 2, the Governess comprehends the extent of her own culpability and failure, and the 'identity theme' returns once more as she sings to Flora (Act 2, Fig. 112):

> My friend, you have forsaken me, at last you have forsaken me.
> Flora I have lost you. She has taught you how to hate me!
> Am I then horrible? Am I horrible? Horrible? No! No!
> But I have failed, failed, most miserably failed, and there is no more
>   innocence in me.

In Quint's nocturnal scene it becomes apparent that the Governess's 'why did I come?' melody is a weaker version of his song. She and Quint share their melodic material in the same way that they share their love for Miles. Britten appears to be suggesting that the songs of good and evil are essentially the same. The full force of this melodic trans-identification is made manifest in the ghost's 'Colloquy' at the start of Act 2.

The 'Colloquy' between Quint and Miss Jessel was one of the most vociferously criticised passages in the opera. James hints that the children's sexuality is awoken by their witnessing the relationship between the two ghosts, but Piper considered

James's characterisation of Miss Jessel to be insufficiently interesting to hold Quint's attention, 'And so, rather lamely, I invented the anti-male note.'[24] Piper followed Britten's suggestion that she should model her text on Verlaine's *Colloque Sentimental* in which two lovers taunt one another with memories of their past affair, but she found that: 'Except for the idea, it was not much help, and I could only emphasise their unhappy self-absorption.'[25] Miss Jessel remains weakly characterised, her situation and fate serving primarily to warn the Governess of her own failings. Quint's power is the focus of the drama and Flora's relationship with Miss Jessel, a significant aspect of James's tale, is diminished in the opera.

However, in some ways the 'Colloquy' is the moral linchpin of the opera. It culminates in Piper's quotation from Yeats's poem 'The Second Coming', set to the 'identity theme' (Fig. 19) [Example 26]. In a theatrical, even hysterical outburst, the two ghosts declaim this phrase, *fortissimo* and in unison, the musical intensity being heightened by the restatement of the 'screw theme' in A♭:

> QUINT AND MISS JESSEL: *Day by day the bars we break,*
> *Break the love that laps them round,*
> *Cheat the careful watching eyes,*
> *'The ceremony of innocence is drowned'.*

Yeats's verse may evoke a nostalgic longing for the past, or alternatively signal a potential escape from the meaningless rituals or 'ceremonies' of a convictionless society:

> Turning and turning the widening gyre
> The falcon cannot hear the falconer;
> Things fall apart; the centre cannot hold;
> Mere anarchy is loosed upon the world,
> The blood-dimmed tide is loosed, and everywhere
> The ceremony of innocence is drowned;
> The best lack all conviction, while the worst
> Are full of passionate intensity.[26]

Yeats's image of the eternally spiralling circle complements James's never-ending 'turns of the screw'; his falcon does not turn in upon itself but breaks free, falling into an abyss which symbolises the violent overthrow of civilised rituals of behaviour. 'Innocence', though perpetuated by meaningless ceremonies, is alone able to challenge the imminent discharge of sexual and social violence, but it may be unable to survive the anarchy which follows the destruction of the ceremonies which sustain it.[27] Britten might be suggesting that it is not innocence itself but the collective rituals of innocence which must be drowned in order to liberate the

---

[24] DH, p. 12.

[25] *Ibid.*

[26] W. B. Yeats, *The Poems*, ed. David Wright (London: Dent, 1990), p. 235.

[27] Yeats's poem looks forward to a 'Second Coming', and remembers another slaughtered 'innocent' who has shed his blood for our sakes. Britten also explored this Christian motif in *Lucretia, Abraham and Isaac* and *Billy Budd*. It is interesting therefore that, following the

Example 26

individual, enabling them to progress physically and emotionally from childhood to adulthood. However, the undercurrents of sexual tension in Yeats's longing for the world to end through apocalyptic change persist in the opera and challenge this moral position: breaking conventions may have good or bad results.[28]

completion of *The Turn of the Screw* he composed his *Canticle III*, a setting of Edith Sitwell's poem, 'Still Falls the Rain':

> *Still falls the Rain –*
> *Dark as the world of man, black as our loss –*
> *Blind as the nineteen hundred and forty nails –*
> *Upon the Cross*
> *. . .*
> *Then sounds the voice of One who like the heart of man*
> *Was once a child who among beasts has lain –*
> *'Still do I love, still shed my innocent light, my blood,/ for thee'*

(Edith Sitwell: *Collected Poems* (London: Macmillan, 1965), pp. 272–3).

28   Britten's reading of Yeats's poem is unclear. However, the line 'The ceremony of innocence

The ghosts' 'Colloquy' fades into the Governess's subsequent scene. Has she seen the ghosts, or heard their cries? Or was the episode construed entirely by her over-active, neurotic imagination? Significantly, in this scene Piper inserts an anguished line for the Governess, who has more self-doubt than James's instruc-tress, which recalls Claggart's cry of despair, 'O beauty, handsomeness, goodness. Would that I never encountered you!':

> GOVERNESS: *O innocence, you have corrupted me, which way shall I turn?*

Piper explained these lines: 'I think that's about her own innocence, that she was a person who was innocent in all her approaches to everything, but that she realised that you can't be innocent, you can't afford to be innocent, so that her innocence has let her down.'[29]

The mental in/stability of the Governess has been one of the most controversial features of *The Turn of the Screw*. The story is essentially *her* narrative, revealed to us by Douglas, and therefore, like Captain Vere she is both the teller of the tale and a character within. The question of her reliability is crucial, and James counsels in his 'Preface':

> It was 'déjà très-joli', in *The Turn of the Screw*, please believe, the general propo-sition of our young woman's keeping crystalline her record of so many intense anomalies and obscurities – by which I don't of course mean her explanation of things, a different matter . . . We have surely as much of her own nature as we can swallow in watching it reflect her anxieties and inductions . . . she has 'authority'; which is a good deal to have given her, and I couldn't have arrived at so much had I clumsily tried for more.

From the start James takes care to emphasise her naivety and impetuous romanti-cism: 'I remember the whole beginning as a succession of flights and drops, a little see-saw of the right throbs and the wrong' (p. 11). This contrasts with Quint's worldliness: 'Quint was so clever – he was so deep' (p. 41).

In James's novella the Governess had recounted, 'It was the first time, in a manner, that I had known space, air and freedom, all the music of summer and the mystery of nature' (p. 22), and in the opera Prologue, she is similarly depicted as 'untried, innocent'. All things outside her limited experience are perceived to be 'dangerous', and in this way the narrow world in which she lives recalls the restricting and oppressive environments of Britten's preceding operas – the Borough, ancient Rome, Loxford, *The Indomitable* and the Elizabethan court.

Having determined that the ghosts were not mere projections of her paranoia, Britten and Piper initially planned a less critical portrait of the young woman. Piper's 'Notebook' records her early ideas:

---

is drowned' does have a rhetorical power, complemented musically, and connects both with the end of Act 1 where Miles's innocence has been in question, and with the Governess's fear of innocence in the subsequent passage.
[29] HC, p. 355.

I see a series of heroic soliloquies.
1) The ordinary fears and doubts of an inexperienced girl faced with responsibility & possibly loneliness and boredom buoyed up by romantic love.
2) The lyrical imagining of an interview with the beloved employer leading up
to the 1st appearance.
3) After the 2nd appearance & the long conversation with Mrs Grose a Heroic
imagining of herself as the influence for good and protection full acceptance of
the role of guardian angel 'I was a screen – I was to stand before them. The more
I saw the less they would.'
4) Realisation that she would not be a protection – that they were already too
deeply involved. (BPL)

They considered portraying the Governess's 'feelings of romantic love for her
employer', the incomplete draft of the libretto containing a passage which depicts
her immaturity and impressionability:

> *Possible*
> *The twilight laden air of summer stirs*
> *My unaccustomed heart*
> *That until now*
> *Only for old habitual things has kept*
> *Looking for each day to play last years* [sic] *part*
> *ending If only I could see him once – see his approval.* (BPL)

However, the first page of Piper's scene synopsis reads: 'for the moment I thought
we would try to leave out the guardian altogether anyway as a sentimental element
in the piece' (BPL). The Governess was to be more level-headed than James's
impulsive young girl and her infatuation with her employer did not accord with
their perception of her as 'very young, fresh, innocent and impressionable, but
not without competence and dignity. One feels that although inexperienced she is
clear-headed and resourceful'.[30] An incomplete draft reveals that after the first
appearance of Quint's ghost, Piper intended her to reflect cautiously upon what
she had seen, and sing 'without panic':

> *Miss A Oh Mrs Grose, I saw . . . [she is about to describe what she saw,*
> *hesitates & decides not to] Why, I saw such a beautiful sky to-night.*
> *Mrs G. Indeed 'twas a beautiful sky to-night [This could develop into a*
> *duet].* (BPL)

This characterisation altered as the libretto progressed and in the final version the
reckless Governess rushes headlong into an elaborate account of her encounter.

It was the addition of the Prologue which undermined Britten and Piper's original impression of the Governess's rationality. Originally, no dramatisation of the
Governess's employment interview was planned but in April 1954 Britten,
concerned that the opera was going to be too short, wrote to Piper after consulting
the producer, Basil Coleman:

We have had one major discussion which he will talk to you about. It arose out

---

30 Scene synopsis p. 1 (BPL).

of a sudden fear that the work is going to be much too short. The first three scenes incidentally play only ten minutes . . . I don't want it to sound as if the proposed alteration comes only because the piece might be too short, because it has been in my head for some little time . . . a prologue? . . . the interview or the ghost story party? probably spoken?[31]

Piper was anxious that the Prologue should not merely repeat the action of the opening of Act 1. She sent two versions to Britten, both of which are housed in the Britten–Pears Library: the first dramatises the interview between the Governess and the children's guardian, while the second outlines the ghost story party which opens James's text. Britten preferred the first, which intimated the Governess's lack of worldliness, her romantic interest in her employer and her identification with her predecessor. As the opera was written for only six singers, the cast was too small to recreate James's 'house-party', but it was decided that the description of the interview would be delivered indirectly by a narrator, thereby confronting the audience with their very own 'Douglas' and allowing Britten to retain what was an important structural feature of the novella. A single singer would take the parts of the Prologue and Quint, thus more directly involving the audience in the opera's moral dilemma. In the first production this singer was Peter Pears, whose role in establishing, and manipulating, the structural and moral frame of the opera recalled his similar function as the Male Chorus in *Lucretia* and Captain Vere in *Billy Budd*.

The Prologue begins with rising arpeggios played by the piano, the 'white' notes indicating the Governess's tonal area, since the story is to be revealed through her eyes. However, Quint's presence is felt in the ornamental gestures which disturb the calmly delivered recitative. At particular moments Quint's 'flat' tonality is evoked (for example, when the Prologue mentions her predecessor), and his arabesques colour specific phrases, such as descriptions of the Governess's doubts or references to her employer. The Prologue closes with the Governess's acceptance of the guardian's offer of employment, her words – 'I will' – imitating a marriage proposal and acceptance. Throughout the opera Miles's attraction to Quint serves as an unavoidable reminder of her own attraction to the guardian.[32]

The struggle between Quint and the Governess takes the form of a fight for 'possession' of the children, and more particularly, Miles. Both adults are desperate to control the children's access to 'knowledge', which as the novella proceeds is increasingly associated with sexuality and experience. Quint urges Miles to spurn the ignorance which is inexperience and to enter the world of knowledge and adventure, of instinct and natural desire. In contrast, the

---

[31] DH, p. 11.

[32] In the 1970 *Scottish Opera* production of *The Turn of the Screw*, Anthony Besch incorporated a mime of the interview at the start of the Prologue, the part of the guardian being mimed by the Prologue/Quint. John Higgins, wrote in *The Times*, 3 April 1970: 'So this is to be a "Screw" based on the neuroses of a governess infatuated with her employer. The ghosts at Bly are entirely of her creation. The death of Miles is to be laid firmly at the feet of a girl totally unfitted for the care and tutorship of two small children.'

Governess aims to force the young boy to speak out and 'tell the truth', to shatter Quint's silent world with a 'confession' which will cleanse his soul of Quint's influence, and by so doing purge her own heart of her disturbing desires.

The protagonists battle for the right to act as surrogate parent and teacher of the uninitiated and inexperienced children who have been neglected and abandoned by their legal guardian. At the preliminary interview James's Governess is informed: 'of course the young lady who should go down as governess would be in supreme authority' (p. 8) and she delights in her conviction that: 'To watch, teach, 'form' little Flora would too evidently be the making of a happy and useful life . . . What I had undertaken was the whole care of her' (p. 13), 'I found it simple, in my ignorance, my confusion and perhaps my conceit, to assume that I could deal with a boy whose education for the world was all on the point of beginning' (p. 22). However, on arriving at Bly she discovers that Quint has assumed this authority: ' "The master believed in him and placed him here . . . So he has everything to say. Yes." – she let me have it – "even about them!" ' (p. 41), 'for a period of several months Quint and the boy had been perpetually together . . . they had been about quite as if Quint were his tutor – and a very grand one – and Miss Jessel only for the little lady' (pp. 53–4). Similarly, in the opera the Governess sings:

> *Poor babies, no father, no mother. But I shall love them as I love my own, all my dear ones left at home.*

She presumes that all knowledge not imparted by herself, or which goes beyond her own limited experience, is untrustworthy or dangerous, and seeks to stifle their natural curiosity. Drafts for the libretto read:

> *But there can be no corruption without knowledge and I have no knowledge*
> *O yes my knowledge is terrible unreal because it is . . . guessed at imagined.* (BPL)

Even public school, the conventional place for a boy's education is 'horrid' and 'unclean'. Hence she is afraid of Quint's power:

> QUINT [to Miles]: *What goes on in your head, what questions?*
> *Ask, for I answer all.*

Ostensibly, it is Miles's expulsion that prevents him from returning to school, but Miles himself senses that the Governess has other motives in keeping him at home:

> 'Well, I think also, you know, of this queer business of ours.' . . .
> 'Of what queer business, Miles?'
> 'Why, the way you bring me up. And all the rest!' (pp. 91–2)

Quint has induced in Miles a yearning for exploration and discovery: 'Then when am I going back? [to school] . . . I want to see more life' (p. 83).

In the opera this episode is reproduced:

> MILES: *Then we can talk and you can tell me when I'm going back*
> *to school.*
> GOVERNESS: *Are you not happy here?*

> MILES: *I'm growing up, you know. I want my own kind.*
> GOVERNESS: *Yes, you're growing up.*
> MILES: *So much I want to do, so much I might do . . .*

The Governess is desperate to prevent this 'growing up' and to preserve Miles's angelic innocence (which resembles the unblemished purity of the apprentice, Lucretia, Albert and Billy), a stasis which can only be achieved through death. She equates the physical process of aging with moral decay, just as Lucretia's blush and Billy's stammer are physical signs of their inner impurity, and she observes that Flora, who is initially 'a vision of angelic beauty', now becomes: 'not at these times a child but an old, old woman . . . her incomparable childish beauty had suddenly failed, had quite vanished . . . she was hideously hard; she had turned common, almost ugly . . . [like a] vulgarly pert little girl in the street' (pp. 105–6). From meagre evidence the Governess construes a monstrous yet unspecified wickedness, equating knowledge with sexual experience and sin. Ignorance is the only possible salvation yet this ignorance suffocates and destroys life. In contrast, the ghosts' gift of knowledge can appear positively liberating, creative and life-giving.

As James's tale unfolds the Governess's fears escalate and inhibit her judgment. At first she had trusted in the innate purity of the children: 'I had seen him on the instant, without and within, in the great glow of freshness, the same positive fragrance of purity, in which I had from the first moment seen his little sister. He was incredibly beautiful . . . [there] was something divine that I have never found to the same degree in any child – his indescribable little air of knowing nothing in the world but love' (p. 21). However, she comes to fear that their apparent lack of guile and their physical perfection – 'their more than earthly beauty, their absolutely unnatural goodness' (p. 72) – may in fact be a trap designed to deceive and ruin her. Her suspicion of their apparent innocence recalls the mistrust of Grimes, Tarquinius and Claggart when confronted with purity of the apprentice, Lucretia and Billy respectively.

Two unanswered questions echo through James's novella and Britten's opera: who has corrupted whom? And what is the nature of that corruption? James's pervasive evil emanates from an indeterminate source. At times he implies that it is the Governess, and not Miss Jessel, who terrifies Flora:

> 'I see nobody. I never have. I think you're cruel. I don't like you . . . Take me away, take me away – oh take me away from her!'
> 'From me?' I panted.
> 'From you – from you!' she cried. (p. 106)

Likewise, the Governess's feelings for Miles are ambiguous, as he becomes a surrogate for her frustrated passion for her employer: 'There were moments when I knew myself to catch them up by an irresistible impulse and press them to my heart. As soon as I had done so I used to wonder: 'What will they think of that? Doesn't it betray too much?' . . . I might occasionally excite suspicion by the little outbreaks of my sharper passion for them' (p. 57). Indeed, Miles later taunts her: ' "You know, my dear, that for a fellow to be with a lady – !" . . . "And always with

the same lady; but after all I'm a fellow, don't you see? who's – well getting on" '
(p. 82). Piper pondered the Governess's culpability in her synopsis of the
bedroom scene:

> *deep affection for the boy and a slightly hysterical attitude towards the situation. It*
> *is the scene in which one feels that she as much as all the other participants is*
> *bringing on the crisis.* (BPL)

However, elsewhere in James's tale it is the Governess herself who is threatened
by the children's precocity. She worries that the children's knowledge outweighs
her own:

> I now feel that for weeks the lessons must have been rather my own. I learnt
> something – at first certainly – that had not been one of the teachings of my
> small, smothered life . . .
>   It was the first time, in a manner, that I had known space and air and
> freedom, all the music of summer and the mystery of nature. (p. 22) . . .
>   I walked in a world of their invention – they had no occasion whatever to
> draw upon mine. (p. 43)

Britten dramatises her fears in Act 2, Scene 6 'The Piano'. Miles's virtuosic recital
arouses the admiration of his audience:

> *O what a clever boy; why, he must have practised very hard.*
> *I never knew a little boy so good.*

His performance is a parody: bitonal dissonances between the Alberti bass left
hand and richly ornamented right hand add a piquancy which explodes in unrestrained cadenzas. Miles's technical skill and the power of his music enchants his
listeners and lulls them to sleep and enables him to escape from the schoolroom in
search of Quint, whose song he imitates.

James first associates cleverness with 'badness' when the letter arrives from
Miles's headmaster forbidding him to return to school. His crime is undisclosed
but it is insinuated that he has contaminated or corrupted his school fellows,
presumably by divulging to them the sexual knowledge which Quint has taught
him. Similarly, the libretto repeatedly focuses on the issue of Miles's 'badness'. In
Act 1, Scene 3, when the letter arrives announcing that Miles has been dismissed
from school, Mrs Grose's 'white note' melody, 'Now all will be well', is interrupted by Quint's celeste and chord cluster. The Governess's E♭ recitation clashes
with the housekeeper's E♮ (Act 1, Fig. 15):

> *GOVERNESS: Mrs Grose! He's dismissed his school! . . .*
> *Tell me, Mrs Grose, have you known Miles to be bad? . . .*
> *MRS GROSE: Never! Not Master Miles. He can be wild, but not bad!*

Britten dramatises the children's sinister precocity in a series of nursery songs and
school room scenes. In the Letter scene Mrs Grose's sustained E♭ on 'bad!' is
silenced by the boisterous entry of the children singing 'Lavender's blue' (Fig. 17).
The superficial purity of this song is betrayed by the asymmetrical five-bar phrases
and the bitonal tensions between the vocal lines. Similarly, in 'The Window', as

Example 27

the children sing 'Tom, Tom, the piper's son', their excessive energy, signified by the harp's flamboyant Quint-like flourishes, borders on violence.[33]

The most important of these songs is Miles's 'Malo Song' [Example 27]. It is his song of self-revelation but the Governess possesses insufficient self-knowledge to decode his ambiguous confession. The stillness and unreality of this song, which is preceded by boisterous Latin games, recalls the calm of Essex's lute-song which had followed the lively 'Quick music is best'. Likewise, the accompanying harp chords echo with the resonances of Essex's strumming lute. Donald Mitchell has observed that the Governess's reaction to this song – 'Why, Miles, what a funny song! Did I teach you that?' – recalls Gloriana's question, 'Robin, a melting song: but who can this unworldly hermit be?'[34] The Governess and Gloriana half-recognise the song but cannot identify the voice as their 'other self'.

Piper's 'Notebook' reveals how the words of this song evolved, and contains her unsuccessful early experiments. An incomplete draft libretto reads:

> *Oh say I am a fool*
> *And a fool is a knave*

---

[33] Jonathan Miller's 1979 production went as far as to hint at an incestuous relationship between the children in this scene. A reviewer in *The Guardian* noted, 8 November 1979: 'Never have Britten's children less deserved to be called The Innocents. When Miles asks "Now chase me", it's a sexual invitation. Likewise, "Tom was beat". Dr. Miller finds it's a Bergmanesque psycho-drama about incest rather than paedophilia, though there may have been some of that too.'

[34] Donald Mitchell, 'A *Billy Budd* Notebook', in Mervyn Cooke and Philip Reed (eds.), *Benjamin Britten: Billy Budd* (Cambridge: CUP, 1993), pp. 124–5.

> *O say I am a fool*
> *And a fool is not brave*
> *But I am Daniel and the lion too*
> *And David whose cunning the giant slew*
> *And so I say beware*
> *Of the fool that's a knave*
> *And so I say beware*
> *Of the knave that is brave*
> *O say I am a fool, O say I am a fool.* (BPL)

Her scene synopsis illustrates the development of her ideas:

Scene 6: Interior school-room . . . I should like if possible to get Miles [sic] *fool song in here. He could have written it and she could make them sing it in parts or canon.*
. . .

   Scene 8: . . . Miles dies. [I simply haven't faced up to this scene – and can't tell until I see how the other scenes with Miles go how this ought to be] I'd like if possible some sort of repetition of the fool song. I think it is the only good thing I have written so far and cling to it a bit because it expresses for me the particular odd mixture old-fashioned imaginativeness . . . But there easily might be something far better. The things one clings to are usually terrible stumbling blocks. (BPL)

Presumably she did not object when Britten suggested alternative text. The strange words of the final version were taken from a Latin mnemonic rhyme which Britten found in an old-fashioned Latin grammar belonging to Piper's aunt. The schoolroom ambience of her original words is retained, as is the 'odd mixture' of convention and imagination. The first two lines summarise the Governess's conservative approach to Miles's education while the final two lines imply the alternative education offered by Quint. Significantly, the melody of the last two lines is an inversion of the first two, words and melody thus clarifying the choice which Miles must make:

> *Malo: I would rather be*
> *Malo: in an apple tree*
> *Malo: than a naughty boy*
> *Malo: in adversity.*

On the Decca recording David Hemmings's performance is confident and secure but his tone has a rawness and a slight sense of strain in the upper registers which imbues his delivery with a tense edginess. His replies to the Governess's query – 'No I found it' – are challenging, even arrogant. In contrast, Sam Pay's style is more lyrical. His tone is purer, the upper registers ringing and echoing. The emphasis in his performance is on the abstract beauty of the vocal timbre, and not on communicating the personality of the rebellious child.

   The mood of stillness and calm in this scene, together with the unearthly timbre of the cor anglais and harp, looks ahead to Quint's 'Night scene'. The interlocking thirds of the 'Malo' melody outline the fourths of Quint's nocturnal call, as if he is directing Miles's voice, shaping his melody and dictating his words. The repetitions of the 'Malo song', and the re-evocation of its distinctive atmosphere, thereby indicate Quint's growing power over Miles. The first of these repetitions occurs in the closing bars of Act 1 (Fig. 89) when the Governess and Mrs Grose discover Miles on his nocturnal escapade in the garden. Quint's broken chord clusters played by the harp accompany Miles's rising fourth motifs, as he sings 'sweetly':

> You see, I am bad. I am bad, aren't I,
> I am bad, I am bad, aren't I?

The melodic fourths are related both to his 'Malo Song' and to the 'who is it?' motif, and this interval dominates the last bars of the scene, as the timpani, whose agitated rhythms had depicted the Governess's arrival at Bly in Scene 1, quietly repeats an E♭–A♭ fourth, the music dissolving and cadencing on a low tremolando A♭. Quint is evidently in the ascendancy.

At the opening of Act 2 Quint announces his ambitions – 'I seek a friend, Obedient to follow where I lead' – and the 'Malo Song' reappears, more crisply articulated, in the accompaniment (Act 2, Fig. 16). Quint's progress towards the satisfaction of his desires is charted by the tonal progression of this Act, his own reappearance in Scene 4 'The Bedroom' being anticipated by the full statement of the 'Malo theme' played by the cor anglais, in E♭ minor. The dramatic struggle between the Governess and Quint for possession of Miles is forcefully depicted by the tension between melody and harmony in this scene. Miles's restatement of the final two lines of the 'Malo Song' traces the Governess's 'white notes', implying a dissonant A minor challenge to the E♭ minor tonality of the scene. However, as the Governess interrogates Miles, Quint's ghostly call reverberates from the shadows: is he tempting the boy into danger or protecting him from the Governess's dubious intentions? She insists 'I want to help you . . . save you', but at this point the candle goes out (Fig. 76) and the cor anglais re-enters with the 'Malo theme', now in E♭ minor. Miles's anguished shriek, a descending glissando recalling the apprentice's cry of death in *Peter Grimes*, looks forward to the following scene where Quint's urgent instructions to Miles to steal the letter take an identical form. His admission ' 'Twas I, who blew it', is punctuated by Quint's cluster chords, the rising fourths, sung 'simply', reminding us of the 'who is it?' motif and thus reinforcing the crisis of identity at the heart of the drama.

It is the Governess herself who sings the last repetition of the 'Malo Song', in a passionate outburst of grief over the dead child's body (Act 2, Fig. 137):

> Ah, Ah, don't leave me now!
> Ah! Miles!
> Malo! Malo! Malo than a naughty boy.
> Malo, Malo, in adversity.

Leaves inserted into Piper's 'Notebook' support her assertion that it was she who suggested that this song should be sung by the Governess at the end of the opera:

> Miles sings his 'Say I am a fool song' again & she sings:
> 'You sang that song the first time I saw you'
> 'Did I? I often sing songs

I know Miles. Sing me one now.
He sings another v. poignant . . .
When he dies she holds him and her last words as curtain falls are his,
but sung instead of spoken
Oh say I am a fool, oh say I am a fool.' (BPL)

Her acknowledgement of shared guilt, 'What have we done between us', is musically represented by the dissonance between the diatonic A major harmony and her vocal line, which emphasises the movement D♯/(E♭)–E. Her phrase concludes with an unresolved G♮ which undermines the perfect cadence in A.

Just as the identification of corrupter, corrupted and potential liberator is unresolved, so the nature of the corruption remains unclassified but is closely aligned in James's text with the concept of freedom. Quint's crime is that he has been 'much too free':

'Too free with my boy?'
'Too free with every one!' (p. 40)

Miles absorbs this passion for freedom: 'I've been ever so far; all round about – miles and miles away. I've never been so free' (p. 120). Piper acknowledged the importance of reproducing James's silence concerning this issue, describing the tale as 'vague in only one thing: in what, if anything, actually happened between the children and the haunting pair'.[35] Her libretto drafts for Quint's words of seduction (Scenes 7 and 8) are more explicit than the final text:

[Scene 7]
Come! for I wait alone
beyond the furthest tree
Come! to the beckoning land
Come! And be free
Come! leave childhood behind
Come. You shall know what I know
Come leave childhood behind
Come for without you [I'm?] lost
Come for I wait
Alone

[Scene 8]
I know the answers to all that you ask
I know the questions that through your . . . mind pass
I know things that you'd better forget
And others not thought of or dreamed of as yet . . .
I am the life that stirs
When the candle is out
The meaning laugh
And the half-heard phrase
The shadowed gesture that dares . . .

---

35 DH, p. 9.

> *In me all half-known roads, all secrets meet . . .*
> *In me all secret ways and all ambitions meet . . .*
> *In me half-formed desires and secrets meet . . .* (BPL)

The synopsis draft indicates that 'Quint and Miss Jessel sing melancholy, romantic and slightly sinister songs . . . intended to attract children on purely nursery or fairy grounds but hold out a promise of knowledge' (BPL). 'The life when the candle is out', 'the shadowed gesture that dares', 'half-formed desires', 'secrets' – these are the freedoms which Quint represents, freedoms which are simultaneously literal and metaphoric, imaginative and physical, innocent and sexual.

Interestingly, Peter Pears did not think that Mrs Grose should say that Quint had 'made free with everyone': 'He feels that "made free" is too particular and suggestive, and that we should save this particular phrase until the beginning of the next page. James merely says "Quint *was* too free with the boy". I think the sexy suggestion should only refer to his relationship with Miss Jessel, don't you? Incidentally it may help to avert a scandal in Venice!'[36] Carpenter describes how it almost did become necessary to avert a scandal when Britten's close relationship with David Hemmings, who sang the part of Miles, exposed Britten to potential accusations that he was becoming a Quint-like seducer. John Amis, whose wife led the English Opera Group orchestra, remembered that 'the composer seemed besotted with the boy. Cast and players noticed that Peter and Ben were at odds', and Basil Douglas confirmed that Britten 'loved David. He was in love with him, but as far as I know there was nothing more . . . Ben was very self-restrained. I took my hat off to him for that. Because he was really smitten, and didn't David know it! He was very advanced for his age.'[37] Was Douglas inferring that it was Hemmings who corrupted Britten? Hemmings himself remembers:

> Was he infatuated with me? Yes, he was. He was a gentleman; there was no sort of overt sexuality about it whatsoever . . . Did he kiss me? Yes, he did. But that was more my need as a young boy alone in his house than it was any threat. I slept in his bed, when I was frightened, and I still felt no sexual threat whatsoever. And I think it would have embarrassed him a damn sight more than it would have embarrassed me at the time . . . Was I aware of his homosexuality? Yes, I was. Did I find that threatening? No, because I learnt an awful lot through it. Did I feel that he was desperately fond of me? I suppose I did, but I must say I thought far more in a sort of fatherly fashion; and I had a very bad father–son relationship.[38]

Pears later told Raymond Leppard how the situation almost escalated beyond control: 'Only one episode did he specially mention as nearly catastrophic . . . David Hemmings . . . at the time of *The Turn of the Screw* in Venice. Ben, it seems, became quite distracted. Peter told me that he had to take Ben away by train or it

[36] Britten to Piper, quoted in HC, p. 336.
[37] HC, p. 356.
[38] *Ibid.*, pp. 357–8.

would have escalated into a major scandal. For how long I don't know, at any rate a cooling off time.'[39] Piper told Carpenter that Britten did talk to her about his friendships with these boys. She portrays Britten as a tormented respecter of the ceremonies of innocence: ' "He would go for long walks – I remember one occasion when he did, perhaps two – and he would say what it was very upsetting for him, worrying. He found it a temptation, and he was very worried about it." She did not know that "he'd gone so far" as to kiss boys, or offer kisses, and is sure that nothing further went on: "I think he kept the rules".'[40]

Hemmings's remarks are curiously 'Miles-like': he, like Miles, occupies ambiguous territory, on the border between ignorance and knowledge. For James, the tale may have been merely a literary game, but Britten was more personally implicated in the drama. In the form of Hemmings he was confronted with a potential transformation of fiction into real experience.

Following the premiere of *The Turn of the Screw* at the Venice Biennale Festival on 14 September 1954, *The Times*'s reviewer commented, 16 September 1954: '[we] ask not whether he has succeeded in his aim but why did he choose this subject, that story or a particular libretto. It is an improper question for criticism to ask, but it recurs so invariably that it must have some relevance to his art.' Writing in *Paris L'Express*, Antoine Golea made one of the first explicit references to Britten's homosexuality in a review of his music, noting that the opera illustrated: 'the composer's customary intense preoccupation with homosexual love and the futility of struggling against it.'[41] Eric Crozier, in his 1966 'Notes' (which were made available to Humphrey Carpenter), recounts Britten's allegation that he had been raped at school and suggests that this may explain Britten's obsession with this theme: 'Having been corrupted as a boy, he seemed to be under a compulsion to corrupt other small boys.'[42]

When asked by Carpenter if the opera might symbolise the struggle between the two opposing sides of Britten's psyche, Piper's replies reveal a naivety which Britten may have considered to be an attractive attribute in a librettist who would be unlikely to probe too deeply into his personal identification with the drama: 'I never thought of that. It seems to me that it may be the two sides of anybody's sexuality.'[43]

Henry James's own private life has been the subject of endless and inconclusive speculation focusing on his suspected homosexuality and a possible incestuous fixation on his brother William. Despite a wealth of extant letters, papers and

[39] *Ibid.*, p. 357.
[40] *Ibid.*, p. 354.
[41] *Ibid.*, HC, p. 360.
[42] *Ibid.*, HC, p. 355. Writing to Britten on 21 November 1964, William Plomer commented, 'Do you know that when Henry James was asked what construction should be put upon The Turn of the S., he said, "The worst possible construction"?' Britten replied on 3 December, 'I must say that when one is rehearsing the boy in T of the S. (as I have been doing the last months) it is difficult to avoid "the worst possible construction" in answering polite queries! But it is extraordinary how children don't put 2 & 2 together, & just get on with the job.'
[43] HC, p. 355.

journals there is little irrefutable evidence that James was homosexual but his texts often seem to resonate with a sexual tension.[44] Richard Hall has analysed the homosexual 'threat' in James's writing,[45] which he proposes is visually expressed by symbols such as window and mirrors. These objects are potent symbols in *The Turn of the Screw*, and in the final pages appear to represent a barrier to understanding or a gap in knowledge: 'The frames and squares of the great window were of a kind of image, for him, of a kind of failure. I felt that I saw him, in any case, shut in or shut out . . . Wasn't he looking through the haunted pane for something he couldn't see' (p. 119), 'For there again, against the glass . . . was the hideous author of our woe –' (p. 127).

This scene is the climax of the opera: Britten represents James's idea of the 'window' or 'gap' by a literal and symbolic 'silence' in his score, i.e. Miles's refusal to confess. It is the Governess's obsessive urgency to fill the gaps in her understanding and to uncover 'the truth' which drives the drama to its tragic denouement. In Act 2, Scene 4, 'The Bedroom', as she coaxes, 'Miles, dear little Miles is there nothing you want to tell me?', Quint appears, signalled by a glockenspiel chord cluster, and repeats his beckoning melisma. Her imploring intensifies in the final scene:

> . . . *tell me what it is then you have on your mind.*
> *I still want you to tell me,*
> *Yes, it would be best, you know.*
> . . .
> *Who is it? Who? Say for my sake . . . Say it! Say it!*
> . . . *Only say the name and he will die forever.*

In contrast, Quint, desperately trying to rescue Miles from the Governess's psychosis, pleads:

> *Beware of her!*
> *Be silent!*
> *Do not betray our secrets! Beware!*

Miles's silence becomes, like the stammers of Albert and Billy, a symbol for all the guilty secrets in the text: Miles is effectively 'on trial', like Grimes, Lucretia, Albert, Budd and Essex before him. The Governess's last lunge for truth is accompanied by a violent physical grasping of the child, and is literally an embrace of death. Miles submits, 'I will tell you everything. I will', and the scene climaxes with the deliberately ambiguous cry, 'Peter Quint – you devil!', quoted directly from James's text. Miles has finally *spoken* out and confessed. Erwin Stein has revealed that Britten was convinced that this remark was aimed at the Governess.[46] The

---

[44] In particular, the short story *The Pupil*, written four years before *The Turn of the Screw*, anticipates the setting, moral issues and narrative conclusion of the later novella.

[45] Richard Hall, 'Henry James: Interpreting and Obsessive Memory', *Journal of Homosexuality*, vol. 8, nos. 3/4, Spring/Summer 1983, 83–98.

[46] In Patricia Howard (ed.), *Benjamin Britten: The Turn of the Screw* (Cambridge: CUP, 1985), p. 145.

result of this reading is a transvaluation whereby a potential saviour is exposed as a destroyer.

The dramatic events which culminate in Miles's death take place above the final statement of the 'screw theme', which gradually unfolds in the form of a passacaglia, recalling Britten's use of this form in association with death in *Peter Grimes, Lucretia* and *Albert Herring*. The first six pitches accompany the Governess's phrase 'O Miles I cannot bear to lose you. You shall be mine, and I shall save you' (Fig. 121). The A major tonality fulfils Britten's need to resolve the harmonic structure of the opera and appears to indicate the Governess's potential victory. However, in addition to balancing the symmetrical A–A♭–A♭–A tonal plan, and resolving the tension between A–E and A♭–E♭, Britten must also sustain the psychological ambiguity which is fundamental to James's novella. Therefore, when the passacaglia bass reaches the pitches of the second half of the screw theme Quint's seductive cry is reintroduced, presaged by the clarinet's rising arpeggios and the reappearance of the celeste (Fig. 125). Quint's E♭ creates a powerful dissonance with the E♮ in the bass and this harmonic bitterness intensifies in the subsequent bars as the passacaglia gets 'stuck' on G♯. This pitch symbolises the adults' battle for possession of the child's soul, as it may be interpreted as the leading note in the Governess's A major, or alternatively as the enharmonic equivalent of Quint's A♭. Britten twists the harmonic screw still further by notating his music bitonally (Fig. 131), a technique that he had employed previously to indicate cross-identification. Quint and the Governess sing in unison for the first time in the opera (Fig. 134):

> GOVERNESS: *Ah, Miles! you are saved!*
> QUINT: *Ah, Miles! we have failed!*

A bass pedal on the pitch A supports their phrases but the tonality and instrumentation is Quint's.

Quint's 'Farewell' (Fig. 135) moves to the Governess's harmonic area while her frantic 'Ah, don't leave me now', is coloured by his A♭ tonality. The implication is that both have lost: she is self-deluded in victory and he is self-knowing in defeat.

The Governess had hoped to 'save' Miles and by so doing to banish her own, barely understood desires. His unforeseen death transforms him from 'saved' to potential 'saviour'. Like Billy Budd, he is a sacrificial victim with the power to forgive and redeem. However, in contrast to Lucretia or Billy, Miles is not a voluntary victim. Whereas Vere is blessed by Billy with a vision of eternal love, the Governess is not redeemed by Miles's death and she ends the opera in despair. In the final scenes of *Billy Budd, Gloriana* and the *Screw* the victim's song is reprised by the destroyer but only Budd's 'far-shining sail' aria has redemptive capacities. The Governess has been 'lost in my labyrinth' seeing 'no truth, only the foggy walls of evil press upon me', but the clearing of the mists which had obscured self-knowledge affords her no consolation. Her restatement of Miles's tender 'Malo Song' in the final bars recalls Gloriana's distorted and fragmented renderings of Essex's lyrical lute melody, which, like a song of death, had symbolised the Queen's self-knowledge and loss.

Piper described Britten's understanding of the Governess's role in the tragedy: 'That evil exists whether in life or in the mind . . . and is capable of corrupting – or perhaps nor corrupting but causing the loss of innocence – he was, I think, quite certain. The governess's good intentions were destroyed by her experiences, whether real or imagined, and her love for Miles was corrupted, in that it became possessiveness and she was aware of it. Hence her last words "What have we done between us?" '[47] Who has corrupted whom, and how? Released from the 'weak specifications' condemned by James, Britten's music, untainted by literalism or referentiality, could express both his personal understanding of the 'innocence' and 'evil' in James's text and excite his listeners' imaginations in order that they might create their own impression of the nature and power of these forces. If the act of speaking out destroys Miles then, by analogy, it might be suggested that the efforts of generations of literary critics to fill in the silences in James's text might likewise 'murder' James's text. Britten's 'reading' is unique in that it can match, even outdo, James's power of suggestion while sustaining the text's fundamental ambiguity. The composer appears to have understood and welcomed this expressive power for when Piper showed Britten her early libretto drafts, which contained many passages reproduced verbatim from James's text, he commented: 'Don't colour them, the music will do that.'[48] She explained that James:

> tells the story with an elaborate fabric of words against which the action and the conversations that take the action further stand out to make the dramatic shape. But nothing that happens is significant without the accompanying density of offered feelings and facts, echoes and memories. Britten used the voice as an instrument that detaches itself from the orchestra to tell the story, but depends for its full dramatic, as well as musical, effect on its relation to the whole fabric of sound and of echoes and memories of sound. He builds up the weight of musical experience as James builds up the weight of evidence and fantasy.[49]

There is a sense that with the completion of *The Turn of the Screw* Britten had arrived at an emotional and professional turning point. The three operas composed between 1951 and 1954 – *Billy Budd*, *Gloriana* and *The Turn of the Screw* – had been characterised by an increasingly explicit exploration of the dialectic between innocence and experience in which the role of Peter Pears, in musically and theatrically dramatising all possible scenarios and denouements, had been crucial. In 'The Art of Fiction' James articulated the dilemma which appears to have obsessed Britten: 'The essence of moral energy is to survey the whole field . . . Full moral awareness is impossible without knowledge but can knowledge remain free from contamination?'[50] The implication in *The Turn of the Screw* is that the two ambiguous abstractions represented by the Governess and

47 Letter to Patricia Howard, 22 February 1982, quoted in Howard, *The Turn of the Screw*, p. 23.
48 DH, p. 9.
49 DH, p. 8.
50 Henry James, 'The Art of Fiction', in *The Critical Muse: Selected Literary Criticism* (Harmondsworth: Penguin, 1987), pp. 186–206.

Quint – innocence and experience – cannot co-exist within Miles. The Governess, Gloriana and Vere do not wish, respectively, Miles, Essex and Billy to die but repeatedly death is the unavoidable outcome. Why is 'love' defeated? Is it Fate? It is a despairing conclusion and the bleakness of this vision may account for Britten's subsequent operatic silence: after ten years of prolific creativity he now ceased operatic composition. Six years passed before he was ready once more to venture into the magic wood in search of the imaginative and emotional riches promised by Quint.

10

Noye's Fludde

> *What is home? Calm as deep water.*
> *Where's my home? Deep as calm water,*
> *Water will drink my sorrows dry*
> *And the tide will turn.*   *Peter Grimes*, Act 3, Scene 2
>
> *Lord Jesus, think on me,*
> *That, when the flood is past,*
> *I may eternal brightness see,*
> *And share thy joy at last.*   *Noye's Fludde*, Congregation Hymn

In the years following the completion of *The Turn of the Screw* Britten's only 'operatic' composition was *Noye's Fludde*, a 'community opera' that was based on one of the Chester Miracle Plays. Britten had had on-going plans to write another children's opera, as a sequel to *The Little Sweep*, and as early as 1951 had considered composing an opera based on Beatrix Potter's *The Tale of Mr Tod*. In 1954 he discussed a 'space travel' themed work with William Plomer: 'I did in fact start on [an opera on astronauts] for children, about ten years ago, with William Plomer – who'd written a superb first scene; we occasionally look back at it and I may finish it sometime. It had a character with the magnificent name of Madge Plato.'[1]

    Noye's Fludde originated in a commission from Boris Ford, then head of schools' programmes at Associated Rediffusion (the London commercial television company), for a new version of one of the English medieval mystery plays. Britten responded enthusiastically, telling Ford that he had been thinking of basing a work on the miracle plays for some time. The subject was taken from the Chester Miracle Plays,[2] and the opera was completed on 15 December 1957 and performed in Orford Church at the 1958 Aldeburgh Festival. The producer was Colin Graham, who also designed the sets, while costume design was undertaken by Ceri Richards.

    Britten's working copy of the medieval mystery plays contains annotations indicating which passages of text correspond to specific musical numbers, such as 'recit' and 'ensemble'; the opera is designed as a series of strophic pieces –

---

[1] Britten in an interview in *The Times* on his return from Russia in 1964; quoted in White, *Benjamin Britten*, pp. 83–4.

[2] Britten's copy of the miracle plays is housed in the Britten–Pears Library: Alfred W. Pollard (ed.), *English Miracle Plays, Moralities and Interludes: Specimens of the Pre-Elizabethan Drama* (Oxford Clarendon Press, 8th edn, 1927); GB–ALb 1–9300358.

'dramatic tableaux' – which are connected by sung dialogue. The dramatic and musical structure is underpinned by three communal audience hymns that are evenly distributed throughout the work. The opera was intended for the same style of performance as the former guild plays. Britten wrote to Owen Brannigan, whom he hoped would take the part of Noye: 'I am writing it for two grown-ups and six professional children, and literally hundreds of local school children. We are doing two or three performances in a very beautiful local church (Orford), very much in the naïve medieval style.'[3]

It is possible to cast the opera almost entirely for children and, as was the case with *The Little Sweep*, Britten's performance instructions are quite detailed and explicit. Adults are required for the Voice of God (though this need not necessarily be a professional actor), Noye (a bass-baritone) and Noye's wife (a contralto). Sem, Ham and Jaffert and their wives should be played by boys and girls between the ages of eleven and fifteen, while Mrs Noye's Gossips should be older girls with strong voices, especially in the lower registers. The animals – forty-nine species divided into seven groups – are played by children. The total cast list is three adults and ninety children. Similarly, the large orchestra of sixty-seven players is to be made up from young amateur players aided by some professionals (namely the solo string quartet, solo treble recorder, piano (four hands), organ and timpani). The very large percussion section includes bass, tenor and side drums, tambourine, cymbals, triangle, whip, gong, Chinese block, wind machine, sandpaper and slung mugs.

The subject of *Noye's Fludde* recalls the father–son drama of *Abraham and Isaac* which Britten had drawn from the same medieval collection.[4] Moreover, it also subtly reconsiders what is a recurring theme in Britten's works – the ambivalent dialectic between innocence and experience, ignorance and knowledge, and between instinct and intellect – a theme which Britten now frames within an explicitly Christian context. The opera starts with a Christian acknowledgement of human frailty and weakness, as the congregation sing the first of the audience hymns, 'Lord Jesus, think on me'. In an admission of guilt, they call upon Christ to restore man to the purity and innocence which they, as adults, have lost, and which the children are about to lose as they travel through the darkness and confusion of the Flood:

> *Lord Jesus, think on me,*
> *And purge away my sin;*
> *From earthborn passions set me free,*
> *And make me pure within.*
> *Lord Jesus, think on me,*
> *Nor let me go astray;*
> *Through darkness and perplexity*
> *Point the heavenly way.*

---

3   7 December 1957; HC, pp. 380–1.
4   Pollard, *English Miracle Plays*.

In 'Through *Noye's Fludde*' Wilfrid Mellers writes: 'We start, that is, with the consciousness of sin and earth-born passion, which we have to encompass before we can see "eternal brightness". Although the Flood is in one sense a destructive force, it is in another sense (as it was in biblical myth) a necessary return to the unconscious waters.'[5] The birth of consciousness heralds the death of innocence. The common people in *Noye's Fludde* are about to undergo a personal trial: like Lucretia, Billy Budd, Albert Herring, Miles and Flora, their child-like simplicity and instinctive faith is under threat.

The first audience hymn is a wild march in a modally inflected E minor. Its principal melodic shape, the descending scale of the appeal 'think on me', becomes a motive of reassurance and confirmation as the opera proceeds.[6] Yet in this opening hymn, the bass line is disconcertingly out of step with the vocal line. The bass traces a sequence of descending fourths, E–B–F♮, the 'disruptive' F♮ injecting a note of conflict and unrest; this unpredictable mingling of 'perfect' intervals with 'imperfect' tritones may signal harmonically the dramatic conflict between guilt and redemption to come [Example 28]. These intervallic progressions in the bass line also underscore the modulatory movement of the succeeding sections of *Noye's Fludde*, modulations which complement and illuminate the dramatic profile of the opera. The use of harmonic opposition in this way recalls the clash of opposing tonal axes which had underpinned the musico-dramatic structures of Britten's early operas, most notably and directly *Peter Grimes*. Indeed in the 'Sunday Morning' scene of *Peter Grimes*, the clash of E and F is exploited within a similar religious context.[7]

In the third verse of the hymn, the prophetic Flood is referred to directly, and at this point Britten's harmonic language become more chromatic. The bass effects a stepwise ascent, mirroring the movement of the rising waters. All voices join in unison for the final verse, and as this verse closes, E–B repetitions in the bass appear to confirm the key as E minor. However, this certainty is undermined by a dissonant F♮ on the last word of the hymn. As the opera progresses, E minor is closely identified with the 'sin' of which humanity must be purged: it becomes what Mellers describes as a 'key of pilgrimage', but at this early stage in the work there is still far to travel and much to endure.

The dramatic significance of the F♮ which undermines the concluding cadence of the hymn is revealed when this pitch is transformed into the thunderous, wrathful voice of God (Fig. 4):

> *GOD'S VOICE [tremendous]:*
> *I, God, that all this worlde hath wroughte,*

---

5   Wilfrid Mellers, 'Through *Noye's Fludde*', in Palmer, *The Britten Companion*, p. 154. The return to unconscious waters echoes the fate of Peter Grimes, Billy Budd, and subsequently Gustav von Aschenbach in *Death in Venice*.

6   The sentiments of this hymn recall the opening chorus of Act 1 of *Peter Grimes*, in which the Borough fishermen and womenfolk ask for God's protection as they struggle with the risks that face them in their daily lives.

7   See Chapter 3.

Example 28

> *Heaven and eairth, and all of naughte,*
> *I see my people in deede and thoughte*
> *Are sette full fowle in synne.*

With the resounding declamation of God, the opera's drama begins. God's spiritual 'otherness' is delineated by his spoken idiom, which recalls the stentorian, disembodied voice of the towering figure of Paul Bunyan. God has created all things, Good and Bad, yet man in sin and guilt has squandered God's blessings; however, mankind may still be saved through the agency of Noye's Ark, which will breast the Flood:

> *Therefore, Noye, my servante free,*
> *That righteous man arte, as I see.*

Throughout God's declamation the bass line reverses its preceding progression, moving from F♮ to B and finally to a pounding pedal E. Repeated crotchets on E are enlivened first with syncopation and then with rhythmic acceleration as Noye formulates his plan, and sings of his joyful acceptance of his fate (Fig. 6):

> *O, Lorde,*
> *I thanke thee lowde and still,*
> *That to me arte in suche will,*
> *And spares me and my howse to spill.*

Noye's lyrical outburst is underscored by a chordal progression, F♯ minor – B major – C♯ major – F♯ minor, while the E pedal continues, gradually assuming the role of the dominant in A major as the voice climbs optimistically to a high E. However, throughout this short passage a quivering E–F♮ semitone motive injects reservation and uncertainty, until (Fig. 7) Noah's energy and conviction lift the music into a more emphatic A major as he summons his children to an act of work and worship.[8]

'Quick and excited', the children gather to build the ark (Fig. 8). Their dancing, pentatonic lines are derived from Noye's call, and the increasing syncopation and mounting canonic entries reveal the eagerness of youth – everyone anticipates, and wants to share in, the transformative experience to come. Similarly, each verse shifts abruptly into a new key and these rapid modulations convey the children's excitement and optimism. In their 'ignorance' they cannot conceive of the existence of sin:

> SEM: *Father, I am all readye bowne;*
> *An axe I have, and by my crowne!*
> *As sharpe as anye in all this towne,*
> *For to goe therto.*

Forebodingly, the ark-building song (Fig. 18) does not shift from F major, for it is a reminder of God's will:

> NOYE: *Now in the name of God I will begyne*
> *To make the shippë here that we shall in*
> *That we may be readye for to swyme*
> *[With the children]*
> *At the cominge of the fludde.*

The falling motive which characterises Noye's solemn declaration, and the melodic shape of the refrain, link this song with the first congregational hymn and recall the fundamental appeal, 'think on me'.

Mrs Noye's is the only voice of dissent. Noye's wife is traditionally portrayed as a cantankerous and difficult woman, and Britten's characterisation repeats some of the parodic representation of *Paul Bunyan*, *Peter Grimes* and *Albert Herring*. She adamantly refuses to play any part, and as such appears to be a less tragic or sincere version of 'the outsider' figure who frequently inhabits Britten's operas. Her argumentative duet with Noye culminates on a pedal E, which progresses once more through B to F, thereby triggering God's ominous and symbolic warning (Fig. 30):

> *Fourtye dayes and fortye nights*
> *Raine shall fall for ther unrightes,*
> *And that I have made through my mightes,*
> *[Dying away]*
> *Now thinke I to destroye.*

---

[8]   However, the second-inversion chord inhibits a full sense of resolution.

In his wrath, God issues further instructions. F♮ continues to pound in the timpani as God prepares to unleash the flood.

At this point, a bugle call is heard for the first time (Fig. 32). Two by two the child-animals march into the ark; the B♭ tonality of the bugle's summons, a tritone distant from the E minor of man's sinfulness, is perhaps indicative of their natural state of innocence. For Britten, the bugle sonority did not necessarily have military associations but rather recalled the world of school. Humphrey Carpenter recounts that David Layton, who was at Gresham's with Britten: 'is convinced that the bugle theme in *Noye's Fludde* is a recollection of the school Officer Training Corps band practising in front of the cricket pavilion, where there was a "grand echo", while he and Britten were nearby in the nets.'[9] Thus the instrument may evoke Britten's own boyhood.

Between the repeated statements of the march tune, coloured by the bugle's repeated calls, the multifarious birds and beasts sing 'Kyrie eleison', a layering of the text which recalls both the Church scene in *Peter Grimes*, and the children's 'Benedictes' in Act 2, Scene 2, 'The bells', of *The Turn of the Screw*. Moreover, the sentiments formerly expressed in *Our Hunting Fathers* and *Paul Bunyan* are brought to mind: the creatures are 'natural', 'preconscious', unsullied by man's consciousness of sin and choice. When the humans enter the ark (Fig. 48) the 'Kyrie eleison' modulates through a series of stepwise rising chords, and expands melodically from a rocking two-note figure to a pentatonic melisma rooted on G (the relative major of E minor and equidistant from E and B♭). This is the first intimation of the pitch that will be the opera's ultimate tonal, and musico-dramatic, goal.

Mrs Noye alone remains defiant, shouting furiously, 'I will not oute of this towne . . . I will not come theirin to-daye'. Noye tries to call her home to God by restating the descending motive of the opening hymn, 'think on me'. Yet she is both dramatically and harmonically alienated from the community, her sharpened sevenths jarring against the flat modal sevenths of the hymn. Moreover, extended trills on D♯, the major seventh of E minor (Fig. 51), persistently prevent an equivocal modulation to G major. Noye's son issues an appeal to his mother (Fig. 53) with a flattened Phrygian version of the hymn phrase 'think on me' which counters her sharp tonality, but still the D♯'s remain. The climax occurs at Fig. 55; the tempo relaxes and the bitonal opposition of Mrs Noye's D♯ and a sustained E minor triad reinforces the vehemence of her statement that she would rather have gossip than salvation. D♯ continues to challenge the E minor ostinato of the 'Flood Song' sung by the chorus of Gossips. Mrs Noye's increasingly frenzied denials – 'That will not I! That will not I' (Fig. 63) – which trace the pitches B–D♯–G, perfectly illustrate this harmonic and expressive conflict.

However, Mrs Noye does show courage and is not ultimately beyond redemption. The children lift her into the boat – and Noye has his ears boxed by his angry wife – as one of the opera's most startling modulations is effected. The *ppp* C

---

[9]   HC, p. 382.

Example 29

minor triad played by the organ enharmonically reinterprets D♯ as E♭ and thereby reconciles the alien harmony. This enharmonic rereading allows for the reaccommodation of Mrs Noah with those who will be saved.

It is at this point (Fig. 67) that God's storm is unleashed, in a large-scale instrumental movement – a passacaglia [Example 29]. The ground bass comprises pairs of ascending minor thirds which rise by whole tone steps: it embraces all twelve notes of the chromatic scale (recalling the 'screw' theme in *The Turn of the Screw*), but is tonally anchored by a strong repeated G. Wilfrid Mellers suggests that this passacaglia theme 'is [also] God's law which is beyond change'.[10] As Noye's family pray (Fig. 70) the first Hymn returns in E minor, and we can see clearly how the melodic contours of this hymn have shaped the ground bass of the storm.

The dramatic grandeur and vast scale of the endlessly repeating ground paradoxically suggest both the epic passing of time and an 'other-worldly' state which is universal, static and timeless. There are twenty-one different variations depicting the rain, rain and wind, thunder, lightning, more wind, waves, wind flapping in the rigging, great waves, the ship rocking and the panic of the animals. The storm opens with a piece of 'nursery-inspired' instrumentation, for Imogen Holst recalled how Britten:

> had the idea of hitting teacups with teaspoons to represent the sound of the first raindrops falling on the ark, but he came round to me one afternoon saying that he'd tried it out at tea-time and it wouldn't work. By great good fortune I had once had to teach Women's Institute percussion groups during a wartime 'social half hour', so I was able to take him into my kitchen and show him how a row of china mugs hanging on a length of string could be hit with a large wooden spoon.[11]

This sound is soon joined by swirling recorders, amateur strings and young percussionists: the storm is made up almost entirely of childlike materials.

At the height of the storm (Fig. 82) the audience join together to ask for deliverance, through the singing of the Victorian hymn, 'Eternal Father, Strong to

---

10 Mellers, 'Through *Noye's Fludde*', p. 158. Britten's use of the passacaglia in this context is reminiscent of Interlude IV of *Peter Grimes*.

11 HC, p. 382.

Save'. This cry of faith from the centre of the storm quells the animals' panic but does not entirely silence the storm. Britten is repeating the practice and function of the audience participation employed in *The Little Sweep*; the audience hymns touch our consciousness and involve us more personally in the drama and its conflicts. Moreover, in a musico-dramatic context, the hymns resurrect the power and function of the communal singing in *Peter Grimes* (where the Borough's 'Old Joe has gone fishing' is intended to banish the storm from the Boar, and from the minds of those who wait inside the inn) and *Billy Budd* (where the sailors' sea shanties hold thoughts of self-pity and despair at bay, stimulating a mood of comradeship and self-reliance).

In *Noye's Fludde*, the angularities in the melody of the second hymn sit less easily with the ground bass than did the gentle curves of the first hymn, although by the second verse, the hymn has tamed some of the elements of the storm. The passacaglia finally disappears with the third verse (Fig. 86). Played by full organ with descant trebles, the untroubled diatonic harmonies of this verse may reassure us that man's 'innocence' has not been lost: the child-animals have survived the storm of passion which has engulfed them:

> O Sacred Spirit, who didst brood
> Upon the chaos dark and rude,
> Who bad'st its angry tumult cease,
> And gavest light and life and peace:
> O hear us when we cry to thee
> For those in peril on the sea.

The silencing of storm also refocuses the congregation's attention on themselves and their own part in the drama: singing together in church, they can reflect on the drama which has both entertained and embraced them. Britten has created a timeless moment – one which lifts the audience out of the drama, and the flood, while simultaneously encouraging them to experience its full significance.

At Fig. 87 the ground resumes. As the storm subsides, the orchestra play the variants of the passacaglia in reverse, alternating with fragments of the hymn tune which are introduced by the solo strings. Pedal Gs intoned by the drums increasingly dominate, and after an augmented recall of the ground (Fig. 94), while Noye watches from his window as the last slow drops of rain ebb away, the movement ends with a profound calm.

Noye now sends out a raven, declaring above a sustained G minor diminished triad:

> And if this foule come not againe
> It is a signe, soth to sayne,
> That dry it is on hill or playne.

Chromatic cello flutterings, unstable rhythms and tonal uncertainty characterise the raven's fast waltz, the final bars restating and emphasising the former opposition of E and D♯, before a lyrical reprise of the passacaglia theme, played by the viola (Fig. 99) reminds us of God's will. Thus Noye despatches the dove, whose graceful waltz strives towards G tonality and tries to resolve the raven's chromatic scales to diatonic concord. When the dove of peace returns with the olive branch (Fig. 106) the passacaglia theme is transformed: it is no longer exclusively confined to the bass, and retrograde elements of the ground infiltrate the melodic lines (Fig. 106). Perhaps this episode reveals that both the raven and the dove are necessary – that the dark and light must mingle and are interdependent. One must pass through the Flood in order to gain redemption.

A C pedal played by the timpani, above which a chord of B♭ is softly articulated by the strings, announces God's forgiveness (Fig. 107) as he commands Noye and his people to disembark. The animals and humans leave the Ark, two by two, singing B♭ 'Alleluias', thus symmetrically balancing the earlier B♭ bugle calls and 'Kyrie eleisons'; moreover, the syncopated rhythms of the 'Alleluias' are also reminiscent of the work song.

According to the musico-dramatic structure which Britten has established, in order for man to be joined with God, G major must be unequivocally articulated and achieved as the opera's tonal destination. Indeed, G is the key of the last of the three audience hymns (Fig. 113), Thomas Tallis's 'The spacious firmament on high'. This hymn affords a vision of the blessed universe in which man takes his place after the covenant of the rainbow:

> *The spacious firmament on high*
> *With all the blue ethereal sky*
> *And spangled heavens, a shining frame,*
> *Their great original proclaim.*
> *[The sun appears]*

This final affirmative communal outpouring assimilates the 'think on me' figure of the first hymn, in both rising and falling diatonic form. In the first two verses, hand-bell clusters clash against a string counterpoint but in the introduction to verse three, the entrance of the bugles in B♭ swings the harmony towards F. As the moon rises, the soothing, dispassionate timbre of the recorder orchestra depicts the serenity of the rising moon, as the divine planets gather in an ordered, universal vision. The ritual bells and bugles continue to sound even when the whole congregation stands to sing Tallis's hymn. Wilfrid Mellers suggests that the bells and bugles: 'remain unaffected . . . for the creatures are what they are, eternally unchanging in their relationship to God's cosmos, whereas man alone can progress from E minor to G major.'[12] Man thanks God for the triumph of his rational mind over preconscious instinct – 'In reason's ear they all rejoice,/ And utter forth a glorious voice' yet still the voice of instinct remains.

One rather peculiar feature of this hymn is the unorthodox *fortissimo* organ cluster-chord passage which is sounded just before the final verse of Tallis's hymn – which the congregation stand to join – resolves into G (Fig. 117), the key representing man's harmony with God. In practical terms, this organ interlude effects this necessary modulation to G, but Peter Evans considers this passage to be a jarring note. In contrast, Humphrey Carpenter argues that Britten meant this

---

12 Mellers, 'Through *Noye's Fludde*', p. 160.

passage to agitate: 'He seems to be portraying people who attain a sense of godliness (G major) by repressing their real natures.'[13] Carpenter contrasts this awkward modulatory sequence for the organ with the passage at Fig. 113, when G major emerges effortlessly and unexpectedly out of the hand-bells' note cluster of B♭ with an added sixth, i.e. the pitch G. This magical moment follows God's speech as the rainbow envelopes the stage:

> *Wher cloudes in the welckine bene,*
> *That ilkë bowe shalbe seene,*
> *In tocken that my wrath and teene*
> > *Shall never thus wrocken be.*
> *[During this speech an enormous rainbow is spread across the stage*
> > *behind the Ark]*

Carpenter suggests that Britten 'intended to show that real godliness, a true sense of oneness with the universe (as opposed to Anglican-style 'churchiness') arises out of a total acceptance of the sensual (the Balinese-style B♭ with added sixth) – a view rarely expressed in Britten's music.'

The Balinese-style note cluster of the hand-bells is also evocative of Quint's nocturnal celeste music. Imogen Holst described how bells got into score:

> They [the ringers] were members of the local Aldeburgh Youth Club, whom Ben used to invite in every now and then . . . And one day, one of the boys said, 'Well, I've got to go now.' And Ben said, 'What are you doing?' And they were practising hand-bells. And Ben said, 'Oh, I'd love to hear them. Will you come and play them to me tomorrow afternoon?' And so they came, and played in his garden – Little Brown Jug I think it was. And he was so thrilled that he gave that marvellous moment in *Noye's Fludde* to those little boys.[14]

This tone colour also reappears in the Church Parables, and Mervyn Cooke[15] has noted that the use of the percussion as an accompanying timbre is interesting not only because it is evidence of Britten's practical interest in Balinese gamelan technique, but also because there is a strong connection, musical and dramatic, between children and percussion timbres in Britten's music. During 1956, Britten was particularly struck by a gamelan composed entirely of adolescent boys which he described enthusiastically in a letter to Roger Duncan, 8 February 1956: 'Jolly good they were too, & enjoying it like fun!' Cooke suggests that this gamelan served as the initial stimulus for the adolescent 'gamelan' in *Death in Venice*, where tuned percussion are a seductive symbol of the powerful attraction which Tadzio holds for Aschenbach.[16]

The final 'Amen' of *Noye's Fludde* releases a kaleidoscope of instrumental colours, symbolising the all-encompassing embrace of God's blessing of Noye [Example 30]:

---

[13] HC, p. 383.
[14] HC, p. 383.
[15] Mervyn Cooke, *Britten and the Far East*, pp. 231–2.
[16] Similarly, this magical and mysterious sound world reappears in the music for the Fairies in *A Midsummer Night's Dream*.

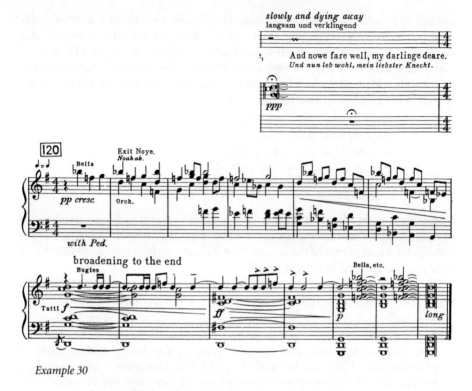

Example 30

My blessinge, Noye, I give thee heare,
To thee Noye, my servante deare,
For vengeance shall noe more appeare,
And nowe fare well, my darlinge deare.

As Noye leaves the stage the music subsides, concluding with three sustained
piano G major chords, above which the hand-bells resonate, trailing into the
silence. Thus, Britten simultaneously depicts a dynamic, human way to God, and
the unchanging, unquestioning and eternal bond between God and Nature.

After the first performance of *Noye's Fludde* Kenneth Clark commented: 'To sit
in Orford Church, where I had spent so many hours of my childhood dutifully
awaiting some spark of divine fire, and then to receive it at last in the performance
of *Noye's Fludde*, was an overwhelming experience.'[17] The opera was generally
well received: Felix Aprahamian, writing in *The Sunday Times*, 22 June 1958,
found it a 'curiously moving spiritual and musical experience', while the *Daily
Telegraph*'s Martin Cooper assessed that 'the future of the work will lie in village
churches such as this and with amateur musicians, for whom Britten has written
something both wholly new and outstanding original'.[18]

Peter Evans observes that: 'Of Britten's typical operatic procedures of

[17] *Ibid.*, p. 109.
[18] *Daily Telegraph*, 19 June 1958.

expansion, whether by development of accompaniment figures and manipulation of phrase lengths in homogenous pieces or by the introduction of significantly contrasted material in others, there is scarcely a trace. And in consequence the work never feels like an opera: "pageant", a term Britten's preface refers to, would probably be its most apt description' (p. 273). However, *Noye's Fludde* does contribute to the inner narrative which was developing in Britten's operatic works. It re-employs various musical techniques found in his preceding operas – such as the binary opposition of harmonic centres and intervals – and extends the musico-dramatic associations of these tonal axes. For example, the opera explores the expressive potential of the relationship between E minor and G major, and establishes the symbolic and dramatic opposition of the semitonal conflict between E and F♮, and the expressive function of B♭ and its associated instrumental timbres. Furthermore, *Noye's Fludde* both revived the mode and spirit of Britten's earlier children's opera, *The Little Sweep*, and was a milestone – for example, in its ritualistic presentation and the use of processions and recessions – on the way to the Church Parables. Likewise the use of familiar hymn tunes looks directly ahead to the use of plainsong in the Parables.[19]

Britten's 'community opera' once more explored the ambiguous relationship between good and evil, innocence and experience, which had been couched in various narrative manifestations in Britten's preceding operas. The harmonic ambivalence at the close of *Noye's Fludde*, recalls a similar unresolved dialectic in *Peter Grimes*, a tension which was associated with a complementary sentiment (Act 1, Scene 1):

> BALSTRODE: *God stay the tide, or I shall share your fears.*
> CHORUS: *For us sea-dwellers, this sea-birth can be*
> *Death to our gardens of fertility.*
> *Yet only such contemptuous springtide can*
> *Tickle the virile impotence of man.*

Until this point, the most transparently Christian treatment of Britten's obsessively revisited theme had been *The Rape of Lucretia*, although in this chamber opera the Christian framework incorporated within Duncan's libretto had seemed dramatically and expressively contrived. Britten's achievement in *Noye's Fludde* was to create a work which could explore this theme within an appropriate genre, and to invest a 'children's opera' with a powerful sincerity and simplicity, accommodating both ambiguity and closure.

---

[19] For example, Cooke, *Britten and the Far East* (p. 222) suggests that the twelve hand bells which colour the speech of God at close of *Noye's Fludde* recreate a Balinese gamelan sonority which emphasises the ritual significance of the spreading of a symbolic rainbow across the stage, and which is reproduced in the timelessness evoked by the set of hand-bells which resonate at the close of *Curlew River*.

11

A Midsummer Night's Dream

> OBERON: *I then did ask of her her changeling child,*
> *Which straight she gave me, and her fairy sent*
> *To bear him to my bower in fairyland.*
> *And now I have the boy, I will undo*
> *This hateful imperfection of her eyes.*
>
> Shakespeare, A Midsummer Night's Dream,
Act 3, Scene 3, lines 58–62[1]

> [Dreaming] gives a chance for your subconscious mind to work when your conscious mind is happily asleep ... if I don't sleep, I find that ... in the morning [I am] unprepared for my next day's work ... [but dreams] release many things which one thinks had better not be released.
>
> Britten, interview with Donald Mitchell[2]

The composition of *Noye's Fludde* was to provide Britten with practical experience of recreating an historical English dramatic form, experience which was to prove invaluable when, in 1959, Britten began working with William Plomer on a new style of operatic genre modelled on Japanese Nō drama. The result was a trilogy of 'church parables' – *Curlew River, The Burning Fiery Furnace* and *The Prodigal Son.*

However, work on the first of these parables was interrupted by the need for Britten to compose a new work for the English Opera Group, which could be performed at the 1960 Aldeburgh Festival, to celebrate the opening of the recently refurbished Jubilee Hall. Britten explained the reasons for the deferment of *Curlew River* to Plomer:

> I fear I must postpone this piece, still near to my heart, for a year. For many reasons ... we are going this coming winter to rebuild the Jubilee Hall, make it a proper little Opera House, with dressing rooms, bigger stage, bigger orchestral pit, changing & increasing the seating, etc, etc, and we must have a new big opera to open it with next June. 'The River' being for a church, wouldn't do, also, it is scarcely festive. So I am going to do the Midsummer Night's Dream – which uses a bigger cast, orchestra, & has the essential advantage of having a libretto ready (it is an old idea of mine, & Peter & I have already done much

---

[1] William Shakespeare, *A Midsummer Night's Dream* (Oxford: OUP, 1994). All subsequent references are to this edition and are given in parentheses in the text.

[2] HC, p. 387.

work, cutting up poor old Shakespeare). I hope you won't be too cross . . . I am determined on doing ['The River'] for the next year.[3]

Elsewhere he explained his choice of subject matter:

Last August [1959] it was decided that for this year's Aldeburgh Festival I should write a full-length opera for the opening of the reconstructed Jubilee Hall. As this was a comparatively sudden there was no time to get a libretto written, so we took one that was ready to hand . . . Operatically, it is especially exciting because there are three quite separate groups – the Lovers, the Rustics, and the Fairies – which nevertheless interact.[4]

Using a pre-existing text of a well-known and popular play was a certainly shrewd commercial decision, one which saved time and the expense of commissioning a new libretto. However, Britten's statement seems somewhat disingenuous given the large quantity of 'unused' librettos which had littered his path and which were theoretically available to him. His librettos were never selected 'for convenience' and it is difficult to believe that his choice was as arbitrary or as objective as he implies.

Shakespeare's *A Midsummer Night's Dream* presents a complex web of possible relationships, one aspect of which is the fight between Oberon and Titania for possession of the exotic Indian changeling boy. The reasons for their battle are never fully explained, and the 'queerness' of this element of the plot is often overlooked. Britten raises their struggle to the centre of his opera and unmasks its sinister undertones. In this way their conflict recalls the previous fights for the possession of an 'innocent' depicted by Britten, most especially that between Quint and the Governess, in which love had been dramatised as both a pure force of goodness and a mania bordering on violence.

The earliest surviving libretto material for *A Midsummer Night's Dream* is a character list and a synopsis of Shakespeare's play in Peter Pears's hand. Having previously collaborated with six different librettists, Britten now decided to write his own text with Pears's assistance. In July 1959 he visited the Pipers to inform them of the project, writing to Pears, 24 July 1959: 'They were thrilled with the idea of *Midsummer Night's Dream* and we discussed it endlessly. I'm just sending off to Myfanwy our projected scheme for it; she has some good ideas about it.'[5] Piper told Carpenter that while she did make a few suggestions, Pears was extremely possessive about his role as co-librettist, and 'didn't want to forgo his collaboration with Ben at all', considering himself 'the literate one'.[6] Britten acknowledged Pears's contribution in a letter to his publisher, Boosey and Hawkes, 16 February 1960: 'Since Peter really did the bulk of the work of

---

3   Britten to Plomer, 12 August 1959, quoted in HC, p. 390.
4   Britten, 'A New Britten Opera', *The Observer*, 5 June 1960, in White, *Benjamin Britten*, pp. 89–90.
5   HC, p. 391.
6   *Ibid.*

adaptation, I think it is only right that he should have the usual librettists [sic] royalties.'[7]

Britten originally intended that Pears himself should sing the part of Lysander, whose phrases are the most independent of the four Lovers (they are seldom differentiated musically), and whose line, 'the course of true love never did run smooth', is the germ of their melodic material.[8] However, early cast lists in Britten's hand suggest that Pears may have been suggested for the role of Flute:

Quince – N. Lumsd (Prologue)	Quince – Lumsden
Snug – T. Anthony (Lion)	Snug – Anthony
Bottom – O. Bran (Pyramus)	Bottom – Branny
Flute – H. Cuenod (Thisby)	Flute – P.P.
Snout – David Tree (Wall)	Snout – Tree
Starveling – (Moon)	Starveling – ?

In the event, Britten's choice, the Swiss tenor Hugues Cuenod who specialised in comic roles, was unavailable and Pears was able to sing his desired part. Pears's performance was reputedly the closest he ever came to camp. Britten's music for the rustics' theatricals in Act 3 was a pastiche of Donizetti, Verdi and Schoenbergian 'sprechstimme', to which Pears added his own parody of Joan Sutherland's performance in Zeffirelli's 1960 Covent Garden production of Donizetti's *Lucia di Lammermoor*.

The libretto which Britten and Pears devised is a substantial truncation of Shakespeare's play, large amounts of the original text being excised in the interests of length and intelligibility. Initially Britten and Pears worked independently from their respective copies of the text, redistributing speeches, inserting repetitions and reordering short, related statements. These amendments were often made for musical reasons: for example, in the Lovers' quarrel, the use of simultaneous speech enabled Britten to assemble the two couples into a quartet, thereby creating a more effective ensemble. Similarly, 'thee' was changed to 'you' and Titania became Tytania, thus facilitating sung pronunciation. Few of the discrepancies between their versions are structurally or thematically significant although interestingly the sources reveal that it was Britten's preferences which were usually retained in these early stages.

It was Shakespeare's opening Act which was subject to the most drastic reorganisation by Britten and Pears. The majority of the first scene was cut, although some of this text was transferred to the final Act of the opera. Thus Shakespeare's formal balance, whereby the action opened and closed in the 'civilised' world of Theseus's court, this world framing the magical woodland scenes, was destroyed. In the play, it is ostensibly Theseus's pronouncement that Hermia must marry

---

[7]   Quoted in Mervyn Cooke, 'Britten and Shakespeare: Dramatic and Musical Cohesion in *A Midsummer Night's Dream*', *Music and Letters*, vol. 74, 1993, 249.

[8]   This phrase is also related to the Fairies' melody 'Over hills over dale' (Act 1, Fig. 1), as well as the line shared by Tytania and Oberon, 'And this same progeny of evils comes,/ From our debate, from our dissension' (Act 1, Fig. 14). Its even, swaying crotchets and stepwise movement infuse much of the melodic material of the opera.

Demetrius which precipitates the action, as it is his rescinding of this judgment which brings about dramatic resolution. Having removed much of the opening scene Britten and Pears were therefore forced, despite Britten's insistence that no changes should be made to Shakespeare's actual words, to insert an additional line – 'Compelling thee to marry with Demetrius' – in order to clarify the characters' motivation. However, Shakespeare also intimates that the discord between the courtly lovers is a direct result of the disharmony in the fairy kingdom. In contrast, in the opera Theseus and Hippolyta are unaffected by Oberon's magic. Their entry in Act 3 occurs too late in the proceedings for them to be established satisfactorily as rounded characters and they can appear stiff, formal and irrelevant to the drama we have witnessed by this point in the proceedings. This weakness was noted by a contemporary reviewer:

> as the music begins for the interlude before the final scene, there is every ground for anticipating a major revelation. But it is precisely at this point of the trial that the opera fails. Already, with the broadly Italianate string melody which heralds the entry to Theseus's court, one senses a certain artificiality, and although the introduction of Theseus at so late a stage is an arduous necessity, there is no reason why he should not be given appreciable musical stature.[9]

Britten was aware of these dramatic shortcomings and discussed with Myfanwy Piper plans for a Prologue. The sources in the Britten–Pears Library contain her drafts for such a scene and a discarded sketch containing four bars of music.[10] In spite of Britten's liking for framing devices he refrained from including a Prologue, presumably because such a passage would have weakened the dramatic effect of his opening scene.

Britten's opera does not open at Theseus's court but throws us immediately into the nocturnal embrace of the wood. By dispensing with Shakespeare's frame he removes the world of social and moral convention against which the

---

9   David Drew, *New Stateman*, 25 June 1960.
10 These read:
    Act One
    Prologue, by a Herald (possibly two Heralds) announcing
    a) Theseus' wedding with Hippolyta,
    b) Hermia compelled by her father's ruling to marry Demetrius or otherwise to enter a Nunnery. (not yet written).
   Piper later supplied the following text:
    <u>1st Herald</u> Know! That the nuptial hour between Lord Theseus and the fair Hyppolita [sic] draws on apace: to-morrow shall the moon, bent in the heavens like a silver bow behold the night of their solemnities
    <u>1st and 2nd Herald</u> Therefore ye youth of Athens, with pomp and triumph and with revelling and mirth, stir up and celebrate.
    <u>2nd Herald</u> Know! This is Lord Theseus will concerning Hermia, Egeus daughter, who, in defiance of her father will not wed Demetrius, but only Lysander, who loves her well. The Athenian Law bids her obey, or leave this world a nun or die, [which last Egeus claims privilige [sic] to enforce]. Lord Theseus gives her till his Nuptial day to make her choice: death, or the cloister, or Demetrius.
    <u>1st and 2nd Heralds</u> Repeat 1st 2 lines to 'apace'.

transgressive events and experiences of the wood might be judged and interpreted. Similarly, in Act 3, Britten and Pears omitted Theseus's monologue:

> THESEUS: Lovers and madmen have such seething brains,
> Such shaping fantasies, that apprehend
> More than cool reason ever comprehends . . .
> And as imagination bodies forth
> The forms of things unknown, the poet's pen
> Turns them to shapes, and gives to airy nothing
> A local habitation and a name.   (V. i. lines 4–6, 14–17)

David Drew interprets this omission as a sign of Britten's confidence that his music had successfully embodied the meaning of Theseus's words:

> There is no surer sign of Britten's present confidence as an opera composer than the fact that he omitted Theseus's speech from his opera. On the surface the speech might appear to parallel the interpretative and moralistic passages in *Billy Budd* and *Lucretia* though of course it is comparatively more natural and integrated. It is the very integration that gives Britten his excuse for omitting the speech, for in opera music has the function of making explicit whatever is latent.[11]

An alternative explanation is possible: that Theseus's speech was cut because it was not relevant to Britten's expressive purpose. In Britten's first three operas the social and psychological dramas had been inseparable, but through *Billy Budd* to *The Turn of the Screw* there had been an increasing internalisation of the dramatic tension and a reduction in the significance and influence of the external forces of oppression. Now, in *A Midsummer Night's Dream*, the forces of social oppression were eliminated entirely and Britten provided no equivalent of the Borough, Roman society, Loxford, naval law, the Elizabethan court or Mrs Grose. 'Coherence' is represented not by 'society' but by 'love'. The dialectic is no longer one between the individual and society, but between 'real' love and self-delusion: it cannot be resolved in the world of convention or normality but only in the world of dreams. Therefore, the opera is framed not by Theseus's pronouncements but by the Fairies song 'Over hill, over dale' and Puck's spoken farewell and invitation:

> PUCK: If we shadows have offended,
> Think but this, and all is mended:
> That you have but slumbered here,
> While these visions did appear.
> Gentles, do not reprehend.
> If you pardon, we will mend.
> Else the Puck a liar call.
> So goodnight unto you all.
> Give me your hands, if we be friends,
> And Robin shall restore amends.

Such 'visions' can only be fully experienced in the imaginative space symbolised by the wood.

---

11 Drew, *New Statesman*, 25 June 1960.

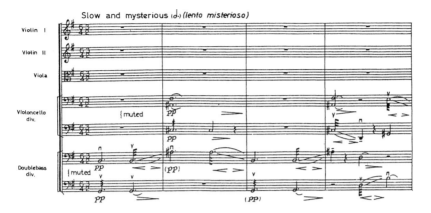

Example 31 (a)

The entire action of the opera is encased within the morally ambivalent domain of the wood, which is elevated to become almost another 'character' in the drama. The sweeping glissandi of the opening bars suggest its all-embracing expanse and its remoteness from human passions, creating a shimmering soundscape which complements the visual effect of half-light and shifting perspectives. It is a land of the night where the Lovers hope to discover the healing power of sleep and dreams, a private place far from prying and judgmental mortal eyes.

The chords which open the opera evoke the deep-breathing, dreamy sighs of sleep [Example 31]. A glistening sequence of carefully orchestrated, kaleidoscopic tone colours, these chords simultaneously suggest 'naturalness' (the chords are diatonic triads) and 'unnaturalness' (they progress in an unrelated sequence). The preciseness of Britten's instrumentation, dynamics and articulation is reminiscent of his notation of the interview chords in *Billy Budd*, while the dodecaphonic character of the chords, which is especially obvious in Act 2, recalls the

slowly animating *(poco a poco animando)*

Example 31 (b)

'screw' theme from *The Turn of the Screw*.[12] Just as these earlier wordless passages had appeared to embody operatic 'meaning', albeit an ultimately undefinable 'meaning', so the 'sleep chords' might be interpreted as a symbol or summary of the expressive 'message' of *A Midsummer Night's Dream*. This is experienced particularly strongly in Act 2 where the chords, whose free repetition and variation in the opening Act establishes an all-embracing sound-world which complements the unified setting, are bonded in a more formal arrangement which frames the Act and punctuates its moments of dramatic intensity.

It is Oberon who is the opera's 'master-of-ceremonies', controlling all events and experiences which take place within the wood. His appearance on stage is theatrically striking, even unnerving. Writing in *The Sunday Times*, 12 June 1960, Desmond Shawe-Taylor described his costume as 'a black magician's gown, half mandarin and half Prospero', while the reviewer in *The Times* found that the experience of the opera 'was that of being gripped by a spell, of being subjected in fact to a dose of Oberon's own medicine'.[13] Visually and aurally Oberon must have unsettled the first audience, challenging their musical and dramatic expectations, for the part was written for male countertenor, a voice which was infrequently employed on the stage at this time. The countertenor's ambiguous vocal

---

[12] Britten's compositional sketches contain several twelve-tone check-lists.
[13] *The Times*, 17 June 1960.

timbre perfectly complements the aura of unorthodoxy which emanates from Oberon, and unites the entire Fairy kingdom in a high, unearthly aural field. However, this vocal casting was not without its problems: for example, in his dramatic struggle with Tytania, Oberon can be musically eclipsed by her virtuosic coloratura, as her unrelenting, piercing phrases overwhelm his lower register. It is not until in Act 3 when Tytania is defeated and forswears her love for Bottom and the Indian boy that her vocal lines, directed by Oberon, become more muted and restrained.

Oberon's magic acts as a unifying force in the opera, and may be viewed as an extension of Peter Quint's power of enchantment.[14] Like Quint, Oberon is identified with the ethereal instrumental timbre of the celeste, harp and percussion. As he wields his power, his music gravitates towards E♭: for example, his instructions to Puck (Act 1, Fig. 51; Act 2, Fig. 89) are recited on this pitch, as is his invitation to Tytania to dance a sarabande with him in Act 3 (Fig. 12). The 'spell' music is the supreme expression of his omnipotence [Example 32]. Its first statement (Act 1, Fig. 20) is introduced by a phrase which chromatically fills the interval, B♭–E♭, recalling the range and shape of Quint's melodies in *The Turn of the Screw*,[15] while the spell melody itself comprises of a series of interlocking thirds whose even, calm declamation seems related to Miles's 'Malo Song'. Accompanied by dissonant seconds played by the celeste (ranging from B♭ to E♭) and a repeated glockenspiel E♭, Oberon's magical song might be considered a synthesis of the music of Quint and Miles. The repetitions of this theme in Act 1 (Figs. 35, 46 and 102) are accompanied by increasingly elaborate orchestral effects, and surrounded by plaintive renderings of the theme performed by solo violin and solo cello. As his spell unleashes its power, Oberon's E♭ and instrumental colouring infiltrate the music of the bewitched characters (see Act 1, Fig. 88, Act 2, Fig. 31, 71 and 81); later, as the dramatic complexities are unravelled, E♭ centred melody and harmony imply that Oberon's spell was the source of the confusion, for example (Act 3, Fig. 9):

> TYTANIA: *My Oberon, what visions I have seen!*
> *Methought I was enamoured of an ass.*
> OBERON: *There lies your love.*
> TYTANIA: *How came these things to pass?*
> *Oh, how mine eyes do loathe his visage now!*

The seductive potency of Oberon's song implies not only the Fairy King's personal authority but also the enchanting power of music itself. Throughout the opera the characters make frequent requests for music, which is often provided by the boy Fairies. As Tytania awakens under the influence of Oberon's spell, she sings to Bottom, beginning with recitation on E♭:

---

[14] It is interesting to note that Oberon's music, and that of the other Fairies, takes the form of closed set pieces, the stillness and decorum of which contrast with the undisciplined 'endless melody' of the four lovers. It is not until Act 3 when Oberon awakens them from their dream that they sing a set-piece ensemble, initiated by Helena's line 'And I have found Demetrius, like a jewel' (Act 3, Fig. 19a).

[15] This interval was also associated with the Governess's lament 'They're lost! lost! lost!'

Example 32 (a)

Example 32 (b)

> *I pray thee gentle mortal, sing again;*
> *Mine ear is much enamour'd of thy note,*
> *So is mine eye enthralled to thy shape,*
> *Thou art as wise as thou art beautiful.*

Similarly, following Tytania's dis-enchantment by Oberon (Act 3, Fig. 11) the Fairy-monarchs cry:

> *OBERON: Tytania, music call, and strike more dead*
> *Than common sleep, of all these five the sense.*
> *TYTANIA: Music ho, ho music, such as charmeth sleep.*

Tytania's phrase stresses the interval B♭–E♭ and in its general shape recalls the 'ceremony of innocence' melody from *The Turn of the Screw*. Britten's music is a 'magic potion': at this point musical concord brings about dramatic harmony but elsewhere its effects are less beneficent.

Similarly, Oberon's magic has both good and bad results. Although his bewitching of Tytania is malicious, Oberon's intentions towards the four Lovers are more benevolent. His spiteful phrase 'And make her full of hateful fantasies, of hateful fantasies' (Act 1, Fig. 51) is immediately succeeded by his instructions to Puck concerning his plans to remedy the Lovers' distress. Despite his apparent authority, he is evidently not fully in control of the power he yields, since his magic does not inform him that Lysander is also in the wood and consequently he fails to warn Puck of the possibility of mistaken identity. His spell, which is both the cause and remedy of disorder, is influenced by an uncontrollable outside agent, which overrides the effects of his power.

Oberon's potion works its magic by the light of midsummer moon, at the moment when the old moon wanes and the new moon rises. Britten had previously depicted the transforming power of the changing moon in *Paul Bunyan*:

> CHORUS OF TREES:
> *But once in a while an odd thing happens,*
> *Once in a while the dream comes true,*
> *And the whole pattern of life is altered,*
> *Once in a while the moon turns blue.*

Shakespeare's moon imagery emphasises the mutability of the moon's influence. Egeus blames the moon for Lysander's enchantment of Hermia:

> EGEUS: Thou hast by moonlight at her window sung   (I. i. line 30)

but when Oberon cancels the spell on Titania, it is a more beneficent symbol:

> OBERON: Be as thou wast wont to be,
> See as thou wast wont to see.
> Dian's bud o'er Cupid's flower
> Hath such force and blessed power.   (IV. i. lines 70–3)

The identification of the changing moon with love may be evidence of the fickleness of romantic love; alternatively, the moonlight may illuminate 'real' love and endow the lover with an enlightened vision. Oberon's spell, working by moonlight, is therefore potentially both liberating and destructive. Latent in his beautiful and erotic melodic strains is the threat of violence: what will happen if he fails to get the boy?

Britten composed the part of Oberon with a particular singer in mind. He wrote to Alfred Deller, a singer with Canterbury Cathedral Choir who, after his 'discovery' by Michael Tippett during the war, was probably single-handedly responsible for reviving the Purcellian counter-tenor voice:

> I see you and hear your voice very clearly in this part.[16]

In the light of the numerous dramatic and musical affinities between the parts of Oberon and Quint it is perhaps surprising that Britten did not envisage Peter Pears in this role. The answer may lie in the 'inhuman' nature of the part of Oberon. In *The Turn of the Screw* Pears's ghostly Quint had projected very real, human emotions through the warm, melodic lyricism of his vocal timbre, in an attempt to achieve a genuine communion with the living boy. In contrast, Oberon's voice is truly a voice from another world, heard only by the Fairies and undetected by the Lovers, the Rustics or the Court. Britten may have considered that the expressive 'otherness' of the countertenor timbre could more effectively establish the required dramatic distance between the mortal and immortal stage characters, and between the Fairies and the audience, than the emotionally burdened tenor of Pears. The audience is briefly admitted into the immortals' sound world but is continually reminded of the 'difference' between themselves and the inhabitants of the wood.

---

[16] HC, p. 391.

Interestingly, though Deller was initially worried about his lack of dramatic experience, Tippett found his dramatic naivety to be a positive feature of his performance, describing his singing as conveying 'almost no emotional irrelevancies [to] distract us from the absolutely pure musical quality'.[17] Tippett is surely mistaken when he says that Deller's singing carried no emotional distractions. At this time, the countertenor voice was relatively rare and was still associated with intimations of effeminacy and emasculation or the irrational and perverse. Wayne Koestenbaum writes: 'Falsetto seems profoundly perverse: a freakish side-show: the place where voice goes wrong.'[18] Conversely, the countertenor is also the descendant of the eighteenth-century castrato, a tradition whereby young boys were surgically castrated to retain their high tessitura. St Paul's decree that 'women should be silent in church' was used to justify their welcome into the Church and the castrato quickly became the *primo uomo* of *opera seria*, singing the 'heroic' roles – kings, warriors, poets, gods – now more usually reserved for the tenor. Although they sometimes performed female stage roles they were not primarily employed as a substitute for women's or boy trebles' voices but were valued for their own peculiar vocal timbre – its power and brilliance, versatility and virtuosity, strangeness and ambiguity – which came to be associated with both transcendence and transsexualism.

The countertenor voice is thus a melting-pot of contradictory expressive and dramatic possibilities. On the one hand it resonates with the spiritual purity of the English cathedral tradition and the music of Purcell; on the other, its 'unnatural' timbre looks back to the eighteenth-century castrato model with its contradictory associations of power and effeminacy. In *A Midsummer Night's Dream* Britten manipulated these ambivalent overtones to create a powerful emotional aura. Later he would further exploit the other-worldly or inhuman qualities of the countertenor timbre and of falsetto singing in *Death in Venice*.

Just as Quint and Oberon appear to share dramatic and musical characteristics, so Puck might be deemed to be a representation of what Miles could have become had he chosen to follow Quint into the wood. Puck is not a prepubescent treble like Miles but is a fully aware adolescent, amoral, agile and gloriously free. Britten cast the role as a speaking part, to be played by a boy acrobat whose voice was on the verge of breaking. He described Puck as 'absolutely amoral and yet innocent': 'I got the idea of doing Puck like this in Stockholm, where I saw some Swedish child acrobats with extraordinary agility and powers of mimicry, and suddenly

---

[17] HC, p. 394. Other observers found Deller's stage inexperience less advantageous. Though he praised Deller's 'exquisite soft singing', Desmond Shawe-Taylor's judgment, in the *Sunday Times* of 12 June 1960, that his performance was 'undramatic', was more typical. For the Covent Garden production in February 1961 Deller was replaced by the American counter-tenor Russell Oberlin. Despite the assertions of his biographers that the experience led to depression, Deller himself had observed the negative effect of his presence among reviewers and had written to Britten: 'delete me when you think fit . . . I shall always be grateful for being given such a wonderful opportunity' (Deller to Britten, 11 June 1960, in HC, p. 396).

[18] Koestenbaum, *The Queen's Throat*, p. 164.

realised we could do Puck that way.'[19] Puck's budding sexuality, symbolised by his breaking (corrupted?) voice, recalls the burgeoning sexual awareness of Albert Herring, Billy Budd and Miles. Furthermore, the trumpet fanfares which accompany Puck's exuberant entries are reminiscent of the trumpet flourishes which had been identified with Billy. Recent reviewers have commented upon the latent pederasty in the relationship between Oberon and Puck and the more general transgressive sexual undercurrents in the opera, in terms which evoke the mood of child-like anticipation present in *Albert Herring* and *The Turn of the Screw*. 'I have always considered this Britten opera as a cute exploitation of choirboys and counter-tenor in baroque pantomime . . . Most extraordinary of all was the athletic entrance and entrancingly obsessive Puck of the 15-year old Kristian Widell, his nose as it were pressed against the glass of the sweetshop window in which all this burgeoning sexuality and passion are displayed.'[20]

Oberon's obsessive longing for the changeling boy is curious since he already has a willing and compliant accomplice in Puck. Perhaps the boy's prepubertal exoticism attracts Oberon because the appeal of the rough and boisterous Puck is fading, just as Britten's relationships frequently cooled as the young boys whom he befriended matured. Stephen Terry, who had sung the part of Harry in *Albert Herring* and who played Puck on the 1966 Decca recording and in the 1967 production, was a frequent guest at the Red House during this period and remembered:

> [Britten] was the kind father/uncle figure. I can remember thinking 'I wish he were my father, I wish I could be his son . . . There was an incredible tenderness as well, not sexuality, but always a great sense of gentle, almost fragile being. And in comparison Peter always seemed strong and severe and slightly judgmental. I think that there was a resentment of me there. I felt Peter as a slightly hostile presence . . . I can remember a paternal kiss on the forehead before going to sleep one night. That's about all. I think there was also the occasional arm around the shoulder, that sort of thing. But it all came across to me as paternal rather than amorous.[21]

Terry described his feelings of rejection when, at the age of seventeen, he asked to stay at the Red House and was told: 'No, you can't because we're too busy, but I'll arrange for you to stay with Jeremy Cullum [Britten's secretary/chauffeur].'[22]

Whatever the root of Oberon's own motivations, he condemns Tytania, his rival for possession of the child, for the 'unnaturalness' of her fixation on the Indian boy. Her refusal to give him up to Oberon is recited on the pitch C, Britten's 'innocent' pitch and the pitch upon which Vere had intoned his responses at Billy's trial (Act 1, Fig. 16):

[19] *The Observer*, 5 June 1960. The original Puck was Leonide Massine II, son of the choreographer.

[20] Tom Sutcliffe, review of Swedish Norlands Opera's production of *A Midsummer Night's Dream*, in *Musical Times*, July 1991, vol. 132, no. 1781, 352–3.

[21] HC, pp. 466–7.

[22] *Ibid.*, p. 467.

> His mother was a votress of my order,
> But she being mortal, of that boy did die.

Tytania is acting aberrantly by coveting the boy and making him 'all her joy' at Oberon's expense. Like Vere she wishes to preserve his unnatural innocence, refusing to let him mature. The Fairies' battle for possession of the strange child is a variant or re-enactment of the fight between Peter Quint and the Governess for control of Miles. Oberon resents Tytania's dotage on the boy and dislodges her obsession by substituting a more absurd one.

His spell tampers with the 'love-sight' of any sleeper into whose eyes the potion falls:

> OBERON: The juice of it on sleeping eyelids laid
> Will make or man or woman madly dote
> Upon the next live creature that it sees.   (II. i. lines 170–2)

Illusion and reality become indistinguishable, as Hermia explains:

> Methinks I see these things with parted eye,
> When everything seems double.   (IV. i. lines 188–9)

Cupid's blindness is both physical and moral:

> HELENA: Things base and vile, holding no quantity,
> Love can transpose to form and dignity.
> Love looks not with the eyes, but with the mind,
> And therefore is winged Cupid painted blind.
> Nor hath love's mind of any judgment taste;
> Wings and no eyes figure unheedy haste.   (I. i. lines 231–7)

In this way, Titania's monomaniacal pursuit of love is exposed as a folly of the imagination, of love untempered by reason, which is dramatised at its lowest level by her passion for an ass.[23]

However, Tytania's love for Bottom is the only relationship in the opera which is not soured by power and possession. Strategically sited at the centre of Act 2, the

---

[23] 'Dotage' or deluded love threatens to make fools of all the lovers: for example, Helena humbles herself before Demetrius:

> 'I am your spaniel, and Demetrius,
> The more you beat me I will fawn on you.
> Use me but as your spaniel: spurn me, strike me,
> Neglect me, lose me; only give me leave,
> Unworthy as I am, to follow you.
> What worser place can I beg in your love –
> And yet a place of high respect with me –
> Than to be used as you use your dog?' (II. i. lines 202–10).

Titania's infatuation with Bottom renders her into an object of ridicule and we are reminded of the actions of Gloriana who, made temporarily irrational by the strength of her passion for Essex, foolishly steals Lady Essex's dress and similarly invites the derision of her subjects. Their humiliation might have acted as a warning to Britten of the consequences of ignoring the rationalising voices of moral convention.

Example 33

coupling of the magical Tytania and the asinine Bottom, representatives of the highest and the lowest orders, may symbolise an ideal synthesis which is truly creative. Is her love ridiculous or sublime? As she and Bottom settle down to sleep upon the bank her phrase cadences on D♯, the enharmonic equivalent of Oberon's E♭ (Act 2, Fig. 46). The reinterpretation of this pitch, now accommodated within a languorous love scene in B major, suggests that, just as this pitch is translated, so is their love transfigured. The climax is Tytania's unaccompanied, lyrical outburst (Act 2, Fig. 56):

> *O how I love thee! O how I love thee! how I dote on thee!*

Her phrase is not ironic. Oberon's menacing interlocking thirds are 'straightened out', in a diatonic declaration of real love [Example 33].

The subsequent extended return (Fig. 57) of the four 'sleep chords' which had opened Act 2 suggests that these chords might symbolise the experience of Tytania and Bottom in the wood: the progression from a dark D♭ major triad (the wood/sleep?) through a B minor seventh chord (their passion?), and E♭ major (Oberon's spell), culminates with a 'pure' major third C–E (an echo of the Fairies' 'Hail! Hail! (Act 2, Fig. 42)). Towards the end of the act, the chords are reiterated (Fig. 94) in a long-term progression interspersed between passages depicting Puck's lively mischief-making and the Lovers' growing weariness. When all the mortals are asleep, the four sleep chords form a passacaglia, or ground bass, above which the Fairies sing a pavane (Fig. 102) [Example 34]:

> On the ground, Sleep sound,
> He'll apply, To your eye,
> Gentle lover, remedy.
> When thou wak'st, Thou tak'st
> True delight in the sight
> Of thy former lady's eye:
> And the country proverb known,
> In your waking shall be shown:
> Jack shall have Jill;
> Nought shall go ill,
> The man shall have his mare again
> And all shall be well, all shall be well, all shall be well.

Is this the opera's brief moment of expressive elucidation? The Fairies' parallel thirds might represent a 'purification' of Oberon's sinister interweaving spell theme and Tytania's erotic outburst, combining the monarchs' melodic thirds in vertical fashion, in a stepwise phrase which mimics the movement of the 'course of true love' melody. The music and text have a preternatural, innocent ambience; indeed, throughout *A Midsummer Night's Dream*, the songs sung by the Fairies as they pass through the wood restoring peace and harmony have a slightly unsettling, sharp, stringent quality. The simplicity of their melodic lyricism is disturbed by asymmetrical rhythms and irregular phrase structures, and by the piquancy of the accompanying timbre (for example, 'Over hills, over dales' (Act 1, Fig. 1) and 'Lullaby' (Act 1, Fig. 98)), in a manner which recalls the children's nursery songs in *The Turn of the Screw*. Their apparent innocence is perturbing since it is beyond our understanding. Britten had written: 'I always feel "Midsummer Night's Dream" to be by a very young man, whatever Shakespeare's actual age when he wrote it.'[24] Perhaps by entering the wood he hoped to rediscover a state of prenescient innocence, of the sort described in his 1941 operetta, *Paul Bunyan*, and in the song cycle *Winter Words*, a setting of seven poems by Thomas Hardy which Britten composed in 1953:

VOICE OF PAUL BUNYAN: *It is a forest full of innocent beasts, There are none who blush at the memory of an ancient folly, none who hide beneath dyed fabrics a malicious heart.*

> . . . *A Time there was as one may guess*
> *And as, indeed, earth's testimonies tell*
> *Before the birth of consciousness,*
> *When all went well.*
> *None suffered sickness, love or loss,*
> *None knew regret, starved hope, or heart burnings;*
> *None cared whatever crash or cross*
> *Brought wrack to things.*

24 *The Observer*, 5 June 1960.

Example 34

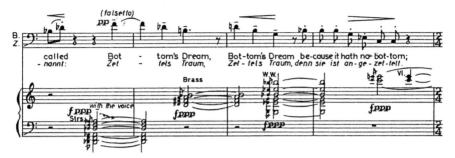

Example 35

> *If something ceased, no tongue bewailed,*
> *If something winced and waned, no heart was wrung;*
> *If brightness dimmed, and dark prevailed,*
> *No sense was stung.*
> *But the disease of feeling germed,*
> *And primal rightness took the tinct of wrong;*
> *Ere nescience shall be reaffirmed*
> *How long, how long, how long, how long, how long?* [25]

In Shakespeare's play, it is Bottom, the 'lowest' of the characters, who alone is afforded a 'dream' – a vision of the Fairy Queen. The synaesthetic confusion of his dream emphasises the wholeness of his perception:

> BOTTOM: I have had a most rare vision. I have had a dream past the wit of man to say what dream it was ... The eye of man hath not heard, the ear of man hath not seen, man's hand is not able to taste, his tongue to conceive, nor his heart to report what my dream was. (IV. i. lines 201–10)

Throughout the play the characters' senses are dislocated and untrustworthy. Bottom alone understands the futility of attempting to solve the riddles and define the undefinable – only the imaginative synthesis of 'art' will supply the 'truth':

> BOTTOM: Man is but an ass if he go about to expound this dream ... I will get Peter Quince to write a ballad of this dream. (IV. i. lines 203–11)

Bottom's 'Dream' is the expressive climax of Britten's opera (Act 3, Fig. 30) [Example 35]. The lilting, regular rhythms and graceful, swaying melodic thirds echo Tytania's words of love, while the woodwind articulate staccato variants of 'the course of true love' motif. Usurping Oberon's falsetto, Bottom pronounces:

> *it shall be called Bottom's Dream, Bottom's Dream because it hath no bottom.*

His melody, which retraces Tytania's falling thirds, is accompanied by the four 'sleep chords'. The last of these chords, C–E–G, is stated by the two harps, vibraphone and cymbals: once again, the chord of 'innocence' has an eerie, exotic

---

[25] Britten, 'Before Life and After', No. 8, *Winter Words, Lyrics and Ballads of Thomas Hardy*, Op. 52.

resonance. The major third, C–E, is taken up by two high solo violins, 'sweetly' quoting a brief fragment of the Fairies' 'Jack and Jill' song.

Britten was fascinated by the world of sleep and dreams, and had previously explored the dream world in the song-cycles *On This Island* (1937), the *Serenade* Op. 31 (1943) – which included a setting of Keats's invocation to sleep, 'O soft embalmer of the still midnight' – and the *Nocturne* Op. 60 (1958). He described the latter, a setting of poems on this theme by Shelley, Tennyson, Coleridge, Middleton, Wordsworth, Owen, Keats and Shakespeare, to Marion Harewood: 'It won't be madly popular because it is the strangest & remotest thing – but then dreams are strange & remote.'[26] The linguistic subtleties of Shakespeare's sonnet 43, which Britten selected for inclusion in the *Nocturne*, recall the complexities of *A Midsummer Night's Dream*:

> When most I wink, then do mine eyes best see . . .
> How would thy shadow's form form happy show
> To the clear days with thy much clearer light.

Do the eyes see most truly when closed, or in dreams do they select only the best? Will the image give as much pleasure as that created by the imagination? These were the questions Britten perhaps hoped to answer in his opera. David Drew proposed that the 'message' articulated in Britten's score was 'nothing less than a statement of a vast and simple truth about creative activity, the truth that reason and imagination are theoretically irreconcilable, but that they meet and become indistinguishable in the work of the true artist'.[27] However, while his operatic characters might indulge their hopes and fears in the imaginative freedom of the wood, Britten himself could find only temporary refuge in his art. The social field which he eradicates from his opera could not be so easily dismissed in reality.

What *do* Britten's lovers find in the wood? Themselves? 'Love'? 'Truth'? When they leave the wood, they recognise that they have been 'translated' by their experiences but they are unable to explain this transformation. We are left with a sense of unease, for Demetrius remains 'bewitched' and Love has been exposed as blind, impulsive, deluded, irrational and compulsive. Britten may be implying that Love may be good or bad, true or foolish, but that it requires the imagination to sustain it. In this way, *A Midsummer Night's Dream* could be Britten's own spell, a musical 'dream' which he hoped would be a realisation of his yearning for a synthesis of imagination and reality.

[26] HC, p. 387.
[27] David Drew, HC, p. 387.

12

The Church Parables

From all ill dreams defend our eyes,
From nightly fears and fantasies;
Tread under foot our ghostly foe,
That no pollution we may know.

'Te lucis ante terminum', from *The English Hymnal*

The composition of *A Midsummer Night's Dream* interrupted a project which Britten had been considering with William Plomer for some time, for a new style of operatic work modelled on Japanese Nō drama. The renewed collaboration between Britten and the librettist of *Gloriana* was to produce a trilogy of works – *Curlew River, The Burning Fiery Furnace* and *The Prodigal Son* – and to lead to the creation of a new genre, the 'church parable'.

In November 1955 Britten and Pears embarked upon a five-month concert tour of Austria, Yugoslavia, Turkey, Singapore, Indonesia, Hong Kong, Japan, Thailand and Sri Lanka. During this tour Britten was able to pursue his strong interest in oriental music, a fascination which had initially been stimulated by his friendship with the Canadian composer and ethnomusicologist, Colin McPhee, whom he had met in America on 7 September 1939.[1] In February 1956, Britten and Pears spent twelve days in Japan, an experience which significantly influenced Britten's subsequent career.[2] Before this visit, Britten had no previous practical experience of Nō theatre or of *Gagaku* (Japanese court music); it was Plomer himself who had recommended that Britten should make the most of the opportunity to immerse himself in these Japanese dramatic arts. Plomer recalled: 'In 1955 Britten was planning a journey to the Far East. Knowing that I had lived in Japan when young, he asked if there was anything he should particularly see or do while there. I strongly recommended the Japanese theatre in its various forms, Kabuki, Bunraku and Nō – particularly the Nō. I remember describing a Nō play and imitating some of the gestures used by the actors.'[3]

---

[1] Britten's first exposure to Indonesian and Balinese music, and his personal friendship and musical collaboration with McPhee, is extensively discussed by Mervyn Cooke, 'Britten and Colin McPhee', *Britten and the Far East*, pp. 23–49.

[2] See Cooke, *ibid.*, 'Japan', 'From Nō to Church Parable' and 'The Later Church Parables', pp. 112–219, for an exhaustive analysis of the influence of oriental music and theatre in Britten's Church Parables.

[3] Edinburgh Festival Programme Book (1968), 28. In fact, remarks by Ronald Duncan, in *Working with Britten*, pp. 112–13, suggest that Britten was interested in Nō plays as early as

Despite the relative 'failure' of his only previous collaboration with Plomer, the Coronation opera *Gloriana*, Britten had retained a sincere professional regard and personal respect for Plomer (as is evident from their extant correspondence, 1948–73).[4] Plomer, like McPhee, had extensive first-hand knowledge of Far East: he had visited Japan in 1926, at the age of twenty-two, and had been so captivated that he had remained for three years. Plomer describes the effect of theatre in Japan:

> And what was the Nō play? To this the European brought that total ignorance which, in its way, made him specially impressionable. One didn't understand the archaic language, the completely strange chanting; one knew nothing of the symbolism, and the briefly outlined plot was so steeped in the mysteries of antiquity, of a remote and venerable culture, of esoteric Buddhism, that one had to rely on little but the evidence of one's senses to perceive the great beauty and refinement and agelessness of a wholly non-popular tradition and convention, which, in present-day jargon, would perhaps be sneered at as 'élitist'.[5]

On 11 February 1956 Britten was taken by Kei-ichi and Hiroshi Kurosawa to the Suidōbashi Nō Theatre for a performance of *Sumidagawa* by Juro Motomasa (1395–1431). Britten was so enthralled by the experience that he insisted on seeing the entire play again before he and Pears left Tokyo,[6] and subsequently acquired a reel-to-reel tape of this production for his own use. In a 1958 broadcast message to Japan, Britten commented: 'I shall never forget the impact made on me by Japanese theatre – the tremendous Kabuki, but above all the Nō plays. I count the last among the greatest theatrical experiences of my life . . . The deep solemnity and *self*lessness of the acting, the perfect shaping of the drama (like a Greek tragedy) coupled with the strength and universality of the stories are something which every artist can learn from.'[7] His sustained enthusiasm on returning from Japan is evident in a letter to Plomer, 13 May 1956: '[I] pray that we can meet – & talk about those No plays, that Court music (I've brought a Shø back with me) . . . Do you know the play Sumidagawa by the way?' It is surprising, therefore, that for more than a year their correspondence remains inexplicably silent on this subject. Plomer seems to have been anxious to work on the libretto of *Sumidagawa* and on 5 July 1957 he revived the idea: 'Somebody brought me a book of Nō plays from Japan the other day & I have been rereading Sumidagawa.

1952. Duncan recalls that, when describing an opera which he and Plomer were planning on the theme of 'outer space', Britten 'had talked to me about its structure because he thought my association with Ezra Pound gave me some knowledge of the Japanese Noh plays, which [Ezra] Pound had translated and which Britten had found fascinating . . . He told George [Harewood] that if Plomer, as he thought likely, would refuse to be diverted from his Noh libretto, then he would like me to write the words of the Gala libretto [i.e. *Gloriana*]'.

4   William Plomer's personal library was bequeathed to the Special Collection at Durham University Library. Originals and copies of the extensive correspondence between Plomer and Britten are also housed at the Britten–Pears Library.

5   William Plomer, *An Autobiography* (London: Cape, 1975), pp. 201–2.

6   He attended a second performance on 19 February 1956.

7   Cooke, *Britten and the Far East*, p. 120.

Have you thought of it again?' Britten may have needed more time to assimilate his Japanese experiences, and also to complete other pressing commitments, for his reply, 10 July, was cautiously positive and restrained: 'The "Sumidagawa" doesn't come into any immediate plans. I've rather put it to the back of my mind; but anytime you feel you'd like to talk about it, it can be brought forward again. It is something I'm deeply interested in, determined to do sometime. Isn't it a curiously moving and disturbing story? I wonder which translation you've got.' Nothing further was heard on the topic until the summer of 1958, when Britten finally seems to have found the time and energy to consider the proposed opera more deeply: 'I can't write about the No play idea now, except to say that it's boiling up inside me, but I have so many things . . . about the style & all . . . before I start on it.'[8] In the autumn of 1958, Plomer produced a draft libretto entitled 'Sumida River', which was essentially a paraphrase of the Japanese Classics Translation Committee's authorised text. However, while Britten praised Plomer's efforts – 'I think the Noh libretto is wonderful'[9] – he was still deferring; and although he declared on 3 April, 'I've more or less finished my Basel chore, & the decks v. slowly clearing for the Noh', a letter of 15 April reveals that a new sticking point had arisen, for Britten and Pears had now had the idea of largely replacing the Zen-Buddhist focus of the original Nô with a more specifically Christian framework:

> I rather hope that you are feeling strong & courageous when you open this letter, my dear, because I feel it's going to be long-winded, & maybe a trifle disturbing . . . A new idea has come into our [Pears and Britten] heads about it – put in, because for many reasons it would be best if done in one of our churches here . . .
>
> This lead [sic] us to the idea of making it a <u>Christian</u> work . . . I have been worried lest the work should seem a <u>pastiche</u> of a Noh play, which however well done, would seem false and thin. I can't write Japanesy music, but might be led into trying if the rest of the production (setting, clothes, moves) were Japanese.

Although 'Christianising' the original might risk losing the magic of the Japanese names and atmosphere, a potential 'problem' could perhaps be resolved in the process, for in a list of points in favour of this modification Britten noted: 'No obvious reason for Pears to do a female part, unless in an accepted style. Actually, to answer the <u>cons</u>, if we made it Mediaeval, or possibly earlier, it would be accurate that no woman should be used; then it wouldn't seem so odd for a woman to be played by a man, especially if the dresses were very carefully & strongly designed.' Plomer replied: 'I have felt all along that the problems & difficulties were formidable, & with anybody but you I should have thought them from the first insuperable . . . I really don't know <u>how</u> the piece could have turned into anything but a pasticcio grosso. But it is a little electrifying to have to think of transposing the story into Christian terms. Think I will, my first thought being that the missing child has

8   12 July 1958.
9   8 March 1959.

come to be regarded locally as a saint . . . & that his grave has already become a place of pilgrimage.'[10]

Coincidentally, 1957 had seen both the first discussions concerning the possible adaptation of *Sumidagawa* and the composition and successful performance of *Noye's Fludde*. The latter was to provide Britten with practical experience of recreating an historical English dramatic form, and Britten now began formulating an unconventional dramatic aesthetic which combined the ancient Japanese conventions with those of the medieval mystery plays.[11]

Extant correspondence and various libretto drafts suggest that much revision took place before March 1959 but further delays ensued and on 17 August Britten apologised: 'I fear I must postpone this piece, still near to my heart, for a year. For many reasons. Partly time; because of my change of location, moving it from Japan to Mediaeval England, we are well behind our schedule. I'm not complaining about this, because I know that this reorientation must happen slowly.'[12] On 29 October the composer wrote to Plomer of his longing to 'see what you have been doing over Sumidagawa, & to talk endlessly with you about it. I am more and more excited about it, & have to keep my ideas in chains in case they don't run parallel to yours.' The two men met in London in mid-November and on 16 November Britten expressed his admiration for Plomer:

> I had hoped so much to have a chance of telling you how excited I am with your Sumida River. You have touched so many of those lame phrases to magic, & yet kept the [to me] moving simplicity & serenity of the original . . . I cannot thank you enough for working with me on it. The more I think of it, the more I feel we should stick as far as possible to the original style & look of it – but oh, to find some equivalent to those extraordinary noises the Japanese musicians made!

Plomer and Britten spent Christmas 1961 at the Red House, but Britten could find little time to devote to the project. The new work was eventually scheduled for the 1964 Aldeburgh Festival and work resumed in earnest at the end of 1963.

Plomer produced a new version of the libretto[13] to which Britten put the finishing touches during February 1964, while staying in Venice:

---

10 17 April 1957. Many of changes involved in this 'Christianisation' were systematic alterations, for example, 'Miyako' became 'west country', and 'willow tree' replaced 'yew tree'. Much of the directly Buddhist philosophy was excised: for instance, 'Ah, but the bond of parenthood/ Cannot survive the grave' was changed to, 'But that would not diminish/ Her yearning for her child'. These changes are discussed in detail in Cooke, *Britten and the Far East*, 'From Nō to Church Parable', pp. 130–89.

11 As early as *Paul Bunyan* Britten had demonstrated his consummate ability to synthesise an eclectic range of stylistic idioms and to make them wholly his own.

12 Moreover, the Jubilee Hall had recently been rebuilt, and a more celebratory and festive opera (*A Midsummer Night's Dream*) was required to open this new venue. However, Britten did reassure Plomer, 23 November, 'Even when deep in the Midsummer Night's Dream I cast nostalgic glances into the future towards 'The River' – still very strong in my fancy & inclination.'

13 2–9100303 (BPL).

A few points. The Ceremonial robing now takes place after the Abbot's prologue (reasons are mostly practical). I've referred to the <u>Land</u> to East (or West) rather than <u>Kingdom</u> (rhythmic problem). To emphasise the river, & Curlew, idea, I like to refer to <u>River</u> people, as opposed to <u>Village</u> p. (less contemporary too, I feel). I liked the idea of keeping the mystery a little longer, & so on page 2 & 4 (typed script), I have kept the burial anonymous (no boy mentioned yet). In the great narration on the boat – I've inserted a reference to the boy as being a <u>Christian</u> – & therefore the <u>Northman</u> as a pagan. Do you mind? . . .

I have omitted referring to the boy's name (Siward) anywhere – it didn't seem necessary . . .

I have concocted a big <u>really</u> Crazy scene for Madwoman on top of 18 – but used nothing, I think, which hasn't appeared before, except one idea pinched from the Nō. I have made her confuse the Curlew River with the bird, & suggested the boy has flown away with the young Curlew birds – 'like the four young birds that left their nest.' . . .

I have a big new idea, which I think is good – I am just approaching the big moment round the Tomb. I would like to use one of those great Gregorian plain-chant tunes. It will somehow tie the whole thing together, & match the entrance and exit chant, (for which I am using '<u>Te lucis ante terminum</u>'). The one I have my eye on is: '<u>Custodes hominum</u>' from the Feast of the Holy Guardian Angels, a magnificent tune & suitable too.[14]

The church opera had now been in Britten's mind for nearly eight years – and the title of the work was still uncertain.

Curlew River

Curlew River was first performed at the Aldeburgh Festival, 13 June 1964. Colin Graham summarised the plot:

> It tells, very simply of a Noblewoman who, driven mad by grief when her son is kidnapped, comes to a ferry. A boat waits to take pilgrims to a miracle-shrine on the further bank, but, because she is mad, the Ferryman refuses to carry her over until her despair moves him and the other pilgrims to feelings of guilt. During the journey he tells of the miraculous happenings at the shrine – the grave of a young child – and the Madwoman recognises her son from the story. At the tomb they are confronted by a vision of the boy and his mother is relieved of her madness.[15]

The Nō theme of the madwoman who crosses a river seeking her lost son and who is subsequently restored to sanity by the revelation at his grave of the boy's consoling spirit, could quite easily be transferred to a Christian context; for it was the dramatic conventions, rather than Buddhist symbolism, which Britten most

---

[14] 15 February 1964.
[15] Colin Graham, 'Staging First Productions 3', in DH, p. 48.

admired in the ancient Japanese theatrical form. Britten's Foreword to the published score stated:

> Was it not possible to use just such a story – the simple one of a demented mother seeking her lost child – with an English background (for there was no question in any case of a pastiche from the ancient Japanese)? Surely the Medieval Religious Drama in England would have made a comparable setting – an all-male cast of ecclesiastics – a simple austere stage setting in a church – a very limited instrumental accompaniment – a moral story?

Obviously the original title, *Sumida River*, had to be changed, and it was Plomer who first suggested *Curlew River* in a postcard dated 26 May 1959. However, as late as 23 October 1963 Britten wrote: 'We [Graham and Britten] did discuss (and with Peter) the title idea & hit on one which struck us as good, & I long to know how you react. "The Other side of the River." That seemed to be the best use of the "River" which seems to us to be such an important part of the whole business.' Other possible alternatives were 'Across the River' and 'Over the River'. On 4 January 1964 Britten worried that 'the title remains a great problem', but the matter was resolved by 15 February: 'Oddly enough, as the work progressed the <u>Curlew</u> grew in significance; & my inclination is to go back to Curlew River as a title!! Colin (who is here now) agrees, & Peter, not wholly.' The curlew, substituted for the Japanese 'Miyako bird', was to be an important verbal and musical element in the opera.

Initially, *Curlew River* had incorporated no quasi–liturgical framework; rather it aimed to be a faithful treatment of *Sumidagawa*, reflecting Japanese characteristics, in which the original Buddhist references were retained. The framing of the dramatic action by the plainsong hymn 'Te lucis ante terminum' emphasises the ritual aspects of the Parable and, in combination with the dry formality of Abbot's address and the ceremonial robing of the monks, recalls the distanced reserve of the Male and Female Chorus in *The Rape of Lucretia*, external observers whose Prologue and Epilogue provide a similar moral context for the action. Moreover, the hymn, a prayer for purity and divine aid in the struggle against moral contamination, recalls the spiritual focus of *Noye's Fludde*. The motivic presence of the chant – the shaping contours of its perfect fourths – is consistently strong throughout, but most especially at moments when Christian overtones are overtly present, as in the Traveller's prayer (Fig. 16), the 'Kyrie' as recalled by the Ferryman (Fig. 65) and the Ferryman's counsel to the Madwoman to pray for her child (Fig. 86).

Thus, the moral framework of *Curlew River* is drawn from the English mystery play, or perhaps rather from the medieval morality plays which formed interludes to these mystery plays, and which involved abstract personifications of vices and virtues.[16] The title 'Parable' suggests that the allegorical dimension of the opera is

[16] Cooke, *Britten and the Far East*, p. 162, observes that Britten owned two extensively annotated volumes of Karl Young's *The Drama of the Mediaeval Church* which had been in his possession from the mid-1950s.

crucially significant, for it emphasises 'a descent out of innocence into sin, and an ascent out of sin to salvation . . . The life of humanity is seen to begin in a potential state of innocence but to lapse in the course of experience into an actual state of sin. This state of sin, in turn, is seen to lead by its own contradictions toward the possibility of a state of repentance.'[17] In the Prologue, the Abbot assures the audience that the play will demonstrate 'God's grace', but even at this early stage in the drama there is a uneasy voice of conflict and restlessness, injected by the nervous tapping of untuned drums[18] and the richly spread chamber organ chord. This ambiguity is also present in the harmonic tensions expressed by the 'river motif', sounded as the Ferryman comes forward (Fig. 8), an undulating scale figure whose rising and falling fourths oppose two modes in semi-tonal conflict [Example 36]. This dichotomy, embodied by the river that divides the land, is developed in the chorus which follows:

> *Between two kingdoms the river flows;*
> *On this side, the Land of the West,*
> *On the other, the Eastern fens.*

Similarly, the Chorus later proclaim:

> *Curlew River, smoothly flowing*
> *Between the Lands of East and West,*
> *Dividing person from person.*
> *Ah, Ferryman, row your ferry boat!*
> *Bring nearer, nearer,*
> *Person to person,*
> *By chance or misfortune,*
> *Time, death or misfortune,*
> *Divided asunder!*

A Traveller arrives, a wanderer who is forever searching, seeking tranquillity on the opposite side of the river. His restlessness is indicated by the augmented fourths of the heavy, trudging double bass crotchets which disturb the harp's sweeping arpeggios; and his melody highlights this tension, rising and falling triads repeatedly turning inwards at the close to emphasise both perfect and augmented fourths:

> *Behind me, under clouds and mist,*
> *Heaths and pastures I have crossed;*

---

[17] Robert Potter, *The English Morality Play: Origins, History and Influence of a Dramatic Tradition* (London: Routledge and Kegan Paul, 1975), p. 190; quoted in Cooke, *Britten and the Far East*, p. 165.

[18] The untuned drums which dominate the texture of all three Parables were inspired by the drums which make up the *hayashi* ensemble in Nō. They are particularly prominent in the Abbot's prologue and epilogue, the tremolo and acceleration effects being derived from Balinese gamelan and Japanese *togaku kakko* techniques. They assume a solo role at key dramatic moments such as the Madwoman's irritated cross-examination of the Ferryman (Fig. 72).

Example 36

Woods and moorlands I have passed,
Many a peril I have faced;[19]

Later he sings of another Traveller who 'at this very place cried: Thinking of his lady love/ Yearning for a woman'. Indeed, *Curlew River* is dramatically propelled by an enduring yearning for 'someone':

> MADWOMAN:
> *I come from the Black Mountains!*
> *Searching for, searching for*
> *Someone . . .*

The Ferryman tells us, 'She too is seeking someone lost, Searching for a son' (Fig. 49). It is a search that will come to an end, 'Now she has reached the Curlew River'.

William Plomer observed that it was a 'strangely fortunate chance' that Britten had seen the one Nō play that was most likely to appeal to him, 'with its motif of innocence wronged'.[20] In a letter of 11 July 1961 he remarked:

> & next week I hope to send you a copy of Richard Rumbold's book <u>My Father's Son</u>. I think there are things in it which may touch you, as you are never insensible to innocence ravaged.
> I sometimes think that the exploration & celebration of innocence in so much of your work as a composer has a profundity and significance that won't be fully understood perhaps until long after your own lifetime.[21]

In the Prologue of *Curlew River*, the Abbot announces:

> *As innocence*
> *Outshineth guilt,*
> *A sign was given*
> *Of God's good grace.*
> ABBOT AND MONKS *[exhorting the congregation]*:
> *O pray for the souls of all that fall*
> *By the wayside, all alone.*
> *O praise our God that lifteth up*
> *The fallen, the lost, the least.*

This story of a 'lost child' recalls the suffering of other 'lost children' in Britten's operas – Peter Grimes's apprentice, Albert Herring, Billy Budd, Miles, the

---

[19] The Traveller's vocal lines turn more consistently to perfect fourths at Fig. 16 as, guided by the Abbot and Monks, he sings, 'May God preserve way-faring men!'
[20] Plomer, *Radio Times*, 18 June (a preview of the broadcast of *Curlew River* at the 1964 Aldeburgh Festival); HC, pp. 434–5.
[21] Britten replied, 4 August 1961, 'How kind of you to send My Father's Son. Peter & I got back last night form Dubrovnik, and I found it waiting for me. It is very painful, but the first 20 pages or so which I have read made me see what a splendid affair it is, & I long to go on with it. How strange, & wrong, that it didn't make the impression that it should have – but I'm sure that in time it will.'

Wingrave boy murdered by his father, even the changeling boy in *A Midsummer Night's Dream.*[22] However, Britten and Plomer chose to concentrate instead on the psychological regeneration of the boy's mother, the Madwoman.

The part of the Madwoman is played by a man in woman's clothes with a small, wooden, female mask, a mask described as 'noble and tragic'.[23] This role, designed for Peter Pears, was inspired by Japanese theatrical tradition, but also carries a hint of the sexual unorthodoxy that Oberon's 'unnatural' counter-tenor timbre had evoked. Pears's understudy, Robert Tear, remembers: 'Peter . . . brought the rehearsal to an end, saying, "Really, Ben, I just can't work in this frock." To which Ben replied to Colin Graham, "Oh for Christ's sake, Colin, give her a crin." '[24] However, Graham recalls that it was in fact Tear who was much more concerned than Pears not to appear effeminate and who infuriated Britten by 'resolutely detaching himself from the role – whereas the whole ethic of Noh-Playing is Total Identification'. Pears himself declared: 'I didn't really find it all that difficult, because I found it so sympathetic . . . I certainly adored doing it.'[25]

The Madwoman is musically introduced by bird-like flutterings played by the flute (Fig. 19); leaping chromatic gestures accompany her offstage cries and portray her agitation (Fig. 20) [Example 37]:

> *You mock me*
> *Whither I go.*
> *How should I know?*
> *Where the nest of the curlew*
> *Is not filled with snow,*
> *Where the eyes of the lamb*
> *Are untorn by the crow,*
> *The carrion crow –*
> ***There** let me go!*

Her vocal exclamations straddle alternating perfect and augmented fourth intervals, derived from (and distorting) the calm fourths of the plainsong. The flute's tremolando swells encompass a major seventh, the composite of these two fourths; this seventh, spanning E to D$\sharp$, is taken up by the muted viola which, as

[22] The part of the boy in the first production was taken by John Newton, who became the recipient of long letters from Britten during the latter's 1965 trip to India. When Britten was ill at the end of that year, Newton visited the composer in the Red House. A letter, 19 January 1966, from Britten to Pears declares, 'He is a dear boy, & was very sweet to me here' (HC, p. 453).

[23] Benjamin Britten, William Plomer and Colin Graham, 'Production Notes and Remarks on the Style of Performing *Curlew River*', published score, p. 145.

[24] HC, p. 430.

[25] Pears in Tony Palmer's film, *A Time There Was*; HC, p. 436. Tear sang the part of the Madwoman at the fourth performance; his performance was well received by critics who praised his precision and control, but Tear recalls that after the performance Pears quipped, 'Lipstick a little too white, I feel'. Steuart Bedford, who later worked with both singers, observed that Tear's top register was much stronger than Pears's and that Pears was aware of this; HC, p. 439.

Example 37

the drama progresses, increasingly becomes identified with the dead child. Thus, in these two gestures Britten musically crystallises the impelling forces of the narrative at the start of the drama.

The Madwoman's soaring voice, together with the flute, is isolated in pitch and timbre from the low-to-middle ranges of the other voices and instruments, and her self-questioning tone recalls the insecurity and angry self-doubts of Peter Grimes. A flute cadenza accompanies her eventual arrival at the bottom of the entrance to the ramp (Fig. 25), the liberal flutter-tonguing, exotic portamenti and glissandi mimicking the ornamental slurs and quaverings of Nō:

> *Let me in! Let me out!*
> *Tell me the way!*

Her words are suggestive of an inner crisis: it is her intense love for her son that has made her mad:

> *All is clear but unclear too,*
> *Love for my child confuses me:*
> ***Where** is my darling now?. . .*

> *Clear and unclear in mind*
> *Eastward I wander on,*
> *In longing for my son.*
> *[She weeps]*

Her child has been 'stolen', 'seized as a slave/ By a stranger, a foreigner'. Gazing into the distance, she commences an account of her life with her son before his kidnapping (Fig. 33), a measured recitation on an eerie monotone, each phrase ending with an unnerving glissando which recalls the seductive vocal colours of another would-be kidnapper, Peter Quint. The Ferryman refuses her a place in his boat unless she entertains the passengers with her crazy singing, insistent choric demands culminating with swooping fourths and sevenths (Fig. 43). In answer, the Madwoman cites 'a riddle' associated with 'this very place', and which is taken up by other singers:

> *Birds of the Fenland, though you float or fly,*
> *Wild birds, I cannot understand your cry.*
> *Tell me, does the one I love*
> *In this world still live?* [26]

As she relates the flight of the curlews to the disappearance of her son, she moves in a circle as if to follow the birds, and her motif, impersonated by the flute, is literally the cry of the curlew. The flute is given increasingly abstract significance as a symbol of the curlews with which she becomes obsessed. Humphrey Carpenter suggests that 'She and the bird seem to be two halves of a divided personality; Britten is once more setting up a pair of balanced opposites. The Madwoman seems to be the mundane, physical aspect of human nature (though with visionary possibilities), the Curlew to be the human spirit purged of the commonplace. It is the age-old tragedy that one side cannot communicate with the other: "Wild birds, I cannot understand your cry." '[27]

The Madwoman is permitted aboard the ferry. As the boat glides from the bank, glissandi in the double-bass and harp re-evoke the erotic and amoral world of the wood in *A Midsummer Night's Dream*.[28] This instrumental timbre persists during the Ferryman's account of the death of the boy, thereby creating an odd contrast between the libretto's plain report of the child's suffering and death and the exotic whirl of the accompanying texture. Upon reaching her son's tomb (Fig. 81), the mother begins a lengthy soliloquy, accompanied only by the solo flute. The bleak sparseness is highlighted by the entry of the other four instruments on the word 'grave'. This passage is the height of vocal stylisation, and recalls both Grimes's 'mad scene' and Peter Quint's hypnotic melisma on Miles's name in *The Turn of the Screw*.

In Plomer's early libretto drafts the dramatic close is swift and simple: the 'lost

---

[26] This enigma was Plomer's own invention.
[27] HC, p. 437.
[28] Indeed, she later asks, 'Am I dreaming?/ Is this a dream?'

child' is discovered to be dead and, after a brief appearance, his Spirit vanishes, leaving the mother weeping on the ground:

> What seemed her son is nothing but a mound,
> A grassy mound alone beside a road.
> Lament for a woman so bereaved,
> And give her the only thing we can – our tears.

In the final text, the first vision of the Spirit of her dead child (Fig. 93) is marked by a melodic fragment – 'Is it you my child?' – which is recognisable as the 'madness theme' of her opening appearance. Britten thereby equates the curlews with the plight of the Madwoman's son, uniting them as joint causes of her psychological distress. In the Japanese version of the tale, at this point the mother grabs wildly at the ghost, an aspect which Plomer had initially incorporated into his libretto but which was subsequently rejected, as Oliver Knussen recalls: 'The music was very fast and nervous . . . which is not only musically out of place in a piece that is predominantly slow and contemplative, but also dramatically (if you can imagine it) very strange indeed – a man dressed as a woman grasping for a small boy . . . The music that replaced it . . . was written as a patch-up over the weekend before the dress rehearsals.'[29] Plomer's draft text had read:

MADWOMAN: Is it you, my child?
GHOST: Is it you, mother?
The GHOST turns towards her. She drops the gong and hammer, and hurries forward to meet it.
The GHOST retreats into the mound.
Dazed and weeping, she looks up, and takes a few steps. The GHOST reappears. She stretches out her arms, runs towards it and tries to embrace it, but it retreats again into the mound, and she collapses. She rises again, approaches the mound, stares at it, retreats slowly, and weeps. During this time the CHORUS has been singing.

> CHORUS: As she tries to take it by the hand
> The shape begins to fade away.
> The vision fades and reappears
> And greater grows her longing.
> Look, there is daylight in the east;
> The ghost has disappeared.
> What seemed her son is nothing but a mound,
> A grassy mound beside a road.
> Lament for a woman so bereaved,
> And give her the only thing we can – our tears.[30]

Following the appearance of the Spirit the slow progress of the story thus far gives way to an immediate closure. The Spirit, represented by the piccolo, returns to the tomb, from whence sounds a thin, barely perceptible cry (Fig. 96):

---

[29] HC, p. 438.
[30] GB–ALb 2–9100297 Sumida River – first draft. Britten does incorporate this gesture earlier in the parable, when the Madwoman sings 'Torn from my nest'.

> *Go your way, mother.*
> *The dead shall rise again*
> *And in that blessed day*
> *We shall meet in Heav'n.*

On the word 'Heav'n' the Spirit's flat modal pitches resolve to an E♮ – the mother
has regained her son and recovered her love. There is a feeling of inevitability: as
the boy's echoes fade and die, nothing more need be said but 'Amen'. Prince
Ludwig of Hesse recalled: 'The mother's grief, a high, swelling Sprechstimme, the
gesturing of the hand to the weeping eyes, the little stroke on the small gong, . . .
the mourning at the grave, the curiously strained and expressive voices, the
sudden stamping with a white foot . . . At the end, the impression of the piece is
moving and profound. It has greatly affected Ben.'[31]

In many ways, the Madwoman's plight reverses Peter Grimes's tragic experience. The theme of the social outcast is pursued in both works and despite the
extreme contrast between the violently insane outbursts of the fisherman and the
ritualistic restraint of the Madwoman, there is a surprising dramatic consistency,
for the works share a quality of dream-like obsession and intense self-exploration
and self-exposure. Donald Mitchell remarks, 'even though they occupy opposite
ends of the theatrical scale, have so much in common'.[32]

The Ferryman has warned us that moral danger lies ahead for those who
abandon the commonplace way of life for something more exotic. However,
whereas Grimes dies mad the Madwoman has her sanity restored. Grimes dies at
sea, yearning for his 'home'; likewise, the boy's spirit has been washed to the sea,
as an early draft revealed:

> *Hoping, I wandered on,*
> *Hoping to find my son.*
> *In hope I came to the river:*
> *The river Sumida*
> *Has washed my hopes away.*

In the final version, the Abbot and Chorus console us:

> *The moon has risen,*
> *The river breeze is blowing,*
> *The Curlew River*
> *Is flowing to the sea.*
> *Now it is night*
> *And time to pray.*

In contrast to Grimes's apprentice, the voice of her lost child *is* heard. The
Madwoman has been isolated in her madness but the community has helped her
to reintegrate: the result is reconciliation rather than disintegration. It may be
revealing that the off-stage voice of the Spirit halts the communal hymn,

---

[31] Quoted in Cooke, *Britten and the Far East.*
[32] Donald Mitchell, 'The Church Parables (I)', in Palmer, *The Britten Companion*, p. 213.

'Custodes hominum', for the mother senses that the answer to her riddle may be found both through reconciliation with her community – 'Let me in!' – and within her own psyche – 'Let me out!'. It is self-knowledge that will free her from her obsession and guilt.

Despite her visionary awakening, the Madwoman makes no reference to Heaven or God until she is freed from her madness by appearance of the Spirit, whereupon she joins with 'Amen'.[33] The Abbot declares that 'in hope and peace, ends our mystery'. Thus the conclusion of *Curlew River* is untroubled by the mists which obscure Crabbe's river landscape and Vere's sea-scape vista. The expanse and spaciousness of the *Curlew River* suggest that the Madwoman's consolation exists outside temporal boundaries.

Britten seemed pleased with the outcome of his renewed collaboration with Plomer, writing on 7 March 1964: 'what a joy it was to have you here & to work with you (you were unbelievably quick to understand what Curlew River was about & what needed to be done)'. The critical reception of the work was generally favourable: William Mann praised Pears's performance and suggested that *Curlew River* might represent 'the start of a new, perhaps the most important, stage in Britten's creative life'.[34] Commenting on a power cut caused by a lightning strike that delayed the start of the première, Leslie Ayres of the *Evening News* remarked that 'there was almost something appropriate about it. For Benjamin Britten's latest dramatic work, *Curlew River*, is full of a mystic sense of powers beyond those of men'.[35]

The Burning Fiery Furnace

> *Friends, remember,*
> *Gold is tried in the fire,*
> *And the mettle of man*
> *In the furnace of humiliation.*   The Abbot, *The Burning Fiery Furnace*

'Got a good idea for another opera in the same style – so be prepared!'[36] So Britten wrote to William Plomer in July 1964, from Amsterdam where *Curlew River* was being performed at the 1964 Holland Festival.[37] On 8 September he told Plomer that he was thinking 'about Church Parable II' and longed to discuss 'Shadrach etc

---

33 In order to clarify the parable conventions, Britten had suggested that a subtitle was necessary to show that the work should be performed in church and was not a conventional opera. Plomer replied, on 3 April 1964: 'Yes, I do like the proposed subtitle: – When young I was taught that a parable was "an earthly story with a heavenly meaning." The Concise Oxford Dic: says "Fictitious narrative used to typify moral or spiritual relations." Exactly!'

34 William Mann, *The Times*, 15 June 1964.

35 HC, p. 433.

36 Undated letter, in HC, p. 440.

37 Britten described the second of his Church Parables in *Faber Music News* as 'much less sombre, altogether gayer affair' than *Curlew River*, quoted in Evans, *The Music of Benjamin Britten*, p. 480.

– or possibly Tobias & the angel. Do you have any feelings?' Plomer sent Britten a carefully considered letter on the merits of these two stories: 'I warmed at once to your suggestion about Tobias & the Angel, a story I'm very fond of, but the problems of making it presentable in the convention of Church Parable I seem, at first sight, rather daunting. Shadrach & company would be surely much more manageable (though much less impressive, lighter, slighter), as being nearer to the Nō tradition of a single magical episode or situation.'[38] Work began in earnest upon Britten's return from holiday in Russia in October 1965. At this stage, the title was not yet decided and the opera was referred to variously as *Strangers in Babylon*, *The Fourth Man* and *The Fiery Furnace*. On 27 October Britten wrote: 'Anyhow I have now got down to the BFF & although I am enjoying it, it can't be really said to have caught fire yet.' Personal ill health and problems within his family involving his sister, Beth, were interfering with the opera's progress, but by early December half of the music was sketched out. Britten's second Church Parable, *The Burning Fiery Furnace*, was completed in February 1966, fully scored by 5 April, and received its first performance in Orford Church on 9 June 1966 at the nineteenth Aldeburgh Festival.

The Burning Fiery Furnace is essentially a lighter counterpart to *Curlew River*, the Old Testament tale incorporating scenes of feasting, comic entertainment, miracles and idolatrous ceremony. It recounts the story, told in the third book of Daniel, of three Jewish exiles (best known by their Babylonian names of Shadrach, Meshach and Abednego) who are appointed by Nebuchadnezzar as governors of the province of Babylon. Although these three Jews are prepared to accept this office, they refuse to defile themselves by partaking of the over-indulgent, self-gratifying eating and drinking customs of the country in which they are living. Similarly, they decline to worship the golden image of the deity Merodak that Nebuchadnezzar has caused to be set up. Thus they incur his intense displeasure and fury, and the King commands that the strongest soldiers in his army should bind the three Israelites and cast them into a furnace which is heated to seven times its usual temperature. This furnace is in fact so fiery that the task force of soldiers is instantly killed by the intense heat; but the three Jews survive, praising, glorifying and blessing Jehovah in the furnace, where an Angel from Heaven in the likeness of the Son of God joins them and protects them. When they are brought out Nebuchadnezzar is amazed to find that they are unharmed. So impressed is he by this miracle that he makes a public proclamation affirming the power of Jehovah and restores the three Jews to their former positions as rulers of Babylon.

As in *Curlew River*, Britten selected a plainsong chant, *Sálus aetérna*, to frame the action structurally and to provide the melodic shapes – once again, predominantly perfect fourths – which assume a symbolic value as emblematic of the Israelites' faith throughout the Parable.

However, as in *Noye's Fludde* and *Curlew River*, perfect fourths intermingle with augmented fourths, a sign not merely of the inevitable challenges which faith

---

[38]   16 October 1964.

must endure, but also of the danger latent in faith of any kind which demands self-negating and self-deceptive obedience and devotion. For example, fourth intervals are also prominent in the music of the Astrologer, the flickering ornaments of his magic being foreshadowed by King Nebuchadnezzar at Fig. 14. Similarly, the faith of the Babylonians as they bow before Merodak (Fig. 65) is expressed in ecstatic howls spanning a fourth, the same interval which represents the truth and constancy of the Israelites' trust in 'Jehovah' (Fig. 50).

The Babylonians and the Israelites are starkly contrasted in terms of their musical style and harmonic language. The music of Babylon is sinuously chromatic, suggesting extravagance and artifice, while the steadfast serenity of the Israelites is evoked by the tonal stability and diatonicism of their vocal lines. In the Abbot's opening address, the 'purity' of the Israelites' faith is contrasted with the chromatic 'wickedness' of Babylon – 'God give us all/ The strength to stand/ Against the burning,/ Murderous world!' Semitonally adjacent intervals, scales and triads, particularly those centring on the chords of D major and E♭ major/minor assume expressive importance. For example, the flexible accompaniment of the alto trombone – the instrument which replaces *Curlew River*'s flute as the principal musico-dramatic sonority – during the Herald's speech (Fig. 7) articulates these opposing semitonal axes. Similarly D and E♭ coexist in the Babylonians' music: at the entrance of Nebuchadnezzar (Fig. 11) – forcefully marked by the abrasive, undeniable clang of the anvil – the voices and organ trace a stepwise rise D–E♭–F–G♭ over a sustained organ D, while the other instruments interject a *sfp* A, perfectly illustrating the potentially expressive enharmonic reinterpretation of these opposing tonal areas.[39]

This tonal ambiguity is present even in the music of the steadfast Israelites, for they have agreed to serve the 'enemy' – 'All honoured with your royal trust/ We pledge ourselves/ To serve you faithfully/ In Babylon' (Fig. 16) – and must now undergo a moral test of their integrity. Thus, at Fig. 19 the D-centred idea which accompanied their renaming gives way to the E♭ of the Chorus of Feasting, 'Good cheer'. The courtiers' jeering cry spans two unequal fourths, E♭–A♭–D, contrasting with the two equal fourth of the Jews' faith – 'They never must in any way/ Betray their faith' (Fig. 3). The climax of this unstable semitonal juxtaposition occurs at Fig. 20, with the entry of the Entertainers, highlighted by the deliberate tread of the organ bass.

Similarly, the Babylonians' unrestrained, orgiastic worship of the golden image, Merodak, is represented by grotesque glissandi across an interval of a fourth, expanding to an augmented fourth: A–D–E♭. In this way, their idolatrous and hypocritical observance is represented by the same interval as the Israelites' sincere devotion. The wild, 'dangerous' chromaticism of the Babylonians' music is most apparent during this procession before Merodak, where the degradation

---

[39] The percussion section in *The Burning Fiery Furnace* is large and diverse, comprising multiple whips, tuned woodblocks, lyra glockenspiel and Babylonian drum. The reverberant acoustic of the church setting encouraged Britten and his percussion consultant, James Blades, to exploit these instruments in inspired fashion.

of their private and public lives is fully revealed. The procession expands the D/E♭ conflict: elaborate instrumental textures alternate the two opposing tonalities in half-bar patterns accompanied by a sustained tremolando D on the Babylonian drum and accumulating perfect fourths played by the organ, building to a climax at Fig. 68 before the Astrologer's pronouncements.

The three Israelites are perceived as a threat to the Babylonian community because they are 'different'. The Astrologer announces:

> *This rash innovation,*
> *Invasion of immigrants,*
> *Puts Babylon in danger.*

Plomer's Foreword to the published score notes: 'It may be felt that in this new version of Nebuchadnezzar, the cult of 'the god of gold', and the resistance movement – ultimately triumphant – of the three young Jewish exiles are not without some relation to our own times.' Similarly, Colin Graham explained in his Production Notes, 'The political aspect of the story, the schism between the Babylonians and the three young Jews, should be continually stressed'. It is undeniable that racism and immigration were increasingly serious and controversial issues in Britain during the mid-1960s. However, the various titles proposed during the early stages of composition suggest that the contemporary political relevance of the opera may have been partially incidental, and that the moral context of the Israelites' trial and triumph was more accurately the defence of one's private conscience in the face of a dictatorial, hypocritical or repressive authority.

Moreover, the three Israelites also sing words which have a more personal and emotional resonance:

> *We do not lack enemies*
> *We might have known jealousy*
> *Would work against us.*

Humphrey Carpenter draws attention to a letter which Britten wrote to Elizabeth Mayer in 1943: 'I have my great friends for my work, and at the moment they seem easily to outweigh my enemies – but for how long, one can't say.'[40] Plomer's libretto declares:

> *They have given us new names*
> *To disguise our true natures . . .*
> *But names cannot change us.*
> *What we are, we remain.*
> *And so must continue . . .*
> *Lord, help us in our loneliness.*

Perhaps it is not too far-fetched to suggest that the testing of the Israelites' moral willpower is suggestive of the plight of homosexuals in Britain in 1966, who were

---

[40] HC, p. 460; LL, vol. 2, p. 1172.

metaphorically thrown into a 'furnace', forced to 'change their names' and deny their sexual identity.[41]

There are those at the Babylonian court, however, who do not condemn; while one set of courtiers denounces, 'Young Jews, a bunch of foreigners!/ Foreigners, foreigners,/ Never trust foreigners!', another group are more tolerant:

> COURTIERS 2:
> O what are you saying?
> They are strangers –
> Do not treat them harshly . . .
> COURTIERS 1:
> Babylon in danger!
> The wise man knows best
> COURTIERS 2:
> He is jealous,
> The young men are harmless . . .
> COURTIERS 1:
> Babylon in danger!
> Down with the foreigners!
> COURTIERS 2:
> To them we are the foreigners,
> These strangers are innocent.

The Babylonians, like all communities, have both dissenting and sycophantic/ hypocritical voices within their midst. Furthermore, the imperial Nebuchadnezzar – the role performed in the first production by Peter Pears – willingly grants the Israelites jobs in his government. During the course of the opera he undergoes a transformation, 'saved' by the shining vision of their faith as embodied in the angelic form which appears amid the flames. Nebuchadnezzar's moral hesitations and self-doubt recall the waverings of Captain Vere when he was similarly called upon to judge and condemn or reprieve a man accused of mutiny and sedition. Both leaders strive to overcome their self-acknowledged 'flaws' and demonstrate genuine concern to make the 'right' moral choice:

> NEBUCHADNEZZAR:
> The stars are against me!
> If the stars are against me
> Then how can I govern?
> My best intentions
> Lead only to confusion and danger!
> Dangerous! Advise me!
> Have I angered the heavens?
> Have I defied the stars?
> What must I do?[42]

---

41 Carpenter notes that in 1943 Plomer had himself nearly been caught by the police for propositioning a sailor on Paddington Station (p. 462).

42 Likewise, just as Vere had rejected Claggart's fawning endeavours to turn him against Billy – 'Now be brief, man, for God's sake . . . Nay! You're mistaken. Your police have deceived you.'

The most significant difference between Plomer's initial drafts and the final libretto of *The Burning Fiery Furnace* is the complete absence from the former of the Entertainment by the boy acolytes at the feast (Fig. 19) (an entertainment which Plomer wittily referred to as the 'cabaret'). This modification is first mentioned in a letter from Britten to Plomer, 28 July 1965: 'Colin has nice ideas of the Acolytes singing and tumbling, which may need some words.'[43] The exuberant mood and movement of this scene look ahead to the balletic children's games in *Death in Venice*. The effervescent energy of the childish entertainers is characterised by woodblocks and sweeping chords on harp, while the text recalls the language of prep school:

> ENTERTAINER 1:
> The waters of Babylon,
>   The flowing waters,
>   All ran dry.
>   Do you know why?
> ENTERTAINER 2:
>   Of course I do!
> ENTERTAINER 1:
>   And so do I!
> COURTIERS:
>   Good cheer indeed!
> ENTERTAINER 2:
> The gardens of Babylon,
>   The hanging gardens.
>   Grew like mad.
>   Do you know why?
> ENTERTAINER 1:
>   Of course I do!
> ENTERTAINER 2:
>   And so do I!

Plomer's words are oddly gauche, but their strangeness may mask a greater significance; for the boys flamboyantly rejoice in a Babylon where Nature has been diverted from its true course, where illicit passions flourish and where self-indulgence is accepted without shame. Thus, beneath the 'harmless' epicureanism of the Babylonians may lie the canker of degeneracy which, masked by hypocrisy, threatens to eat away at the façade of public decency.

The three Israelites reject the seductiveness of the Entertainers' music. They are summoned before Nebuchadnezzar: above a tremolo drum roll on D, the King

---

Don't come to me with so foggy a tale. That's the young fellow I get good reports of' – so Nebuchadnezzar repels the Astrologer's poisonous utterances: 'Must you disturb me while I pray? Let me alone! . . . Must you bring complainings at this time? Go away! Go away!' After the miracle of the furnace, the Astrologer is conclusively expelled: 'And you, Chaldean,/ What have you to say?/ Consulter of the stars/ Pretentious fraud,/ Where is your wisdom now?'

[43] A carbon copy of the typescript of the first draft of the libretto (GB–ALb 2–9500545) contains annotations and further material in Plomer's hand, including the acolytes' text on two inserted pages.

demands, 'Is it true, O Shadrach, Meshach and Abednego,/ You do not serve my god, the god of gold, of Babylon?' (Fig. 72). His melodic contours recall the courtiers' celebratory cries, 'O joyful occasion' (Fig. 9), arcs centred in E♭ giving way to D with the word 'Babylon'. In canon, Nebuchadnezzar, the Astrologer and the courtiers pound out the Israelites false names (Fig. 75), the D-based fourths culminating on a sustained D – 'answer!'. D and E♭ continue to battle for precedence during the Israelites' resistance:

> O King, Nebuchadezzar,
> Our God whom we serve is able to deliver us.
> If he wishes, he will deliver us – Out of thy hands,
> But, if not –
> We would not offend you, O King.
> We will not serve thy God,
> Nor worship the image of gold
> Which you have set up, in Babylon the Great.

Their 'innocence' is dramatised in the heart of the fire (Fig. 80), where they are joined by another young boy, an Angel, whose semitonal vocalise 'purifies' the wild excesses of the Babylonian fire and momentarily resolves the music's asymmetries to two perfect fourths, F–B♭–E♭, followed by a B♭ major triad [Example 38].[44] Andrew Porter, writing in *The Financial Times*, 11 June 1966, described the Angel's melody as 'shining unelaborated notes . . . casting a steady celestial radiance on the song of human praise rising below'. In contrast, Jeremy Noble declared that the wordless cry reminded him only of Miles's ecstatic 'I'm here' in *The Turn of the Screw*.[45]

Out of the furnace roar rises the opening of *Benedicte*,[46] perhaps suggesting the power of music to cleanse and heal. After the miracle in the furnace, the Abbot draws the moral of the parable:

> Friends, remember,
> Gold is tried in the fire,
> And the mettle of man[47]
> In the furnace of humiliation.

He prays:

> God give us all
> The strength to walk
> Safe in the burning fiery furnace
> Of this murderous world.

The musicians process out. There is no answer: 'They never must in any way betray their faith'. *Sálus aetérna* – what we are, we remain.

---

44 Draft GB–ALb 2–9500545 p. 19 (Fig. 80 in printed score) contains the pencil addition '3 + Angel' in Britten's hand. Another 'child' – like Grimes's apprentice, Billy Budd and Tadzio before him – must play a redemptive role.
45 *New Statesman*, 17 June 1966.
46 In the margin of p. 22 of libretto draft GB–ALb 2–9500545, Britten marked, 'Latin hymn for all' alongside Nebuchadnezzar's words, 'Hear my decree:/ There is no god except this God'.
47 Draft GB–ALb 2–9500545 reads, 'And acceptable men'.

Example 38

The Prodigal Son

No voice so dear
As your voice reheard.   Father and Younger Son, *The Prodigal Son*

On 30 December 1966 Britten and Pears visited the Hermitage Gallery in Lenin-grad where they marvelled at Rembrandt's 'The Return of the Prodigal': '(with his broken back, shaven head, worn sole to his one foot out of its shoe, the father all loving-understanding, the three diverse characters looking on, judging, grudging and surprised). Of course, this is the subject for the next Church Parable.'[48] Shortly after their return from Russia Britten wrote to Plomer, 6 January 1967: 'P.S. Does the idea of the Prodigal Son attract you for a new Ch. Par.' Plomer responded positively and on 17 March Britten committed himself to the project: 'I'm so glad that you liked the idea of the Prodigal Son so much. Alas, I couldn't get a postcard of the Rembrandt, but it is in most of the R. books . . . For several reasons (which I won't bore you with now) I do want to do it for next year – it would be wonderful to complete the trilogy when one's mind is working in this direction.' Britten was clearly eager to commence the opera, for one month after the 1967 Aldeburgh Festival, he wondered, 'Dare I ask you if you have had time to put pen to paper over "Prodigal Son" '.[49] A rough version of the libretto was sketched by 27 July which Plomer revised, producing a fair hand-written copy on 16 August.[50] On 22 November Britten wrote: 'I am launched on the Prodigal – i.e. I have found a splendid Plain-song to start me off, & useful ideas are popping up. I am having a meeting with Colin, early in December, & I & he have several matters we want to discuss . . . My chief worries are still the nature & presentation of the temptations, & the character of the Tempter which I still haven't found the exact prototype for.' Britten decided to go to Venice to complete composition of the score: 'I have started my routine of working all the morning, & in the afternoons wandering, looking into churches . . . & generally [being] fascinated by this beautiful, but very much lived in, museum of a city.'[51] Despite Britten's evident enthusiasm, his focus seems to have waned during the final stages of composition. Mervyn Cooke suggests that a debilitating illness in the preceding spring and the realisation that the score contained moments of uncharacteristic weakness may have been the reasons behind Britten's hesitancy. Perhaps, like Aschenbach in *Death in Venice*, Britten experienced amidst the passionate splendour of this city, a loss of confidence, an apprehension that his art could become formulaic or over-reliant on tried and tested procedures.

The theme of *The Prodigal Son* had been explored by Britten twenty years

---

[48] Peter Pears, *Moscow Christmas: December 1966*, privately printed; HC, p. 471.
[49] 20 July 1967.
[50] GB–ALb 2–9700609 and GB–ALb 2–9700610 respectively. Britten's annotations to these early drafts demonstrate the way in which the forms and techniques of the Church Parables had been absorbed into a highly individual musico-dramatic style.
[51] Britten to Plomer, 20 January 1968.

earlier, in *Albert Herring*. Strictly speaking it is the only one of the three Church Parables which *is* a 'parable'. In the Foreword to the printed score, Plomer explained, 'With its unforgettable climax of reward and rejoicing being lavished not upon virtuous correctness but upon a sinner, this parable celebrates the triumph of forgiveness. The story seems to bring into the clearest possible focus the Christian view of life'. *The Prodigal Son*, drawn from Luke Chapter 15, re-presents the social comedy of *Herring*, with comparable tenderness and compassion, but within a more unambiguously moral context: like Albert, the Prodigal Son wins his emancipation and is ultimately enriched by his experience.

The most significant alteration made by Plomer and Britten to the original biblical tale was the introduction of a Tempter and the elaboration of the Temptations which he places before the errant son.[52] Pears was to play the part of the Tempter – 'Lucifer, rather than Mephistopheles'.[53] He is thus a fallen angel, and this 'doubleness' is effectively emphasised by the dramatic presentation, for the Tempter is the Abbot in disguise:

> *Ah – you people, listening here today,*
> *Do not think I bid you kneel and pray*
> *[The Tempter slowly moves past the congregation towards the acting area]*
> *I bring you no sermon,*
> *What I bring you is evil.*

Accompanied by the organ and cymbal, his vocal line is characterised by alternating major and minor thirds which disturb the modal simplicity of the preceding chant, *Jam lúcis órto sídere*. He sets the scene:

> *You are about to see*
> *A country patriarch,*
> *A father with his family.*
> *With property and progeny*
> *In order,*
> *So orderly, so dutiful,*
> *He enjoys*
> *The harvest of a well-spent life.*

After the first entrance of the Tempter, Plomer had originally included a chorus:

> *Who is this evil one?*
> *Never seen him before!*
> *Why doesn't he speak to us?*
> *What is he doing here?*
> *Where is he going now?*

---

[52] The temptation scenes were elaborately extended by the time that the third typescript was complete (GB–ALb 2–9700611). Cooke suggests that Britten and Plomer were influenced by the four Tempters who appear in T. S. Eliot's *Murder in the Cathedral* (1935), and identifies at least two instances where the phraseology of the libretto recalls Eliot closely (Cooke, p. 211).

[53] Britten to Plomer, 12 December 1967.

> *Never been here before!*
> *Who is this evil one?*

These lines recall the Governess's cries of concern upon the first appearance of Quint in the tower:

> *No! No! Who is it? Who?*
> *Who can it be?*
> *Some servant – no! I know them all.*
> *Who is it, who?*
> *Who can it be?*
> *Some curious stranger? But how did he get in?*
> *Who is it, who?*
> *Some fearful madman locked away there?*
> *Adventurer? Intruder?*

The chorus's questioning was subsequently crossed out by Britten. In *The Prodigal Son*, the chorus does not function as an external commentator (in contrast to the Male and Female chorus in *The Rape of Lucretia*). Instead, the Elder brother provides a contrasting note of objectivity and perspective.[54]

The Tempter attacks the bourgeois sterility and stagnation of the Younger Son's home life:

> *Ah – what a worthy family!*
> *What a quiet life*
> *Habit has made them dull,*
> *Dull and self-satisfied.*

Indeed, the Father's words, together with the secure B♭ tonality and the prevalent perfect fourths recalling the moral certainty of the framing chant, depict the warmth, stability and frugality of the home life; but they do invoke an overtly moralising tone (Fig. 10):

> *Evil lurks everywhere*
> *Watching for idleness,*
> *When evil is lurking*
> *Repel it by work.*

Originally the Tempter had been even more critical:

> *TEMPTER: Two sons, the elder stern,*
> *The younger full of life,*
> *Hungry for happiness,*
> ~~*Excitement, anything*~~
> ~~*Away from family routine.*~~
> *He is the one I'll use*
> *To break* ~~*it up*~~ *this harmony*
> ~~*This family*~~ *See how I break it up.*[55]

---

54 Moreover, at this stage in the drama, the Tempter is visible only to the Younger Son, for he is an externalisation of his longings.

55 GB–ALb 2–9700609 libretto first draft.

He is an agile Peter Quint, urging the Young Son to 'Act out your desires' accompanied by glistening harp textures and the trumpet's suggestive, slippery portamenti which outline major and minor thirds (Figs. 19, 21):

> *Imagine, imagine,*
> *What you are missing.*
> *Imagine, imagine,*
> *Before it's too late,*
> *High living, secret delights,*
> *And beauty, beauty*
> *To kindle your senses,*
> *While you are still young,*
> *While you are young.*

The Tempter anticipates the curious 'strangers' who will cross the path of Aschenbach in *Death in Venice*, embodying the inner voices which lead him into temptation. Moreover, there are also echoes from the past, for the Tempter's words recall Britten's 1937 setting of Auden's 'Underneath an Abject Willow' – 'Act from thought should quickly follow'.

Britten was quite specific that the Tempter was 'also the other side of the Younger Son's nature'.[56] During the initial confrontation between the Tempter and his 'victim', the Younger Son asks:

> *What right have you to speak?*
> *You, a stranger to me,*
> *To tell me how to live!*
> TEMPTER:
> *I am no stranger to you,*
> *You know me very well,*
> *I am your inner voice, your very self.*

The Tempter is both in and outside the drama, coldly luring the boy to his self-destruction and passionately involved in that degradation. They echo one another in close canon at the unison (Fig. 34), an aural interweaving which may have been made more powerful by the similarity between the vocal timbres of Pears and Robert Tear, who played the role of the Younger Son.[57] In *The Turn of the Screw* the voice of Quint had called:

> *I seek a friend –*
> *Obedient to follow where I lead,*
> *Slick as a juggler's mate to catch my thought,*
> *Proud, curious, agile, he shall feed*
> *My mounting power.*

The Governess too had offered moral guidance in the guise of friendship – 'I stay

[56] Letter to Plomer, 20 August 1967.
[57] The voice of temptation which haunts the Younger Son revives memories of John Claggart's inner torment, and of the emotional ambivalence which troubles and confuses the protagonists of *Peter Grimes*, *Gloriana* and *The Turn of the Screw*.

as your friend, I stay as your friend'. The Father and his servants do not recognise that, as the Younger Son abandons his childhood, he too will have a 'friend' to accompany him on his adventure:

> FATHER: Think of the dangers of the journey,
> Leaving without guide or friend . . .
> SERVANTS: We see you departing,
> Without any protector,
> Without any friend.

Only the Younger Son can hear the voice that speaks so reassuring to him: 'Free! Free! At last I am free! Be what I want to be, Do what I want to do, Be guided by you'.

As Peter Quint urged Miles to be 'free', so the Tempter challenges the Younger Son to break out of the 'prison' which restricts and confines him:

> Have you never thought
> 'If I go on living life
> Of long monotonous days,
> When shall I ever know
> The strong sweet taste
> Of life outside?'

The youth is surprised by the accuracy of these words – 'How can he be informed/ Of my secret longings in this way,/ Giving them shape as I have never dared to do?' Likewise, Quint had reassured Miles:

> What goes on in your head, what questions?
> Ask, for I answer all . . .
> What goes on in your dreams? Keep silent!
> I know, and answer that too.

The growth of corruption is indicated by increasing chromatic distortion. The Tempter infiltrates the Father's B♭ tonality (Figs. 23–6) – 'You might learn little save what is bad' echoes the Tempter's intervals – and the accompanying semi-quaver waver is subsequently revealed as symbolic of the Tempter's own desires (Fig. 57, 'I have done what I wanted, Acted out my desires'). The Younger Son's music oscillates between two voices, juxtaposing the diatonic 'goodness' of his Father with the disruptive intervallic characteristics of the Tempter, as he justifies his appeal for freedom with the music and arguments he has learnt from his new guide. He is an adolescent, his character still being formed, and the Tempter personifies his adolescent fantasies.[58] Youth is a time to dream, a sentiment expressed in many of Britten's operas and song settings:

> ELDER SON AND SERVANTS:
> There is time, there is time when young
> To live inside a dream,
> Before things show themselves
> Not what they seem.

[58] Similarly, Miles tells the Governess, 'I'm growing up you know. I want my own kind.'

Peter Pears had accompanied Britten when he travelled to Venice to complete the score of *The Prodigal Son*, but had left soon after on a recital tour. Subsequently, Colin Graham, Rosamund Strode and Mary Potter all arrived in the Italian city. Britten told Plomer: 'we started discussing the Temptations immediately. I had the idea of seductive, acolyte, voices "off" to add to the night-mare atmosphere'.[59] The boys' howling voices form a refrain between the episodes of degradation, the first depicting the perils of alcohol, the second the sins of the flesh, and the third the dangers of gambling. As in *The Turn of the Screw* and *A Midsummer Night's Dream*, Britten powerfully exploits the rich variety of the limited but eclectic accompanying ensemble, the instrumental timbre adding a psychological dimension to the narrative of dissolution. When the Tempter joins the Son on his journey to the city (Fig. 34), the viola commences a steady tread, while the harp adds a wealth of arabesques until the trumpet announces their arrival at the city. The virtuosity of these new colours is dazzling: organ clusters, viola harmonics, flute tremolandi. For example, a trumpet *obbligato* on the Tempter's brassy thirds underscores the son's first taste of wine (Fig. 44), while the seediness of the second episode is conveyed by the free, lurching rhythms and aching vibrato of the trumpet's postlude (before Fig. 50). During the third episode (Fig. 53) rippling *fortissimo* harp chords, alto flute tremolandi, tumbling trumpet triplets, sustained organ chords built from unequal fourths, and the palindromic rhythms of the tuned wood blocks combine to create a dream-like atmosphere, a quality which looks ahead to the orgiastic instrumental colours of *Death in Venice*. Similarly, selected instruments – harp, solo horn, and drums – portray the shedding of the Younger Son's innocence, as the Tempter strips the Son of his Father's robe at the successive stages of his defilement. The introduction of *sprechstimme* in the city scene injects a histrionic, uncontrollable quality, and is reminiscent of the whispering of distant voices in *The Turn of the Screw* and *Death in Venice*. 'My boy, indulge yourself! Show yourself to be a man!': Humphrey Carpenter observes that 'my boy' is an address that occurs frequently in Pears's letters to Britten, and that the Tempter's goading may have been made more personal in this scene by Pears's speaking voice.[60]

It is during the torment of the Younger Son's dialogue with the viola (Fig. 63) that we understand the dark profundity of his despair and witness the ultimate triumph in him of the virtues represented by the framing plainsong [Example 39]. He has learnt that 'experience has its price'. The viola introduces a theme whose contorted twists chromatically fill out unequal fourths, and evoke both his pitiful wretchedness and the terrible memory of his whole experience. Viola and voice treat this material in dialogue as the purging process begins. Gradually the chromatic complexities of the melodic strands are filtered out until, at the moment of realisation, 'While even my father's servants can eat', the second line of the plainsong hymn is recalled (thereby mirroring the farewells fashioned from the hymn

---

59   20 January 1968. The use of off-stage boys' voices looks ahead to the ballad refrain in Act 2 of *Owen Wingrave*.
60   HC, p. 480.

Example 39

as the youth embarked upon his adventure). The thoughts of this 'lost son' keep turning to 'home': his announcement, 'I will arise and go' (Fig. 65), is related to the organ chord which introduced the Tempter (Fig. 1), thus reinforcing the dramatic symmetries. This melody is repeated more confidently and then taken up by the viola, as the voice quotes the plainsong hymn 'Father, I have sinned' in a simple major mode.

The Younger Son's homeward journey is a luminous instrumental fantasia on the work's germinal plainsong, in four free parts, supported by a percussive ostinato of weary footsteps: it is a stark distillation of his misery and poverty. During the journey, the alto flute articulates and elaborates his previously rehearsed 'confession', turning towards B♭ when his Father is seen in the distance.

In the biblical tale, the end of the parable is the most important section. Whereas in *Curlew River* and *The Burning Fiery Furnace* the moments of revelation were marked by the communal hymns, *Custodes hominum* and *Benedicte*, in *The Prodigal Son* it is the Father's words of forgiveness that fulfil this prophetic function:

> For this son of mine was dead, and is alive again,
> Was lost, and is found.

The canticle, *Cantate Domino*, is now presented over a solid ground bass (Fig. 71). Although the ground begins on a Lydian E, it outlines the B♭ tonality associated with 'home' and the recollection of motifs from the past by the servants and accompanying instruments (while father and son marvel at their reunion) assures us of the 'triumph of forgiveness'. However, at this point Britten also moves beyond the confines of the parable's narrative. As the servants rejoice 'O sing unto the Lord a new song,/ For he have done marvellous things' we are reminded once again of the conciliatory and redemptive power of music itself.

Yet, a note of unrest lingers. The Tempter reappears and reclothes himself in the Abbot's habit to deliver the concluding homily (Fig. 86). At his words, 'and prodigal come home', a chromatic reminder of the Son's city nightmare and the echoing reminiscences of the servants' 'Go if you must go' inject a sad recognition of human weakness. The framing reprise of the Latin chant is introduced by the blessing of the Tempter/Abbot, 'And may the Lord bless you and keep you'. The agent of temptation is also the provider of consolation: Pears's voice both tantalises and tempts, and provides a lyrical reassurance of redemption and salvation.

The three Church Parables are linked by their narratives of the renewing of faith. Britten and Plomer progress from personal introspection in *Curlew River* to a social drama of conflict between personal belief and the dictates of authority in *The Burning Fiery Furnace*. The final parable, *The Prodigal Son*, explores the evil which arises from self-indulgence but which may be defeated by love.

Many commentators have observed that the second and third Parable were weaker, dramatically and musically, than *Curlew River*. Writing in the *Sunday Times*, 12 June 1966, Desmond Shawe-Taylor lamented that although *The Burning Fiery Furnace* possessed a 'modern relevance', it lacked 'the intense pathos and single-minded purity of *Curlew River*'. Several critics attacked the dramatic insipidity of the temptation scenes in *The Prodigal Son*: for example, Martin Cooper felt that 'the city's allurements' were 'palely described . . . mild and unreal . . . hardly more than perfunctory',[61] while Peter Heyworth complained

---

[61] *Daily Telegraph*, 13 June 1968.

that 'the prodigal's sinful living never looks remotely like rocking the piece's moral edifice'.[62]

Similarly in 'The Church Parables (II): Limits and Renewals', Robin Holloway[63] declares that the second and third Parables lack the freshness, inevitability and inward concentration of *Curlew River*, being characterised by musical monotony and repetition. They are over-didactic, their presentations of Hope, Faith and Love too 'neat': 'In the depiction of Babylonian Gold-lust and the debaucheries of the Big City a tone can be heard that is not so much ascetic as prim and even priggish. This music renders abandon with monkish distaste; there is no imaginative understanding of the ambiguity within "sinfulness".'[64] Holloway suggests some of these short-comings are inherent in the church parable conventions, but they may also be the result of more general 'limitations', for Holloway's main complaint appears to be that Britten glosses over the 'ambiguity' inherent in his material. In the same way, Carpenter notes a lack of tension in *Curlew River* between the Christian force of words, particularly the plainsong, and the exotic musical timbres, note-clusters, glissandi and gamelan-like tremolandi which recall the seductive world of *The Turn of the Screw* and *A Midsummer Night's Dream*: 'At moments the music is purely Christian – the boy's "Go your way in peace, mother,/ The dead shall rise again" sounds like part of the Mass – but at other times becomes oriental and seductive. The child's final "God be with you, mother" ends on a sighing glissando like Miles responding to Quint, while the Madwoman's response to this, a melismatic "Amen", might evoke Quint even if the two roles had not been sung by the same performer.'[65] As the framework closes on each story and the Abbot comes forward to preach (in a manner reminiscent of the Chorus in *The Rape of Lucretia*), we may feel a unintended discomfort.

Holloway writes: 'as in *The Burning Fiery Furnace* the climax is somehow missed (though everyone knows where it should be); moreover in *The Prodigal Son* the reserve upon which the genre depends for its expressive manner gives way in two crucial places to a direct appeal – to pathos in the father's forgiveness, to reconciliatory warmth in the final ensemble; and in both cases the result is ineffectual.'[66] Peter Heyworth was also doubtful about the 'sincerity' of the genre: 'somehow the props . . . the village church at twilight, the hooded monks, the plainsong . . . finally seem more theatrical than conventional theatre, and the other-worldliness they evoke less a confrontation with the world than a germ-free refuge from it.'[67]

The accusation is that in the Church Parables Britten refrains from fully

---

62 *The Observer*, 16 June 1968.
63 Robin Holloway, 'The Church Parables (II): Limits and Renewals', in Palmer, *The Britten Companion*, pp. 215–26.
64 *Ibid.*, p. 222.
65 HC, p. 438. Even so, Martin Cooper in *Daily Telegraph*, 15 June 1964, noted a 'questionable note' injected by having Christian denouement in middle of 'East–West cross-fertilization'.
66 Palmer, *The Britten Companion*, p. 222.
67 *The Observer*, 16 June 1968.

exploring the multiple implications which arise from his material, retreating from the dramatic ambiguities which had darkened and deepened his previous operatic works, preferring to frame his narratives within unequivocal Christian structures. This attempt to effect a definitive and consoling dramatic resolution renders the inherently ambivalent material one-dimensional. He is afraid to let the voices speak, yet unable to totally silence them; and a full unleashing of these tensions does not occur until *Death in Venice*. In the Church Parables the theme of 'renewal' may frustrate, just as surely as did Vere's vision of the 'far-shining sail', for such certainty and closure do not allow for the unavoidable mingling of 'good' and 'bad' in the human soul. Nor does it allow one's individual conscience to effectively oppose the social and religious moral frameworks which may seek to repress and silence 'difference' and dissent. We are reminded of Auden's complaint: 'I am certain too that it is your denial and evasion of the ~~attractions~~ demands of disorder that is responsible for your attacks of ill-health, ie sickness is your substitute for the Bohemian.'

13

Owen Wingrave

> OWEN: *I cannot forget them, the bully and the boy*
> *stalking their way to the room which saw their deaths . . .*
> *Walking, walking – these two:*
> *the old man and the boy,*
> *for ever in each other's company.*
>
> Myfanwy Piper, *Owen Wingrave*, Act 2, Scene 1

My destiny is . . . to die in harness.   Britten, to Sidney Nolan[1]

In 1954, the year in which *The Turn of the Screw* was completed, Britten wrote to Eric Walter White that he had just read another short story by Henry James with 'much the same quality as the Screw'.[2] This story was *Owen Wingrave*, a tale which James had written for the 1892 Christmas issue of *The Graphic*, and which was republished in the collection, *The Wheel of Time*, in 1893. Thirteen years after he had first encountered this tale, Britten asked Myfanwy Piper to adapt it for his next opera, a 'television opera' commissioned by the BBC.[3] Her primary task was to develop characters only superficially sketched by James and to fill out scenes from mere hints in the original. Although she was aware that James had himself dramatised his short story, in a play entitled *The Saloon*, Piper was later to claim that she had not utilised this text. However, in an undated letter to Britten, she wrote: 'I have been reading & rereading Owen Wingrave & the Saloon & have come to several conclusions . . . I agree there are some good things in the Saloon – & some bad ones too' (BPL). In addition, a spiral Notebook containing Piper's early ideas for the libretto reads: 'Look up Shaw's letter of rejection of 'The Saloon' for the stage . . . about Dec 1908 or Jan 1909 . . . Kate's red dress good for colour T.V. I think. Exchange between Coyle and Wingrave Saloon Page 657. excellent' (BPL). Evidently *The Saloon*, in which James had expanded ideas merely sketched in his original narrative, was a useful source text.

In many ways, *Owen Wingrave*, set in a country house which is home to super-natural presences, is a companion piece to *The Turn of the Screw*. The

---

[1] Sidney Nolan in interview with Donald Mitchell, 11 June 1990; quoted in HC, p. 512.
[2] HC, p. 508.
[3] The televisual character of the opera does not seem to have affected the aesthetic or emotional discourse contained within the work. However, the narrow visual focus did exacerbate the effects of inappropriate casting and the over-literalism of the producers in the 'ghost scenes'.

276 THE OPERAS OF BENJAMIN BRITTEN

single-minded focus and intensity of the earlier opera is revived, and issues such as the complexity of the teacher-pupil relationship and the struggle between individualism and conformity resurface. The Governess has evolved into the less 'sinister', but similarly maternal and affectionate, figure of Mrs Coyle. (Similarly, her husband, Mr Coyle, shares many of Captain Vere's characteristics and anxieties, fears which he openly acknowledges when in his role of military instructor he finds himself increasingly, and disturbingly, attracted to his protégé's ideals of 'peace'.)

Alternatively, *Owen Wingrave* might be interpreted in the context of its relationship to *A Midsummer Night's Dream*. Britten's Shakespearean opera is essentially a self-indulgent foray into the world of dreams and the imagination, a world from which moral censure is eradicated and where all possible desires can be fulfilled. *Owen Wingrave* is almost a photographic negative of this liberal landscape: at Paramore, the forces of social oppression and moral convention as represented by the Wingrave clan dominate the setting. In this world, devoid of all compassion or sympathy, the repressive spirit of the Borough or Loxford is magnified and its malignancy increased. The musical palette of the opera is similarly limited, characterised by the strident rhythms, harmonic dissonances and angular melodic intervals which symbolise the claustrophobic weight of the Wingraves' militarism, and it lacks the melodic richness and lyrical expansion of Britten's earlier works.

A Midsummer Night's Dream and *Owen Wingrave* may perhaps be viewed as 'sequels' to *The Turn of the Screw*, developments which dramatise the potential outcomes of the choice which Miles must make: in *A Midsummer Night's Dream*, Miles has followed Quint into the wood, while in *Owen Wingrave* the domineering will of the Governess has prevailed. However, Owen, a few years older than Miles, is dissatisfied which the path he has chosen. Rebellious voices continue to beckon him but these voices no longer sing Peter Quint's powerful seductive song; they are symbolic inner voices which are ambiguously identified with the ghostly presences of Owen's dead Wingrave ancestors.

The instrumental prelude to *Owen Wingrave* similarly brings together the techniques and expressive symbolism of *The Turn of the Screw* and *A Midsummer Night's Dream*. The pounding chords which open the opera literally assault the listener's ear, just as Owen will be physical and mentally attacked by the Wingraves' aggression which the chords represent. They comprise all twelve notes of the chromatic scale, arranged in the form of three dominant and diminished triads, thus suggesting the unnatural yet inescapable nature of the family's oppressive grip. Previously Britten had transformed such chord sequences to imply dramatic progression – for example, the turns of the psychological screw, or the translating power of sleep. However, in *Owen Wingrave* these dissonant clashes are static and reappear in a virtually unaltered form in the orchestral interludes which punctuate the scenes: the Wingraves' violence is unrelenting and inflexible, bolstered by history and tradition, confident of its continuance and future. However, there are musical hints that this self-assurance is delusory. The chords are played by the percussion section which, although providing an

Example 40

appropriately militaristic colour, has been previously identified with the exotic sound world of Peter Quint's magic casements and the liberality of the dreamers' wood. This duality suggests that the force of the Wingraves' violence might be intended to repress the dangerous impulses that could threaten the family's stability [Example 40].

In bar 4 of the orchestral prelude there is an abrupt change of musical atmosphere as the family portraits which line the walls of Paramore come into view. As each painting is highlighted in succession, a single pitch is added to a sustained chord until it contains eleven pitches.[4] The eleventh note, E♭, resolves to D, the pitch which is identified with Owen himself. This is the first indication of the harmonic conflict (E♭–A♭/A–D) which will underpin the dramatic battle between the Wingraves and Owen. It is interesting that the E♭ axis, associated with the Wingraves, had previously been employed by Britten to represent two seemingly irreconcilable forces. In *Peter Grimes*, *Albert Herring*, *Billy Budd* and *Gloriana*, E♭-centred music indicated oppression, conformity and convention. In contrast, in *The Turn of the Screw* and *A Midsummer Night's Dream*, Quint and Oberon appropriated this pitch and transformed it into an exotic aural symbol of

---

4   The illumination of the fifth portrait, 'a double one of a ferocious old Colonel and a young boy', is accompanied by a piercing piccolo melody which is associated with the ghosts throughout the opera. Similarly, the tenth portrait, of Owen's father, is marked by the addition of E♭ (Sir Philip Wingrave's pitch) to the accumulating chord cluster.

enchantment and love. Perhaps Britten is suggesting that both forces are present, and inseparable, at Paramore.

The multitude of possible musical and dramatic readings implies that behind the ostensibly simple tale of youthful rebellion against family tradition there lies a more complex network of half-illuminated ideas. Indeed, in *Owen Wingrave* there are essentially two stories which are never satisfactorily brought together. In the first, Owen challenges the bigotry of his militaristic family. The second tale tells of a former Wingrave youth who refused to fight a childhood acquaintance and was beaten to death by his furious father. Now both murderer and victim haunt the corridors of Paramore. What is the relationship between Owen and the dead boy? As well as their similar ages, they share their rejection of violence, but they appear to have an emotional, even spiritual, need for one another that is not explained by circumstantial factors. What might account for Owen's conviction that a personal sacrifice is required on his part to lay the disturbed, wandering spirits of the past to rest? The dead Wingrave ancestor had refused to fight his 'friend': perhaps we might connect this with Owen's refusal to engage in rivalry with his 'friend', Lechmere, for Kate's favour. What does this 'pacifism' symbolise? Do they share a secret, a guilt, a shame? Will the answers be found in the locked room?

Owen Wingrave is frequently referred to as Britten's 'pacifistic' opera. Henry James's own pacifism certainly influenced his tale, which on one level is an overt expression of the views which he and his brother William had held since the American Civil War. Exempted from active service by a back injury which his family suspected was psychosomatic, James nevertheless remained envious of his younger brothers' military exploits and eagerly read many military memoirs. The inclusion of some of these historical details in *Owen Wingrave* suggests that the story may have been a way for James to lay to rest his own family ghosts.

James's 'Notebooks' contain references to the origin of *Owen Wingrave*:

[26 March 1892] The idea of the soldier – produced a little by the fascinating perusal of Marbot's magnificent memoirs. The image, the type, the vision, the character, as a transmitted, heredity, mystical, almost supernatural force, challenge, incentive almost haunting, apparitional presence, in the life and consciousness of descendant – a descendant of totally different temperament and range of qualities, yet subjected to a superstitious awe in relation to carrying out the tradition of absolutely 'military' valour – personal bravery and honour. Sense of the difficulty – the impossibility, etc.; sense of the ugliness, the blood, the carnage, the suffering. All these things make him dodge it – not from cowardice, but from suffering. Get 'something' it is enjoined upon him to do – etc . . . a brave soldierly act – an act of heroism – done in the very effort to evade all the ugly and brutal part of the religion, the sacrifice, and winning (in a tragic death?) the reward of gallantry – winning it from the apparitional ancestor.[5]

[8 May 1892] . . . there is a kind of degradation, and exposure to ridicule, and ignominy in his apostasy. The idea should be that he fights, after all, exposes

5   *The Complete Notebooks of Henry James*, ed. L. Edel and Lyall H. Powers (Oxford: OUP, 1987), pp. 66–7.

himself to the possibilities of danger and death for his own view . . . It is a question of a little subject for the 'Graphic' so I mustn't make it 'psychological' – they understand no more than a donkey understands a violin . . . It seems to me that one might make some 'haunting' business that would give it a colour without being ridiculous . . . He must die, of course, be slain, as it were on his own battlefield, the night spent in the haunted room in which the ghost of some grim grandfather – some bloody warrior of the race – or some father slain in the Peninsular or at Waterloo – is supposed to make himself visible.[6]

These passages contain all the elements of the finished tale, introducing the notion of the disgust or disgrace which Owen's action will induce and hinting that his refusal to fight will be considered 'unmanly'. Two aspects stand out: first, that the protagonist's pacifism derives from 'suffering', and second, that his act of heroism is an act of 'sacrifice'. In this way, Owen's dilemma and fate – his passive response to oppression, his voluntary self-sacrifice – have much in common with the experiences and actions of Lucretia and Billy Budd.

Britten's pacifistic beliefs were publicly well-known and formed at an early age. As head boy of Lowestoft preparatory school he had led a campaign to stamp out bullying; at South Lodge School he wrote an essay attacking blood-sports and the cruelty of war; while at Gresham's School he had refused to join the Officer Training Corps. Britten was probably sensitive to Owen's 'outsider' status since, in 1939, when he and Pears followed Auden and Isherwood to America, public disapproval was vociferous and a correspondence arose in the popular press denouncing 'absentee intellectuals'.[7] From the start of his career Britten's pacifism influenced his music. During the 1930s he worked on Paul Rotha's film *Peace of Britain* and composed a *Pacifist March* for the Peace Pledge Union. Colin Graham declared that *Owen Wingrave* was written in direct response to the Vietnam War, and more specifically to the shooting of student demonstrators on the Kent Campus in Ohio; however, Myfanwy Piper contradicted Graham, asserting that Britten first talked of an opera based on James's tale before he composed the *War Requiem* in 1961, and considered it a 'very personal coda to follow up the War Requiem'.[8]

The ambiguous relationship between convictions held in life and those articulated in art is exemplified by Britten's own self-contradictory description of the *Sinfonia da Requiem*, commissioned in 1940 by the Japanese government to commemorate the 2600th anniversary of the Japanese Empire: 'I'm making it just as anti-war as possible. I don't believe you can express social or political or economic theories in music . . . I'm dedicating this symphony to the memory of my parents . . . all I'm sure of is my own anti-war convictions as I write it.'[9]

When Henry James refused to participate actively in the American Civil War

---

[6] *Ibid.*, pp. 67–8.
[7] For a detailed account of this correspondence and other attacks on Britten see LL, vol. 2, pp. 869–73.
[8] DH, p. 15.
[9] In an interview, *New York Sun*, 27 April 1940.

he insisted that, as an artist, his role was to continue creating and not to contribute to the destruction. Similarly, Owen prefers the poetry of Goethe to the prose of Clausewitz, and James emphasises Owen's artistic sensibility, which is at odds with the military temperament of his family:

> The spring day was warm to his young blood, and he had a book in his pocket which, when he had passed into the Gardens and, after a short stroll, dropped into a chair, he took out with the slow soft sigh that finally ushers in a pleasure postponed. He stretched his long legs and began to read it; it was a volume of Goethe's poems. He had been for days in a state of the highest tension, and now that the cord had snapped the relief was proportionate; only it was characteristic of him that this deliverance should take the form of an intellectual pleasure.[10]

Britten shared James's opinions of the 'role' of the artist in times of war. He had written to his publisher, Ralph Hawkes, 7 October 1940:

> I am afraid what you say about performances of my things in England & what some people are saying doesn't surprise me, much as it hurts me . . . both of us again asked official advice on what we had better do. The answer is always the same – stay where you are until called back; you can't do anything if you do go back; get on with your work as artistic ambassadors etc. etc.[11]

In the opera, Owen articulates this view:

> OWEN: I'm not afraid.
> Courage in war is false.
> Courage in peace,
> The kind that poets know,
> Wins everything.

Art is a possible means of defiance, resistance or salvation and Owen is one of a line of 'artists' in Britten's operas – like Grimes, Budd, Essex and Quint, his imaginative vision contributes to his condemnation and tragic fate. His melodies strive for diatonic lyricism, in contrast to the Wingraves' piercing chromaticism. In the prelude, with the introduction of the final portrait which he resembles, the horn melody which identifies him is stated for the first time (Act 1, Fig. 11). It is an expansion of the phrase heard in bar 4, its gentle chains of descending thirds recalling Tytania's outpouring, 'O how I love thee', which is echoed by Bottom in his 'Dream'. The last four pitches of the horn melody (G♯, F♯, E, D) melodically trace the distance between Owen and his family. His elderly but formidable aunt, Jane Wingrave is described by James as possessing 'too little imagination' (p. 49). The Wingraves stifle Owen's creativity and ensure, through his death, that their own family line becomes extinct. Thus the restatement of Owen's theme at the end of Act 1 (Fig. 195) is truncated; when its triadic shapes reappear at the

---

[10] Henry James, *Owen Wingrave* in *The Turn of the Screw and Other Stories* (Oxford: OUP, World Classics, 1992), p. 42. All subsequent references are to this edition and are given in parentheses in the text.

[11] LL, vol. 2, p. 867.

opening of Act 2, with the treble voices' 'Trumpet blow' motif, it is in the context of a tale of violence and death.

Ironically, Spencer Coyle, the man entrusted with Owen's military instruction, is also presented as 'an artist in his line', 'caring only for picked subjects and capable of sacrifices almost passionate for the individual . . . He was a person exactly of the stature of the great Napoleon, with a certain flicker of genius in his light-blue eye: it had been said of him that he looked like a concert-giving pianist' (p. 40). Coyle, like Vere and the Governess, is initially presented as a figure of authority and balanced judgment, as one of Piper's Notebooks record:

> *I have the pick of*
> *Of all the youth of England both*
> *to spread her influence, her laws*
> *her riches overseas*
> *I have the Power to spread her glory over seas*
> *to protect and spread her justice.*

In the final libretto he sings:

> *COYLE: Oh! I thought I knew them all, the foibles of the young.*
> *Straight out of school they come to me, full of themselves,*
> *Impatient of advice, careless, hot-headed and rash – mere boys.*
> *My task is to instil a needed discipline*
> *A core of ordered facts to set reality*
> *Beside their gallant dreams,*
> *And yet not to cool the heroes' blood*
> *That makes me choose to teach them.*

Charged with the responsibility for 'saving' Owen from the consequences of his rebellion, Coyle, whose own name implies tension and repression, finds himself attracted to the young man and his ideals. James reveals that Coyle 'had taken a particular fancy to Owen Wingrave' (p. 40), and that his wife shares this affection: 'he had accused the good lady more than once of being in love with Owen Wingrave. She had admitted that she was, she even gloried in her passion' (p. 56).[12] Piper noted that she must take care to express: '1 Mrs Coyles attraction to O & affection for C. Loyalty. 2 Mr Coyles slight pessimism & beginnings of realisation of Owens toughness & brainpower' (BPL).

As the drama proceeds the teacher–pupil relationship is destabilised and James insinuates that, like Miles, Owen might 'enchant' his tutor: 'He liked ardent young men . . . This young man's particular shade of ability, to say nothing of his whole personality, almost cast a spell and at any rate worked a charm' (p. 40). Coyle begins to mistrust his pupil's intellectual superiority but is influenced, albeit reluctantly, by Owen's precocity and the 'freedom' of his ideas: 'The tone of his favourite pupil now expressed, without intention indeed, a superior wisdom

---

[12] Interestingly, when Mrs Coyle sings 'They are all, all sons to me' (Act 1, Fig. 71) Britten introduces a fourths-based melody on solo violin, solo cello and harp which recalls the melodic shape of the 'screw theme'.

that irritated him' (p. 40); 'young Lechmere . . . had never before observed the head of the establishment to set a fellow such an example of bad language . . . The first thing that struck young Lechmere in the case was the freshness, as of a forgotten vernacular, it had imparted to the governor's vocabulary' (pp. 42–3), '[Coyle's] own spirit had been caught up by a wave of reaction . . . There was something in the young fanatic's very resistance that began to charm him' (p. 57). In the opera, Coyle declares:

> But Owen, he most gifted, heroic, of them all,
> Is moved by some new ferment, unknown to me.
> Owen, whom I delight in, in whom I believe,
> Surely he must retract – though I fear his mood.

It may be overstating the case to suggest that Owen 'corrupts' Coyle, but it is true that Coyle fears that Owen will, like Miles, adversely influence his fellow students: 'He oughtn't to talk to you in that way. It's corrupting the youth of Athens. It's sowing sedition' (p. 44).

The Wingraves' primary accusation is that Owen will bring disgrace upon the family name: ' "I'll do what I can – I'll tell him its a regular shame." "Yes, strike that note – insist on the disgrace of it" ' (p. 44), 'Oh they had made him feel they were ashamed of him; they accused him of putting a public dishonour on their name' (p. 59). Piper includes this episode in the libretto:

> LECHMERE: Right you are, sir.
> I'll go for him and tell him,
> Tell him it's a shame.
> MRS COYLE: Shame and Owen – no!
>
> COYLE: More than shame, disgrace!
> MRS COYLE: Disgrace and Owen, no! . . .
>
> SIR PHILIP: Insulting the family,
> Dragging our name in the dirt –
> Disgusting!
> MISS WINGRAVE: Public dishonour to Wingraves,
> Our noble name scorned –
> Obscene!

Recalling Gloriana and Tytania, Owen's actions will expose him, and by implication his family, to public ridicule: 'He saw that her only present fear could have been that of the failure to prevent her nephew's showing publicly for an ass, or for worse' (p. 49). Owen's pacifism is interpreted as a sign of madness or mental derangement: ' "Upon my honour you must be off your head!" cried Spencer Coyle . . . "don't you know your mind from one day to the other?" ' (p. 39). The force of the Wingraves' objections is suspicious, and James hints at a hidden motive (although Piper omits this detail from her libretto): ' "Of course he's intelligent; what else could he be? We've never, that I know of, had but one idiot in the family!" said Jane Wingrave . . . Poor Philip Wingrave, her late brother's eldest son, was literally imbecile and banished from view; deformed, unsocial, irretrievable, he had been relegated to a private asylum and had become among the friends of the family only a little hushed legend' (pp. 45–6). The Wingraves have incarcerated Owen's elder brother in a lunatic asylum: it appears that the family has a tradition of banishing its guilty secrets to locked chambers. They charge Owen with both mental instability and physical sickness; his pacifism is a form of deviancy, one which resonates with sexual threats. Miss Wingrave warns: 'I'll talk to him and I'll take him down to Paramore; he'll be dealt with there and I'll send him back to you straightened out' (p. 50). James suggests that 'Paramore' may house repressed emotional currents: these are 'closeted' away in the 'locked room', which becomes a sort of psychic repository for deviancy.

The musical representation of Owen's rebellion suggests the ambiguous origins of his ideals. Alone in the park he sings (Act 1, Fig. 43):

> *At last it's out.*
> *No doubt old Coyle will rage,*
> *but in the end*
> *he'll see*
> *I'm strong, not mad, or weak –*
>
> *One little word: no! no! no! no!*
> *And I'm am released for ever*
> *from all the bonds of family and war.*

The sweeping harp septulets which accompany his lines come from Quint's magic casements: it is as if Quint is providing Owen with the courage to challenge his family. Rebuked by Miss Wingrave, Owen retaliates, encouraged by the return of the harp (Fig. 50):

> *I'm not afraid,*
> *Courage in war is false,*
> *Courage in peace, the kind poets know, wins everything.*

Although he is impressed by the sight of the horse guards on parade, Quint's harp reminds Owen (Fig. 58):

> *No, it is false, false plumes and pride, obedience that ends in destruction and*
> *murder.*

Likewise, when Owen arrives at Paramore, 'to face them, all of them, the living and the dead' (Act 1, Fig. 116), he 'opens the door with a flourish', his determination and energy represented by the trilling D of the sustained horn and the climbing arabesque of the harp.

The Wingraves consider Owen's pacifism to be a symbol of his evasion of adult, 'masculine', responsibilities. The homosexual and the pacifist both reject the idea that violence can act as a means of 'proving' their manhood. This idea is forcefully expressed in the opera, the Wingraves' hysterical outbursts recalling the exaggerated gestures of Loxford's elite in *Albert Herring*:

> *MRS JULIAN: Scruples are for milksops.*
> *SIR PHILIP: Scruples are for women.*
> *KATE: Scruples are for parsons.*

> *MISS WINGRAVE: Scruples are for weaklings.*
> *ALL FOUR: Scruples are for adolescent boys.*

In *Opera, Ideology and Film*, Jeremy Tambling proposes that the presence in the locked room of the ghosts of an ancestral bully and his victim establishes this room as a Freudian site of primal instincts and paternal power.[13] The Oedipal burden against which Owen must struggle is implied in the opera:

> *OWEN [talking to the family portraits]:*
> *Father! Father! You must understand.*
> *I am as resolute as you at Kandahar.*

The spirit of patriarchal tyranny is represented by Owen's grandfather, Sir Philip Wingrave. The producer, John Culshaw, had imagined that this relatively small, but dramatically significant, role would be taken by a 'grisly old bass', but Britten declared he was writing the part for Peter Pears. Pears, whose family had a strong service tradition, modelled his character on a military uncle whom he had often visited as a child: '[He was] high-spirited, high-spoken very military-minded, it seemed, and very conventional . . . I remembered all sorts of things about him – in fact, I made up as near as I could to my Uncle Dick.'[14] Throughout the opera Sir Philip is identified with the pitch E♭ (for example, Act 2, Fig. 178). Similarly, his later entry in Act 2 (Fig. 215) is marked by an abrupt modulation to this key: as the members of the household successively cry 'Sir Philip', a low pedal E♭ is sustained, until he leaves with Owen for the interview. The characters speculate about this hidden scene, as a chromatic bass progression slowly unfolds, B♭–A–A♭–G–F♯–G–A–B♭–D♭–E♭ (Figs. 216–18): this sequence implies a long-range perfect cadence in E♭ and, indeed, this tonality is unambiguously restored as Sir Philip throws open the door and Owen reappears (Fig. 222). Owen's phrase, 'It's over, I'm disinherited. He turns me out forever!', is accompanied by a low tuba E♭ (Fig. 223); it was this identically pitched instrument which had formerly signified Grimes's defeat at the hands of the Borough. The connection between the two operas is further reinforced at the conclusion where, despite his excommunication from Paramore, Owen retains a sense of hope and asks Kate to share a new life with him (Fig. 266):

> *OWEN: We two, the only young things here,*
> *Could build a new life.*
> *Kate come with me.*
> *It's not too late.*
> *KATE: I can't, I can't.*
> *I was prepared to sacrifice my life to you, and your fate;*
> *Even in death your glory would be mine.*

Significantly, their duet is in E♭: Kate fails him, as Ellen had 'failed' Grimes, and it

[13] Jeremy Tambling, 'Owen Wingrave and Television Opera', in *Opera, Ideology and Film* (Manchester: Manchester University Press, 1987), pp. 113–25.

[14] Quoted in Headington, *Peter Pears*, p. 239.

is no surprise when her final exclamation, 'And Owen he's dead', closes on E♭ (Fig. 294).

Sir Philip's voice is the voice of convention, of social and familial authority, yet there are also more sinister undercurrents in the relationship between 'father' and 'son', which replicate the violence and tension which is reputed to have destroyed their Wingrave predecessors. During his interview with Sir Philip, Owen sings:

> *I half thought the old man would knock me down – or worse.*

The 'father–son' relationship in *Owen Wingrave* continues the pattern of violent, sexually repressed relationships in Britten's operas – Grimes and the apprentice, Claggart/Vere and Budd, Quint and Miles. When Sir Philip confronts Owen off-stage it is as if the closeted interview between Vere and Billy Budd has recommenced, now made more explicit. Sir Philip's voice is heard challenging Owen, whose replies are represented by the muted horn:

> *SIR PHILIP: You have disgraced yourself . . . you must obey . . . What is there left to be said . . . Can you deny your behaviour's unmanly?*

The final words of *Owen Wingrave*, before the reprise of the ballad song, are Sir Philip's 'My boy!' Piper disliked this method of address – 'I didn't think it was very successful – it's not really dramatic'[15] – but Pears insisted upon its retention. Perhaps Piper was unaware that this was how Pears had addressed Britten in their early letters. Its revival in this context may imply that Sir Philip's tyranny is a subconscious allusion to an oppressive dimension of Pears's love for Britten.

Owen's failure to conform to expected patterns of 'manly' behaviour destroys his relationship with Kate, his intended wife. Lechmere, 'a nice manly boy', is invited by Miss Wingrave to Paramore to 'do her wretched nephew some good' (p. 56), but his flirtations with Kate merely confirm Owen's reluctance to play the role of 'suitor'. Kate rejects Owen as a 'poor creature' – 'such conduct doesn't begin to be that of a gentleman!' (p. 69) – and Coyle realises that 'she was at any rate a damsel who placed her ideal of manhood – damsels doubtless always had their ideals of manhood – in the type of the belted warrior' (p. 70). Piper attempted to persuade Britten that Kate was as much a victim of her background as Owen, and emphasised her gentler side in one of the libretto's more lyrical passages, 'I came to look for a jewel from my brooch'.[16] Likewise, the role's first interpreter, Janet Baker, explained that she found it difficult to empathise with her character and tried to draw out a more sympathetic dimension: 'Kate is full of fear too, of insecurity and the vulnerability of youth . . . she behaves badly but there are reasons for her behaviour.'[17] However, according to Piper, Britten found

---

15 HC, p. 513.
16 One of Piper's Notebooks records her first impressions of Kate: 'Kate Young/ unsophisti- cated/ tough/ brought up with one idea/ spirited/ fatalistic/ asks nothing better of life/ than to suffer her father's fate through her husband ie. Owen./ capable of cruelty because life is cruel and she doesn't expect anything of it. Hopelessly the victim of her circumstances./ not clever, or rather, not educated, therefore narrow' (BPL).
17 DH, p. 2.

her 'an impossible and arrogant girl, not worthy of the thoughtful Owen'[18] and in the opera, Kate's sexuality emerges as an aggressive challenge to Owen's perceived effeminacy. The sexual tension between Kate and Owen is later intensified, in a scene loaded with Freudian connotations:

> OWEN: Tell me what you want
> Some drunken officer's trick?
> Thrust my sword through my hand?
> Pin it to the table,
> To amusing the gaping ladies.

Cast as a mezzo-soprano, Kate's relatively low register implies an exclusion of the feminine from her personality. She alone is not afraid of Sir Philip, and laments:

> KATE: Why was I not a man?

Owen's invitation, 'Come turn your key?', further emphasises his own emasculation. Owen's interview with Kate is the most dramatic moment in the opera. She challenges him to confront his own sexuality, although this is not made fully explicit in the opera.

Owen's retaliation against repression takes the form of an aria to 'peace'. The text for this aria caused Piper some difficulties and her Notebooks contain copious reworkings. Some evocative lines were excised from the completed libretto, including:

> peace is not a hiding away
> it is active, passionate, positive
> committing, like the act of war
> peace is not self-less
> Peace walks alone
> Peace is the right to walk alone
> to decide alone
> To accept . . .
> In Peace a man can rejoice to be amongst men
> and yet walk alone . . .
> he can love without demanding
> he can believe without interfering. (BPL)

The final text reads (Act 2, Fig. 246):

> In peace I have found my image,
> I have found myself.
> In peace I rejoice amongst men,
> and yet walk alone . . .
> peace is not silent it is the voice of love . . .
> only in peace can I be free.

This passage is reminiscent of Billy Budd's 'far-shining sail' aria, although Owen is more articulate than Billy, whose naivety and stammer inhibited free expression

[18] DH, p. 14.

Example 41

[Example 41]. Owen's 'song of love' is a lyrical outpouring which contrasts with the silence and repression practised by his family. He has implored the portraits 'Is there not one of you to help me, you? you? You are all silent too, but your eyes, your nostrils speak' (Act 1, Fig. 129), and has recalled Coyle's advice 'Good soldiers in a mist, we're told, keep silence, no friendly murmurs, no scream of pain betray their position to the enemy'. Now he breaks his silence, his music 'betraying' his own emotional position.

As Owen sings of his tranquillity, the two strands of accompaniment evoke the inner and outer forces he confronts. Heavy, diatonic woodwind chords, directly recalling the weight and colouring of the 'interview chords' in *Billy Budd*, pass through a sequence, the root pitches tracing the notes of the Wingraves' twelve-tone series. Above these chords, a gamelan-like shimmer erupts from the glockenspiel, harp, vibraphone, piano and xylophone, possibly symbolising the momentary ascendancy of love. Britten endeavours to make this passage sound affirmative but there is only transient hope not permanent resolution. Ominously when the bass progression reaches D♯/E♭ (Fig. 253) there is a lengthy pause and a complete tone row is sounded. The soothing curves of Owen's phrases are interrupted by the Wingraves' angular motifs, and he confronts them, 'Peace is not won by your wars.' The cycle resumes (Fig. 255) until eleven notes have been sounded, the missing root being A♭. Exhausted by the effort of speaking out, Owen lapses into half-spoken text, as 'the apparitions of the old man and the boy slowly walk across the hall, and up the stairs' (Fig. 257). As Owen addresses the portraits, the lyrical power of his peace music ebbs away, its transcendent strains silenced:

> *Ah! I'd forgotten you!*
> *Come on, then, come on, I tell you.*
> *You two will never walk for me again . . .*
> *[to the boy] you made your stand too young –*
> *but I have done it for you – for us all.*
> *Tell the old man, tell your fearful father,*
> *Your fate and his no longer frighten me,*
> *Tell him his power has gone and I have won,*
> *And at last I shall have peace.*

Like Grimes, Owen is defiant. However, his final phrase closes on G♯, reinforced by an A♭ in the bass, as Kate re-enters: this is the missing pitch from the twelve-tone row, and issues a tritonal challenge to Owen's D. The significance of this harmonic opposition is fully revealed in the final bars of the opera (discussed below).

What part do the Wingrave ghosts play in Owen's death? In keeping with his practice in *The Turn of the Screw*, James gave no indications in *The Saloon* that any ghostly apparitions should actually appear on stage, directing only that the stage should be plunged into darkness at the theatrical climax. When, in 1911, the actress-producer Gertrude Kingston, who was fascinated by psychic phenomena, elected to materialise the ghosts, James complained that there was 'absolutely no warrant or indication for this in my text . . . Let me earnestly request you then to suppress the 'figure'.[19] In the opera, the visual effect of the family portraits which line the corridors and stairways of Paramore plays a crucial part in evoking the presence of ancestral spectres, but Piper was aware of the dangers of over-literalism, as her Notebooks reveal:

---

[19] *The Complete Plays of Henry James*, ed. L. Edel (New York: J. B. Lippincott Co., 1949), pp. 648–9.

The [televisual] technique should be used, not to create ghostly appearances, making figures walk out of frames etc but simply to draw attention to the hallucinatory powers of a heightened imagination – so that a double take of a portrait at slightly different angle might give exactly the same impression as that, half seen by a person on the lookout for a manifestation of life or interest – another glance and one is not <u>sure</u> if the figures actually moved or grimaced, or made a sign, an impression of following glances easily achieved. The same slight approach should be used for the walking ghosts, a movement a shadow, a possibility made more positive by the watching nervous subject. (BPL)

Owen, like Peter Grimes, is haunted from within and without, and the ballad which frames Act 2 is the most potent musical expression of this doubly oppressive torment. Initially Britten and Piper had intended to reveal the story of the former boy's death through dialogue between Coyle and Owen, and sketches for this scene appear in Piper's drafts. Piper provided additional explanation for the boy's refusal to fight, writing to Britten, 19 August 1968: 'I'm finding everyday that problems in O.W solve themselves. I don't mean the final expression of them because that is fluid of course – but little cross-currents, relationships echoes – in particular I find a very strong identification of Owen and the murdered boy has taken over and left me feeling much happier about the Ghost story and the way to use it' (BPL). The original plan was abandoned and it was decided that the tragic history would be disclosed in a ballad, sung by a narrator, thereby increasing the dramatic weight of the episode and establishing a historical perspective by which the violent destruction of innocence would be seen as part of a recurring pattern at Paramore. Thus, the ballad would become an epitaph for all Wingrave victims. The part of the ballad singer was to be taken by Peter Pears. In a manner recalling the technique employed in *The Turn of The Screw*, where Pears had sung the parts of Quint and the Prologue, he was now to be both the agent of present oppression and the communicator of past tragedy. In both scenarios, the individuality of Pears's vocal timbre provided Britten with the opportunity to produce a musical 'double exposure', which possessed powerful dramatic consequences.

Piper was concerned to stress the literal and spiritual connections between Owen and the dead boy. On 17 July 1969 she wrote to Britten: 'I've been working hard at a revised version of the ballad. It seemed to me inconsequential and I wanted to make it link up more with Owens character and attitude . . . I wanted to be rid of the archaisms too' (BPL). Britten's music clarifies the indissoluble fusion of past and present as time, place and character are coalesced in the Act 2 Prologue [Example 42]. The Narrator's first two phrases explore a mixolydian mode on D, Owen's pitch, encompassing an octave and beginning and ending on the pitches D–A. The distant trumpet rhythms represent the house itself, having been introduced in this context in the third interlude of Act 1, while the trebles' triadic melodies are related to Owen's own horn melody. The simple memorability of the ballad singer's unaccompanied phrases renders it instantly recognisable, and thus increases the dramatic effectiveness of the varied restatements of this theme. For example, in Owen's peace aria, the ghosts glide across the hall to the accompaniment of woodwind trills outlining the opening pitches of the ballad, while the

Example 42

oboe restates the scalic melody from the Act 1 Prelude which had been identified with their portraits (Act 2, Fig. 257). Similarly, these pitches return in a vertical arrangement when Kate issues her challenge to Owen – 'Sleep in the haunted room'. He is forced from his tranquil reveries and, realising that his sense of peace is transitory, acknowledges that his battle is with both the living and the dead (Act 2, Fig. 273):

> OWEN: *Ah! I thought I'd done with that,*
> *With the Wingraves and the house*
> *Would you drag me back? . . .*
> *The anger of the world is locked up there,*
> *the horrible power that makes men fight:*
> *Now I must take it on,*
> *I must go in there.*

What happens in the locked room? The drama has implied that this secret chamber houses not only the ghosts of a repressive military tradition but also the spirit of repressed love. In James's story it is revealed that Owen has already spent a night in the haunted room but will not disclose what he has witnessed:

> '. . . I'm sure he did see something or hear something,' [Lechmere] added.
> 'In that ridiculous place? What makes you so sure?'
> 'Well, because he looks as if he had. I've an idea you can tell – in such a case. He

behaves as if he had.
'Then why shouldn't he name it?'
Young Lechmere wondered and found 'Perhaps it's too bad to mention'. (p. 76)

What is it that cannot be named? We might hope for musical elucidation from Britten, an explanation or intimation of the 'meaning' of the events which lead to Owen's death. The Coyles' conversation (Act 2, Fig. 280) is supported by a ballad-derived ostinato which evokes both the sense of time passing in the present and the inescapable pulse of the past. The motif passes through a descending sequence A–D (Figs. 279–90), reversing and resolving the direction of the original ballad and thus emphasising that the tragic patterns of history are being re-enacted behind the locked door. Significantly, as Lechmere relates that Owen has entered the room (Fig. 287) the clarinet, piano and harp restate Quint's sweeping runs.

The descending harmonic sequence ends:

> KATE: Ah, Owen, Owen you've gone! . . .
> ALL: Kate what is it?
> KATE: Ah, Owen, Owen, it's my fault, it's my fault.

As she stands over Owen's lifeless form, we half expect Kate to reprise the Governess's 'What have we done between us?' Indeed, Piper's drafts reveal that she was influenced by this earlier scene:

> KATE: Ah Owen, Owen, Owen, You're gone [in pencil above]
>   What have I <u>done</u>.

At this point the ballad returns in its original tonality, D. Like Miles's 'Malo Song', it is a song of death, and has silenced Owen's aria of peace. Owen must be sacrificed in order for the forces of convention to be defeated. But, is Owen's death redemptive? There are five crucial bars between Kate's declaration that Owen is dead and the beginning of the ballad restatement. The defining cadence in the bass, D♭–A♭, undermines the sense of closure implied by the large-scale progression A–D, and above a pedal A♭, the Wingraves' diminished intervals are sustained. As Owen's life is extinguished, the xylophone's repeated D diminishes rhythmically and dynamically. All that remains is Sir Philip's 'My boy!' ringing in the silence.

Why does Owen die? In *The Saloon* Coyle asks Kate if she wants 'so much to send him off to be killed?' The choice for Owen is between conformity and a 'living death', and defiance and a 'literal death', grim alternatives that are unequivocally outlined in *The Saloon*:

MRS JULIAN: You speak as if you were dead!
OWEN: What else is left a fellow so thoroughly treated as dead? . . .
OWEN: Ah, there you are with your low measure of Success. You want too much to live!
KATE: For Honour.
OWEN: Well, my dear, I'm ready to die for it.[20]

---

[20] Henry James, *The Saloon* in *The Complete Plays of Henry James*, pp. 651–80. All further references are to this edition and are given in parentheses in the text.

Owen lives and dies like a soldier, his body discovered on the exact spot where his ancestor was slain: 'He was all the young soldier on the gained field' (p. 78). Described as 'a young lamb so visibly marked for sacrifice' (p. 66), Owen cannot evade the patterns of sacrifice which have destroyed generations of Wingraves.

Rejecting *The Saloon* on behalf of *The Incorporated Stage Society*, George Bernard Shaw criticised James for allowing the ghosts to 'defeat' Owen:

> What do you want to break men's spirits for? . . . Do you seriously think that you would have been beaten by that ghost? . . . In the name of human vitality WHERE is the charm in that useless, dispiriting fatalism . . .
>
> It really is a damnable sin to draw with such consummate art a houseful of rubbish and a dead incubus of a father waiting to be scrapped; to bring on for us the hero with his torch and his scrapping shovel; and then, when the audience is saturated with interest and elated with hope, waiting for the triumph and the victory, calmly announce that the rubbish has choked the hero, and that the incubus is the really strong master of all our souls.[21]

He later added:

> The question whether the man is to get the better of the ghost or the ghost of the man is not an artistic question: you can give victory to one side just as artistically as to the other . . . You have given victory to death and obsolescence: I want you to give it to life and regeneration.[22]

James replied:

> There was only one question to me, that is, that of my hero's . . . getting the best of everything, simply; which his death makes him do by, in the first place, purging the house of the beastly legend, and in the second place by creating for us, spectators and admirers, such an intensity of impression and emotion about him as must promote his romantic glory and edifying example for ever . . . Danger there must be . . . It's exhibited by the young man's lying there gracefully dead – . . . Really, really we would have howled at a surviving Owen Wingrave, who would have embodied for us a failure – and an ineptitude.[23]

Evidently for James the matter was an 'artistic' one. He ignored Shaw's perceptive criticism, since for James the story was merely a literary riddle, a piece of hack work for a popular magazine. Although he may have identified with the theme and his hero, he maintains an authorial detachment which enabled him to treat the work as a literary abstraction. In contrast, Britten's personal identification with the fate of the protagonist appears to have been far more intense. Presumably he hoped that the audience, sympathising with Owen, would be able share the brief experience of illumination or truth which occurs at the moment of Owen's death. However, there is a danger that Owen's death will be interpreted as another example of the 'dispiriting fatalism' demonstrated by several of Britten's previous

---

[21] Letter from Shaw to James, 17 January 1909, quoted in *Complete Plays of Henry James*, pp. 642–3.

[22] *Ibid.*, p. 646.

[23] *Ibid.*, pp. 646–7.

operatic protagonists. Even, Piper appears to have had misgivings, as her Note-books record: 'Logically Kate and or both Wingraves should die at the end of the piece as well – but something in what they all sing, except Coyle, could – or must indicate a sense of Death, of finality as far as the Wingrave household is concerned. This, Owens death, is the end' (BPL).

It is important for Britten that Owen's death is established as both a private and personal validation of 'self'. His 'peace' has little to do with pacifism but symbolises his inner calm, acceptance and love. However, in the opera, the private haunting blends uneasily with the public pacifism. Act 1 is too long and is dominated by the 'first story', which is practically a manifesto for pacifism. Indeed, the Owen of Piper's first Act – in contrast to James's hesitant, dreamy idealist – is an articulate and inflexible spokesman for pacifism. The libretto begins neither with James's confrontation between Owen and Coyle, nor with the after-dinner scene at Paramore which opens *The Saloon*, but plunges us immedi-ately into the actual details of life in a military crammer. Although Piper recog-nised that Owen's personality undergoes a major transformation under the strain of the rebukes he receives at Paramore,[24] her libretto was not subtle enough to provide any justification for the change. The ghosts and their legend are intro-duced too late for an effective relationship to be established between the dead Wingrave boy and Owen. Just as the ballad which frames Act 2 marks a move-ment into a different musical world, so the dramatic landscape of Act 2, which deals almost exclusively with the hero's psychological suffering, is entirely alien-ated from Act 1. In this way, there is little musical or dramatic continuity between the two Acts and the musical conclusion of the second Act is too equivocal for the dramatic tensions of the entire work to be resolved. Indeed, throughout *Owen Wingrave* issues are raised or insinuated but are neither verbally nor musically developed and resolved.

Previously, when dramatic and musical resolution was ambivalent or inade-quate, Britten had attempted to provide reassurance by emphasising or adding a Christian dimension, as occurs in *The Rape of Lucretia* and *Billy Budd*, or by composing another work which might function as an operatic 'epilogue', as in the Canticles *Abraham and Isaac* and *Still falls the Rain*. The composition which immediately followed *Owen Wingrave* was the *Canticle IV* (Op. 86), a setting of T. S. Eliot's poem 'The Journey of the Magi'. This is not a particularly strong piece, and was designed principally as a vehicle for its first three performers, Peter Pears, John Shirley-Quirk and James Bowman. However, at the close the idea of 'sacri-fice' is once again expanded to assume a more general significance:

All this was a long time ago, I remember,
And I would do it again, but set down

---

24 Piper wrote to Britten: 'To me a very important thing is the contrast between his bravery *before* going home – that is the clear way in which he has faced the problem, knowing it's going to be hell but worth it, and his grim tenacity afterwards (do you remember he looked *five* years older) when he found it was infinitely worse than he'd imagined' (undated letter, BPL).

> *This set down*
> *This: were we led all that way for*
> *Birth or Death? There was a Birth, certainly,*
> *We had evidence and no doubt. I had seen birth and death,*
> *But had thought they were different; this Birth was*
> *Hard and bitter agony for us, like Death, our death.*
> *We returned to our places, these Kingdoms,*
> *But no longer at ease here, in the old dispensation,*
> *With an alien people clutching their gods.*
> *I should be glad of another death.*

In *Owen Wingrave* Britten had been determined to emphasise Owen's youthful energy:

> I think we need a sort of musical flowering bit for Coyle and Mrs C. in the first scene and what has occurred to me could be a little number about <u>youth</u> for Coyle . . . (instead of 'the boy is mad'). Something about rashness, madness, pomposity etc. of youth . . . And for Mrs Coyle (this is very tentative perhaps somewhere in Scene iii. possibly in her retort to C. about favourites) . . . a rather lyrical bit about the attractiveness, excitement of youth.[25]

Similarly, an earlier letter from Piper to Britten, 28 October 1967, advised:

> I'm also interested to discover that Owens first soliloquy in the park after telling Coyle is one of extreme optimism – It just works out like that, he has made the first effort and is so relieved that, in spite of his knowing the difficulties ahead he is certain that he'll get away with it. I hope you'll agree that this helps dramatically and also helps to underline his extreme youth and youthful self-importance and confidence. [BPL]

However, in the finished opera Owen sings, 'I am so tired': these are not the words of a young, energetic man but of one who has been aged by the struggle he has undergone, a man not unlike Britten himself at this stage in his life and career. Similarly, Owen's words to Kate might have been spoken by Britten himself:

> OWEN: *I was surrounded with love*
> *Nursed in hope,*
> *Spoiled with admiration,*
> *But for all the image they made of me,*
> *for the man they planned to make of me.*
> *Now I am nothing.*

Having faced, and apparently overcome, the Wingraves' attacks, why does Owen not simply leave Paramore? Having conquered a 'real' problem, he is then killed by a metaphor for that problem, which suggests that the 'metaphor' is in fact, something quite different. It appears Owen believes that only through his sacrificial example will violence, of all kinds, be eradicated: thus he embraces suffering, as Auden had once urged Britten: 'If you are really to develop to your

---

[25] Britten to Piper, 14 May 1969, quoted in DH, p. 14.

full stature, you will have, I think, to suffer, and make others suffer . . . against every conscious value that you have.'[26] Owen may have reminded Britten that it is:

> So easy to conform.
> So easy to accept.

However, James had emphasised that Owen was a fighter: despite the musical and dramatic irresolution at the end of *Owen Wingrave*, the opera may have given Britten the courage to enter his own locked room, a step which he finally took in his last opera, *Death in Venice*.

---

[26] Auden to Britten, (31 January 1942?), in LL, vol. 2, p. 1016.

14

Death in Venice

'You see, Aschenbach has always only lived like this' – and the speaker closed the fingers of his left hand tightly into a fist – 'and never like this' – and he let his open hand hang comfortably down along the back of the chair.

Thomas Mann, *Death in Venice*[1]

Ben is writing an evil opera, and it's killing him!   Peter Pears[2]

Thomas Mann's novella *Death in Venice* is a tapestry of unnamed secrets: sickness, sexuality, deviancy and danger are closeted within its pages, concealed by silence, self-delusion and self-denial yet simultaneously disclosed through Mann's symbolic patterns and ironic narrative method. The tale tells of the moral and physical decline of the aging writer, Gustav von Aschenbach. Dignified, successful and highly respected, he has devoted his life to the service of his art but now finds the disciplines and ideals by which he has lived undermined by a vision of Beauty in the form of a young Polish boy, Tadzio, whom he encounters during a visit to Venice. Although he is initially determined to sublimate his desire in his art, Aschenbach eventually concedes victory to his passionate impulses over his aesthetic discipline. This psychological self-honesty triggers a physical and moral collapse: Aschenbach abandons all pretence at dignity and shadows Tadzio and his family through the streets of Venice. He succumbs to the cholera plague which pollutes the Venetian waters and dies an ambivalent death on the shore of the Lido beach, as Tadzio beckons to him from the sea.

During the filming of *Owen Wingrave* in September 1970, Britten invited Myfanwy Piper and John Culshaw to work with him on his next opera, which he intended to base on Mann's text. She described her response: 'My first thought when I heard its subject was that it was impossible; the second that if Britten said so, it could be done.'[3] Certainly there were practical difficulties: for example, the novella might be considered to be particularly 'non-operatic', with a non-dramatic plot constructed from lengthy monologues and dense prose. Yet, why should Pears say that the opera was 'evil'? Perhaps it was the uncanny

[1] Thomas Mann, *Death in Venice*, trans. David Luke (London: Secker and Warburg, 1990), p. 203. All further references are to this edition and are given in parentheses in the text.
[2] Peter Pears to Sidney Nolan, in HC, p. 546.
[3] Myfanwy Piper, 'The Libretto', in Donald Mitchell (ed.), *Death in Venice – Cambridge Opera Handbook* (Cambridge: CUP, 1987), p. 45.

concordance between the events depicted in Mann's text and Britten's own life which so alarmed Pears and other observers. Ronald Duncan remembered:

> Dramatically, I could see it lacked conflict, musically, I thought it erred by having too much recitative within a limited range amounting to a vocal monotony. But these were not the reasons why I was unable to listen to the entire opera: I could not bear the public revelation of private agony . . . Though the over-tones of the confessional in the opera alarmed me, I was entirely alarmed and distressed when I heard later Ben had had himself flown to Venice. I knew his mind. I saw the immediate threat to himself when imagination and reality become fused and identified. I wrote to George [Harewood] expressing my fear that this act of self-dramatisation meant that Ben was, as it were, scoring his own epilogue, and that his end must be near.[4]

Duncan is probably close to the truth, for in Mann's *Death in Venice* Britten appears to have discovered an explicit account of the very subject which his own operas had repeatedly striven towards, but whose unambiguous expression he had avoided through strategies of evasion and equivocation.

The events of Mann's novella were based upon his recollections of a Venetian visit of May 1911: 'Nothing is invented: the wanderer at the Northern Cemetery in Munich, the gloomy ship from Pola, the foppish old man, the suspect gondolier, Tadzio and his family, the departure prevented by a muddle with the luggage, the cholera, the honest clerk at the hotel agency, the sinister singer.'[5] Mann and Aschenbach shared several attributes: a residence in Munich, a mixed ancestry, a disciplined bourgeois background, a slow and methodical working method, and a concentration in their writing on a certain 'type' of character. However, through his ironic narrator and the objective and subtly critical authorial perspective, Mann is able to distance himself from the sufferings of his protagonist. We are provided with a detailed account of Aschenbach's personal history and psychological and literary development, which exposes the extent of his self-deception and prepares the reader for his inevitable degradation. In this way, Mann demonstrates that Aschenbach's 'fall' is caused neither by Tadzio nor by the plague which he contracts but derives from his lack of self-knowledge.

As a mature artist Aschenbach has rejected such 'knowledge' in his pursuit of pure 'classical' form, 'in the recognition that knowledge can paralyse the will, paralyse and discourage action and emotion and even passion, and rob all these of their dignity' (p. 206). Ironically it is this artistic strategy which ensures his personal tragedy since it entails the abandonment of critical analysis, and by implication self-scrutiny and moral enquiry, and thus removes an ethical framework against which he might judge his own motives: 'Aschenbach was no longer disposed to self-criticism; taste, the intellectual mould of his years, self-respect, maturity and late simplicity all disinclined him to analyse his motives and decide whether what had prevented him from carrying out his intention [to speak to

---

4   Duncan, *Working with Britten*, pp. 153–4.
5   Thomas Mann, *A Sketch of A Life*, quoted by Luke in his translation of *Death in Venice*, p. xxxv.

Tadzio] had been a prompting of conscience or a disreputable weakness' (pp. 240–1).

If Mann was able to partially disassociate himself from Aschenbach, the reverse seems true in Britten's case. Previously he had identified with his protagonists but now he seems almost to have desired to become Aschenbach and to fulfil his own desires through Aschenbach's fictional experiences. Pears described Britten's profound identification with Aschenbach's fate: 'For Ben, the opera was, in some sort of way, a summing-up of what he felt, inspired even by the memories of his own idyllic childhood . . . At the end, Aschenbach asks what it is he has spent his life searching for. Knowledge? A lost innocence? And must the pursuit of beauty, of love, lead only to chaos? All questions Ben constantly asked himself.'[6] In the opera, there is no distanced narrator and events are related through Aschenbach's recitatives and Britten's musical translations of Mann's prose. There is little ironic disclosure in the libretto and consequently Aschenbach's 'fall' from grace is potentially greater. In fact, the libretto of Death in Venice is less explicitly sexual than that of Peter Grimes, Billy Budd, The Turn of the Screw or A Midsummer Night's Dream, and almost all the sexuality in the opera is sited in the music. In Death in Venice Britten appears to have overcome the sometimes sterile and parodic self-reference which had been a feature of Owen Wingrave, and revived the freshness, lyricism and rich invention of his earlier operas. The score is densely motivic but theatrically intense: Britten, Pears, Aschenbach, even the audience, become 'trapped' in its claustrophobic musical embrace, all inescapably involved in the unfolding tragedy.

There was one crucial difference between Mann and Britten: whereas Mann was only thirty-six years old at the time of writing his novella, Britten's personal circumstances were closer to those of Aschenbach, a fifty-three year old artist, a pillar of the cultural establishment, who finds himself in poor health and lacking creative confidence and energy. At this time, Britten's own health was giving grave cause for concern. In 1972 Ian Tait, Britten's Aldeburgh doctor, had diagnosed aortic valve disease and it was apparent that a major operation was necessary. Tait recalls that Britten seemed to sense 'that this might be his last major work'[7] and the composer disclosed in a interview with Alan Blyth: 'I wanted passionately to finish this piece before anything happened. For one thing, it is probably Peter's last major operatic part; for another, it was an opera I had been thinking about for a very long time, and it had already been postponed once.'[8]

Mann had described how Aschenbach's life 'had begun its gradual decline and his artist's fear of not finishing his task – the apprehension that his time might run out before he had given the whole of himself to doing what he had it in him to do – was no longer something he could dismiss as an idle fancy' (p. 200). He has lived a disciplined, repressed life, adhering to a self-imposed rigid daily routine:

---

6   Peter Pears, in Tony Palmer's 1980 film A Time There Was, quoted in Michael Kennedy, Benjamin Britten (London: Dent, 1981, revised 1993), p. 101.

7   HC, p. 543.

8   Alan Blyth, 'Britten returns to Composing', The Times, 30 December 1974.

'Perfectionism, of course, was something which even as a young man he had come to see as the innermost essence of talent, and for its sake he had curbed and cooled his feelings' (p. 201). In the opera, Aschenbach sings of, 'the growing fatigue, that no one must suspect and that I must not betray by any sign of flagging inspiration', and Britten acknowledged his own need for self-discipline in a letter to his brother-in-law, Kit Welford, as early as March 1942: 'I have come to an identical point-of-view (re discipline and obedience) – but in art, as you know, the bias is to the other direction, that of anarchy and romantic 'freedom'. A carefully chosen discipline is the only possible course.'[9] However, as Auden warned Britten shortly afterwards, secrecy and repression may plant seeds of subversion and sickness in the life and work of the artist. Indeed, Mann describes how Aschenbach's fictional heroes, and by implication Aschenbach himself, conceal: 'from the world's eyes until the very last moment a state of inner disintegration and biological decay; sallow ugliness, sensuously marred and worsted' (p. 205). In this way, the 'sickness' which afflicts Aschenbach is a symptom of the very repression required to sustain his art: it may indicate his artistic sensitivity but also implies his moral decadence and decline, i.e. both the Apollonian and Dionysian forces within him.[10] Similarly, the musical score which is the literal manifestation of Britten's creative powers also subtly encodes his, and Aschenbach's, physical and psychological flaws. Aschenbach's Platonic adoration of Tadzio is represented by A major, while his subversive impulses towards sexual love are symbolised by E major. Paradoxically the affinity between these two tonal areas is underlined by a dissonance, A–G♯, the latter pitch being both the major third in E and the leading note in A. This harmonic relationship clarifies the dramatic potential of Britten's score: whereas Mann's literary language can merely describe and account for the distance between these two forces, Britten's music can bridge this gulf and, in the absence of verbal communication between man and child, bring about a musical consummation which might radically alter the 'meaning' of Mann's text.

Britten's *Death in Venice* is virtually a monologue for Gustav von Aschenbach. In this role, Pears was forced to become the public voice of Britten's private, possibly pederastic passions.[11] However, Pears was not merely an agent of communication but took an active interest in shaping the part, especially the text, an intervention which Piper found 'very tiresome, absolutely maddening'. The free recitatives employed to convey Aschenbach's introspective self-reflections,

---

9 Quoted in Mitchell, *Death in Venice*, p. 22.
10 In Mann's fiction the teeth are frequently a site for inherent weakness, and decaying teeth can be interpreted as a symbol of psychological sickness and as an indication of an inescapable genetic degeneracy. It is therefore an uncanny coincidence that in November 1971 Britten underwent a major operation to have several teeth removed, as it was believed that they had contributed to the severe endocarditis that had afflicted him in 1968.
11 Pears was suffering from high blood pressure at the time. Thomas Hemsley told Carpenter that when Britten informed Lucie Mann, with whom Pears was studying, of the part he was planning, she was alarmed: 'You realise that you'll probably kill him, don't you?' Britten allegedly replied, 'I can't imagine a better way for him to go' (HC, p. 546).

passages which Britten had originally envisaged as being spoken, were modelled on the undefined rhythmic notation of the Passions of Schütz, and were an extension of the unmeasured notation which Britten had used in the church parables. Furthermore, the melodic shapes of the recitatives were based upon the inflections which Pears gave the words as he read the text. He described the flexible rhythmic method required: 'I was aware from the first just what a challenge it was going to be, but then Ben built the role around my voice and some things that might seem difficult to another singer may be quite natural for me . . . That technique was second nature to me and I had no trouble whatsoever with it.'[12]

The opera opens with Aschenbach alone on stage: there is no visible antagonist, no oppressive Borough or enticing Quint, for the ensuing conflict essentially takes place in Aschenbach's own mind. He is the agent of his own destruction:

ASCHENBACH: *My mind beats on, my mind beats on and no words come.*

The opening recitative is a twelve-tone row whose tortuous ascent suggests the creative and spiritual struggle which lies ahead, the dry coolness of the piano accompaniment evoking the dispassionate, Apollonian side of Aschenbach's temperament [Example 43]. The second phrase is a retrograde version of the opening row and together they give rise to an overwhelming sense of stasis. These phrases define the opera's harmonic conflict: tonal inflections within the rows hint at half-cadences in E and A major, while the tessitura spans from F to E, the pitches associated with Apollo and Dionysus respectively. The forthcoming battle between these two Gods in the Act 2 dream sequence is anticipated in this opening scene by the repetitive rhythmic pattern on a low F which is persistently and painfully challenged by a muted E played by high trombone and low tuba. The dramatic significance of the tuba is profound, as it carries symbolic resonances from Britten's previous works. Britten had identified its deep, ominous timbre with the plague in the 'Rats Away!' movement of *Our Hunting Fathers*, with the fog-horn which summons Grimes to his death, and with the oppressive weight of military tradition in *Owen Wingrave*. Now the tuba's dark tone, later specifically associated with the Venetian cholera, suggests the physical and spiritual sickness which will destroy Aschenbach. Subversion and instability are intensified in this opening scene by the rhythmic tolling of the clarinets and muted horns, and the harp's flamboyant glissandi, which are complemented by fluctuating tempi, frequent pauses and wide-ranging dynamics. As Aschenbach walks in the garden it is as if Quint is lurking in the musical shadows, heard but unseen.

As Aschenbach struggles to subdue his Dionysian leanings and restore the Apollonian to the ascendancy, the key signature, which literally alternates between F major and E major, and the rising melodic phrases which strive upwards from E to F (a feature which returns at important dramatic moments (for example, Figs. 17, 83, 114, 226 and 305)) reveal the futility of his efforts. His proud, confident Grimes-like entry on a high E – 'I, Aschenbach, famous as a

12 Headington, *Peter Pears*, p. 248.

SCENE 1: Munich.
München.
ASCHENBACH is walking in the suburbs of Munich on a spring evening.
ASCHENBACH geht langsam durch die Vorstädte von München an einem Frühlingsabend.

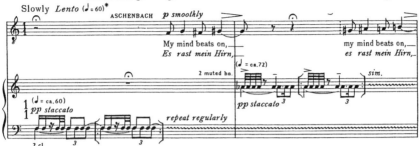

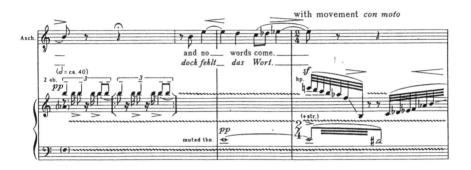

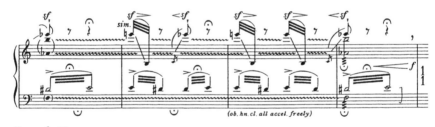

Example 43

master writer, successful, honoured' – is undermined by the mocking quality of the trumpet accompaniment. In these opening moments Aschenbach reels, like Grimes, between defiance and vulnerability. He may protest, 'I reject the words called forth by passion', but the music of his repressed inner life will not be silenced.

The dark side of Aschenbach's nature is personified by a series of ambiguous Figures. Piper compressed these Figures (the traveller in the cemetery, the gondolier, the elderly fop, the hotel manager, the hotel barber and the leader of the players) into a composite 'Stranger-Traveller', to be sung by a single singer. This synthesis was supported by Mann's account of their shared distinguishing features – yellow clothing or colouring, snub noses, red hair and eye-lashes, goat-beards, protruding or diseased teeth. On one level these Figures represent death,[13] but their latent homoeroticism suggests that they are also an invitation to sexual abandon.

The first of these Figures is the Traveller whom Aschenbach encounters in the Munich cemetery. His manner is aggressive and he has 'an air of imperious survey, something bold or even wild about his posture . . . the man was in fact staring at him so aggressively, so straight in the eye, with so evident an intention to make an issue of the matter and outstare him, that Aschenbach turned away in disagreeable embarrassment' (p. 199). His red hair and unflinching gaze are reminiscent of Peter Quint, whose sudden appearance and confrontational stare had similarly alarmed the Governess. The encounter has a startling emotional effect on Aschenbach, who senses 'an extraordinary expansion of his inner self, a kind of roving restlessness, a youthful craving for a far off place, a feeling so new or at least so long unaccustomed and forgotten' (p. 199).

In the opera, the Traveller's presence (Fig. 12) is heralded by fleeting whole-tone tetrachords which return in association with the Leader of the Group of Players in Act 2 (Fig. 257). The Traveller's sinuous opening phrase, 'Marvels unfold' (Fig. 14) is derived from the semitonal movement of Aschenbach's first melodies, thereby establishing his status as a symbol of Aschenbach's inherent corruption. The aura of danger is enhanced by the unpitched, throbbing drum and chromatic woodwind arabesques. The effect of the Traveller upon Aschenbach's musical style is radical: his stifling serialism is swept aside by a remarkable free, expressive outburst (Fig. 16):

> Strange, strange hallucination, inexplicable longing.
> . . . What is this urge that fills my tired heart,
> A thirst, a thirst, a leaping, wild unrest, a deep desire!

The contrary motion tetrachords which conclude this passage (Fig. 18) converge on the pitch E. Quint had urged Miles to follow him on a nocturnal adventure: so Piper's Traveller invites Aschenbach to:

> Go, travel to the South.
> Great poets before you
> Have listened to its voice.[14]

Aschenbach is intoxicated by the tempter's seductive song. In Mann's novella he envisages:

---

[13] Piper's symbolism was somewhat heavy-handed. In Act 1, Scene 2 the gondolier sings:
> Passengers must follow
> Follow where I lead
> No choice for the living
> No choice for the dead.

and his words are echoed by the Hotel Manager in Act 2, Scene 17:
> Be silent –
> who comes and goes is my affair.

[14] Likewise, Auden had proposed, 'North must seem the "good" direction, the way towards heroic adventures, South the way to ignoble ease and decadence', in W. H. Auden, 'England: Six Unexpected Days', *Vogue*, no. 128, 15 May 1954, 62.

a tropical swampland under a cloud-swollen sky, moist and lush and monstrous, a kind of primeval wilderness of islands, morasses and muddy alluvial channels; far and wide around him he saw hairy palm-trunks thrusting upwards from rank jungles of ferns, from the thick fleshy plants in exuberant flower . . . shadowy-green, glassy waters where milk-blossoms floated as big as plates, and among them exotic birds with grotesque beaks stood hunched in the shallows . . . between the knotted stems of the bamboo thicket the glinting eyes of a crouching tiger; and his heart throbbed with terror and mysterious longing. (pp. 199–200)

This is a vision of Quint's nocturnal wilderness, whose alluring promise of freedom and liberation was partially fulfilled in *A Midsummer Night's Dream*. Indeed, Mann suggests Aschenbach's translation to a dream-state: 'something not quite usual was beginning to happen, [that] the world was undergoing a dream-like alienation, becoming increasingly deranged and bizarre' (p. 211). The jungle which promises fertility and life is also the source of the plague which brings death. Aschenbach does not intend to travel 'that far, not quite to where the tigers were', but once within the wood his senses are confused and reason gives way to obsessive love, or 'dotage': 'So it was that in his state of distraction he could no longer think of anything or want anything except this ceaseless pursuit of the object that so alarmed him: nothing but to follow him, to dream of him when he was not there, and after the fashion of lovers to address tender words to his mere shadow' (p. 248).

At this stage in the opera Aschenbach's embrace of freedom is tentative. As the Traveller mysteriously vanishes (Fig. 19) his tetrachords are transformed into scalic runs in E major, underscored by a sustained pedal which increasingly demands resolution. The play of antagonistic forces is literally embodied in the rapidly changing key signatures (Fig. 20):

> *Should I go too beyond the mountains.*
> *Should I let impulse be my guide.*
> *Should I give up the fruitless struggle with the word?* (E major)
> . . .
> *(Aschenbach takes from his pocket a small book. the symbol of the*
>   *novelist's trade.)*
> *I have always kept a close watch over my development as a writer,*
> *over my behaviour as a man.* (C major)
> . . .
> *So be it! I will pursue this freedom* (E major)
> *and offer up my days to the sun and south.* (F major)
> *My ordered soul shall be refreshed at last.* (C major)

Aschenbach decides to visit Venice, a city whose fragile beauty is permanently endangered by the poison latent in the waters upon which it is built. Thomas Mann described 'that magical life between the warm sea in the morning and the ambiguous city in the afternoon. Ambiguous is really the humblest adjective that can be applied . . . and for all the city's modern silliness and corruptness . . . this musical magic of ambiguity still lives . . . For certain people there is a special

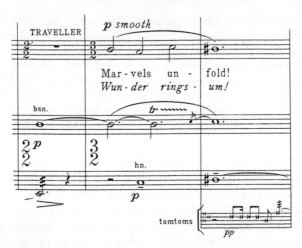

Example 44 (a)

melancholia associated with the name of Venice.'[15] Piper's libretto develops this depiction:

> ASCHENBACH: *What lies in wait for me here,*
> *Ambiguous Venice,*
> *Where water is married to stone*
> *And passion confuses the senses?*
> *Ambiguous Venice.*

The city's ambiguity is represented musically by two related melodic motifs which are derived from the 'Marvels unfold' phrase – the 'Serenissima' motif and the 'plague' melody [Example 44 a, b, c].

The soothing 'Serenissima' melody is introduced (Fig. 25) by the exuberant Youths on board the boat which transports Aschenbach to Venice, its slow-moving minims evoking the city's timeless serenity. When Aschenbach arrives at the hotel he is enchanted by the beauty of Venice and the sea, and he translates the promise of fulfilment, implied by the 'Serenissima' motif, into purely Platonic aspirations (Fig. 46):

> ASCHENBACH: *Serenissima! Serenissima!*
> *Where should I come but to you*
> *To soothe and revive me,*
> *Where but to you*
> *To live that magical life*
> *Between the sea and the city?*

The calm lyricism of the melody is complemented by the comforting, rhythmic rock of the lapping waters, although the increasing emphasis on off-beats in the bass has an unsteadying effect. Aschenbach's hope that his visit will restore his spiritual peace is symbolised by the modulation to C major for the 'view theme'

---

15 Letter to Erika and Klaus Mann, 1932. Thomas Mann, *Letters*, vol. 1, trans. Richard and Clara Winston (London: Secker and Warburg, 1970), p. 187.

Examples 44 (b) & (c)

which depicts the vista of the beach (Fig. 59), but his inevitable disillusionment is revealed by the minor inflections which later colour this theme (Fig. 65), and which are preceded by the restatement of his proud opening phrases (Fig. 62) and the Traveller's whole-tone shadings (Fig. 63). Indeed, the harmonic structure of the 'view theme' itself suggests the precarious fragility of Venice's beauty. Although the arching melody is wide-ranging and confident, it is supported by a series of unresolved second-inversion chords which portray the weak foundations upon which the city rests.

The portentous Figures that cross Aschenbach's path signal the dangers which await him. The first of these is Elderly Fop. Disgusted by the old man's overt lasciviousness and synthetic attempts at youthful rejuvenation, Aschenbach fails to recognise in the degraded Figure before him, his own potential 'other self'; the Fop is an object of ridicule, such as Aschenbach will subsequently become when he too mistakenly decides that the surrender to one's desires is less destructive than the sublimation of one's urges. Aschenbach's transformation in the make-up scene in Act 2 may either be an act of defiance or a sign of his decadence, but it exposes him, like Gloriana, to public ridicule, as insinuated by the song of the Travelling Players, which crudely proclaims 'how ridiculous you are' (Fig. 252).[16]

---

[16] It is interesting that Desmond Shawe-Taylor, writing in *The Sunday Times* 24 June 1973,

The Fop and the Leader of the Singers are further united by their use of falsetto which, recalling the unnatural timbre of Oberon, hints at a transsexual nature.

In a letter to Carl Maria Weber, Mann claimed that his aim in *Death in Venice* had been to establish an 'equilibrium of sensuality and morality' between 'the Dionysian spirit of lyricism, whose outpouring is irresponsible and individualistic, and the Apollonian, objectively controlled, morally and socially responsible'.[17] It is Tadzio, poised between innocence and half-conscious coquetry, who is the meeting-point of the self-disciplined Apollonian cult of beauty and the dark, destructive longings of Dionysus. In two 'Hellenising' passages influenced by Plato's *Phaedrus* and Plutarch's *Erotikos*, Mann formulates a theory of the relationship of beauty to man's spiritual and intellectual life: the value of the beautiful lies in the higher reality it partakes of, and points to, a world beyond corruption which the artist seeks to recreate in his work. Indeed, Aschenbach's fatal attraction arises from his aesthetic tastes: he begins by admiring Tadzio as if he were god-like, or a work of art: '– there, like a flower in bloom, his head was gracefully resting. It was the head of Eros, with the creamy lustre of Parian marble, the brows fine-drawn and serious, the temples and ear darkly and softly covered by the neat right-angled growth of the curling hair' (p. 223). Emphasising Tadzio's statuesque qualities, Aschenbach's devotion is explicitly linked with his own creative ambitions:

> And yet the austere pure will that had here been darkly active, that had succeeded in bringing this divine sculptured shape to light – was it not well known and familiar to Aschenbach as an artist? Was it not also active in him, in the sober passion that filled him as he set free from the marble mass of language that slender form he had beheld in spirit, and which he was presenting to mankind as a mirror and sculptured image of intellectual beauty? (p. 237)

> And what he craved, indeed, was to work on it in Tadzio's presence, to take the boy's physique for a model as he wrote, to let his style follow the lineaments of this body which he saw as divine, and to carry its beauty on high into the spiritual world. (p. 239)

However, long before he has abandoned all pretence, doubt has been cast on Aschenbach's motives. The narrator comments: 'It is as well that the world knows only a fine piece of work and not also its origins, the conditions under which it came into being; for knowledge of the sources of an artist's inspiration would surely shock them, and the excellence of the writing would be to no avail' (p. 239). The purely visual relationship which exists between man and boy is shown to be delusory: 'Nothing is stranger, more delicate, than the relationship between people who know each other only by sight . . . Between them is uneasiness and overstimulated curiosity, the nervous excitement of an unsatisfied, unnaturally

found this stripping of Aschenbach's dignity to be the 'most moving episode of all', and declared that the climax of Act 2 was not the Dionysian nightmare but the scene in which 'Aschenbach, although by now grotesquely transformed into the semblance of the painted dandy of the earlier boat scenes, sings the words of Socrates' tender dismissal of Phaedrus'.

17 Mann, *Letters*, p. 102.

suppressed need to know and to communicate . . . desire is born of defective knowledge' (p. 243). Furthermore, recalling the flaws which mar the beauty, virtue and precocity of Lucretia, Albert, Billy Budd and Miles, Mann's Tadzio is far from the ideal specimen of Aschenbach's first impressions. Later he observes that: 'Tadzio's teeth were not as attractive as they might have been: rather jagged and pale, lacking the lustre of health and having that peculiar brittle transparency which is sometimes found in cases of anaemia' (p. 228). This description links Tadzio with the other tempters in the text: the stranger in the cemetery whose 'lips seemed to be too short and were completely retracted from his teeth, so that the latter showed white and long between them'; the elderly fop whose 'upper set of false teeth dropped half out of his jaw', and who 'licked the corners of his mouth with the tip of his tongue in a repellently suggestive way; and the travelling singer who 'lasciviously lick[ed] the corner of his mouth', and with a 'sly obsequious grin bared his prominent teeth'. Piper's libretto is explicit: Tadzio is not a passive victim but a potential destroyer of a flawed but tortured soul:

ASCHENBACH: *There is a dark side even to perfection. I like that.*

Above all, it is Tadzio's knowingness and coquetry that unsettle Aschenbach, who notes that his own 'interest and attention were not wholly unreciprocated'. The boy's invitational glances grow in frequency – he looks 'over his left shoulder to where his lover was sitting' and passes 'unnecessarily close to him, almost touching his table or his chair'. These approaches culminate in a smile 'that was provocative, curious and imperceptibly troubled, bewitched and bewitching' (p. 244). Mann informed Weber that although his story had originally had no homo-erotic content and had actually been based on the aged Goethe's passion for a young girl from Marienbad: 'What was added to the amalgam at the time was a personal, lyrical travel experience that determined me to carry things to an extreme by introducing the motif of "forbidden love".'[18] This 'experience' was Mann's infatuation for a young Polish boy (since identified as Wladyslaw-Moes) as described by Mann's wife, Katia: 'He immediately had a weakness for the youth, he liked him inordinately, and he always watched him on the beach with his friends. He did not follow him through all of Venice, but the youth did fascinate him, and he thought about him often.'[19] Britten's personal interest in Mann's

---

[18] *Ibid.*

[19] Katia Mann, *My Unwritten Memoir*, quoted in Thomas Mann, *Death in Venice*, ed. Clayton Koelb, Norton Critical Edition (New York: Norton & Company, 1994), p. 214. Robert Tobin ('Why is Tadzio a Boy?', in Mann, *Death in Venice* (Koelb), pp. 207–32) and Albert Braverman and Larry David Nachman, 'The Dialectic of Decadence: An Analysis of Thomas Mann's *Death in Venice*', *Germanic Review*, vol. 45, 1970, 289–98, provide comprehensive accounts, supported by Mann's letters and diaries which supply evidence of his homosexual passion for a series of young men, such as Armin Martens, Willri Trimpe, Paul Eurenberg, Klaus Heuss, and even his own son, Klaus. Mann's diaries contain many references to these infatuations, for example: 'In love with Klaus these days . . . Germ of a Father-Son novella (5 July 1920) . . ./ It seems to me that I'm finally done with the feminine? . . . delight in Eissi [Klauss's nickname] who is frigheningly cute in the bath. Find it natural that I'm falling in love with my son' (25 July 1920, quoted in Mann, *Death in Venice* (Koelb), pp. 214–15).

novella sprang from remarkably similar origins. Colin Matthews told Carpenter that he was convinced *Death in Venice* had:

> some relationship to Britten's infatuation with David Hemmings at the time of the premiere of *The Turn of the Screw* in Venice. I think I was probably wrong, but at the time I couldn't comprehend what had led Ben to choose the subject, and I clearly remember that the impression I had was of Aschenbach as almost a caricature of Peter, as if the role wasn't written so much out of love for him as out of some strange desire to wound. That's a simplistic and one-sided way of looking at it, but there is a very dark side to the work that I still can't claim to understand.[20]

In fact, at the time of the composition of *Death in Venice* Britten was involved in two new 'friendships', with Charles Tait, the son of his doctor, and Ronan Magill, a gifted young pianist whom Britten had begun to help financially and musically in 1970, and whom he nick-named 'Tyger'.[21] At the start of 1972 Britten travelled to Wolfsgarten to visit Peg Hesse and begin sustained work on the score, yet he found time to write to Charles: 'I was very pleased to get your letter . . . I certainly miss you too . . . I upset almost half a bottle of bubble-bath stuff into the bath the other evening, & the room smelt like a chemist shop all night – & I looked rather like you did in your bubble-bath at the Red House: almost invisible.'[22] Charles Tait was a shy, naive boy but, looking back, he told Carpenter that Britten was probably 'very tempted' sexually by their friendship.[23] In contrast, Ronan Magill was a mature eighteen year old, and he felt personally implicated in the subject matter of Britten's opera:

> Britten was a homosexual; I wasn't. There was a time, when I was in Horham with him, when he wanted to, and I said, 'No.' I have to be quite honest. But that didn't mean to say there weren't moments of deep affection, on a very high level.
> . . . And I knew that I was probably being very cruel. He felt fragile, and he had an awful lot of things on his mind, and I didn't know the half of it at the time.
> He probably thought I was some sort of escape, a sort of Tadzio-like youth, and I think there's certainly a relationship [to the opera] there. The theme in the opera when Tadzio is winning all the games, wanting to succeed, wanting to show how good he is, there's certainly a link there. But Tadzio – the fragility of the man, being devastated by it – that's why, whenever I hear that motif, it's with very deep emotion . . . I remember holding him, and hearing his heart beat – this was in Horham . . . It had a sort of hollow bang to it.[24]

20 HC, p. 546.
21 Stephen Reiss proposed another possible model for Tadzio, the son of the recently employed caretaker at the Maltings: 'I think he was more or less the prototype for the boy in *Death in Venice*. Ben and Peter were crazy about him' (HC, p. 524). Likewise, Fidelity Cranbrook recalled 'this pretty boy of seventeen', in whom Britten's and Pears's sexual interest was 'so blatant' (HC, p. 525).
22 Britten to Charles Tait, 26 January 1972, quoted in HC, p. 537.
23 HC, p. 538.
24 Ronan Magill to Carpenter, 27 June 1991, quoted in HC, pp. 538–9.

In the first production of *Death in Venice* the part of Tadzio was performed by Robert Huguenin; it seems that Pears too became infatuated, for later he wrote: 'I miss Bob Huguenin very much. This boy . . . has <u>not got</u> It at all!! Oh dear! I wouldn't dream of looking at him for more than 5 seconds.'[25] However, Pears's remark demonstrates a self-conscious irony which Britten's comments, and his music, entirely lack. In this way, Magill's recollections draw attention to two important features of *Death in Venice*: his own unintentional cruelty and Britten's vulnerability. Similarly, it is clear that Aschenbach is not simply a pederast preying upon innocence and youth but is also a 'victim', destroyed by his knowledge of the innocence which he has lost and which cannot be regained.

Aschenbach sings:

> *As one who strives to create beauty, to liberate from the marble mass of language the slender forms of an art, I might have created him. Perhaps that is why I feel a father's pleasure, a father's warmth in the contemplation of him.*

In the music accompanying Tadzio's first entrance (Fig. 73) Britten metaphorically sculpts Tadzio in a shimmering gamelan-like chord [Example 45]. Donald Mitchell described the genesis of this motif:

> Britten told me, he had brought his composition sketch to the point of Tadzio's first entry *without*, it seems, any clear idea of what the boy's musical profile – his distinguishing theme – would be . . . [the next morning he resumed work and] the theme came to him . . . What was surprising . . . was the character and special properties of the theme itself, which, to quote Britten's own words, 'used up the notes that had been left unused the night before'.[26]

The air of timelessness, emphasised by frequent musical pauses, contrasts with the preceding noisy activity of the other hotel guests. For the first time in the opera the drum is silenced, as the slowly unfolding vibraphone melody expands from A to G♯, delineating the harmonic progression-resolution which is required to bring about a spiritual union between Aschenbach and Tadzio. This phrase initiates Aschenbach's struggle with his opposing physical and spiritual impulses which continues to the end of the opera. Although at times sublimation seems possible – as when the 'view theme' expands through Tadzio's warm major thirds (Fig. 77); or when Aschenbach, refreshed by his vision of Tadzio, resolves to leave Venice and devote himself to his art, departing with the words 'May God bless you' which trace Tadzio's melodic arc (Fig. 125) – in reality Aschenbach's senses are confused by Tadzio's bewitching aura and self-knowledge remains unattainable.

Tadzio's statuesque power is dramatised in the 'Games of Apollo', a balletic episode which relies on gesture, mime and pose to communicate, and which foreshadows the Dionysian dance of Aschenbach's Dream in Act 2. Despite Piper's Notebook observation that it was necessary to 'avoid the obviousness of the

---

25 Pears to Britten, 12 October 1974, quoted in HC, p. 557.
26 Mitchell, *Death in Venice*, p. 3. The sustained chord which supports Aschenbach's observations of the Hotel Guests contains seven pitches – the remaining five are used in Tadzio's melody.

Example 45

'homosexual theme', in a letter to Britten, 28 February 1972, she made a surprising suggestion:

> Another little discovery – on page 299 of the book 'Hessian Tapestry' 'Little naked boys were turning somersault on the horizontal bars at the swimming pool' . . .
> I think the way to deal with the beach scenes is to have the 1st beach ballet, as I have already suggested, much more clothed & then have the 2nd one, as far as the boys are concerned, really naked so as to remove the whole thing slightly from reality, as the whole of Aschenbach's attitude is removed from reality . . .
> At the end when Tadzio is mixed up with grownups he could simply have his white beach towel. (BPL)

Britten replied that the idea was 'excellent, & could be wonderfully beautiful, Hellenically evocative. There may be some objections – Fred Ashton might raise some – & I am worried lest the work might cause a certain interest that none of us really wants!'[27] Fortunately, the idea was abandoned but 'The Games' did prove problematic. Colin Graham considered them too long and numerous, and he described how Ashton, who choreographed the scene, was somewhat stumped when confronted by long-jumps and sprinting races.[28] Physically the dances

---

27 HC, p. 539.
28 Colin Graham, 'The First Production', in Mitchell, *Death in Venice*, p. 71. 'The Games' were criticised by reviewers of the first production. Ned Rorem condemned the literal embodying of Aschenbach's fantasy in the form of a dancer which he believed made the opera, 'the saga of a flirty boy who lusts for an old man but whose mother interferes so he drowns himself. If the Silent Ideal must be depicted within a medium whose very purpose is noise, then, mime,

proved difficult for children to perform and the dancers required athletic physiques which contradicted Mann's descriptions. However, while Piper's text for the 'Games' is the least inspired section of the libretto, the episode was evidently central to Britten's interpretation of Mann's text as a glorification of Hellenic philosophy, demonstrating the doctrine that the Divine is manifest in the perfect human form.

For this reason the position of the 'Games' sequence in the opera was crucial. Although Piper maintained that 'In Mann's story the order of events is essential; everything depends upon what went before',[29] in practice she made a subtle but significant alteration.[30] In Mann's *Death in Venice* the turning point for Aschenbach comes after his foiled departure from the city. Returning to his hotel room, he observes Tadzio playing beneath his window and this vision initiates a total reversal of his philosophy as he surrenders to his intoxication. Piper reduces the significance of the lost luggage episode and postpones the emotional climax until after the 'Games of Apollo'. In this way, the latter come to symbolise the pinnacle of Aschenbach's idealism and not the beginning of his decline. Piper's addition of a single line of text encourages a reading of 'The Games' as the embodiment of Platonic idealism:

Often what is called disruptive is not directed against life, but is invigorating, a renewal.

In his 'Working Notes' Mann had noted that 'Apollo ... is the pure god of light, but at the same time the horrible sender of epidemics and a quick death',[31] yet the libretto does not hint at the latent danger of the sun with which Tadzio is associated:

CHORUS: *No boy, but Phoebus of the golden hair*
Driving his horses through the azure sky
Mounting his living chariot shoulder high,
Both child and god how he lords it in the air.

He is the peak of perfection and purity, residing at the top of the pyramid, the victor of all sporting competitions. Only in the final contest, the wrestling match, is there any hint of homoerotic tension, deepened by the gradual rise in pitch, tempo and dynamics, and by the gusts of the wind machine:

while a bit illegal, is probably the only solution ... [but] when the Silent Ideal is rendered as a champion athlete the careful craft of Thomas Mann, without a word changed is utterly violated' ('Britten's Venice', *The New Republic*, 8 February 1975, 31–2). Bayan Northcott, writing in *The New Statesman*, 22 June 1973, came to a similar conclusion: 'Coming at the end of an Act 1 running an hour and a half and glorifying Robert Huguenin's rather glum Tadzio, the prep-school nostalgia of this lengthy Ancient Greek sports day strikes me as both dramatically gratuitous and disturbingly at variance in spirit with what is for the most part so faithful a transposition of Mann's original.'

29   Mitchell, *Death in Venice*, p. 47.
30   See Clifford Hindley, 'Contemplation and Reality: A Study of Britten's *Death in Venice*', *Music and Letters*, November 1990, vol. 71, 511–23.
31   Quoted in Mann, *Death in Venice* (Koelb), p. 74.

> CHORUS: *Measure to fight,*
> *face your man,*
> *forehead to forehead,*
> *fist to fist,*
> *limbs coiled round limbs,*
> *panting with strain,*
> *tear apart and close again,*
> *immobile now, tensing! tensing!*

One of the sequences in 'The Games' is a formal solo dance for Tadzio (Fig. 158). This physical set-piece is the closest which movement can come to the stylised stillness which embodies perfection. The chorus sing:

> *Beauty is the only form*
> *Of spirit that our eyes can see*
> *So brings to the outcast soul*
> *Reflections of Divinity.*

However, the danger inherent in this worship of the body is implied by the subversive, quasi-sexual aura of the accompaniment, played by the harp, double bass, pizzicato cello, gong and tom-tom.

Although there is little in the libretto to clarify the ambiguous nature of Apollo's influence as embodied in Tadzio, Britten's music powerfully evokes the God's equivocal power and charm. Originally Britten had intended that the Voice of Apollo be sung by a boy treble, thus identifying the boy's 'voice' with that of the God. Piper wrote to Britten, 28 February 1972:

> I've made an interesting discovery which I think would wholly justify your using a voice that could be Tadzio's for Apollo in the dream . . . There is no doubt in my mind that Aschenbach was a devotee of Apollo – that Apollo is the God whom he puts up against Dionysus and that Tadzio therefore also can and does represent Apollo in his mind so that in his distraught state a voice that could be Tadzios would be dramatically right if you think we can get away with it. (BPL)

However, Pears suggested that the 'unnatural' timbre of the counter-tenor might be more dramatically appropriate: 'I still like the idea of a boy's voice there but Peter has had a stranger idea, but possibly a better one – why not a counter-tenor, colder, not manly or womanly, & a sound there [sic] hasn't been used before.'[32] After hearing James Bowman perform Britten's *Canticle IV* Piper wrote enthusiastically to Britten, 30 May 1972: 'the thrilling quality of the counter tenor [which] really does make one's flesh creep in terror <u>and</u> delight. If we could manage to get the counter tenor, in completely different moods, into both the end of Act I and the dream in Act II, I think it would be wonderful' (BPL). Thus the unearthly, asexual cry of Oberon is revived by Apollo in *Death in Venice*: indeed, during 'The Games' (Fig. 143) he sings 'He who loves beauty worships me. Mine is the *spell* which binds his days' (my italics). Apollo never appears on stage but is

---

[32] Britten to Myfanwy Piper, 6 February 1972, quoted in HC, p. 539.

present as a powerful disembodied voice, a voice whose mastery and moral authority is precarious, as implied by the precious rarity of its own strange timbre.

Following 'The Games' Aschenbach glories in the embodied ideal which he has witnessed:

> *The boy, Tadzio shall inspire me.*
> *His pure lines shall be my style.*
> *The power of beauty sets me free.*
>
> *I shall write what the world waits for rejoicing in his presence.*

Although the key signature and harmony are securely based in A major, Aschenbach's melodies expose his latent lust, as they modulate from C major (Fig. 177) to E major (Fig. 179), through strategic emphasis on the pitch E and a proliferation of D#'s. The climax of this passage occurs with the phrase 'Then Eros is in the word', sung to Tadzio's motif, but the lyricism rapidly disintegrates and is replaced by a disturbing rhythmic energy. Crucially, as Aschenbach despairs – 'this is frenzy, absurd. The heat of the sun must have made me ill' – the tuba is reintroduced. It rises chromatically from a low E, gradually spanning an octave, signifying the unstoppable advance of both the plague and Aschenbach's sickness. As Tadzio passes on the way to the hotel, accompanied by the trembling of the glockenspiel, he smiles (Fig. 187):

> *ASCHENBACH: Ah! don't smile like that! No one should be*
> *   smiled at like that.*
> *(realising the truth at last)*
> *I love you.*

The final phrase unequivocally establishes the E major tonality which Aschenbach has struggled to deny; but the final cadence is imperfect, suspended and unresolved: at the close of Act 1 spiritual transcendence remains a possible outcome.

In the second Act Aschenbach's continued attempts to sublimate his passion leave him feeling degraded and debauched. He has been a 'devotee of solitude and silence' but now finds his self-imposed repression unwelcome, desiring to 'naturalise' his emotions by speaking to the boy. Such communication is, of course, impossible, as Tadzio is the literal symbol of Aschenbach's inner silence or sickness: 'Why, Tadzio, there you are again too! But at the same instant he felt that casual greeting die on his lips, stricken dumb by the truth in his heart' (p. 233). Piper understood the significance of the verbal impasse which was at the heart of his spiritual and creative paralysis: 'although we know everything that he thought about Tadzio we know nothing of Tadzio's thoughts about him . . . The important thing from our point of view was that, unlike the Ghosts in *The Turn of the Screw*, what he thought or said would have been of no interest to us. Here what needed to be underlined was not communication but the lack, indeed the impossibility of it.'[33] Tadzio 'walks in the silence obliquely across the room', and communicates only with a 'smile' or 'a murmured word': he is not a 'real' boy

---

[33] Piper, 'Working for Britten', in DH, p. 17.

and in this way he seems closer to the apprentice, Albert or Billy, than to Miles or Puck.

Aschenbach's sickness is replicated by the Asian cholera concealed beneath Venice's beautiful facade. The plague which will ravage his body springs from the same sources as the disease which pollutes his soul: 'Originating in the sultry morasses of the Ganges delta . . . that primitive island shunned by man, where tigers crouched in bamboo thickets, the pestilence had raged' (p. 256). The 'ceremonious silence' which prevails in the hotel masks the knowledge of this latent danger, a concealment which intensifies Aschenbach's sense of guilt: ' "They want it kept quiet!" . . . "They're hushing it up!" . . . this guilty secret of the city, merged with his own innermost secret [and] which it was also so much in his own interest to protect' (p. 246). In Britten's opera Aschenbach sings:

> Ugh! rumours, rumours. They should be silent.
> The city's secret, growing darker every day, like the secret in my
>   own heart.

The appearance of the word 'sickness' in the libretto signals the tuba's introduction of the 'plague motif' (Fig. 198) which, like the 'Serenissima' phrase, is derived from the Traveller's 'Marvels unfold'. Significantly, the suppression of truth gives rise to an outbreak of crime and disorder in Venice which Mann associates with the exotic, 'extravagant' impulses 'indigenous only to southern Italy or oriental countries.' Eventually, however, 'The truth seems to have leaked out, and however tightly the interested parties closed ranks, panic could no longer be stemmed' (p. 261).

The silence in *Death in Venice* is partly a result of the failure of language itself, as Mann indicates: 'He was more beautiful than words can express, and Aschenbach felt, as so often already, the painful awareness that language can only praise sensuous beauty, but cannot reproduce it' (p. 244). Perhaps music might overcome this inadequacy, bridging the silence without resorting to clichés and literalisms.[34] Mann had described the 'uneasiness and overstimulated curiosity, the nervous excitement of an unsatisfied, unnaturally suppressed need to know and to communicate'. As Aschenbach pursues Tadzio and his family through Venice's polluted backwaters, Britten's music seems to be literally a harmonic manifestation of this desire for communication and sublimated union.

Aschenbach's delirious pursuit is supported by an ostinato-like progression, initiated by the tuba and double bass (Fig. 211), which passes through the opera's principal tonal centres. The circular pattern E–F♯–G–G♯–E, which traces the major third of Aschenbach's 'I love you', concludes with a sustained pedal E (Fig. 213), before recommencing on Tadzio's pitch, A (Fig. 217). This modulation seems to encapsulate the desperate chase through the city as Aschenbach sings 'Careful search now leads me to them, cunning finds them out.' Although a brief move to F major indicates Aschenbach's struggle to reassert his Apollonian will (Fig. 216), his degradation is confirmed as E major is restored (Fig. 230):

---

[34] In a letter to Marianne Lidell, a violinist, 8 October 1944, Mann had written: 'How I envy music for needing no translation!' (Mann, *Letters*, vol. 2, p. 453).

Ah, Tadzio, Eros, charmer, see I am past all fear, blind to danger, drunken, power-less, sunk in the bliss of madness.

Throughout *Death in Venice* Aschenbach's worship of beauty struggles to be aesthetic rather than earthly and passionate, and this confrontation climaxes in 'The Dream'. The voice of Apollo does battle with the voice of Dionysus, the latter sung by the singer who also takes the composite part of the Stranger-Traveller. In Britten's 'Dream' the opposing forces are assigned different key signatures – E major for Dionysus and F major for Apollo. Apollo's defeat is confirmed by the definitive establishment of E major (Fig. 283): his fading phrase descends through an octave of A, as the bells ring out the dissonance A/G♯:

APOLLO: *I go, I go, I go, I go now.*

Unable to control or contain the subversive voices which his own spell has released, Apollo is vanquished. The dancing followers of Dionysus appear and an orgasmic musical liberation ensues. Mann had described the resulting aural frenzy: 'from wooded heights, between tree trunks and mossy boulders, it came tumbling and whirling down: a human and animal swarm, a raging rout, flooding the slope with bodies, with flames, with tumult and frenzied dancing' (p. 260). Bottom's tender fantasy has become a Dionysian nightmare and the magical forces of the Gods are unleashed in uncontrolled wordless howls – 'Aaoo!' – which outline the major seventh of Tadzio's motif. Initially Tadzio's foreign language had charmed Aschenbach – 'the sound of the foreign boy's speech exalted it to music . . . it was liquid melody to his ears' (p. 236) – but as it is trans-formed, first into the 'unintelligible dialect' sung by the vagrant balladeer, and now into the revellers' orgiastic shrieks, enchantment is replaced by torment:

> from far off a hubbub was approaching, an uproar, a compendium of noise, a clangour and blare and dull thinking, yells of exultation and a particular howl with a long-drawn out u at the end – all of it permeated and dominated by a terrible sweet sound of flute music . . . And the god's enthusiasts howled out the cry with the soft consonants and long-drawn out final u, sweet and wild both at once . . . But the deep, enticing flute music mingled irresistibly with everything. (pp. 259–60)

The drums whose pulsing rhythms have been omnipresent now let loose a wild, frenzied pounding, depicting a primitive and violent sexual energy, but perhaps also implying the uncontrollable, irregular beating of Aschenbach's (Britten's?) heart. It is as if Aschenbach's aesthetic urges are being 'raped' by his lustful desires. This violation is a complete reversal of Tarquinius's rape of Lucretia, where phys-ical violence was notably absent from the score.

For Mann, *Death in Venice* seems to have been essentially a literary experiment. Shaped by his own homoerotic leanings it was the medium through which he could explore his suspicion of 'passion': Aschenbach's passion is homosexual but Mann was able initially to ignore the physical dimension of Aschenbach's desire and to focus on Tadzio's status as an embodiment of the Platonic Beauty which may inspire Aschenbach, through aesthetic rebirth, to attain spiritual revelation.

Some critics assumed that the degeneration of the protagonist demonstrated that Mann's novella was intended as anti-homosexual propaganda but Mann countered these accusations in his letter to Weber:

> But that the novella is at its core of a hymnic type, indeed of hymnic origin, cannot have escaped you . . . there is a naturalistic bent in my generation which compelled me to see the 'case' also in a pathological light, and to alternate this motif (climacterium) with the symbol motif (Tadzio as Hermes-Psychopompos). Something still more a matter of intellect, because more personal was added: the altogether non-'Greek' but rather Protestant, Puritan ('Bourgeois') basic state of mind not only of the story's protagonist but also of myself; in other words, our fundamentally mistrustful relationship to passion in general . . . Passion as confusion and as a stripping of dignity was really the subject of my tale.[35]

Mann's ironic narration exposes Aschenbach's self-deceptions and emphasises the precariousness of the dignity and status which the duped Artist believes he commands.[36] Aschenbach's death does not represent an apotheosis: Plato's theory of Eros had provided Mann with a framework for an exposition of a love which was both sexual and visionary yet he refrained from using it to endorse Aschenbach's desire. Essentially the moral victory in *Death in Venice* does not centre on homosexual love, but is an artistic victory for Mann the writer, who now rejects Aschenbach's literary style, a style which he had himself employed in his earlier works.

Britten's priorities were more complex: the problems facing him were not Mann's objective abstractions but Aschenbach's subjective dilemma – how might his 'suffering', his homosexuality, become art? Whereas Mann appears to have considered homosexuality to be essentially a visual, non-physical phenomenon, Britten's sexuality was altogether more complex. Consequently the operatic dramatisation of his desires was a painful and gradual process, one which had occupied his entire creative life, and which now left him feeling vulnerable and 'exposed'. He wrote to Frederick Ashton that *Death in Venice* was 'either the best

---

35 Mann, *Letters*, p. 102.

36 Mann emphasised the importance of his theme in his 'Working Notes': 'Understanding, that the artist cannot be worthy of dignity (that he necessarily goes the wrong way) remains a Bohemian (gypsy, libertine) and an eternal adventurer of the emotions' (quoted in Mann, *Death in Venice* (Koelb), pp. 158–9). The early chapters of *Death in Venice* describe the public recognition and honour which Aschenbach has received: 'he thought of his fame, reflected that many people recognised him in the streets and would gaze at him respectfully, saluting the unerring and graceful power of his language – he recalled all the external successes he could think of that his talent had brought him, even calling to mind his elevation to the nobility' (p. 227). Britten was created a Companion of Honour in June 1953, recieved the Order of Merit in March 1965, and was made a life peer in 1976. Much of his career he had been safeguarded from adverse criticism by well-intentioned friends and colleagues but he was becoming increasingly aware of the fickleness of the artist's public status. Carpenter describes his growing professional insecurities, which were exacerbated by his fear that, whereas the music of Michael Tippett was growing in popularity and esteem, his own compositions were considered unfashionable and reactionary (HC, pp. 535–6).

or the worst music I've ever written', and said he had a 'terrible dread of playing the piece to anyone'.[37] Does Britten flinch back from the abyss? Is his opera merely another dramatisation of timidity and non-doing? Or does he finally confront his own dark side?

In his review in *The New Statesman*, 22 June 1973, Bayan Northcott asked the question which must have troubled Britten himself: 'In tackling as overt and ripely obsessive a treatment of a theme so long latent in his output was Britten not risking self-parody?' Other commentators were blatantly hostile; for example, Joan Cross condemned the work as an apologia for paedophilia, 'Preaching to the converted'.[38] In August 1989 Kent and Sussex LEAs banned performances of *Death in Venice* by Glyndebourne Touring Opera in the counties' schools, on the grounds that it might promote homosexuality, although, as Philip Brett noted, the opera was more likely to act as a warning against 'being gay or pederastic: [because] you will stoop to any indignity (such as painting your face) to lure your young prey, and you will die alone, rejected, and in misery'.[39] In contrast, Robert Tear attacked Britten's failure to commit himself: 'Musically, it's a masterpiece. But there's a cop-out. It mustn't be called sexual lust. It's Beauty, or it's Greek. And that's a cop-out.'[40] Colin Matthews recalls that 'around *Death in Venice* time, Britten read out to me an article in *Opera* magazine which said, "All Britten's opera are concerned with the loss of innocence." And he said, "This is absolute *rubbish!*" and picked up the thing and threw it to the other side of the room. And I've regretted ever since that I didn't have the courage to say, "Well, what are they about, then?" '[41] Perhaps Britten's anger arose from his belief that the reviewer's comments were intended as a personal attack upon himself. Matthews does not remark upon the fact that in *Death in Venice* it is not Tadzio who suffers and is sacrificed but Aschenbach himself. He is not the seducer but the seduced. Britten's musical rendition of this tragedy may have been an attempt to communicate the anguish which he had suffered as a result of his homosexual and pederastic desires, as well as what Mitchell describes as 'the obligatory consequential constraints, the absence of which – of the 'carefully chosen' and shouldered 'discipline' – was ultimately Aschenbach's undoing.'[42]

Indeed, Britten is more emphatic than Mann in blaming 'society' for Aschenbach's tragedy. The Polish family's disapproval of Aschenbach is underlined by the addition of an aria at the close of Act 2 for the Lady of the Pearls who draws Tadzio away from Aschenbach. Clifford Hindley observes: 'she (and

---

37 21 October 1972, quoted in HC, p. 545.
38 HC, p. 552.
39 Philip Brett, *Musical Times*, 1990, vol. 131, 10–11.
40 HC, p. 552.
41 HC, p. 536.
42 Mitchell, *Death in Venice*, p. 207. Significantly, in Act 1, Scene 5 of *Death in Venice*, Aschenbach sings a passage not included in Mann's novella: 'Yes, Aschenbach you have grown reserved . . . dependent not upon human relationships but upon work, and again – work. How much better to live, not words but beauty, to exist in it, and of it. How much better than my detached and solitary way.'

through her, society) must share in the responsibility for deflecting Aschenbach from a potentially ideal relationship which could have brought him fulfilment as an artist and as a man.'[43] In *Peter Grimes*, the Borough had been similarly implicated in Grimes's failure. Moreover, Piper's lines for the Chorus in *Death in Venice* – 'We who live by summer's trade guard the city's secret . . . There's no danger if we watch and do as we are told' – are oddly reminiscent of the Borough's pronouncement:

> We live and let live, and look
> We keep our hands to ourselves.

Britten and Aschenbach are both searching for a brief, inebriating vision of union and understanding: at the close of *Death in Venice* are their dreams fulfilled? Britten told Donald Mitchell, '*Death in Venice* is everything Peter and I have stood for'.[44] However, Philip Brett disagrees: 'If, as Donald Mitchell insists, *Death in Venice* is a testament, then it is a testament to the power, not of love, but of the destructive effects on the personality of the dynamics of the closet.'[45] Perhaps the answer may be found in the final pages of the score which illustrate Britten's attempts to immortalise the union between Aschenbach and Tadzio, who *is* literally a 'musical moment', in his art.

The closing pages of the score appear to chart Aschenbach's ultimate physical collapse and moral dissolution. Following his consumption of the rancid strawberries (Fig. 306) there begins a restatement of the bass progression from E to G$\sharp$ which had accompanied Aschenbach's earlier pursuit of Tadzio, together with sustained chords constructed from Tadzio's pitches.[46] Aschenbach repeats his proud phrases from the opening of the opera, but his attempts to re-establish his former identity are ineffectual. Following a final Hellenising episode in C major (Fig. 308) the tuba returns (Fig. 311). The reappearance of the plague motif (Fig. 322) and the contraction of the intervals of the 'view theme' (Fig. 320) suggest the withered, diminished state of Aschenbach's mind and body.

As in *Peter Grimes*, the closing bars of *Death in Venice* portray the protagonist's disintegrating consciousness. However, the final 'word' is Tadzio's. The off-stage female chorus softly intone his name, 'Adziu', in a comforting musical caress which is taken up by Aschenbach. As Tadzio beckons him from the sea,

43 Hindley, 'Contemplation and Reality'.
44 HC, p. 552.
45 Brett, *Musical Times*.
46 Aschenbach's self-destructive surrender to his desires is symbolised by this wilful consumption of the strawberry-seller's over-ripe fruit. In a similar way, Britten's own decision to postpone his urgently needed heart operation, to prevent his work on *Death in Venice* from being interrupted, might be considered a comparable abandonment of caution in the interests of 'experience'. Ian Tait remembered discussing the problem with Britten who was concerned that hospitalisation might prevent his completion of the opera and was consequently 'very keen not to interrupt his work on *Death in Venice*, which he expressed as being his priority above all else' (HC, p. 543). However, according to Donald and Kathleen Mitchell, Britten was aware of the dangers involved in delaying surgery, and understood that his heart might give out before the opera was completed.

Aschenbach's 'sweet' cry rises from A to G$\sharp$, initiating a dissonance which is sustained to the final bar. Above a low rumbling trill on G$\sharp$ approached by a grace note A, Tadzio's sensuous vibraphone tremor is accompanied by a slow wood-wind, horn and string ascent through A major, spanning five octaves. The simultaneous sounding of these two pitches, A and G$\sharp$, may indicate that man and boy must remain apart, that resolution is impossible. Alternatively, this aural simultaneity may be the only possibly resolution. In the final bar the music reaches to the heights and depths, embracing 'everything', as Aschenbach and Tadzio are united in sound and in the silence which follows [Example 46].

The presence of the sea is crucial, for Tadzio is a god of the sea: 'this living Figure, lovely and austere in its early masculinity, with dripping locks and beautiful as a young god, approaching out of the depths of the sky and sea, rising and escaping from the elements' (pp. 226–7). Aschenbach gazes at the expanse of ocean as he contemplates his decision to remain in Venice:

> What better place could I find? And with his hands folded in his lap, he let his eyes wander in the sea's wide expanse, let his gaze glide away, dissolve and die in the monotonous haze of this desolate emptiness. There were profound reasons for his attachment to the sea: he loved it because as a hard-working artist he needed rest, needed to escape from the demanding complexity of phenomena and lie hidden on the bosom of the simple and tremendous; because of a forbidden longing deep within him that ran quite contrary to his life's task and was for that reason very seductive, a longing for the unarticulated and immeasurable, for eternity, for nothingness. To rest in the arms of perfection is the desire of any man intent upon creating excellence; and is not nothingness a form of perfection? (p. 224)

He shares his passive longing for watery oblivion with Britten's earlier operatic protagonist, Peter Grimes. Grimes had asked 'Where's my home? Deep as calm water': the grave which he welcomes will drown the Borough's shrieks of persecution, and resonate with a wordless music which he believes will harbour him from 'terrors and tragedies'. It is necessary to go through the flood to reach salvation, and this is the music which soothes Aschenbach in his dying moments. The jovial 'Addios' of the travelling youths, the gondoliers' 'Aou!', the wild whoops of the Dionysian revellers, the children's tender elongation of Tadzio's name, cries which have 'both a sweetness and a wildness' and have provoked a sensual response in Aschenbach who 'listened with closed eyes to this song as it began music deep within him' (p. 227) – now these syllables are united in the music which emanates from the sea as Tadzio beckons to Aschenbach on the shore: 'There the watcher sat . . . to him it was as if the pale and lovely soul-summoner out there were smiling to him, beckoning to him; as if he loosed his hand from his hip and pointed outwards, into an immensity rich with unutterable expectation. And as so often, he set out to follow him' (p. 267).

Ultimately, however, the musical union between Aschenbach and Tadzio cannot be made atemporal, cannot exist outside the confines of Britten's score. The only possible end for Aschenbach is death, as Piper's libretto drafts had clarified:

Example 46 (a)

Example 46 (b)

ASCHENBACH: Literature is death, and I shall never understand how one can become enslaved by it without hating it bitterly . . .
   One must die to life, in order to be entirely a creator.[47]

Yet for Britten *Death in Venice* was not the 'end': despite Pears's fears, this 'evil opera' did not kill him. Although his heart operation was marred by complications, by the summer of 1974 he was well enough to begin composing again. In July he completed the *Canticle V: The Death of Narcissus*, after T. S. Eliot, and the first performance was given on 15 January 1975, by Pears, accompanied by the harpist, Osian Ellis. Britten apparently professed to Rosamund Strode, 'I haven't the remotest idea what it's about'[48] but the poem could be describing Tadzio, retracing the path trodden in Britten's preceding operas:

> *Struck down by such knowledge*
> *He could not live men's ways, but became a dancer before God*
> *If he walked in city streets*
> *He seemed to tread on faces, convulsive thighs and knees.*
> *So he came out under the rock.*
>
> *First he was sure that he had been a tree,*
> *Twisting its branches among each other*
> *And tangling its roots among each other.*
>
> *Then he knew that he had been a fish*
> *With slippery white belly held tight in his own fingers,*
> *Writhing in his own clutch, his ancient beauty*
> *Caught fast in the pink tips of his new beauty.*
>
> *Then he had been a young girl*
> *Caught in the woods by a drunken old man*
> *Knowing at the end the taste of his own whiteness*
> *The horror of his own smoothness,*
> *And he felt drunken and old.*
>
> *So he became a dancer to God*
> *Because his flesh was in love with the burning arrows*
> *He danced on the hot sand*
> *Until the arrows came,*
> *As he embraced them his white skin surrendered itself to*
>   *the redness of blood, and satisfied him.*
> *Now he is green, dry and stained*
> *With the shadow in his mouth.*

[47]   GB–ALb 2–9900066.

[48]   HC, p. 565. Throughout the *Canticle* there is an unsettling disharmony between the voice and harp. The vocal phrases repeatedly commence and conclude on the pitch E, and there is a constant striving towards E major. As in *Death in Venice*, tension is created melodically by the juxtaposition of E and F. At the close of the first section of the *Canticle*, as the harp descends the voice rises, sustaining a long E before fleetingly resolving on F. This harmonic ambivalence is resolved at the end of the work. The phrase, 'With the shadow on his mouth', ascends to a held D which resolves briefly on E. However, this time the harp also traces an upward, aspiring path. It reaches an E, which is repeated three times and spans four octaves, in the final bar.

15

Conclusion

...it is you who have given me everything, right from the beginning, from yourself in Grand Rapids! through Grimes & Serenade & Michelangelo & Canticles –
one thing after another, right up to this great Aschenbach – I am here as your
mouthpiece and I live in your music –   Pears to Britten, 21 November 1974[1]

> PROLOGUE: *It is a curious story.*
> Myfanwy Piper, *The Turn of the Screw*, Prologue.

At the heart of the analyses in the preceding chapters lies a problematic question
concerning the complex, and perhaps ultimately indefinable, nature of musical
expression: how might music, which does not possess easily graspable social,
ideological and symbolic values, express ideas which can be understood by the
performer and the listener? I have attempted to answer this question, indirectly,
by posing two further questions: What is Benjamin Britten himself trying to
express and how? And in what way does he evade expression and why?

Far from being troubled by the protean character of musical 'meaning', Britten
appears to have found this fluidity to be creatively advantageous. The reticence
which characterises musical communication and the discretion inherent in
musical form and language enabled him to formulate a personal language of
self-expression. This language is not exclusively musical but is an *operatic*
discourse, one which fuses the aural, visual and theatrical elements of musical
notation and performance, embracing word, melody, harmony, texture, timbre
and setting, as well as the actual articulation of these elements. He creates an
invigorating language in which tonal, harmonic, melodic, orchestral and verbal
strategies accrue symbolic force through free association, repetition and variation. It communicates both rationally and irrationally, stimulating the listener
intellectually and emotionally. Why did Britten choose opera as the site for his
experiments in expressivity? Perhaps he located in its combination of musical and
verbal discourses – its union of non-literal and literal elements – unique opportunities for the simultaneous concealment and disclosure which his practical situation and emotional predicament seem to have required.

The librettos and scores of Britten's operas pulse with a 'queer' energy.
Half-concealed by an obvious pattern of recurring narrative themes (innocence,
the outsider etc.) are aesthetic and emotional tensions (creativity, silence,

---

[1] HC, p. 569.

sickness) which suggest the presence of a subversive and dangerous dynamic. Thus, partially shielded by the 'literariness' of his chosen source texts, Britten was able to repeatedly revisit a number of homoerotically charged situations, dramatising his personal responses to the covert currents in his operas in his musical score.

In *Peter Grimes*, the 'hero' sings:

> *Who can turn skies back and begin again?*

The accumulation of musical and verbal echoes in Britten's operas gives rise to the impression that the operas are essentially a reworking of a single theme, an obsessive recapitulation which indicates a desperate attempt to achieve order, stability and resolution. Each recommencement represents a 'fresh' beginning, but one which incorporates specific 'constants' which confirm its connection to previous versions of the tale. These 'constants' are not simply textual and musical leitmotifs but are literally embodied in the appearance and reappearance of real and fictional characters – i.e. the individual singers who took roles in a number of Britten's operas, and the characters they represented, who often displayed similar physical and psychological characteristics despite the different narrative contexts in which they appeared – reinforced by aural and visual details. Voices and figures thus become phantoms of anxiety and uncertainty which inhabit and revisit the texts and scores. In this way, the idiosyncratic vocal timbre and technique of Peter Pears's voice functions as an aural signifier of re-enactment and revisitation. Similarly, the reappearance of characters such as Quint, Oberon, Apollo, Dionysus, the Stranger-Traveller, the Wingrave ghosts – perhaps even the implied presence of the ghosts of Grimes's father and the murdered apprentices which Britten eliminates from Crabbe's poem – indicates the existence of ambiguous, manipulative forces, which are ineradicable but indefinable.

This persistent musical and textual 'redoing' – restructuring, reinterpreting, rearticulation – is a form of creative elaboration which finds musical expression in the 'variation' form, a technique which has a significant dramatic function in Britten's operas. At moments of dramatic and theatrical intensity Britten employs this form to musically delineate his protagonists' contemplative self-interrogations. These vocal and orchestral variations are not quests for definition or resolution but imaginative reflections on potentials or possibilities, which can unfold slowly, can meander in non-linear fashion, can begin again, can experiment and transform. Although Britten's emotional involvement may differ in degree from opera to opera, within each work he seems to systematically provide opportunities to include these reflective forms, which assume an almost 'editorial' function. The overall effect of the variation technique is one of intensification, a sharpening of focus or narrowing of vision and, in this way, these passages serve as a musical microcosm of Britten's entire operatic method and ambition.

At other moments, Britten does not turn back the clock, but stops it completely, suspending the impression of linear time and temporarily entering and occupying an atemporal space. Situations and emotions are not merely represented on stage but are transformed by a process of translation which involves the transfer of 'idea', performer and listener to a realm far removed from the narrative action. The 'idea' may assume a physical manifestation, such as Billy Budd hanging from the yard-arm or Tadzio poised in statuesque immobility, objectified and suspended like a work of art. This stillness releases undefined narrative and emotional expectations: there is a sense that moments such as these may embody the essential 'meaning' of the work.

At these hiatuses – for instance, Grimes's 'Great Bear' aria, the 'interview chords' in *Billy Budd*, Quint's nocturnal enticement scene, Miles's 'Malo Song', Oberon's spell music, Bottom's 'Dream', Owen Wingrave's peace aria or Tadzio's entrance music – the operatic conventions of the 'set piece' are appropriated and transformed by Britten. Extraordinary pinnacles of transcendence are attained which are experienced by composer, performer, operatic protagonist and audience, demonstrating how Britten's music is more than mere self-gratification and communicates directly, powerfully, even magically, with the listener. Such communication relies not just on music in its notational, 'textual' form but also on the *physical* effects of musical sound, accompanied by other theatrical elements. The linear progression of the unfolding drama is interrupted and an operatic 'moment' is created in which sound, sight, voice and body fuse in a union which is deeply sensual and erotic.

However, these climactic, synaesthetic events, which temporarily assume a status almost independent of the work which contains them, are inevitably reassimilated within the forward movement of the literary and musical narrative. The promise of fulfilment is denied, the symbol does not disclose its meaning and the narrative resumes, its events and characters – and by implication the performer and the listener – untransformed by the existential peak which Britten has climbed.

The actual processes of expression and self-expression involve a transfer of ideas from the internal to the external world. Artistic creation may begin with introversion, contemplation and self-exploration but the art work which is born of these reflections must ultimately be 'given up', freed from the creator's possessive grasp and handed to an interpreting audience who may or may not understand its 'meaning'. In this way, the *performance* of the work – the medium, method and act of communication – is an essential part of the artistic process, the link between creator and receptor, a potential life-line to the essence of the work. Rendition, interpretation and control are profoundly relevant to music which, it might be argued, actually exists only in performance. Thus, the recreative, interpretative strategies of the performing musician might be considered integral to the 'meaning' of the composition, and to the listener's understanding of this 'meaning', since they mark the point at which the composer must yield control over his material.[2]

These issues are deeply pertinent in the case of Benjamin Britten whose works

---

[2] Writing to congratulate Britten on the speech that he made upon receiving the Aspen Award in 1964, William Plomer commented, 'the whole gist of your speech is that every piece of music is a special communication & becomes a collaboration between composer, executant

were nearly always composed for specific performers, most especially Peter Pears. Moreover, Britten is perhaps the last of the historic line of musicians who consistently performed their own compositions. His performances and recordings with Pears of a large body of songs and song-cycles enabled him to retain a form of 'ownership' and control over his work and also established an interpretative frame of reference for subsequent performers. However, whereas in song Britten and Pears literally shared the stage as author and performer, in his operas Britten was forced to entrust Pears alone with the task of bringing forth the secrets embodied in his music and texts. Britten frequently directed the performance from the conductor's rostrum, both in the theatre and in the recording studio, but the conductor's contribution is a 'hidden' one: concealed below the stage in the orchestral pit, he is unobserved and unacknowledged by the audience who are captivated by the sights and sounds raised before them. In this way, Pears, occupying centre-stage, might temporarily be perceived as the work's 'creator'. His interpretations have gained an authority and 'rightness' by virtue of his privileged position in Britten's life and his access to the composer's personal and professional desires, and thus he has literally become Britten's 'other voice'. Moreover, Pears might achieve self-definition through this performance: he is not only Britten's 'mouthpiece' but also 'lives in' his music.

Much has been written about the idiosyncratic timbre and delivery of Pears's voice but little is known of Britten's own thoughts concerning its nature and expressive power. Was it for him an abstract, disembodied medium associated with a pure essence of feeling? Did he perceive it to be 'gendered' or 'asexual'? Was it a sexual current whose peculiar expressivity was a result of its emanation from the *body* of his lover? Roland Barthes refers to the erotic and penetrative power of the voice in his reading of Balzac's tale, *Sarrasine*. When the sculptor Sarrasine hears the voice of Zambinella, a castrato, for the first time: 'the beauty of the prima donna and her voice fill him with desire; because of his proximity to the stage, he hallucinates, imagines he is possessing La Zambinella; penetrated by the artist's voice, he achieves orgasm; after which, drained, he leaves, sits down and muses: this was his first ejaculation.'[3] The aural and visual gender confusion implicit in the figure and voice of the castrato is sexually stimulating. Furthermore, Barthes draws attention to the implicitly sexual relationship between the listener who is 'passive' and the singer who is 'active': 'The voice is described by its power of penetration, insinuation, flow; but here it is the man who is penetrated; like Endymion 'receiving' the light of his beloved, he is visited by an active emanation of femininity, by a subtle force which 'attacks' him, seizes him, and fixes him in a situation of passivity.'[4] This situation is complicated if the listener is the actual composer, particularly if the song he hears is his own gift to his lover. Who is 'passive' now?

& auditor. It is so strange that so basic & vital an idea is so seldom made explicit' (16 October 1964).
[3]   Roland Barthes, *S/Z*, trans. Richard Miller (New York: Noonday Press, 1988), p. 119.
[4]   *Ibid.*, p. 118.

The creative and emotional debt which Britten owed Pears is evident in a letter which he wrote, 17 November 1974:

> My darling heart . . . I must write a squiggle which I couldn't say on the tele-phone without bursting into those silly tears – I do love you so terribly, not only glorious *you*, but your singing. I've just listened to a re-broadcast of *Winter Words* (something like Sept. '72) and honestly you are the greatest artist that ever was – every nuance, subtle & never over-done – those great words, so sad & wise, painted for one, that heavenly sound you make, full but always coloured for words & music. What *have* I done to deserve such an artist and *man* to write for?[5]

Pears's reply is quoted at the opening of this chapter: clearly Britten's gratitude was reciprocated. Was Pears's performance a perfect aesthetic and sexual consummation which crystallised for Britten the musical and emotional 'essence' of his work?

On the operatic stage, Britten could see and hear Pears as he enacted Britten's own dreams and desires. He was implicated in, but not endangered by, the experi-ences which his surrogate underwent. Thus the negative effects of his self-elimination from the final stages of the communicative process might be partially overcome by the unique potential of opera for imaginative self-dramatisation and self-recreation. Britten's decision to commit himself to oper-atic composition was made at an early stage in his career. During the Second World War Britten and Pears became close friends with Michael Tippett, who recalled how they had discussed their ambitions: 'Ben and I discussed what we thought our futures were. And Ben said: "I am possibly an anachronism. I am a composer of opera, and that is what I am going to be, throughout." '[6] As noted at the start of this chapter, the strength of Britten's conviction and determination suggests that he considered opera to be a peculiarly appropriate medium for self-expression. What did he locate in opera – a hybrid genre, magnificent, malleable and ambiguous – that could salve his artistic and emotional anxieties?

Opera is an extravagant art, characterised by theatrical artifice, aggrandisement and exaggeration. The members of the audience may recognise, magnified and raised before them, the passions and experiences of their own lives. However, opera may also trigger emotional impulses which in the actual lives of the listeners are scarcely acknowledged or completely repressed. In this way, as they witness from the safe distance of the auditorium the dramatisation of their potential selves and 'alternative' lives, the audience may encounter, in the excessive emotions of the operatic bodies and voices before them, their own unheeded or unarticulated passions. Such confrontations may be cathartic and healing or disturbing and dangerous, but ultimately order is restored through dramatic and musical resolution.

However, latent within these temporary liberations is the threat of revolution

---

[5] HC, p. 568.
[6] *Ibid.*, pp. 193–4.

and anarchy. Ambiguity is encoded within the conventions of opera and this ambiguity is inherently transgressive. As disguise and masking are integral to the operatic mode, it proffers an unparalleled range of opportunities for the subversive overthrow of traditional classifications, particularly those associated with identity, gender and sexuality. The *travesti* roles which proliferate in opera from the late eighteenth century[7] – in which a female singer *looks* like a man and enacts a male role, but *sounds* like a woman – give rise to an erotic interplay of cross-identification and gender confusion which is designed, among other things, to be sensual or titillating. Consider, for example, the homoerotic vocal dynamic which is initiated when Cherubino avows his/her love for Barbarina/Susanna/the Countess, or when the rhapsodic vocal lines of Octavian, Sophie and the Marschallin inter-penetrate in the closing moments of *Der Rosenkavalier*.[8]

There are some crucial differences between opera and spoken drama. The absolute suspension of disbelief which opera demands enables singers to perform parts for which they are physically unsuited, and this incongruity results in a separation of voice and body culminating at specific moments in the almost exclusive focusing on the disembodied voice. This division is further intensified by the common practice of performing operas in languages which are foreign to the audience. It is a paradox of opera that a genre which draws so heavily on visual and theatrical elements should be characterised by the dismissal of the entire visual and signifying order at moments of climactic intensity. In *The Angel's Cry: Beyond the Pleasure Principle in Opera*, Michel Poizat describes the 'falling away' of the rational consciousness, as experienced by the listener:

> These moments are not exactly moments of jubilation, or are so only very rarely; rather they are moments of physical thrill, of stupefaction, as the listener seems on the verge of disappearing, of losing himself, of dissolving in the voice, just as the singer on stage becomes sheer voice, sheer vocal object . . .
>
> . . . what characterises this emotion is that . . . it occurs as an acute, irrepressible irruption linked to specific musical passages in which all that is visual and all that tends towards signification fails and falls away. In these instants pure voice alone persists.[9]

---

7 This increase was partially due to the decline of the castrati at the end of eighteenth century. Parts formerly composed for castrati were now taken by mezzo-sopranos 'in drag', reversing and further complicating the gender tensions inherent in the transgressive timbre of the original vocal designation.

8 See 'What are These Women Doing in Opera?', in *En Travesti: Women, Gender Subversion, Opera*, ed. Corinne E. and Patricia Juliana Smith (New York: Columbia University Press, 1995), pp. 59–98. Ralph P. Locke details instances of the reverse practice, whereby male singers appropriate female parts. He describes a 1990 production of Kurt Weill's *Seven Deadly Sins* in which the role of Anna I – originally written for the soprano voice of the young Lotte Lenya – was sung by a tenor, Ludwig Boetteger, presumably in some combination of falsetto and high tenor. Furthermore, he reports on a current trend for countertenors to assume male parts written for women, revealing that Brian Asawa is to play Baba the Turk – the bearded lady – in a forthcoming video of Stravinsky's *The Rake's Progress*, and that he may soon tackle the part of Cherubino.

9 Michel Poizat, *The Angel's Cry: Beyond the Pleasure Principle in Opera*, trans. Arthur Denner (Ithaca and London: Cornell University Press, 1992), pp. 3–4, and 31–2.

There are obvious differences between the experience of opera in the theatre and that of listening to a recording, but Poizat finds the potential for operatic 'jouissance' even in the latter:

> Every opera lover knows at first-hand the experience of the libretto falling out of your hands: you are listening to a recording of your favourite opera, installed comfortably in an easy chair, book in hand so as to follow better the subtleties of inflection, the expressivity of the interpretation. Inevitably, if the work is beautiful and the interpretation is good, certain passages will wrest your attention from the printed words: you lean back in your chair and lose yourself in listening, for all the world oblivious of the printed text. It is then that the libretto falls from your hands. Your attitude conflicts with your original project of listening attentively to the verbal exchange, as it is precisely in these powerful moments, when the singer's expressive qualities and the meaning of the words ought to come together in the deepest sense, that you should be most attentive to the literary text. Yet somehow you feel a radical antagonism between letting yourself be swept away by the emotion and applying yourself to the meaning of each word as it is sung.[10]

For Poizat, the aesthetic power of opera is located in these moments beyond words, and is intensely physical and sensual.[11]

Opera contains its latent subversions within strictly prescribed, and understood, structural, dramatic and theatrical conventions. Rigidly enforced external boundaries enable creator, performer and audience to act out their most dangerous fantasies, safe in the knowledge that the musical and dramatic resolution demanded by the form will ultimately protect them from self-destruction or social fragmentation. Moreover, contained within the established formulae there resides a flexibility which enables opera to break through the boundaries laid down in the narrative and score, and to translate performer and listener to a place beyond the literal theatrical space. This emotional, atemporal realm is a sort of 'closet': by unlocking the door to this closet, opera releases a song which literally embodies sexuality, both as pleasure and danger. Such is opera's erotic power: it provides a momentary release from anxiety and a temporary sensation of ecstasy. Yet, these opportunities for rebellion and transgression are transient and must be subdued in the interests of formal, cultural and social stability, and the silencing of the subversive voice is an essential part of this process. In *Opera, or the Undoing of Women* Catherine Clément locates a conspiracy in the operatic canon, whereby plots are structured around female victims, who function as symbols of perceived feminine weaknesses – hysteria, irrationality, insanity – and who are sacrificed

---

10 *Ibid.*, p. 36.
11 In *Opera in the Flesh* Sam Abel describes his personal response to opera in similar, if more explicit, language: 'I want to know why opera feels so much like sex' (p. 4). Later he answers his own question: 'Opera feels like a sexual act because it is a sexual act. That is the secret of opera's irrational appeal and of its overwhelming effect on an audience that gives itself over to opera's excesses. When I engage my desire with an operatic performance, I feel its stimuli in all the muscles of my body' (pp. 82–3).

(silenced) as a cathartic means of restoring the emotional wholeness and social cohesion which their explosive coloratura outbursts have endangered.[12]

Opera possesses both universalising and minoritising tendencies. It is a potential haven for minority groups, a rich site for transgressive exploration where pre-established practices can be extended and manipulated in the search for alternative patterns which might accurately and imaginatively encode and communicate their experience. The grandness of its luxuriating gestures may encourage or impel any listener to 'speak out', to dare to confess, but the anonymity guaranteed in this covert space might appeal particularly to the homosexual who finds empowerment within opera's liberating parameters. By exploiting the expressivity of half-concealment, the homosexual composer or singer might develop an intricate technique of self-presentation and self-preservation which energises and eroticises the dramatic surface. Because, in contrast to heterosexual passion, homosexual desire has seldom been theatrically enlarged, explored and contained in a visual sense, the threat which the homosexual or transsexual character poses may be focused almost exclusively in opera's aural dimensions.[13] The singer's voice is charged with an energy and dynamic which is never explained, only instinctively felt, and consequently the tension between visual and aural, or intellectual and sensual, discourses is greater. This enforced equivocation may result in aesthetic dissatisfaction if the visual or dramatic ending is incongruous with the musical or vocal dialectic.

12 Catherine Clément, *Opera, or the Undoing of Women: Towards a Feminist Criticism of Music*, trans. Betsy Wing (London: Virago Press, 1989). While Clément's analyses are incisive and pertinent in the context of nineteenth-century operatic practices, she disregards the entire genre of comic opera, and ignores those female operatic heroines who are depicted as challenging and defeating social adversity, e.g. in *Fidelio*. Michel Poizat takes Clément's thesis one step further and proposes that the death of the diva is not necessitated by her status as a dissident dramatic symbol but by the erotic danger latent in the actual sound of her voice: the diva's song evokes repressed primal pleasures which must be violently annihilated. Operatic women, even as victims, possess a vocal assertiveness which commands the audience's attention and compels their deeper involvement, but which ultimately demands containment.

13 Even in 'heterosexual opera' the theatrical production may ignore or submerge radical gestures in the text and music in accordance with cultural and social norms and expectations. For example, in *Don Giovanni* it is conventionally perceived that Donna Anna welcomed Don Giovanni's advances, and is in some way complicit in her own rape. This interpretation can be traced back to E. T. A. Hoffmann's description of the hero's 'superhuman sensuality... [which] made her powerless to resist' (quoted in Julian Rushton (ed.), *Mozart: Don Giovanni Cambridge Opera Handbook* (Cambridge: CUP, 1981), pp. 129–31). In fact, there is no evidence for this interpretation of her character in either libretto or score. It is clear that at the start of the opera Donna Anna has broken free but is 'holding him by the arm' attempting to prevent his escape in order that she might identify her assailant. As Giovanni threatens her with further violence, she shouts for help and repeats her avowals of vengeance. Furthermore, the creative tensions between text, score and production in 'homosexual opera' may be diminished or lost now that homoerotic subjects are being openly dramatised. An example of one such work is the lesbian opera, *Patience and Sarah* by Paula Kimber, with a libretto by Wende Persons based on a cult novel of the same name by Isabel Miller, which was performed at the Lincoln Center, New York, in 1998.

The silencing of the singer's voice is a potent symbol for the homosexual. It may be a metaphor for the social oppression and self-repression experienced by the homosexual, for the singer who 'loses' his or her voice is disabled, musically 'dead'. Alternatively, this 'lost' voice may merely be displaced and, like the cry of Quint, Oberon, and the Stranger-Traveller, return to haunt the original owner with tantalising echoes of a lost identity. Operatic silence is ambiguous and multifarious. It may represent an unspeakable idea; or it may take the form of a silent cry or scream, an aural vacuum which signifies the pain of the mute sufferer. It may be a 'nothingness' or it may be a space replete with aesthetic advantages for those who are able to exploit its potential for a different mode of communication. It is a type of open secret, which does not disguise knowledge, but merely disguises knowledge of that knowledge. Choosing silence could be either an act of defiance, a weapon against a repressive society, or an act of passive surrender.

The most extreme form of silence is death. Sam Abel notes the way in which the gay community frequently finds celebration in death, pain and failure, which they commonly locate in opera: 'gay men flock to the opera in a cult of death, a glorious but ultimately futile gesture of symbolic self-immolation in the face of a hostile society and impossible love'.[14] He is dismissive of 'opera queens' for whom opera *is* death, or is a form of transfiguration in which the dangers of sexual transgression are assuaged by music which eases their burden of shame, secrecy, failure, loneliness and disjuncture. Typically, Wayne Koestenbaum portrays opera as a sublimation or substitute for failed or absent love – 'Opera has always suited those who have failed at love.'[15] Yet for Koestenbaum, opera's own erotic exchanges are always frustrated and are merely an illusion that staves off inevitable death and dissolution. Abel rejects this negative vision:

> Is opera nothing but a sublimation of failed desire? . . . I refuse to embrace this portrait of the tragic opera queen to explain my own passion for opera . . . The gay population still has a stake in opera, as a powerful means of embodying our desire. But we do not need to latch onto opera as a death cult to engage with this embodiment. Opera provides other avenues for sorely needed, positive public expressions of desire in the gay community.[16]

Abel's comments are supported by those of Alex Ross, in a review of Koestenbaum's book in the *New Yorker*, 12 April 1993: 'Opera has nothing to do with the lives of most gay men, past or present. Conversely, most operagoers, fanatics included, are not gay in the least. Opera cannot serve as a synonym for homosexuality, because opera-going expresses no essential sexuality, gay or straight.' Opera's unique generic, formal and expressive qualities, its flaunting of erotic excess, enable it to function as a field of undifferentiated, unspecified desire. Opera can thus serve as a space for the imaginative fulfilment of illicit passion, for the homosexual and heterosexual alike.

---

[14] Abel, *Opera in the Flesh*, p. 59.
[15] Koestenbaum, *The Queen's Throat*, p. 18.
[16] Abel, *Opera in the Flesh*, pp. 61–3.

*

Superficially, the operas of Benjamin Britten might reinforce the impression that opera is riddled with death, disease and madness. Within his works the boundaries between sickness and sexuality, madness and imagination, silence as rebellion and silence as defeat, are ambiguous and obscure. Disease is strongly identified with both creativity/musicality and sexual perversion:[17] the pursuit of fulfilment in either field invariably ends in sacrifice, silence and death. On the one hand, free, creative experimentation and elaboration is depicted as a healthy extension of the boundaries of art and life. On the other hand, the impulses which are creatively enabling are also revealed to be spiritually and physically destructive, and their cancerous presence is exposed by physical weaknesses and flaws which are manifestations of increasing moral decadence and spiritual decay.

Self-denial and repression are the catalysts which transform the sickness which emancipates the imagination into the sickness which suffocates the body and soul. In Thomas Mann's *Doctor Faustus* the Devil declares that 'sickness' is empowering, a pathway to creative and spiritual liberation:

> creative, genius-giving disease, disease that rides on high horse over all hindrances, and springs with drunken daring from peak to peak, is a thousand times dearer to life than plodding healthiness ... You [Adrian Leverkühn] will lead the way, you will strike up the march of the future, the lads will swear by your name, who thanks to your madness will no longer need to be mad. On your madness they will feed in health, and in them you will become healthy ... Not only will you break through the paralysing difficulties of the time – you will break through time itself, by which I mean the cultural epoch and its cult, and dare to be barbaric, twice barbaric indeed, because of coming after the humane, after all possible root-treatment and bourgeois raffinement.[18]

There is a strong resemblance between the Devil's words to Adrian Leverkühn and Auden's words to Britten, previously quoted:

> As you know I think you [are] the white hope of music; for this very reason I am more critical of you than anybody else, and I think I know something about the dangers that beset you as a man and as an artist because they are my own.
>
> Goodness and Beauty are the results of a perfect balance between Order and Chaos, Bohemianism and Bourgeois Convention.
>
> Bohemian chaos alone ends in a mad jumble of beautiful scraps; Bourgeois convention alone ends in large unfeeling corpses.
>
> Every artist except the supreme masters has a bias one way or the other ...
>
> For middle-class Englishmen like you and me, the danger is of course the second. Your attraction to thin-as-a-board juveniles, i.e. to the sexless and innocent, is a symptom of this. And I am certain too that it is your denial and

---

[17] Philip Brett explores the connections between 'homosexuality' and 'musicality' in 'Musicality, Essentialism and the Closet', in Brett, Wood and Thomas, *Queering the Pitch*, pp. 9–26.

[18] Thomas Mann, *Doctor Faustus*, trans. H. Lowe-Porter (New York: Random House, 1966), pp. 242–3.

evasion of the ~~attractions~~ demands of disorder that is responsible for your attacks of ill-health, i.e. sickness is your substitute for the Bohemian.[19]

Auden's poem 'Underneath an Abject Willow' (1936) seems similarly to convey a persuasive warning on the subject of sexual repression, encapsulating the poet's thoughts on Britten's reluctance at that time to engage in warm, presumably sexual, relationships. Britten's perception of his predicament is revealed in his diary, 5 June 1936: 'Life is a pretty hefty struggle these days – sexually as well. Decisions are so hard to make, & its [sic] difficult to look unprejudiced on apparently abnormal things.'[20] Key words in the poem are 'cold', 'desolation', 'sombre', 'unloving', 'coldest' and 'numb'; Auden recommends action – 'Coldest love will warm to action': only the warmth of physical consummation will bring about 'satisfaction'.[21]

Perhaps Britten perceived Auden as sort of 'demon', persistently whispering and articulating the words of his own inner voices. Yet Donald Mitchell, who was with Britten when he received the news of Auden's death in September 1973, attests that although the two men had not communicated for thirty years Britten was devastated by this loss: 'it was the only time I'd ever seen Ben weep'.[22]

Auden's voice was perhaps a voice which Britten could live neither with nor without. Significantly, at the 1974 Aldeburgh Festival excerpts from their operetta *Paul Bunyan*, which had been unheard since 1941, were performed on two occasions. Rosamund Strode suspected that Britten was unwilling to revive the piece before this time as this would have necessitated working with Auden again; now 'Ben could take his own decisions'.[23] On 1 February 1976 *Paul Bunyan* was performed complete, for the first time in thirty-three years, on BBC Radio Three. Donald Mitchell and Pears, who had sung the part of Johnny Inkslinger, were with Britten when he listened to a tape of the performance: 'Ben was profoundly moved by re-encountering this forgotten work from a forgotten – virtually suppressed – past. He hadn't remembered that it was such a 'strong piece' – his words; and the impact of the music, combined with all the memories it aroused – of Auden, of the American years, of his own youth, energy and vitality – overwhelmed him . . . when we got to the end of the work . . . Ben was shattered, and

---

[19] Auden to Britten (31 January 1942?) in LL, vol. 2, pp. 1015–16.

[20] LL, vol. 1, p. 66.

[21] In his setting of this poem, Britten apparently chose to ignore the advice of his self-appointed 'sexual mentor': the poetic mood is passionate yet Britten's music has an impersonality and distance. The *vivace* tempo, dance-like, impetuous semi-quavers and playful trills in the accompaniment hint that Britten is refusing to take the message seriously. Moreover, by setting the poem as a duet, Britten refuses to assume the role of protagonist and eliminates the possibility of a personal response. Only in the final three lines, 'Walk then, come,/ no longer, numb,/ Into your satisfaction', does the music flourish, employing repetition, chromaticism, vocal range and dynamic heights to powerfully express the poetic sentiments.

[22] HC, p. 561.

[23] *Ibid.*, p. 564.

broke down.'[24] This might partially explain Britten's remark, 'Auden is in all my operas'.[25]

Are Britten's operas able to transcend the homosexual dynamic which infuses text and score and communicate a more universal experience?[26] He strove for consolidation and affirmation – to attain a balance between the Bourgeois and the Bohemian, to reconcile the Apollonian with the Dionysian – in order to create the Goodness and Beauty which might be embodied in his art. Although his operas might be considered an exteriorisation of his inner life, an artistic experiment with his actual and potential selves and attitudes, this aspiring for the redemption which could be achieved in and through art was not merely a personal quest but one of universal human significance, a search for values which might be personally sustaining and healing but which were also culturally rewarding.

The contradictions inherent in the artistic challenge which Britten set himself were further complicated by the antagonistic forces within him. From an early age he seems to have been driven by irreconcilable impulses, by the desire to rebel and the need to conform. For example, actions and behaviour such as his pacifist convictions and Conscientious Objector status, and the candour with which he conducted his relationship with Pears, suggest a courageous individualism and radicalism which seem incompatible with the reactionary, pro-Establishment leanings and social ambitions of the man who complained to Michael Tippett: 'I would be a Court composer, but for my pacifism and homosexuality.'[27]

We are reminded of one of Auden's maxims – 'It is folly to imagine that one can live two lives, a public and a private one. No man can serve two masters . . . In the struggle between public life and the private life, the former will always win because it is the former that brings home the bacon.'[28]

In a similar way, having invested profound creative and emotional energy in musically vitalising the homosexual dynamic in his operas, Britten appeared content for these works to be received simply as musical settings of 'classic' texts,

[24] Mitchell to Carpenter, *ibid.*, p. 577.

[25] *Ibid.*, p. 248.

[26] A comparable question arises in Elizabeth Wood's investigation of lesbian musical discourse. In her essay 'Sapphonics', in *Queering the Pitch*, pp. 27–66, Wood appears to argue that the lesbian musical space which she locates in the music of composers such as Ethyl Smyth is only accessible to lesbian listeners. Similarly, in 'I am an Opera', in Blackmer and Smith, *En Travesti*, pp. 99–131, Judith A. Peraino declares that her sexuality permits her a privileged understanding of Purcell's *Dido and Aeneas* which enables her to 'identify with the opera itself – as a rebellious and queer participant in an entrenched outline of history and culture . . . My goal is not only to proclaim the hidden relevance of a neglected work of art for a neglected audience but also to practise musicology from a neglected though insightful perspective: the perspective of the margin.'

[27] HC, p. 194.

[28] Mendelson, *The English Auden*, p. 401. The opening movement of *Our Hunting Fathers* had described 'the poles between which our desire unceasingly is discharged . . . A desire in which love and hatred so perfectly oppose themselves that we cannot voluntarily move'. Britten must surely have struggled to unravel the contradictions, and to confront this emotional and physical 'immobility'.

allowing the literary status of the sources to serve as a justification for, and a distraction from, the subversive nature of the narratives. On rare occasions Britten did acknowledge privately his personal involvement in the subject matter of his operas. For example, two months after the premiere *The Turn of the Screw* he wrote to Eric Walter White: 'I am delighted in your reaction to my latest baby – one is always so delighted that one's sympathetic friends find the last work the best. It was certainly a difficult work to bring off technically and spiritually.'[29] To Desmond Shawe-Taylor he was even more explicit: 'I think in many ways you are right about the subject being, as it were, nearest to me of any I have yet chosen (although what that indicates of my own character I shouldn't like to say!).'[30]

Was Britten, as Ronald Duncan declared, 'a reluctant homosexual, a man in flight from himself, who often punished others for the sin he felt he'd committed himself.'[31] The common perception is that while Pears was comfortable with his sexuality Britten was not. After Britten's death Pears remarked that although he had been pleased by the increasing public tolerance of homosexuality, 'The word "gay" was not in his vocabulary . . . He resented that [word], I think'.[32] Stephen Reiss recalled how Britten even attempted to down-play the significance of his relationship with Pears: 'He would all but say to me that his relationship with Peter was nothing. He would try and submerge that whole aspect of himself. He wanted to be just an absolutely normal person.'[33] Yet he told Mitchell, who was to be his biographer, 'I want you to tell the truth about Peter and me'.[34]

What was this 'truth'? Is it possible that, in spite of his reluctance to openly embrace or actively promote homosexuality, Britten's love for Pears was in fact the perfect realisation of the integration of his creative and sexual energies, a union which achieved its fullest expression in his operas? Perhaps his insecurity and longing for social acceptability were driven by the self-knowledge that darker secrets might be disclosed if the respectable surface was breached in any way.

Britten might convince himself that homosexuality was 'normal' or 'natural' but pederasty definitely was not, although even this issue is ambiguous and contradictory. Despite the inferences earlier mentioned, only one of the young boys whom Britten befriended recalls a specific incident where Britten made a direct sexual advance. In an interview with Humphrey Carpenter, Jonathan Gathorne-Hardy recalls an incident from his late adolescence:

> one day as I got out of the bath and came in in my towel, Ben came up with an extremely soppy, sentimental look on his face, and put his arms round me, and kissed me on the top of the head. And I made the speech which I'd long prepared. I said, 'No, Ben, it is not to be!' Ben didn't break out into guffaws – he must have felt slightly surprised; it might have been in an opera, really. In fact I

29 5 November 1954, HC, p. 361.
30 6 November 1954, *ibid.*
31 Duncan, *Working with Britten*, p. 28.
32 HC, p. 578.
33 *Ibid.*, p. 445.
34 *Ibid.*, p. 578.

should have sung it! And we sort of manoeuvred.

Ben sort of went into the bathroom, gulped, came back and again approached me – he wasn't put off by this – and again put his arms round me, and again – I don't know if I actually repeated my aria, but I said, 'No, no, Ben, I can't', or something. And he was perfectly nice. We went down and had our Martini and wine . . . But I felt that there was no question that, had I relaxed, we would have been in that double bed.[35]

Britten's reaction to unsavoury rumours about his friendships with children was one of anger. During the preparations for the premiere of *Noye's Fludde* at the 1958 Aldeburgh Festival, Charles Mackerras remarked that the work had 'more boys than any Britten work to date – masses of boys!', a comment which unfortunately was reported back to Britten by John Cranko. Mackerras then received a letter from Pears saying: ' "You've ruined the pleasure of *Noye's Fludde*." I was told to go to the Red House, and when I got there Ben said to me, "Because I like to be with boys, and because I appreciate young people, am I therefore a lecher?" '[36] Colin Graham attempted to explain Britten's possible pederastic feelings: 'I am sure that those compulsorily platonic relationships did put a lot of strain upon him. But I also believe it was always in *loco parentis* that he saw himself, and the father–son relationship is a very strong one.'[37] Supporting Graham's assertion, Ronald Duncan describes a conversation he had with Britten in 1955:

'Ronnie, I've got a problem. I love children and as you know, I can't marry.'
'Yes, I know. Why don't you adopt one?'
'That's what I want to do.'
'Then there's no problem.
'You don't understand. It's Roger I like. I want to be as a father to him. But I don't want to put your nose out of joint. Will you allow me to give him presents, visit him at school, and let him spend part of his school holidays with me – in other words share him?'
'Of course. He's fond of you too. And as you see, we've always got Briony.' . . .
'Thank you. That fills a gap in me. But I wouldn't want you to think I was trying to replace you. I want to be as his father.' . . .
For the next ten years Ben was a second father to my son, giving him affection and advice as he grew up. He wrote to him once or even twice a week . . . These letters show Ben at his best. They reveal his sympathy for and his understanding of children. Their language is childlike and often schoolboyish: they are not from a man writing down to a child, but letters from somebody who is relaxing into the nature of a child within himself.[38]

Similarly, on 7 October 1952 Imogen Holst wrote in her diary that Britten had:

35 *Ibid.*, pp. 350–1. Gathorne-Hardy's musical metaphors are peculiarly appropriate, for it is when they are confronted with similar dangerous choices that Britten's operatic protagonists withdraw into musical realms which transform potentially degrading events into spiritually uplifting experiences.
36 *Ibid.*, p. 385.
37 *Ibid.*, p. 368.
38 Duncan, *Working with Britten*, pp. 132–3.

told me that he was thinking of adopting two children from the Hessen's displaced persons camp in Germany: – he wanted a boy and a girl but it would probably have to be two boys because of regulations about a predominantly male household. He said he'd been thinking about it for ages because he realised that it was unlikely that he'd ever marry and have children of his own, and he'd got such an immense instinct of love for them that it spilled over and was wasted.[39]

As early as 1937 these paternal feelings seems to have been evident. Searching for a 'successor' to the maturing Piers Dunkerley, Britten was introduced to a disadvantaged boy from London whom he took on holiday to Cornwall. Carpenter reports that after two weeks Britten had had a 'slight over-dose' of the child but was undeterred by the experience and, at the suggestion of a friend of Peter Burra who was working in Spain, decided to 'adopt' a Basque boy and bring him to Snape for a year.[40]

Perhaps Britten's desires sprang partially from a longing to restore what he perceived as his own 'lost innocence'. Significantly, in the last years of Britten's life the nature of his relationship with Pears changed markedly, as Britten's illness and infirmity forced him to remain in Aldeburgh while Pears continued touring and performing. Rita Thomson, who had nursed Britten during his heart operation, now moved into the Red House and undertook his full-time care, and some observers judged that Britten began to indulge himself in the role of eternal school-boy. For example, Colin Matthews thought that 'Britten had reverted to his schoolboy days', while Pears told the young tenor Neil Mackie, whom he was teaching, 'I've lost Ben. Rita's taken over'. Thomson herself described Britten as 'the best brought-up little boy you could imagine.'[41]

Ultimately it is probably futile to attempt to classify the nature of Britten's feelings towards the young boys whom he befriended in simplistic, dualistic terms. Neither his homosexual nor his pederastic desires are reductive. Like his operatic 'heroes' – Grimes, Vere, Quint, Oberon, Aschenbach – Britten's love for these boys appears to have been essentially paternal. Any menace or danger latent in this love was probably more likely to harm Britten himself than the children he sought to love and protect.

Perhaps we should look instead at the operas themselves, where Grimes, Vere, Quint and Aschenbach similarly seek to transmute sexual feelings into paternal ones. Britten may have hoped that operatic composition would be an act of purgation or purification involving the transference of the darker side of his desires from life into art where they might be dramatised and redefined, a process that might be spiritually and artistically enriching. However, Leonard Bernstein's comments in the film *A Time There Was*, concerning the musical consequences of the contradictory emotions which tormented Britten, suggest that these desires were not transfigured but merely displaced, and that the operas became sites of

---

[39] HC, p. 353.
[40] *Ibid.*, p. 111.
[41] *Ibid.*, pp. 569–70.

emotional tension which were in fact intensified and enlarged by the process of theatricalisation: 'Ben Britten was a man at odds with the world. It's strange, because on the surface Britten's music would seem to be decorative, positive, charming, but it's so much more than that. When you hear Britten's music, if you hear really hear it, not just listen to it superficially, you become aware of something very dark. There are gears that are grinding and not quite meshing, and they make a great pain.'[42]

Certainly both life and art seem to have been a continuous juggling or balancing act for Britten but one which was essential if his creative energy was to be sustained and constantly enriched. All impulses and desires had to be maintained in continuous motion if his creative processes were to remain fertile and vitalised. Similarly, in music itself resolution implies closure; the final consonant cadence is followed by silence/death. In contrast, dissonance, however subtle, continues to disturb the air with unresolved tensions which invite fresh creative explorations.

The effort required to perpetuate this creative dissonance seems to have become an almost unbearable burden as Britten's health declined in later years. Owen Wingrave had sung 'I am so tired', and there are signs in Britten's later compositions of the physical and emotional strain which weighed upon him. In January 1975 he completed the song cycle *Sacred and Profane*, the movements of which alternate devotional sentiments with more worldly reflections. The last song, entitled 'A death', is an unsentimental account of the decay of the body as death approaches which ends with the lines, 'For the whole world I don't care one jot'. Even more revealing is the dramatic cantata *Phaedra*, for mezzo-soprano and small orchestra, which was first performed by Janet Baker at the 1975 Aldeburgh Festival. Derived by Britten from Robert Lowell's *Phaedra – A Verse Translation of Racine's Phèdre*, it dramatises the insanity and death of Phaedra as she confronts her guilty lust for her husband's son. Despite the passion and frenzy in the text, the music is calm and assured, particularly at the moment of Phaedra's imminent death by self-poisoning. She sings:

> *Death will give me freedom; oh it's nothing not to live.*
> *. . . chills already dart*
> *along my boiling veins and seize my heart,*
> *A cold composure I have never known*
> *gives me a moment's poise . . .*
> *My eyes at last give up their light, and see*
> *the day they've soiled resume its purity.*

Her words are accompanied by a 'pure' C major triad with an added sixth and ninth, expressive pitches which Christopher Palmer suggests imbue this resolution with a pentatonic, oriental ambience.[43]

In the final scenes of *Death in Venice* both Aschenbach and Britten strive to

---

[42] *Ibid.*, p. 591.
[43] Palmer, *The Britten Companion*, p. 410.

attain this 'freedom', 'cold composure' and 'purity'. Their efforts recall Grimes's longing for a harbour which 'shelters peace . . . Where night is turned to day', and Budd's vision of the 'far-shining sail'. The 'purity' or 'innocence' which they all seek might be termed 'Beauty', 'Goodness', 'Innocence', 'Love' or 'Eros': whatever its name, its possession requires a compromise between harmonious and discordant forces, between light and darkness. Perhaps this is not a conflict between 'good' and 'evil' but between incompatible 'goods', between irreconcilable social and human forces. The motivating, forward energy which drives Britten and his protagonists, threatens to propel them into realms of moral anarchy and paradoxically requires a counterforce of stillness and cessation. The words of Lucretia – 'Even great love's too frail/ To bear the weight of shadows' – hint at the difficulty, perhaps even the futility, of this search for balance and wholeness.

The final chord of *Death in Venice* may therefore serve as a metaphor for the paradox which is latent in Britten's art and life: resolution must be achieved through the simultaneous sustaining of dissonance and consonance. In November 1975 Britten returned to Venice, having completed his Third String Quartet in the previous month. The links between this quartet and his last opera are strong: the final part is called 'Serenissima' and the score resonates with echoes from the opera, particularly Aschenbach's 'I love you' motif which is constantly reiterated in countless tortuous permutations. The final movement repeatedly strives towards Aschenbach's 'own' key, E major, yet significantly this redemptive resolution is once more withheld. In the final two bars the viola and cello resist the efforts of the violins to assert an unequivocal E major, producing a semitonal discord, after which the cello sustains a D♮ alone. Britten himself said: 'I want the work to end with a question.'[44]

Music is the only art capable of simultaneously holding such contradictions in suspension, of both consoling and disturbing, without fracturing its own structural cohesion or destroying its expressive logic. It is this unique power which Britten exploits in his operas and which enables him to satisfy his inner need for both self-expression and evasion. From *Paul Bunyan* to *Death in Venice*, Britten creates literal and symbolic voices, communicating his 'meaning' in sound and in silence. Ultimately, the song which these voices sing expresses and embodies the essential reticence of Music itself, a reticence which Britten might have called its innocence.

[44] Blyth, *Remembering Britten*, p. 179.

Bibliography

This bibliography omits (a) performance reviews and public correspondence consulted but not cited in the text, and (b) some secondary sources relating to literary works discussed.

Primary sources

Albert Herring, Op. 39. London: Boosey & Hawkes, 1948.

Billy Budd, Op. 50. London: Boosey & Hawkes, 1961, revised edition.

The Burning Fiery Furnace, Op. 77. London: Faber Music Ltd, 1966.

Cabaret Songs, for high voice and piano. London: Faber Music Ltd, 1980.

Canticle I: 'My Beloved is Mine and I am His', for high voice and piano, Op. 40. London: Boosey & Hawkes, 1949.

Canticle II: 'Abraham and Isaac', for alto, tenor and piano, Op. 51. London: Boosey & Hawkes, 1953.

Canticle III: 'Still falls the Rain', for tenor, horn and piano, Op. 55. London: Boosey & Hawkes, 1956.

Canticle IV: 'Journey of the Magi', for counter-tenor, tenor, baritone and piano, Op. 86. London: Faber Music Ltd, 1972.

Canticle V: 'The Death of Narcissus', for tenor and harp, Op. 89. London: Faber Music Ltd, 1976.

Curlew River, Op. 71. London: Faber Music Ltd, 1965.

Death in Venice, Op. 88. London: Faber Music Ltd, 1975.

Fish in the Unruffled Lakes, for high voice and piano. London: Boosey & Hawkes, 1947.

Gloriana, Op. 53. London: Boosey & Hawkes, 1953.

The Little Sweep: The Opera from "Let's Make an Opera" An Entertainment for Young People, Op. 45. London: Boosey & Hawkes, 1950.

Noye's Fludde Op. 59. London: Boosey & Hawkes, 1958.

A Midsummer Night's Dream, Op. 64. London: Boosey & Hawkes, 1960.

Our Hunting Fathers, Op. 8. London: Boosey & Hawkes, 1964.

Owen Wingrave, Op. 85. London: Faber Music Ltd, 1977.

Paul Bunyan, Op. 17. London: Faber Music Ltd, 1978.

Peter Grimes, Op. 33. London: Boosey & Hawkes, 1945.

Phaedra: dramatic cantata for mezzo-soprano and small orchestra, Op. 93. London: Faber Music Ltd, 1997.

The Prodigal Son, Op. 81. London: Faber Music Ltd, 1968.

The Rape of Lucretia, Op. 37. London: Boosey & Hawkes, 1946.

Sacred and Profane: Eight Medieval Lyrics, for unaccompanied voices, Op. 91. London: Faber Music Ltd, 1977.

String Quartet No. 3, Op. 94. London: Faber Music Ltd, 1977.

The Turn of the Screw, Op. 54. London: Boosey & Hawkes, 1955.

Underneath the Abject Willow. London: Boosey & Hawkes, 1937.

War Requiem, Op. 66. London: Boosey & Hawkes, 1962.

Winter Words: lyrics and ballads of Thomas Hardy, for high voice and piano, Op. 52. London: Boosey & Hawkes, 1954.

Secondary sources

Abel, Sam. *Opera in the Flesh: Sexuality in Operatic Performance*. Oxford: Westview Press, 1996.

Alexander, Peter F. 'The Process of Composition of the Libretto of Britten's *Gloriana*', *Music and Letters*, vol. 67, April 1986, 147–58.

Altman, Dennis. *Homosexual: Oppression and Liberation*. London: Allen Lane, 1974.

Auden, W. H. *The Dyer's Hand*. London: Faber & Faber, 1946.

—— *Paul Bunyan*. London: Faber & Faber, 1988.

Banks, Paul (ed.). *Britten's 'Gloriana': Essays and Sources*. Aldeburgh Studies in Music 1. Woodbridge: The Boydell Press, 1993.

Barthes, Roland. *S/Z*, trans. Richard Miller. New York: Noonday Press, 1988.

Bayliss, Stanley. 'Not a Great Britten', *Daily Mail*, 10 June 1953.

Bernstein, Leonard. *The Unanswered Question*. Cambridge, Mass.: Harvard University Press, 1976.

Blackmer, Corinne E., and Patricia Juliana Smith (eds.). *En Travesti: Women, Gender Subversion, Opera*. New York: Columbia University Press, 1995.

Blair, J. G. *The Poetic Art of W. H. Auden*. New Jersey: Princeton University Press, 1965.

Blake, William. *Songs of Innocence and Songs of Experience: Showing the Two Contrary States of the Human Soul* (introduction by Richard Holmes). London: The Folio Society, 1992.

Blyth, Alan. 'Britten Returns to Composing', *The Times*, 30 December 1974.

—— *Remembering Britten*. London: Hutchinson and Co., 1981.

Bonavia, Ferrucio. Review of *Peter Grimes*, *Daily Telegraph*, 8 June 1945.

Braverman, Albert, and David Nachmann. 'The Dialectic of Decadence: An Analysis of Thomas Mann's *Death in Venice*', *German Review*, vol. 45, 1970, 289–98.

Brett, Philip. '*Albert Herring*', *Musical Times*, vol. 127, October 1986, 545–7.

—— 'Are You Musical?', *Musical Times*, vol. 135, June 1994, 370–6.

—— (ed.). *Benjamin Britten: Peter Grimes*. Cambridge Opera Handbook. Cambridge: Cambridge University Press, 1983.

—— 'Britten and Grimes', *Musical Times*, vol. 118, 1977, 995–1000.

—— 'Character and Caricature in *Albert Herring*', *Musical Times*, October 1987, 545–7.

—— '*Death in Venice*', *Musical Times*, vol. 131, 1990, 10–11.

——, Elizabeth Wood and Gary C. Thomas (eds.). *Queering the Pitch: The New Gay and Lesbian Musicology*. New York and London: Routledge, 1994.

Britten, Beth. *My Brother Benjamin*. Buckinghamshire: The Kensal Press, 1986.

Burridge, Christina J. ' "Music such as charmeth sleep." Britten's *A Midsummer Night's Dream*', *University of Toronto Quarterly*, vol. 151, no. 2, Winter 1981/2, 149–60.

Cairns, David. *Responses: Musical Essays and Reviews*. London: Secker and Warburg, 1973.

Canning, Hugh. Review of *Gloriana*, *Sunday Times*, 26 December 1993.

Capell, Richard. Review of *Gloriana*, *Daily Telegraph*, 13 June 1953.

Carpenter, Humphrey. *Benjamin Britten: A Biography*. London: Faber & Faber, 1992.

Citron, Marcia J. *Gender and the Musical Canon*. Cambridge: CUP, 1993.

Clément, Catherine. *Opera, or the Undoing of Women*, trans. Betsy Wing. London: Virago, 1989.

Cooke, Mervyn. *Britten and the Far East: Asian Influences in the Music of Benjamin Britten*. Woodbridge: The Boydell Press, 1998.

—— 'Britten and Shakespeare: Dramatic and Musical Cohesion in *A Midsummer Night's Dream*', *Music and Letters*, vol. 74, May 1993, 246–68.

—— and Philip Reed (eds.). *Benjamin Britten: Billy Budd*. Cambridge Opera Handbook. Cambridge: Cambridge University Press, 1993.

Cooper, Martin. Review of *The Turn of the Screw*, *Daily Telegraph*, 15 September 1954.

Corse, Sandra. 'From Narrative to Music – Benjamin Britten's *The Turn of the Screw*', *University of Toronto Quarterly*, vol. 51, no. 2, 1981, 161–74.

—— and Larry Corse. 'Britten's *Death in Venice*: Literary and Musical Structures', *Musical Quarterly*, vol. 73, no. 3, 1989, 344–63.

Crabbe, George. *The Complete Poetical Works*, ed. Norma Dalrymple-Champneys and Arthur Pollard. 3 vols. Oxford: Clarendon Press, 1988.

Crozier, Eric (ed.). *Benjamin Britten: Peter Grimes*. Sadler's Wells Opera Books No. 3. London: Sadlers Wells, 1945.

—— (ed.). *The Rape of Lucretia: A Symposium by Benjamin Britten, Ronald Duncan, John Pier, Henry Boys, Eric Crozier, Angus McBean*. London: Bodley Head, 1948.

Culshaw, John. 'The Making of *Owen Wingrave*', *The Times*, 8 May 1971.

Dean, Winton. 'Britten's "Inner Insecurity" ', *Opera*, vol. 43, no. 5, May 1992, 536–41.

—— '*Death in Venice*: Festivals, Aldeburgh', *Musical Times*, vol. 114, August 1973, 819–20.

Donaldson, Ian. *The Rape of Lucretia – A Myth and Its Transformations*. Oxford: OUP, 1982.

Drew, David. Review of *A Midsummer Night's Dream, New Statesman,* 25 June 1960.

Duncan, Ronald. *All Men are Islands.* London: Rupert Hart-Davis, 1964.

—— *How to Make Enemies.* London: Rupert Hart-Davis, 1968.

—— 'How *The Rape of Lucretia* Became an Opera', *Shakespeare Quarterly,* no. 1, Summer 1947, 95–100.

—— 'The Problems of a Librettist: Is Opera Emotionally Immature?', *The Composer,* no. 23, Spring 1967, 6–9.

—— 'A Sketch of Benjamin Britten', *World Review,* no. 11, January 1950, 18–19.

—— *Working with Britten: A Personal Memoir.* Devon: The Rebel Press, 1981.

Elliot, Graham. 'The Operas of Benjamin Britten: A Spiritual View', *Opera Quarterly,* vol. 4, no. 3, Autumn 1986, 28–44.

Evans, John, Philip Reed and Paul Wilson (eds.). *A Britten Source Book.* Suffolk: Britten-Pears Estate, 1987.

Evans, Peter. *The Music of Benjamin Britten.* London: Dent, 1979.

—— '*Death in Venice*', *Music and Letters,* vol. 62, 1981, 112–14.

—— '*Gloriana,* An Opera in 3 Acts Op. 53', *Music and Letters,* vol. 72, no. 3, 1991, 498–9.

Felman, Shoshan. *Literature and Psychoanalysis: The Question of Reading Otherwise.* Baltimore: John Hopkins University Press, 1982.

Forster, E. M. *Aspects of the Novel.* London: Arnold, 1938.

—— 'George Crabbe: The Poet and the Man', *The Listener,* 29 May 1941.

—— *Maurice.* Harmondsworth: Penguin, 1972.

—— *Selected Letters,* ed. Mary Lago and Philip Furbank. 2 vols. Glasgow: Wilkins and Son Co., 1983–5.

—— *Two Cheers for Democracy.* London: Arnold, 1972.

Garbutt, J. W. 'Music and Motive in *Peter Grimes*', *Music and Letters,* vol. 44, 334–42.

Glock, William. Review of *Albert Herring, Time and Tide,* 28 June 1947.

Gray, Cecil. Review of *The Rape of Lucretia, The Observer,* 14 July 1946.

Hall, Richard. 'Henry James: Interpreting an Obsessive Memory', *Journal of Homosexuality,* vol. 8, nos. 3–4, Spring/Summer 1983, 83–98.

Harewood, George. *The Tongs and the Bones: The Memoirs of Lord Harewood.* London: Weidenfeld and Nicolson, 1981.

Hayford, Harrison, and Morton M. Seatts Jnr. *Billy Budd, Sailor: Reading Text and Genetic Text, Edited from the Manuscript with Introduction and Notes.* Chicago: University of Chicago Press, 1962.

Headington, Christopher. *Peter Pears.* London: Faber & Faber, 1992.

Herbert, David (ed.). *The Operas of Benjamin Britten: The Complete Librettos Illustrated with Designs of the First Productions.* London: The Herbert Press, 1989, revised edition.

Higgins, John. Review of *The Turn of the Screw, The Times,* 3 April 1970.

Hillman, Roger. 'Deaths in Venice', *Journal of European Studies,* vol. 22, no. 88, 1992, 291–311.

Hindley, Clifford. 'Britten's *Billy Budd*: The "Interview Chords" Again', *Musical Quarterly*, vol. 78, no. 1, Spring 1994, 99–126.

—— 'Contemplation and Reality: A Study of Britten's *Death in Venice*', *Music and Letters*, vol. 71, November 1990, 511–23.

—— 'Homosexual Self-affirmation and Self-oppression in Two Britten Operas', *Musical Quarterly*, vol. 76, Summer 1992, 143–68.

—— 'Love and Salvation in Britten's *Billy Budd*', *Music and Letters*, vol. 70, August 1989, 363–81.

—— 'Platonic Elements in Britten's *Death in Venice*', *Music and Letters*, vol. 73, November 1990, 407–29.

—— 'Why Does Miles Die? A Study of Britten's *The Turn of the Screw*', *Musical Quarterly*, vol. 74, no. 1, 1990, 1–17.

Holroyd, Michael. *Lytton Strachey: The New Biography*. New York: Farrar, Strauss and Girous, 1994.

Holst, Imogen. 'Working for Britten', *Musical Times*, vol. 118, February 1977, 202–6.

Howard, Patricia (ed.). *Benjamin Britten: The Turn of the Screw*. Cambridge Opera Handbook. Cambridge: CUP, 1985.

—— *The Operas of Benjamin Britten*. London: Barrie and Rockliff, 1969.

Howes, Frank. Review of *Albert Herring*, *The Times*, 21 June 1947.

—— Review of *Peter Grimes*, *The Times*, 8 June 1945.

James, Henry. *The Art of the Novel*. London: Scribner's, 1934.

—— *The Complete Notebooks*, ed. Leon Edel and Lyall H. Powers. Oxford: OUP, 1987.

—— *The Complete Plays of Henry James*, ed. Leon Edel. New York: J. B. Lippincott Co., 1949.

—— *The Critical Muse: Selected Literary Criticism*. Harmondsworth: Penguin, 1987.

—— *The Turn of the Screw and the Aspern Papers*. Hertfordshire: Wordsworth Editions, 1993.

—— *The Turn of the Screw and Other Stories*. Oxford: OUP World Classics, 1992.

Jed, Stephanie H. *Chaste Thinking: The Rape of Lucretia and the Birth of Humanism*. Bloomington: Indiana University Press, 1989.

John, Nicholas (ed.). *Peter Grimes/Gloriana*. ENO Opera Guide. London: John Calder, 1983.

Jones, Lewis. *Silence and Music*. Sussex: The Book Guild, 1992.

Keller, Hans. 'Resistances to Britten's Music: Their Psychology', *Music Survey*, vol. 2, no. 4, Spring 1950, 227–36.

—— 'Three Psychoanalytic Notes on Peter Grimes', ed. Christopher Wintle. Institute of Advanced Musical Studies, King's College London, in association with the Britten–Pears Library, Aldeburgh, Suffolk, 1995.

—— and Donald Mitchell (eds.). *Benjamin Britten: A Commentary on His Works from a Group of Specialists*. London: Faber & Faber, 1952.

Kennedy, Michael. *Benjamin Britten*. Master Musicians Series. London: Dent, 1981.

Koestenbaum, Wayne. *The Queen's Throat: Opera, Homosexuality and the Mystery of Desire.* New York: Poseidon Press, 1993.

Lago, Mary. *E. M. Forster: A Literary Life.* London: Macmillan, 1995.

Law, Joe K. 'We Have Ventured to Tidy Up Vere', *Twentieth Century Literature*, vol. 31, Summer/Fall 1985, 297–314.

Leppert, Richard, and Susan McClary (eds). *Music and Society: The Politics of Composition, Performance and Reception.* Cambridge: CUP, 1987.

Lindenberger, Herbert. *Opera – The Extravagant Art.* New York: Cornell University Press, 1985.

Mann, Thomas. *Death in Venice*, ed. Clayton Koelb. Norton Critical Edition. New York: Norton & Company, 1994.

—— *Death in Venice*, trans. David Luke. London: Secker and Warburg, 1990.

—— *Doctor Faustus*, trans. H. Lowe-Porter. New York: Random House, 1966.

—— *Letters*, trans. Richard and Clara Winston. 2 vols. London: Secker and Warburg, 1970.

Martin, Robert. 'Saving Captain Vere: Billy Budd from Melville's Novella to Britten's Opera', *Studies in Short Fiction*, vol. 23, Winter 1986, 49–56.

Mason, Colin. Review of *The Turn of the Screw. The Guardian*, 15 September 1954.

Maupassant, Guy de. *Madame Husson's Rose-King.* London: Dent, 1977.

Mayhead, Robin. 'The Case of Benjamin Britten', *Scrutiny*, vol. XIX, no. 3, Spring 1953.

McClary, Susan. 'Of Patriarchs . . . and Matriarchs, Too', *Musical Times*, vol. 135, no. 1816, June 1994, 364–9.

McClure, Paul. 'Britten and the Seraphic', *Durham University Journal*, vol. 82, no. 1, 1990, 89–99.

Melville, Herman. *Billy Budd, Sailor and Other Stories.* Harmondsworth: Penguin, 1985.

Mendelson, Edward (ed.). *The English Auden: Poems, Essays and Dramatic Writings 1927–1939.* London: Faber & Faber, 1977.

Milnes, Rodney. Review of *Gloriana, The Times*, 20 December 1993.

Mitchell Donald (ed.). *Benjamin Britten: Death in Venice.* Cambridge Opera Handbook. Cambridge: CUP, 1987.

—— *Britten and Auden in the Thirties: The Year 1936.* London: Faber & Faber, 1981.

—— *Cradles of the New – Writings on Music 1951–1991*, ed. Mervyn Cooke. London: Faber & Faber, 1995.

—— 'Public and Private Life in Britten's *Gloriana*', *Opera*, vol. 17, October 1966, 767–74.

—— and John Evans (eds.). *Pictures from a Life: Benjamin Britten 1913–76.* London: Faber & Faber, 1978.

—— and Philip Reed (eds.). *Letters from a Life: The Selected Letters and Diaries of Benjamin Britten 1913–1976*, 2 vols. London: Faber & Faber, 1991.

Newman, Ernest. Review of *Albert Herring. Sunday Times*, 29 June 1957.

—— Review of *Gloriana. Sunday Times*, 14 June 1953.

—— Review of *The Rape of Lucretia. Sunday Times*, 28 July 1946.

Northcott, Bayan. Review of *Death in Venice. New Statesman*, 22 June 1973.

Palmer, Christopher (ed.). *The Britten Companion.* London: Faber & Faber, 1984.

Pears, Peter. 'Neither a Hero nor a Villain', *Radio Times*, 8 March 1946, 3.

Piper, John. '*Billy Budd* on the Stage: An Early Discussion between Producer and Designer', *Tempo*, Autumn 1951, 21.

Piper, Myfanwy. 'A Collaboration Recalled: Myfanwy Piper Talks to Roderic Dunnett', *Opera*, vol. 46, no. 10, October 1995, 1158–64.

Pollard, Alfred W. (ed.). *English Miracle Plays, Moralities and Interludes, Specimens of the Pre-Elizabethan Drama.* Oxford, Clarendon Press, 8th edn, 1927.

Plomer, William. *An Autobiography.* London: Cape, 1975.

Poizat, Michel. *The Angel's Cry: Beyond the Pleasure Principle in Opera*, trans. Arthur Denner. Ithaca and London: Cornell University Press, 1992.

Rorem, Ned. 'Britten's Venice', *The New Republic*, 8 February 1975, 31–2.

Schmigall, Gary. *Literature as Opera.* New York and Oxford: OUP, 1977.

Sedgwick, Eve Kosofsky. *Between Men: English Literature and Male Homosocial Desire.* New York: Columbia University Press, 1985.

—— *Epistemology of the Closet.* California: University of California Press, 1990.

Shakespeare, William. *A Midsummer Night's Dream.* Oxford: OUP, 1994.

—— *The Poems*, ed. George Wyndham. London: Senate, 1994.

Shawe-Taylor, Desmond. Review of *Death in Venice, Sunday Times*, 24 June 1973.

—— Review of *Gloriana, New Statesman*, 13 June 1953.

—— Review of *Peter Grimes, New Statesman*, 8 June 1945.

Sigworth, Oliver F. *Nature's Sternest Painter: Five Essays on the Poetry of George Crabbe.* Tucson: University of Arizona Press, 1965.

Sitwell, Edith. *Collected Poems.* London: Macmillan, 1965.

Slater, Montagu. *Peter Grimes and Other Poems.* London: Bodley Head, 1946.

Solie, Ruth (ed.). *Musicology and Difference: Gender and Sexuality in Music Scholarship.* California: University of California Press, 1993.

Spender, Stephen. 'Forster's Queer Novel', *Partisan Review*, vol. 39, 1972, 113–17.

Spiegelman, Willard. 'Peter Grimes: The Development of a Hero', *Studies in Romanticism*, vol. 25, Winter 1986, 541–60.

Stallybrass, Oliver (ed.). *Aspects of E. M. Forster: Essays and Recollections written for his 90th Birthday.* London: Arnold, 1969.

Still, Judith. 'Lucretia's Silent Rhetoric', *Oxford Literary Review*, vol. 6, 1984, 70–86.

Strachey, Lytton. *Elizabeth and Essex: A Tragic History.* London: Chatto and Windus, 1932.

Sutcliffe, Tom. Review of *A Midsummer Night's Dream. Musical Times*, vol. 132, no. 1781, July 1991, 352–3.

Tambling, Jeremy. '*Owen Wingrave* and Television Opera', in *Opera, Ideology and Film.* Manchester: Manchester University Press, 1987.

Tranchell, Peter. 'Britten and the Brittenites', *Music and Letters*, April 1953.

Tracey, Edmund. 'London Music', *Musical Times*, vol. 107, January 1954, 36–7.

Turner, W. J. Review of *The Rape of Lucretia, The Spectator*, 6 September 1946.

Vickers, Jon. 'Jon Vickers on *Peter Grimes*', *Opera*, vol. 35, no. 8, August 1984, 835–43.

White, Eric Walter. *Benjamin Britten: His Life and Operas*. London: Faber & Faber, 1983.

Whittall, Arnold. *The Music of Britten and Tippett: Studies in Themes and Techniques*. Cambridge: CUP, 1982.

Wilcox, Michael. *Outlines: Benjamin Britten*. Somerset: Absolute Press, 1997.

Wilson, Edmund. *Europe without Baedeker: Sketches among the Ruins of Italy, Greece and England*. London: Secker and Warburg, 1948.

—— *The Triple Thinkers*. Harmondsworth: Penguin, 1962.

Unpublished source material

Peter Grimes

The Elizabeth Mayer Collection, BPL (GB–ALb 2–9401375 to 2–9401388), including Elizabeth Mayer Collection

(a) Printed text: *The Life and Works of the Revd. George Crabbe*, edited by his son, in one volume (London: John Murray, 1851)

(b) Draft outline of Act 1 in Britten's hand

(c) Draft outline of Acts 1, 2 and 3, in Pears's hand, including a libretto sketch for Act 2, Scene 2, written on the reverse side of typed carbon copies of programme drafts for Pears's Elizabethan Singers

(d) Draft scenario in Pears's hand written on Axel Johnson line paper

(e) Draft scenario in Britten's hand

(f) List of characters in Britten's hand, written on the reverse of a letter from Elizabeth Mayer, 1 June 1942

(g) Draft libretto, incomplete

(h) Draft libretto, second version, also incomplete

(i) Water colour sketch of *The Borough* by Kenneth Green

(j) Libretto

(k) Libretto, carbon copy

(l) Libretto, carbon copy, used by Eric Crozier during the first production

(m) Letter dated 3 December 1944, from Slater to Britten

BPL Additional Material

Libretto: Peter Grimes (London: Boosey and Hawkes, 1945)

Libretto: Peter Grimes (London: Boosey and Hawkes, 1961)

Libretto: Peter Grimes (London: Boosey and Hawkes, 1979)

The Rape of Lucretia

BPL

(a) Microfilm A60

  (i) Fragment of carbon copy of a letter from Erwin Stein to G. A. M. Wilkinson, 1 April 1946

  (ii) Text of Act 2 Interlude, in Britten's hand, headed 'Ronnie'

(b) Draft libretto, carbon copy, typescript, with many annotations (GB–ALb 2–9100355 RL)
(c) Microfilm X24: On loan from Humanities Research Centre, The University of Texas, Austin, Texas
  (i) 9 pages of text in Duncan's hand, with revisions
  (ii) 59 pages of notes, in a notebook, in Duncan's hand
(d) Typescript of 1946 Boosey & Hawkes libretto – 56 pages with deletions and notes. Additional notes by Erwin Stein loosely laid in the Ronald Duncan Papers, The New Collection, University of Plymouth

The Ronald Duncan Papers, The University of Plymouth
(a) Manuscript drafts of *Working with Britten* and other autobiographical papers
(b) Typescript drafts of *Working with Britten*: uncorrected proofs, corrected proofs
(c) 'Benjamin Britten: A Pen Portrait', single sheet, 3 March 1950
(d) Unpublished typescript notes for *Benjamin Britten: A Personal Memoir* by Ronald Duncan, assorted leaves
(e) Correspondence between Ronald Duncan, Miranda Weston-Smith and W. H. Allen, concerning Ronald Duncan's Britten biography, December 1978
(f) Correspondence between Ronald Duncan, Donald Mitchell, Miranda Weston-Smith and Eric Glass, concerning Ronald Duncan's Britten biography, November 1980
(g) Correspondence between I. Caplan, A. Davis, Donald Mitchell and Rosamund Strode, concerning imminent revisions, factual discrepancies and publishing of Ronald Duncan's Britten biography, December 1978
(h) 56 letters and 30 postcards from Britten to Duncan
(i) Essay, 'An Answer to Auden/ Adolescent Opera/ Libretti: Some Technical Aspects', photocopy reproduction, unpublished versions

Albert Herring
BPL
Typescript Libretto (contains no annotations)

The Little Sweep
BPL, including material donated to the BPL by Eric Crozier in 1980
(a) Letter from EC to BB; first ideas for a children's opera (GB–ALb 2–9500472)
(b) Draft scenario, 'Sweep, Sweep!' (GB–ALb 2–9104591)

Billy Budd
This includes Eric Crozier's libretto material, donated to the BPL in 1980
(a) Earliest materials – January 1949. List of characters and dramatic situations in Britten's hand. Sketch of a ship by Britten with annotations by Forster
(b) 5 scene synopsis
(c) Draft libretto in 3 Acts – January to March 1949
(d) Complete draft libretto (3 copies) – March 1949

(e) Libretto in 4 Acts (Crozier's copy) – August 1949
(f) Libretto in 4 Acts (Britten's copy) – August 1949
(g) Supplementary material – includes text for the sea shanties which were not written until 1950, Forster's notes from Melville concerning characterisation and dialogue, and final text for Vere's Epilogue in Britten's hand

The Forster Papers, Modern Archive Collection, King's College, University of Cambridge:
(a) Letters from Britten to Forster, 1944–69
(b) Letters from Forster to Bob Buckingham, including enclosures

Gloriana
BPL (GB–ALb 2–9200291 to 2–9200302)
(a) Earliest scenarios (July 1952)
(b) 3 National Gallery postcards
(c) 12 pages of detailed descriptions of royal entertainments 1559–1602, from E. K. Chambers's *The Elizabethan Stage* (Oxford)
(d) Draft libretto (July 1952–January 1953): in Plomer's hand, with extensive annotations and revisions
(e) Second draft libretto (Autumn 1952-January 1953): typescript top copy with revision leaves
(f) Letters between Plomer and Britten
    (i) 1948–51
    (ii) 1952
    (iii) 1953–4

The Turn of the Screw
BPL Microfilm A69
(a) Earliest materials
    (i) Notebook in Piper's hand
    (ii) Incomplete draft
    (iii) Loose pages
(b) Synopsis of scenes
(c) Libretto drafts
(d) Britten's working libretto
(e) Letters from Piper to Britten
    (i) 1952–4
    (ii) Undated

Noye's Fludde
BPL (GB–ALb 2–9100372)
Typescript Libretto

A Midsummer Night's Dream
BPL Microfilm A60
(a) Character list and synopsis in Pears's hand

(b) Incomplete draft in Britten's hand
(c) Two copies of Shakespeare, *A Midsummer Night's Dream*, G. R. Harrison (ed.) (Harmondsworth: Penguin, 1953)
(d) Two draft outlines in Britten's hand
(e) Britten's working libretto
    (i) Act 1
    (ii) Complete
    (iii) Prologue by Myfanwy Piper
(f) Act 2, Imogen Holst's copy

Curlew River
BPL (GB–ALb 2–9100297 to 2–9100303)
(a) Alfred W. Pollard (ed.), 'Sumida River', libretto first draft
(b) Alfred W. Pollard (ed.), Corrected first draft
(c) Alfred W. Pollard (ed.), Second draft
(d) Alfred W. Pollard (ed.), Britten's annotated typescript
(e) Alfred W. Pollard (ed.), Typescript libretto
Alfred W. Pollard (ed.), *English Miracle Plays, Moralities and Interludes, Specimens of the Pre-Elizabethan Drama* (Oxford, Clarendon Press, 8th edn 1927) (GB–ALb 1–9300358)

The Burning Fiery Furnace
BPL (GB–ALb 2–9500545 to 2–9500555)
(a) Libretto, second draft – typescript
(b) Carbon copy of (a) with WP corrections and new handwritten material
(c) Fourth draft, typescript
(d) Fourth draft, with amendments by Colin Graham

The Prodigal Son
BPL (GB–ALb 2–9700609 to 2–9700614)
(a) Libretto first draft
(b) Libretto second draft
(c) Corrected typescript, 5 March 1958
(d) Britten's copy, typescript
(e) Final typed version (corrected by Britten, Easter 1968)

Owen Wingrave
BPL
(a) Five spiral-bound notebooks containing early drafts, synopsis, sketches, checklists and miscellaneous material, in Piper's hand
(b) Miscellaneous assorted leaves, handwritten and typescript, of libretto in various stages of development
(c) Letters from Myfanwy Piper to Benjamin Britten
    (i) undated file
    (ii) 1952–69
    (iii) 1970–6

Death in Venice
BPL (GB–ALb 2–9900066)
(a) Letters Myfanwy Piper to Benjamin Britten 1970–6
(b) 8 Notebooks of librettos drafts
(c) Miscellaneous sheets and typescripts

Supplementary sources

Interviews
Carpenter, Humphrey. 14 July 1997, Canterbury
Cowie, Edward. 21 March 1996, Canterbury
Hemsley, Thomas. 2 April 1996, London
Holroyd, Michael. 11 September 1996, Canterbury

Private correspondence
Evans-Crozier, Nancy, OBE. 2 May 1995
Langridge, Philip, CBE. 20 April 1995

Index